W9-DEV-661

SAGA OF THE SWAMP THING BOOK SIX

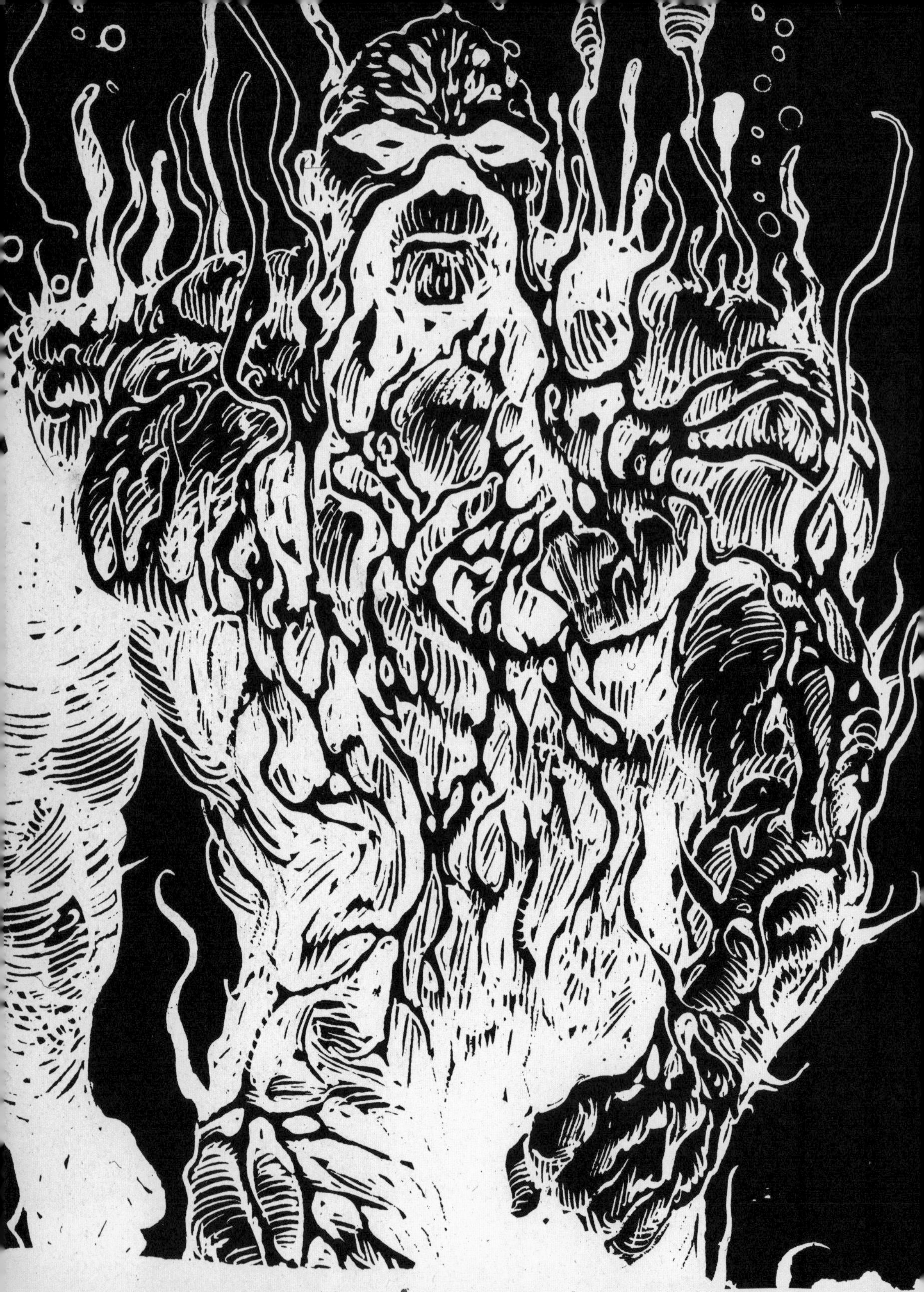

Introduction

Originally written by Stephen R. Bissette in 1988 as two separate pieces for the tenth and eleventh volumes of Titan Books' black and white SWAMP THING collections, the following introduction has been updated and expanded by Bissette for this new hardcover edition.

"Gee, this is nice. How long is it gonna last?"

All good things must end.

In the waning summer of 1987, after over forty issues' worth of fantasy, horror, and science fiction, Alan Moore's tenure as the writer of *Swamp Thing* ended with issue #64.

Though the artists that he worked with (yours truly included) certainly left their mark on the character and the series, there can be no doubt that Alan was the anchor and the navigator. After his departure, Rick Veitch (who had become the book's regular penciller) took over both writing and drawing the monthly title, and Alan went on to chart his own course in other directions — with other characters, other series, other graphic novels and other media, many of which were enormously successful. But *Swamp Thing* will always remain, for many readers, Alan's maiden voyage.

For the final issues collected in this volume, there were also a few other cooks in the (vegetarian) kitchen — Alfredo Alcala continued in his now-established position as Rick's inker; John Totleben and I each contributed an issue of art and scripting, respectively; Rick took his first stab at filling Alan's shoes by scripting as well as pencilling the story "Wavelength" for #62; and, for the final installment, original *Saga of the Swamp Thing* artist Tom Yeates returned to lend a hand (more on all that below).

That the saga ended — *truly* ended, with a deliberate and satisfying conclusion that also simultaneously managed to lay the foundation for Rick's continuation of the series — is another testament to Alan's dedication to and, yes, love for the characters. Believe you me, the final stretch was difficult and sometimes less than happy; nevertheless, Alan's careful planning paid off as editor Karen Berger (the too-often unsung guiding hand behind the title's good fortunes) orchestrated all of the title's collaborators toward an appropriately lush finale.

But first, there was a new beginning...

*****

As noted in the introduction to *Saga of the Swamp Thing Book Five*, Alan's writing underwent a real transformation from horror to science fiction and fantasy beginning with *Swamp Thing #51*'s "Home Free" — a change which became more manifest in *Swamp Thing #56*'s "My Blue Heaven" and which was reflective of Alan's willingness to adapt to the interests and orientation of his creative partner, Rick Veitch.

As I discussed in that previous introduction, Rick's predilection for science fiction and fantasy rather than horror was central to the new storyline that began in "My Blue Heaven," but I must emphasize that at the same time Alan was also beginning major new paths in his own personal and professional life. I don't betray any confidences in citing this — he was, after all, well inside the public eye with his ongoing work on *Marvelman/Miracleman*, *Watchmen* and other multiple-Earths-shaking collaborations.

While readers today know *Watchmen* primarily as a single graphic novel, it was, in fact, originally a twelve-issue limited series with the final issue cover dated October 1987. To say that Alan was over-extended and exhausted during this period would be a gross understatement — his collaboration with Dave Gibbons on *Watchmen* was completed at the same time that he was juggling a host of other work, including the monthly *Swamp Thing* issues collected herein. In early 1987 there was an *enormous* burden upon Alan's shoulders. The completion of *Watchmen* was running behind schedule (the final issue was originally slated for an April 1987 release), and the pressure not only to deliver but also to live up to the high expectations created by the initial issues was and remains impossible to quantify.

It was under this burden that Alan scripted a fresh science fiction run of *Swamp Thing*, firmly rooted in Homer's epic poem *The Odyssey*. Simply reading the stories without knowing this context, however, you would never detect the writer's stress. Inspired rather than depleted by his own "I've done it all" feelings vis-à-vis horror, Alan launched into a happy collaboration with Veitch mining DC's Silver Age science fiction heroes and titles (which they had both grown up reading) with the same marvelous sense of adventure and invention that he brought to everything he wrote. Together they explored the science fantasy and mythic potential of both Swamp Thing and the DC universe with the same insight and energy that the earlier "American Gothic" storyline had brought to the horror genre.

The science fantasy bloomed with the first two issues in this collection, "Mysteries in Space" (*Swamp Thing* #57) and "Exiles" (*Swamp Thing* #58). The heroic co-star of these issues is Adam Strange, a childhood favorite of Veitch's. Strange dated from the formative years of DC's Silver Age — he was editor Julie Schwartz's Space Age follow-up to the successful debut of the Flash in the pages of *Showcase*. Strange first appeared in *Showcase* #17 (December 1958) under the subtitle "Adventures on Other Worlds," an overture for Schwartz's new science fiction direction for the title. Originally a Flash Gordon/John Carter imitation, Earth archeologist Adam Strange was transported to the distant planet Rann by a novel concept called the Zeta-Beam, a teleportational ray of light fired towards Earth by scientists on Rann. The first time it struck Strange was pure happenstance, but after his initial adventures and the beginning of his love affair with Rann native Alanna, Strange made the bitter discovery that when the beam "wears off" (typical comic book "science") he is flung back to Earth. The Zeta-Beam was a classic *coitus interruptus* conceit, forever wearing off at the moment when Adam and Alanna finally got a second to themselves. Finding that he can calculate when and where the beam will strike Earth again, he then hazards any obstacle to make sure that he is struck by the mysterious ray and returned, however briefly, to his lover's arms and his life as a hero.

The first four pages of "Mysteries in Space" bring Adam Strange crashing into the 1980s as he has to intercept the Zeta-Beam in a decidedly inconvenient locale. Moore and Veitch put the character through their revisionist paces, bringing the series' sexual undercurrents and fetishistic elements (Strange's costume, for instance, along with that of the Thangarians) to the fore. As well as showing us the contempt in which the elite of Rann hold the "ape" from Earth, they pit Strange against a planetary catastrophe that no cleverness of Gardner Fox (Adam Strange's original Silver Age writer) could resolve: depletion of the soil and mass famine. Moore also reinterprets Strange as an intergalactic Clint Eastwood — a violent "Dirty Harry" whose blunt tactics are in marked contrast to the reasoning detective that he was in the 1960s. This expression of his inner violence (driven, no doubt, by the fact that the damned Zeta-Beam keeps interrupting his sex life on Rann) is also in keeping with the eroticism that pervades both chapters.

This eroticism, and the nature of the relationship between lovers — as well as the *distance* between lovers — is deeply felt, and continues the threads that Alan had begun with "Home Free" in *Swamp Thing* #51. The questioning of values in intimate relationships, the doubts that plague lovers who are forcibly separated and/or thrown together, and the enduring quality of a love that transcends time, distance and the bonds of flesh — this, too, echoed Odysseus, and reflected much of what was happening in Alan's personal life. This became the core of the final fourteen issues of Alan's work on *Swamp Thing*.

*****

When Karen suggested that I try my hand at writing a fill-in issue, I was careful to weave a narrative thread appropriate to Alan's thematic tapestry into my first contribution as a writer to the series, "Reunion" (*Swamp Thing* #59). I haven't the distance or wherewithal to judge the quality of the result; I leave that to you. I can only hope that the various narrative voices aren't too tangled, and that it touches you. I can also offer some background on the tale.

It's odd that a British writer (especially one of Alan's caliber) could write a comic book set in America with more insight and fidelity to local history and color than any American writer had yet brought to the title (only one actual southerner — Arkansas-born Nancy A. Collins — has written *Swamp Thing*), and yet totally ignore the European heritage of one of his key characters: Abigail Cable, *née* Arcane. Alan always imbued Abby with remarkable depth and caring, even maintaining a rhythm of speaking that embodied the type of American woman she had become. And yet — what of her roots? Her mother country? Her family, her heritage?

In our often lengthy exchanges of story ideas, Alan, John Totleben and I had fostered a catalyst for a story that would bring back Abby's father, Gregor. In the third issue of the original Len Wein and Bernie Wrightson *Swamp Thing* series (February-March, 1973), the mortal remains of Count Gregori Arcane — a.k.a. Gregor — had been salvaged from an explosion and rebuilt by his brother, Anton Arcane, into a Frankensteinian monstrosity called the Patchwork Man. In what was presumably an attempt to push the character towards his own series, the Patchwork Man was brought to American shores in a one-shot cover story in *House of Secrets* #140 (February-March, 1976). Building upon that connection and our original collaborative idea — the long-absent, presumed dead father turning up on Abby's doorstep as he feels himself dying — I wrote "Reunion."

In using the Patchwork Man to embody the extreme ravages of old age, I chose to portray Abby as working in a nursing home for the aged to set the stage emotionally for the story's climax. There were two nursing homes in the neighborhood in which I grew up in Colbyville, Vermont, and I knew many of the people who lived and worked there as well as those who owned and ran the homes. I did my best to honestly convey my impressions of those people and places in this story. It resonated, too, with the location used in the three-part Demon/Kamara story that Alan, John and I had co-plotted (*Saga of the Swamp Thing* #25-27): a home for autistic children (a setting based on the now-defunct Green Meadows School, a structured living facility for autistic children in Wilmington, Vermont, where my first wife, Marlene O'Connor, worked in the 1980s; Alan visited Green Meadows during his visit to our Vermont home).

Though I look back on "Reunion" as being a rather misshapen story — it was my first attempt to write a full 23-page comic, and I fear I tried to cram too much into it, making it a sort of "Patchwork Story" — I've since experienced the death of dear friends, up close and personal, from age or terminal illness, and I have to say that the emotional content still rings true for me. In any case, Rick did a marvelous job illustrating it, and I still find Abby and her father's shared embrace moving. That particular page is as heartfelt and piece of writing as I'd ever managed up to that point in my life, and I dedicate it with a father's love to my own daughter, Maia Rose.

Oh, and one last thing about "Reunion" — specifically about the framing story with Anton Arcane in Hell. The thing about Arcane is that he is such an unrepentant, irredeemably nasty bastard; he's truly one of the most repulsive villains ever to besmirch the pages of a comic book. I always thought that Alan missed the boat in "The Brimstone Ballet" (*Saga of the Swamp Thing* #31) when Arcane is finally consigned to eternal damnation. As he fell, screaming in fear and outrage like a beaten bully, I remember thinking, "Much too tame." Even though Alan certainly made up for it with Arcane's subsequent appearance in "Down Amongst the Dead Men" (*Swamp Thing Annual* #2), I still longed to see him damned to Hell in proper style, shrieking bile and pissing blood.

Others played with Anton Arcane in later *Swamp Thing* incarnations (including, Heaven help us, a born-again Arcane), but that's neither here nor there. If I never get to try my hand with Arcane again, I'm pleased with how I left him: burning in Hell, but rejoicing in the agony he was still causing to those he hurt in life, death and undeath.

*****

Swamp Thing #60's "Loving the Alien" — its title is a nod to the 1985 David Bowie song from the *Tonight* album — brought John Totleben back as a guest artist. I'll never forget standing in

Totleben's studio in Erie, Pennsylvania (my only visit there) and getting my first look at the pages of art he was sculpting (yes, *sculpting*) for this story. They were still raw and unfinished, but already they were as riveting as any drawing John had ever done, and as audacious as any piece of Pop Art ever created in any artist's studio in the 1960s.

There was a rippling spread picturing Swamp Thing with his form flowing like melted marrow, his internal organs exposed in an organic collage of still-functioning watch parts that writhed with their own clockwork secrets. Metallic scraps shared space with pasted-down photos of machinery on a base of heavy illustration board, a crazy quilt of almost Gigeresque "biomechanics" that easily weighed five pounds or more. At the center of each page was our beloved protagonist, composed of retouched photographs of a tiny model of the character that John and I had molded out of Super-Sculpy (a plastic-based sculpting material that can be baked and built upon), various resins and actual bits of mold and vegetation. It was not so much an exercise in storytelling — that was Alan's worry — as it was an externalization of John's own perverse geometry and inner landscapes. It was stunning, and I'm sorry to say that as beautiful as the printed version is, it is but a pale shadow of what I saw and held that night. If only today's computer production techniques could resurrect what that original art embodied!

What can be thoroughly enjoyed is the remarkable story that grew out of the unique cat-and-mouse game played by a writer and an artist at the peak of their creative powers. John completed half the issue as pure imagery, unfettered by even the germ of a story idea. Alan brooded over the pages until the raw Totlebenian expression began to suggest a narrative — a tale that would eventually coagulate into a portrait of inhuman desires and hunger culminating in a savage and appropriately unsettling rape sequence. It is a strange, otherworldly experience, an experiment that remains an outrageous high-water mark in the *Swamp Thing* saga, and in my judgment it claims the honor of being John and Alan's finest moment working together.

*****

"All Flesh Is Grass" (*Swamp Thing* #61) grew out of a concept I had suggested to Karen as a follow-up to "Reunion." When I had to decide between scripting #61 or working with Alan on his final issue, I chose the latter option and passed my idea for the former on to Alan. My initial concept had Swamp Thing growing a body on a planet whose dominant species are highly-evolved plant beings. A mass of these individuals then become the cells of an outsized Swamp Thing, who in turn is driven mad by the cacophony of voices and consciousnesses. As usual, Alan nurtured this germ of an idea into a much more ambitious and moving tale. The loopy, revisionist Adam Strange from #57-58 also makes a return visit here, in a bitterly amusing epilogue. As in his earlier tale, Strange comes across as being — well, *strange*: a hero displaced in time and space, and a bit of a buffoon for it.

"Wavelength" (*Swamp Thing* #62) proved that Rick Veitch, writing and drawing solo, was up to the task of taking over the title. Rick had, of course, been writing and illustrating his own work since the late 1970s, most notably in the pages of *Epic Illustrated* ("Abraxas and the Earthman") and in his graphic novel *Heartburst*, but scripting and pencilling a monthly comic book was quite another feat. Consider, dear reader, the Herculean feat that Rick went on to perform each and every month: writing *and* drawing full issues of *Swamp Thing*. Precious few creators can manage it — Jack Kirby, John Byrne, Dick Briefer, etc. — and fewer still can do it with the intensity of vision and originality that Rick brought to *Swamp Thing* during his tenure. I am in constant awe of the man, and you should be too.

Rick's role model was, of course, the late, great Jack Kirby. Metron, the prime mover of "Wavelength," was one of the fascinating characters that Kirby created for his "Fourth World" series in the mid-1970s. Kirby was himself a prime mover in American comics at that time, having left a legacy of titles, concepts, and characters behind him that remains the foundation of the entire Marvel Comics line. DC had successfully courted the King (as Kirby was rightfully called), and he began his brief but dazzling contributions to the DC universe by invigorating their least interesting title, *Superman's Pal, Jimmy Olsen*. A torrent of ideas and characters, each more mind-boggling than the last, soon spilled over into three new titles that Kirby created to tell his saga of war between the superhuman forces of Apokolips and New Genesis on battleground Earth. Together, *The New Gods*, *The Forever People* and *Mister Miracle* were arguably Kirby's finest hour — harbingers of the 21st century torrent of summer movie spectacles that we now take for granted — and at their core was the stone-faced Darkseid, whose quest for the Anti-Life Equation threatened disaster and subjugation for all other living beings.

It is one of the great tragedies of American comics that the powers-that-were cancelled the "Fourth World" titles before Kirby could conclude his grand fable. DC revived the characters years later, and in 1985 they reprinted the series with a new "resolution" in the form of *The Hunger Dogs*, a graphic novel for which Kirby had been courted back to DC. In the meantime, between the termination of the original titles and the publication of *The Hunger Dogs*, Kirby had moved to other publishers and attempted to retell his grandiose parable in a different guise (*The Eternals*, etc.), but he was never able to muster the magic to do it justice, much less finish it properly. It was an ignoble fate for the King and his creations. Veitch was true to the spirit of both in "Wavelength," and the appearance of the New Gods and their cosmic struggles provided an appropriate foreshadowing of the direction in which Rick would take *Swamp Thing* from issue #65 onwards.

*****

The tales told in Alan's last two issues have to speak for themselves. *Swamp Thing* #63's "Loose Ends (Reprise)" resurrected the horrific atmosphere and explosive (literally, in the case of Dwight Wicker's fate) potential for violence that characterized the original Moore/Bissette/Totleben collaborations, while "Return of the Good Gumbo" (*Swamp Thing* #64) brought it all to a fitting conclusion — a moving and bittersweet finale to the entire Alan Moore symphony of the Swamp Thing.

Behind the scenes, it was an event to be savored: the framing sequences (pages 1-3 and 20-24) were drawn by the original *Saga of the Swamp Thing* artist, Tom Yeates, who used to share a house with Veitch, Totleben and myself in our post-Kubert School daze. Rick and inker Alfredo Alcala drew pages 4-7, while I pencilled the central sequence (pages 8-19) — my farewell to the series as an artist. Alan and I co-plotted the pages over the phone. I pencilled them and added a few notions (including the glimpses of primordial Swamp Things that pepper pages 15-16, inspired by Walt Kelly and John O'Reilly's 1952 illustrated book *The Glob* — though Tom Veitch argues that he provided some inspiration here too, so I'll give him his due as well), and Alan scripted the pages over faxed photocopies of the artwork. The dream was to see John Totleben ink my pencils one last time; alas, it didn't work out, as John was already knee-deep in work on *Miracleman*. Alfredo came through, inking my final pencils, but Karen did manage to coax a lovely painted cover from John for the issue that was nominated for that year's UK Eagle Award for Best Cover.

Over a decade later, John and I *did* reunite for one more Swamp Thing story — the 10-page tale "Jack in the Green" in the Vertigo collection *Neil Gaiman's Midnight Days*. Neil orchestrated that return against considerable odds, and once told me that he was very pleased with the results, because John and I were still working up to the level that we'd brought to our best work in *Swamp Thing* in the 1980s.

That was also my final story for mainstream American comics, period. Karen made sure that my "farewell" signature on the last page I drew made it into print, a fine and noble parting gift.

Goodbye, Swampy and Abby.

I miss you.

All good things must end.

— Stephen R. Bissette
October 1988/July 2011
Mountains of Madness, Vermont

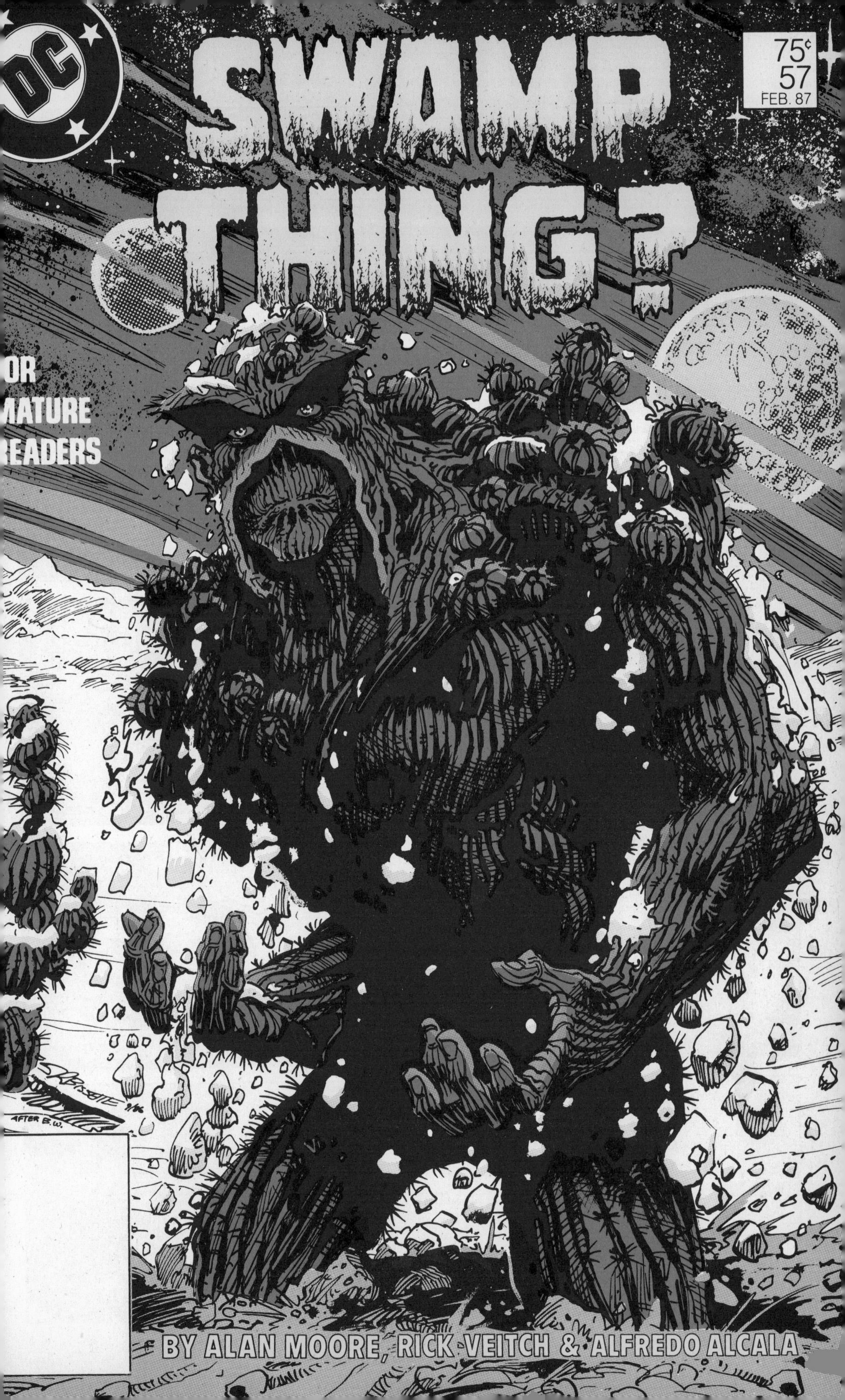
DC
SWAMP THING
75¢
57
FEB. 87
OR
MATURE
READERS
AFTER B.W.
BY ALAN MOORE, RICK VEITCH & ALFREDO ALCALA

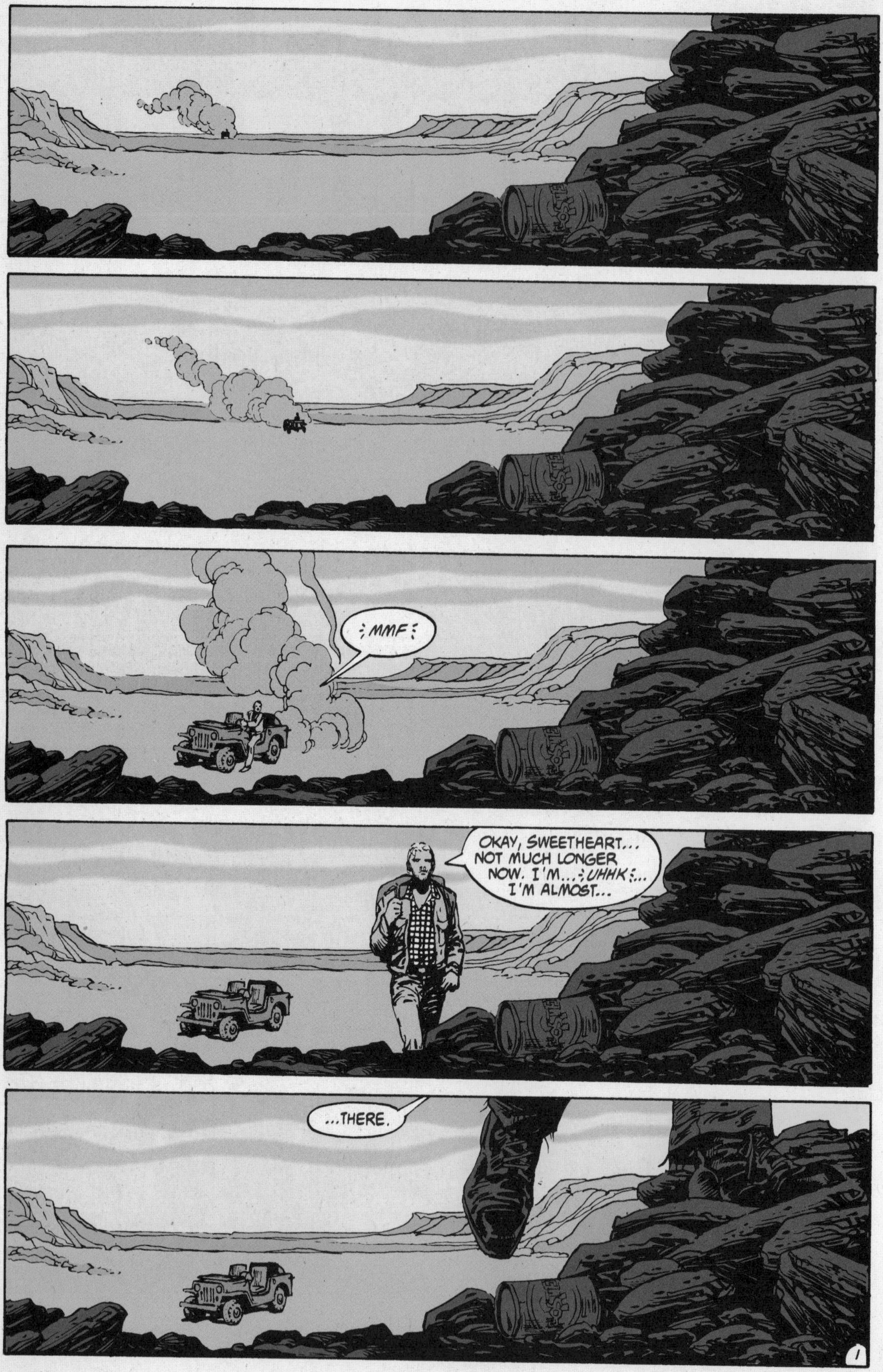
MMF
OKAY, SWEETHEART... NOT MUCH LONGER NOW. I'M... UHHK... I'M ALMOST...
...THERE.
1

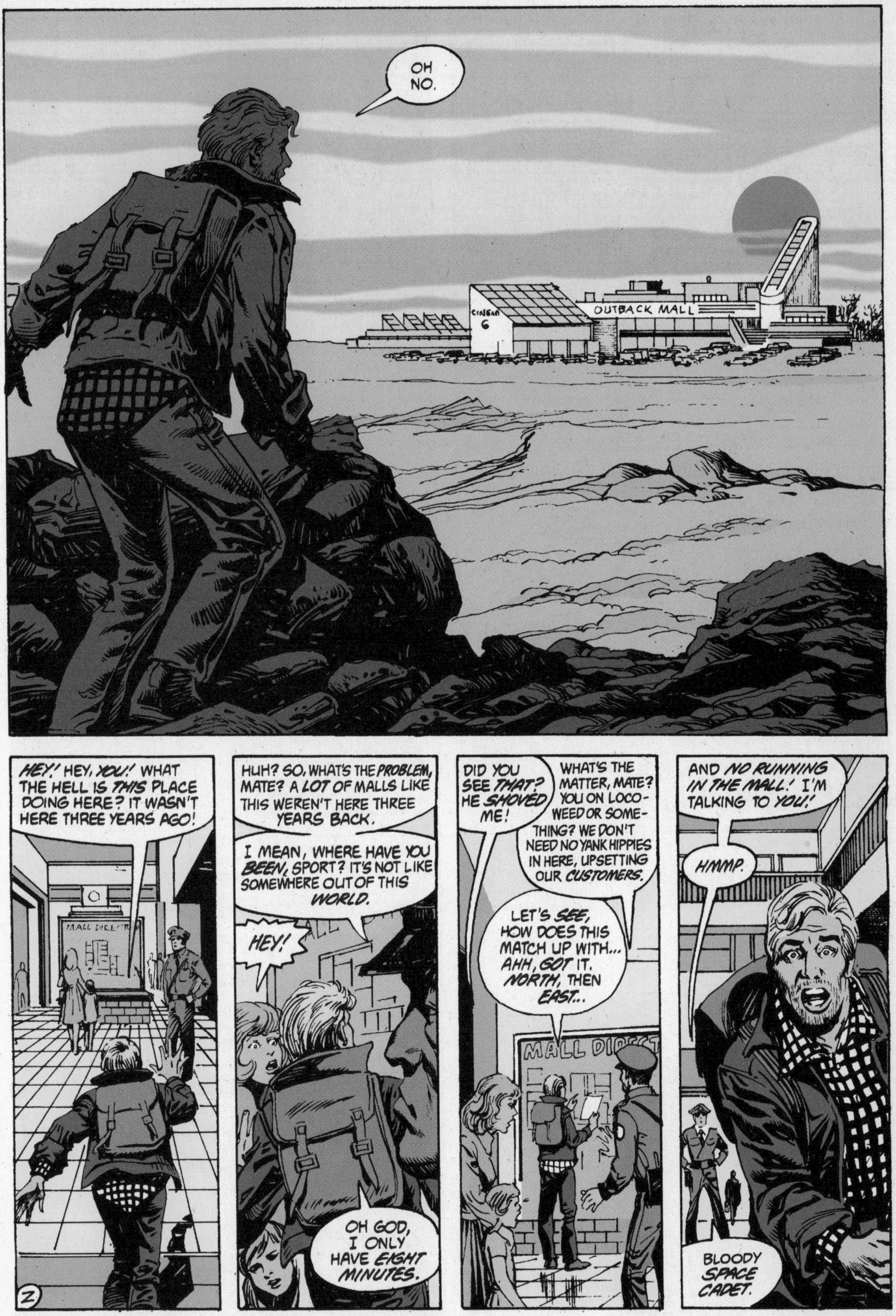
OH NO.
CINEMA 6
OUTBACK MALL
HEY! HEY, YOU! WHAT THE HELL IS THIS PLACE DOING HERE? IT WASN'T HERE THREE YEARS AGO!
2
HUH? SO, WHAT'S THE PROBLEM, MATE? A LOT OF MALLS LIKE THIS WEREN'T HERE THREE YEARS BACK.
I MEAN, WHERE HAVE YOU BEEN, SPORT? IT'S NOT LIKE SOMEWHERE OUT OF THIS WORLD.
HEY!
OH GOD, I ONLY HAVE EIGHT MINUTES.
DID YOU SEE THAT? HE SHOVED ME!
WHAT'S THE MATTER, MATE? YOU ON LOCO-WEED OR SOMETHING? WE DON'T NEED NO YANK HIPPIES IN HERE, UPSETTING OUR CUSTOMERS.
LET'S SEE, HOW DOES THIS MATCH UP WITH... AHH, GOT IT. NORTH, THEN EAST...
MALL DIRECT
AND NO RUNNING IN THE MALL! I'M TALKING TO YOU!
HMMP.
BLOODY SPACE CADET.

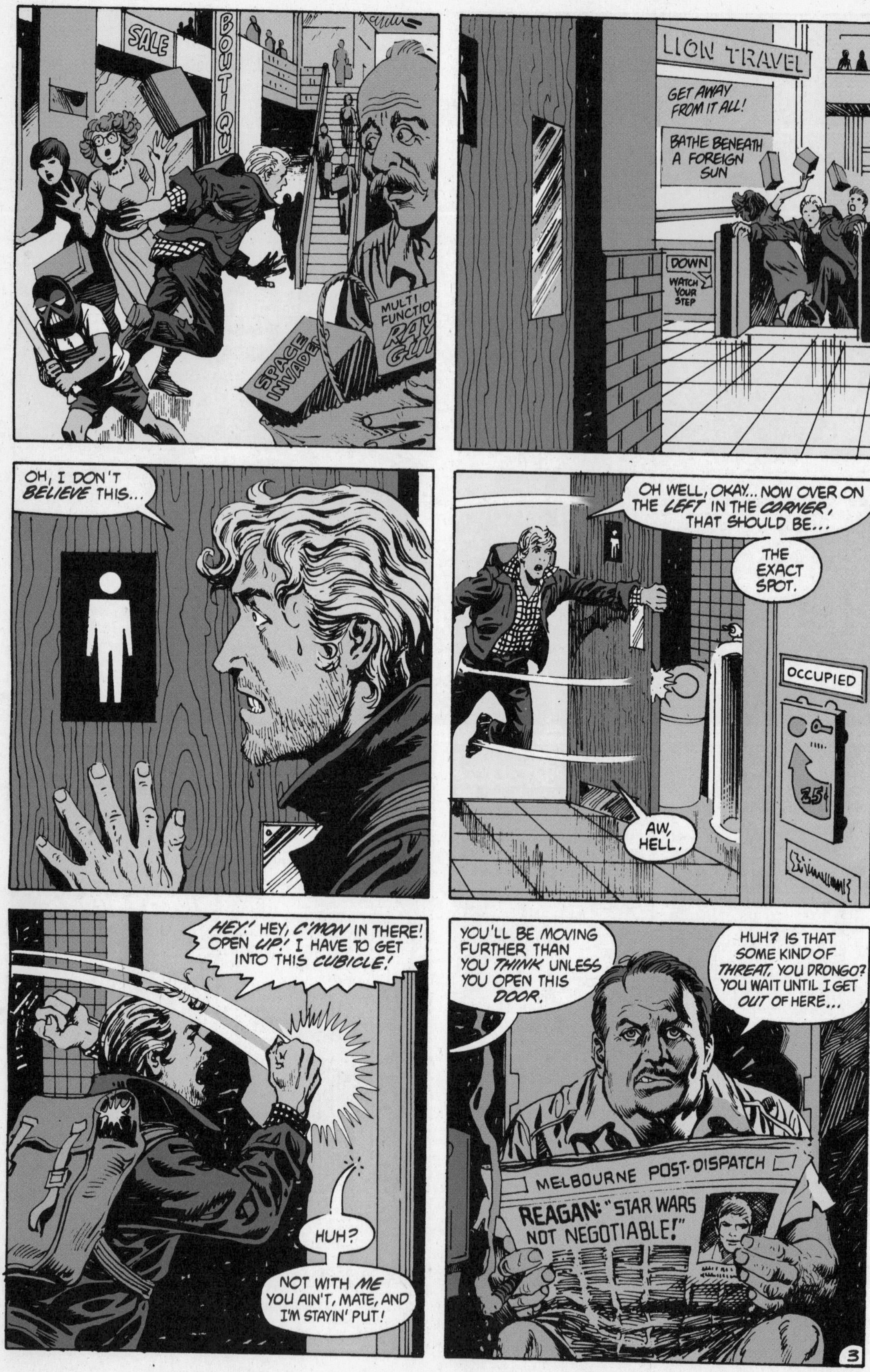
SALE
BOUTIQU
MULTI FUNCTION RAY GUN
SPACE INVADERS
LION TRAVEL
GET AWAY FROM IT ALL!
BATHE BENEATH A FOREIGN SUN
DOWN
WATCH YOUR STEP
OH, I DON'T BELIEVE THIS...
OH WELL, OKAY... NOW OVER ON THE LEFT IN THE CORNER, THAT SHOULD BE...
THE EXACT SPOT.
OCCUPIED
35¢
AW, HELL.
HEY! HEY, C'MON IN THERE! OPEN UP! I HAVE TO GET INTO THIS CUBICLE!
HUH?
NOT WITH ME YOU AIN'T, MATE, AND I'M STAYIN' PUT!
YOU'LL BE MOVING FURTHER THAN YOU THINK UNLESS YOU OPEN THIS DOOR.
HUH? IS THAT SOME KIND OF THREAT, YOU DRONGO? YOU WAIT UNTIL I GET OUT OF HERE...
MELBOURNE POST-DISPATCH
REAGAN: "STAR WARS NOT NEGOTIABLE!"
3

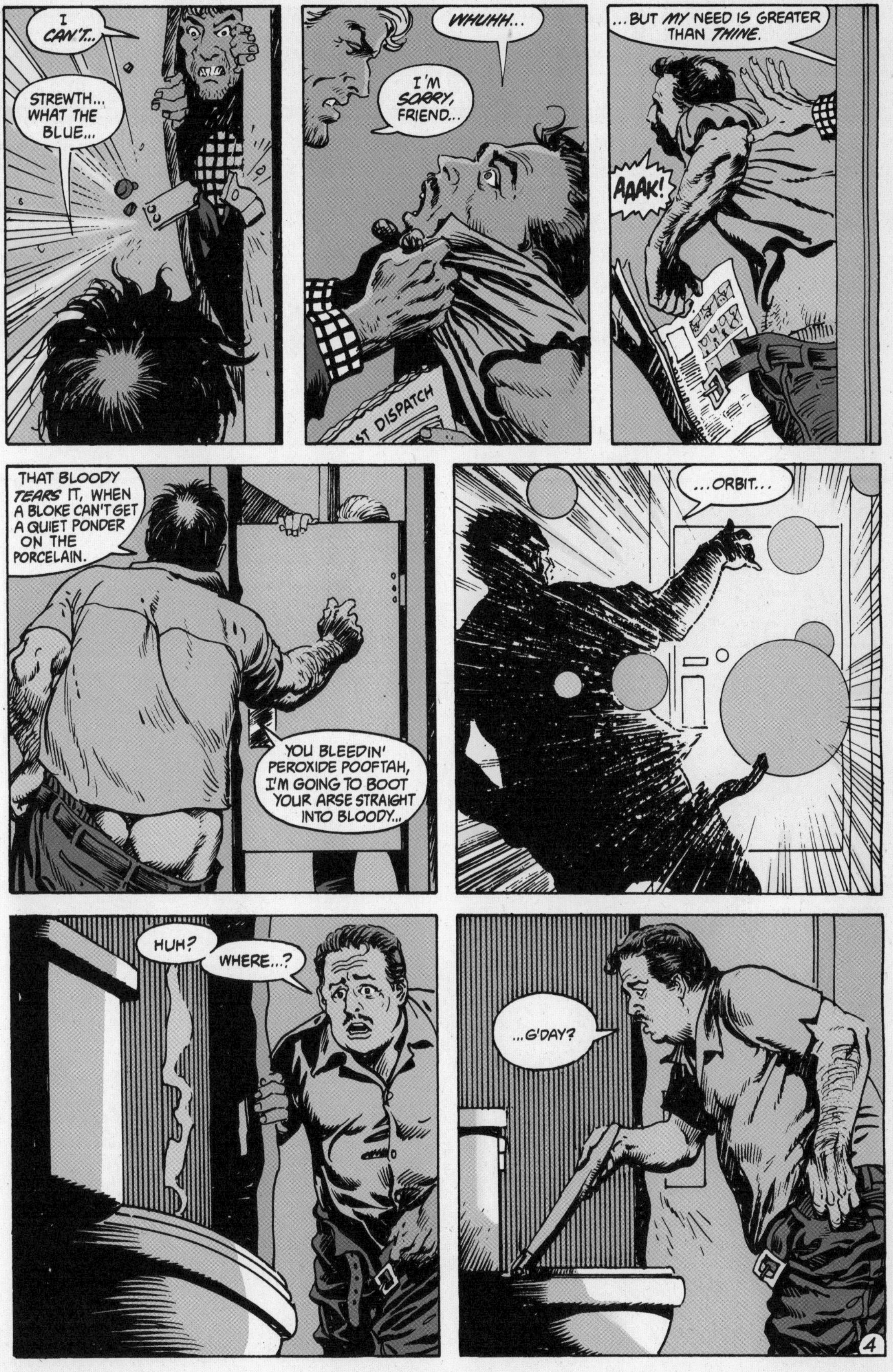
I CAN'T...
STREWTH... WHAT THE BLUE...
WHUHH...
I'M SORRY, FRIEND...
...BUT MY NEED IS GREATER THAN THINE.
AAAK!
THAT BLOODY TEARS IT, WHEN A BLOKE CAN'T GET A QUIET PONDER ON THE PORCELAIN.
YOU BLEEDIN' PEROXIDE POOFTAH, I'M GOING TO BOOT YOUR ARSE STRAIGHT INTO BLOODY...
...ORBIT...
HUH?
WHERE...?
...G'DAY?
4

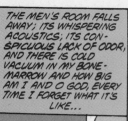

THE MEN'S ROOM FALLS AWAY; ITS WHISPERING ACOUSTICS; ITS CONSPICUOUS LACK OF ODOR, AND THERE IS COLD VACUUM IN MY BONE-MARROW AND HOW BIG AM I AND O GOD, EVERY TIME I FORGET WHAT IT'S LIKE...

...AND FALLING AND FALLING, BUT INWARDS, LIKE SHRINKING, AND THEN...

TENDRILS SQUIRM IN CRUMBLING BROWN PLANET-FLESH...

IN THE LABORATORY, A BOMB, HE BURNED...

THE WHITE-HAIRED WOMAN, GONE...

THE BLUE WORLD, HE JUMPED AND THEN...

WHAT? WHAT? COLLISION! IN NOWHERE. I HIT SOMETHING, IMPACT, THAT SMASHING GREEN FIST, I CAN'T...

⑤

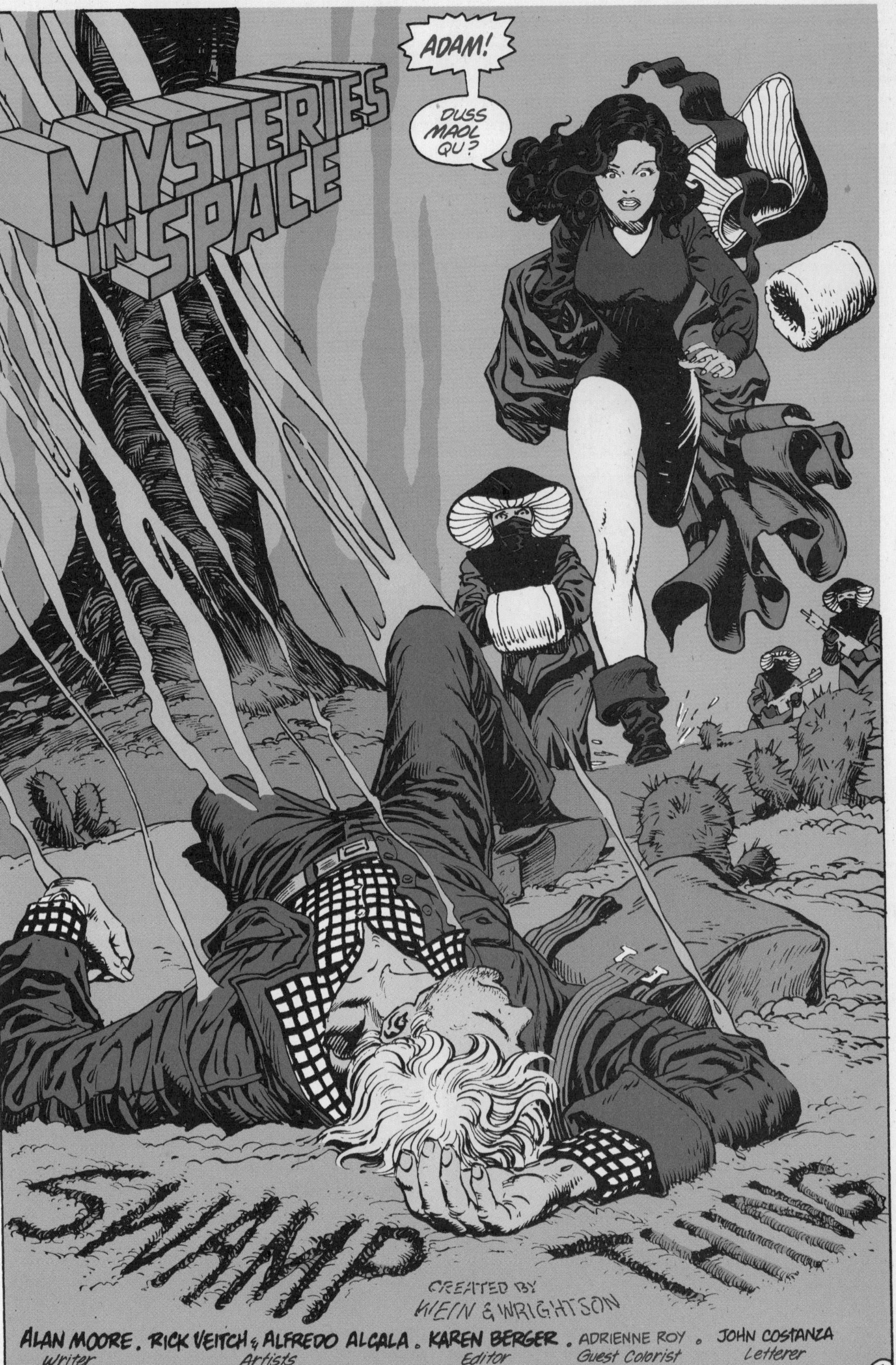
MYSTERIES IN SPACE
ADAM!
DUSS MAOL QU?
SWAMP THING
CREATED BY WEIN & WRIGHTSON
ALAN MOORE . Writer
RICK VEITCH & ALFREDO ALCALA . Artists
KAREN BERGER . Editor
ADRIENNE ROY . Guest Colorist
JOHN COSTANZA Letterer
6

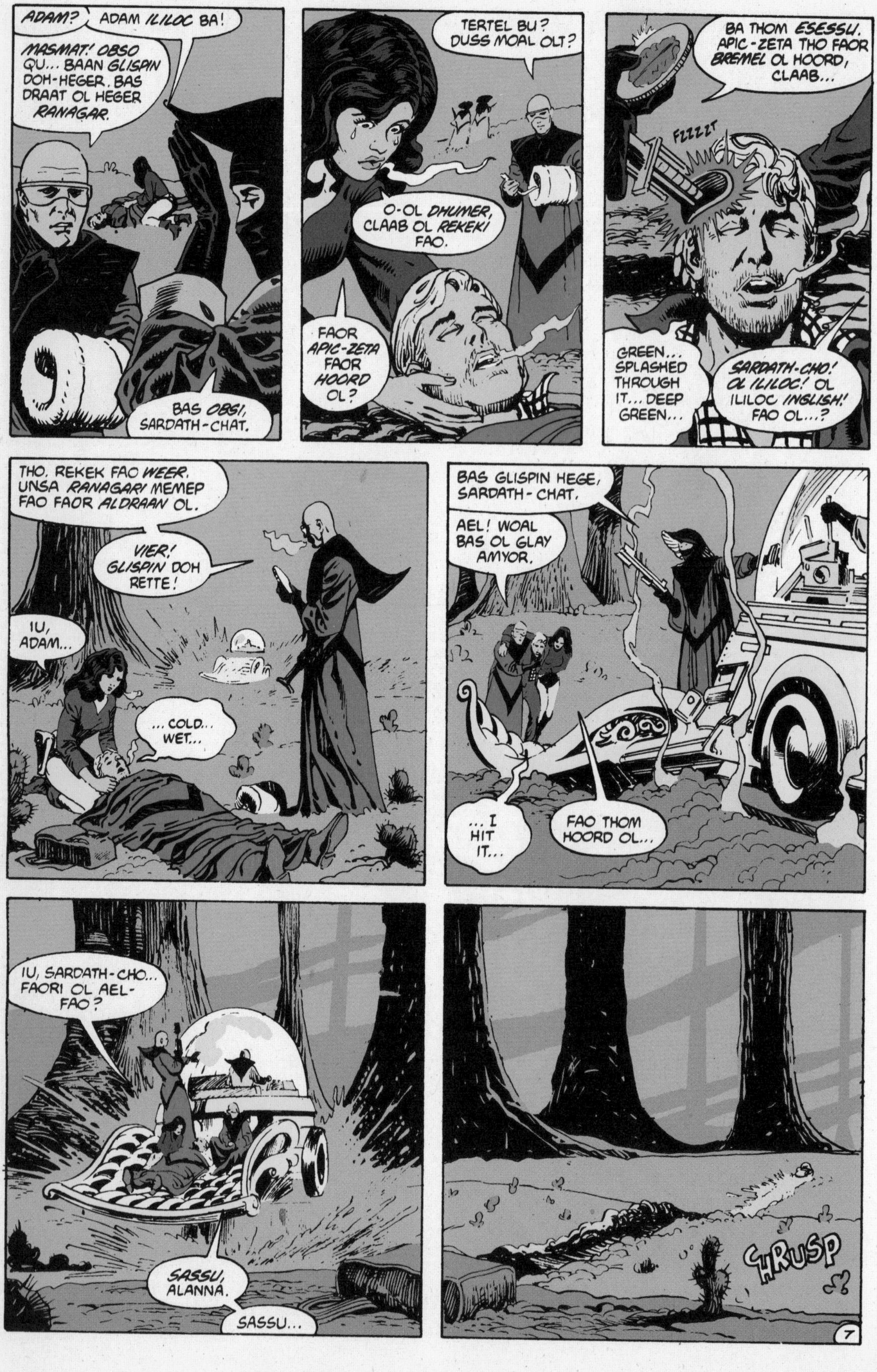
ADAM?
ADAM ILILOC BA!
MASMAT! OBSO QU... BAAN GLISPIN DOH-HEGER. BAS DRAAT OL HEGER RANAGAR.
BAS OBSI, SARDATH-CHAT.
TERTEL BU? DUSS MOAL OLT?
O-OL DHUMER, CLAAB OL REKEKI FAO.
FAOR APIC-ZETA FAOR HOORD OL?
BA THOM ESESSU. APIC-ZETA THO FAOR BREMEL OL HOORD, CLAAB...
FZZZZT
GREEN... SPLASHED THROUGH IT... DEEP GREEN...
SARDATH-CHO! OL ILILOC! OL ILILOC INGLISH! FAO OL...?
THO. REKEK FAO WEER. UNSA RANAGARI MEMEP FAO FAOR ALDRAAN OL.
VIER! GLISPIN DOH RETTE!
IU, ADAM...
...COLD... WET...
BAS GLISPIN HEGE, SARDATH-CHAT.
AEL! WOAL BAS OL GLAY AMYOR.
...I HIT IT...
FAO THOM HOORD OL...
IU, SARDATH-CHO... FAORI OL AEL-FAO?
SASSU, ALANNA.
SASSU...
CHRUSP
7

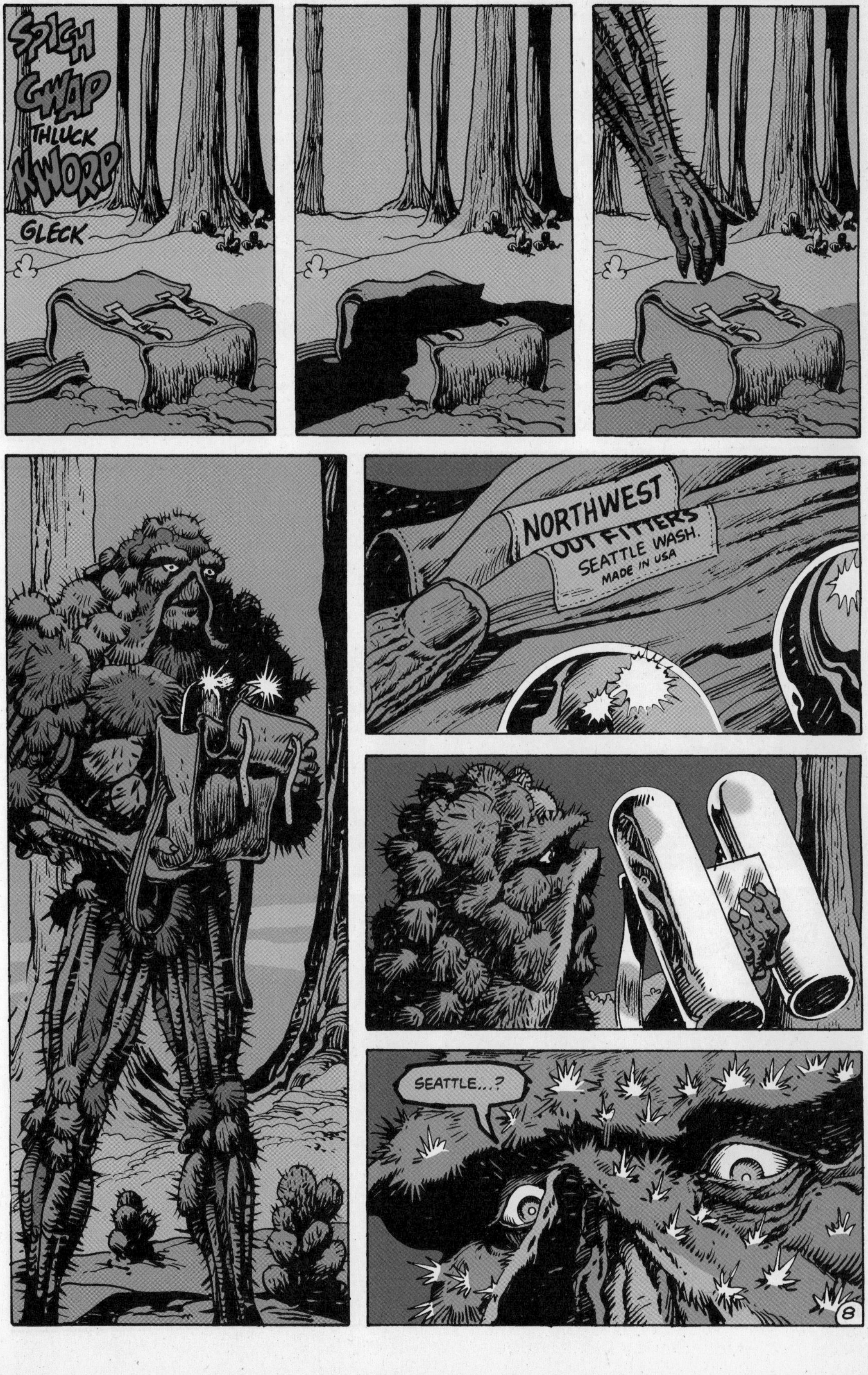
SPLCH
GWAP
THLUCK
KWORP
GLECK
NORTHWEST
OUTFITTERS
SEATTLE WASH.
MADE IN USA
SEATTLE...?
8

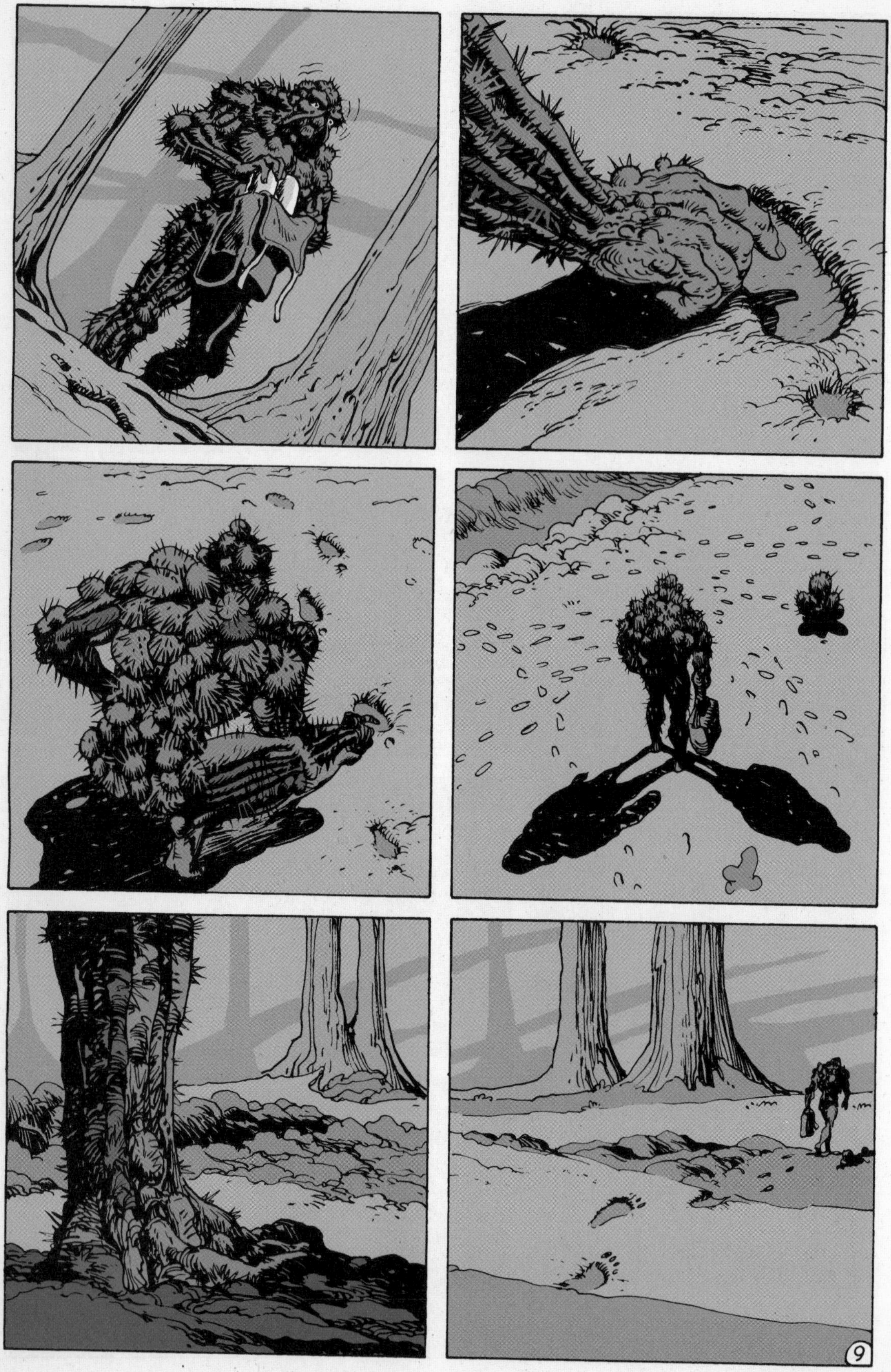
9

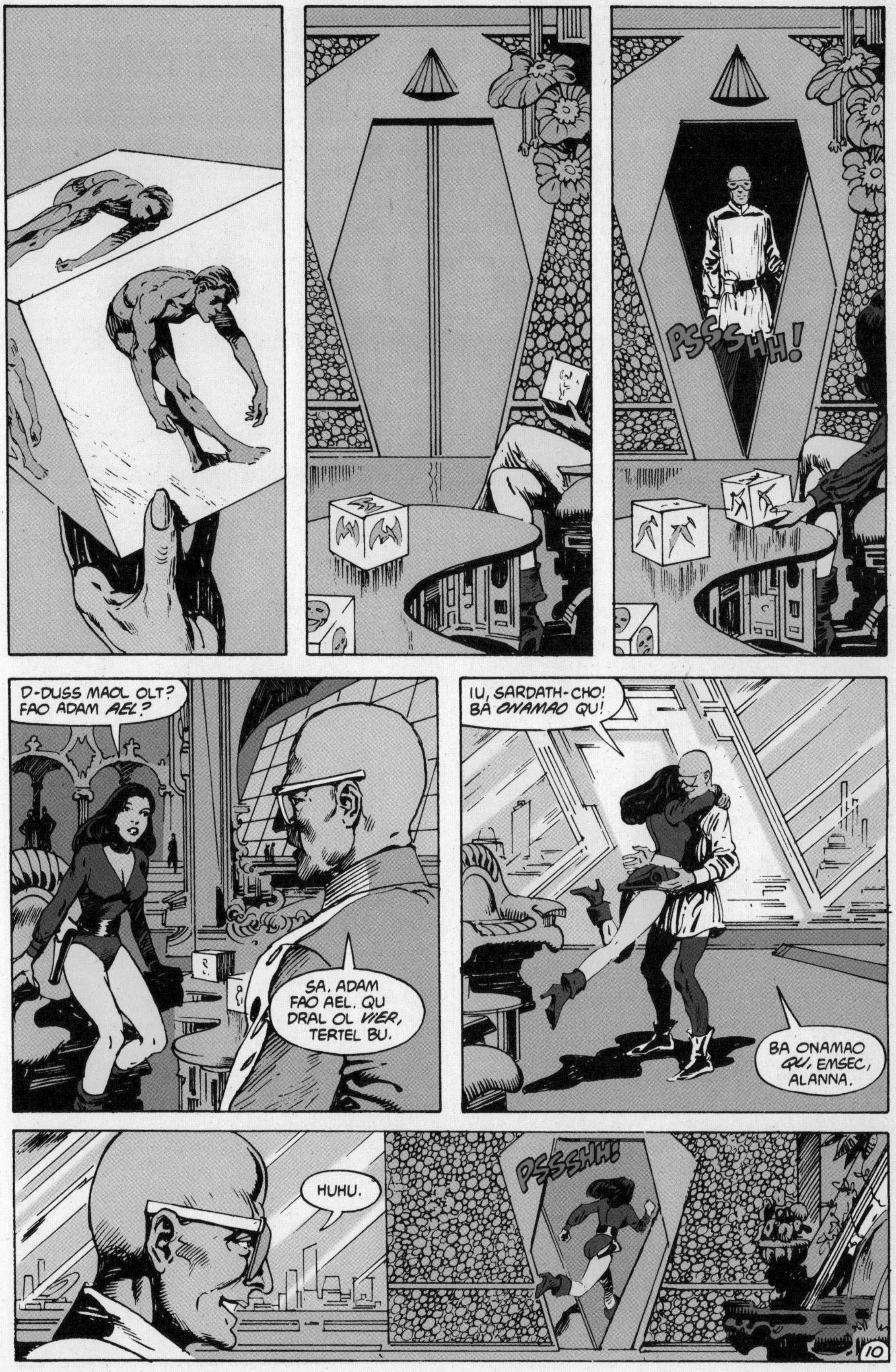
PSSSHH!
D-DUSS MAOL OLT? FAO ADAM AEL?
SA, ADAM FAO AEL. QU DRAL OL VIER, TERTEL BU.
IU, SARDATH-CHO! BA ONAMAO QU!
BA ONAMAO QU, EMSEC, ALANNA.
HUHU.
PSSSHH!
10

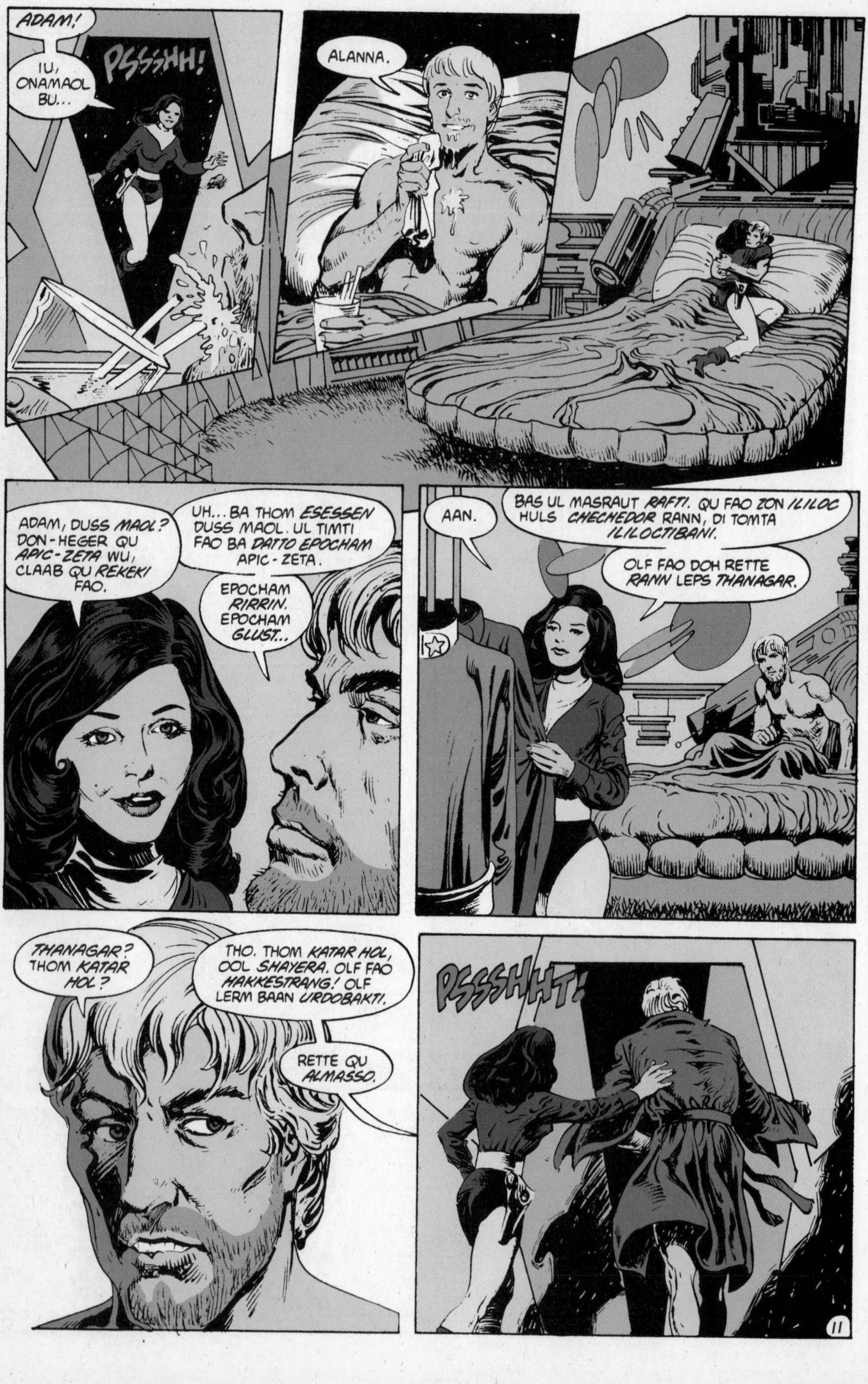
ADAM!
IU, ONAMAOL BU...
PSSSHH!
ALANNA.
ADAM, DUSS MAOL? DON-HEGER QU APIC-ZETA WU, CLAAB QU REKEKI FAO.
UH... BA THOM ESESSEN DUSS MAOL. UL TIMTI FAO BA DATTO EPOCHAM APIC-ZETA.
EPOCHAM RIRRIN. EPOCHAM GLUST...
AAN.
BAS UL MASRAUT RAFTI. QU FAO ZON ILILOC HULS CHECHEDOR RANN, DI TOMTA ILILOCTIBANI.
OLF FAO DOH RETTE RANN LEPS THANAGAR.
THANAGAR? THOM KATAR HOL?
THO. THOM KATAR HOL, OOL SHAYERA. OLF FAO HAKKESTRANG! OLF LERM BAAN URDOBAKTI.
RETTE QU ALMASSO.
PSSSHHT!
11

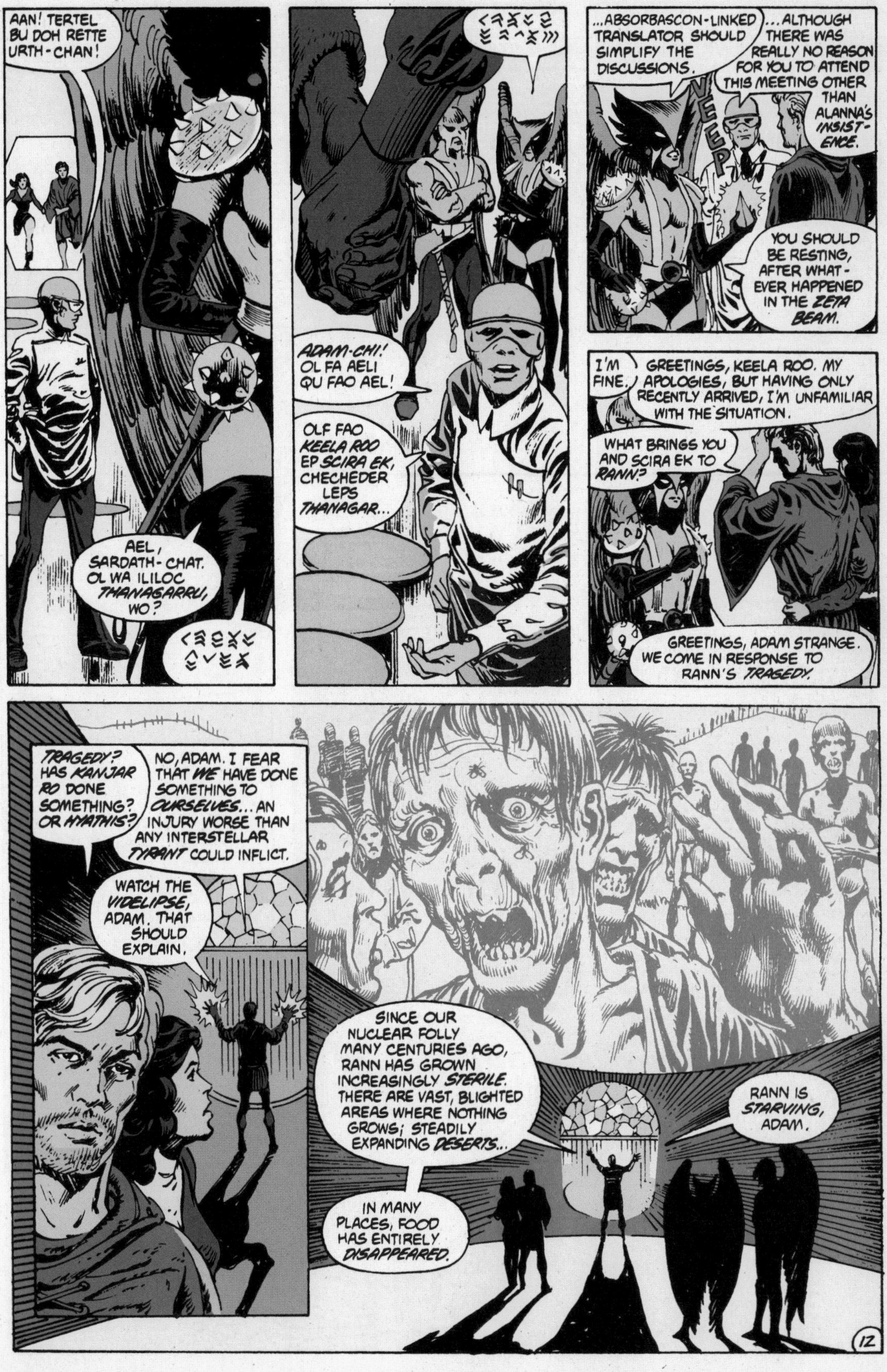
AAN! TERTEL BU DOH RETTE URTH-CHAN!
AEL, SARDATH-CHAT. OL WA ILILOC THANAGARRU, WO?
ADAM-CHI! OL FA AELI QU FAO AEL!
OLF FAO KEELA ROO EP SCIRA EK, CHECHEDER LEPS THANAGAR...
...ABSORBASCON-LINKED TRANSLATOR SHOULD SIMPLIFY THE DISCUSSIONS.
VEEP
...ALTHOUGH THERE WAS REALLY NO REASON FOR YOU TO ATTEND THIS MEETING OTHER THAN ALANNA'S INSISTENCE.
YOU SHOULD BE RESTING, AFTER WHATEVER HAPPENED IN THE ZETA BEAM.
I'M FINE.
GREETINGS, KEELA ROO. MY APOLOGIES, BUT HAVING ONLY RECENTLY ARRIVED, I'M UNFAMILIAR WITH THE SITUATION.
WHAT BRINGS YOU AND SCIRA EK TO RANN?
GREETINGS, ADAM STRANGE. WE COME IN RESPONSE TO RANN'S TRAGEDY.
TRAGEDY? HAS KANJAR RO DONE SOMETHING? OR HYATHIS?
NO, ADAM. I FEAR THAT WE HAVE DONE SOMETHING TO OURSELVES... AN INJURY WORSE THAN ANY INTERSTELLAR TYRANT COULD INFLICT.
WATCH THE VIDELIPSE, ADAM. THAT SHOULD EXPLAIN.
SINCE OUR NUCLEAR FOLLY MANY CENTURIES AGO, RANN HAS GROWN INCREASINGLY STERILE. THERE ARE VAST, BLIGHTED AREAS WHERE NOTHING GROWS; STEADILY EXPANDING DESERTS...
IN MANY PLACES, FOOD HAS ENTIRELY DISAPPEARED.
RANN IS STARVING, ADAM.
12

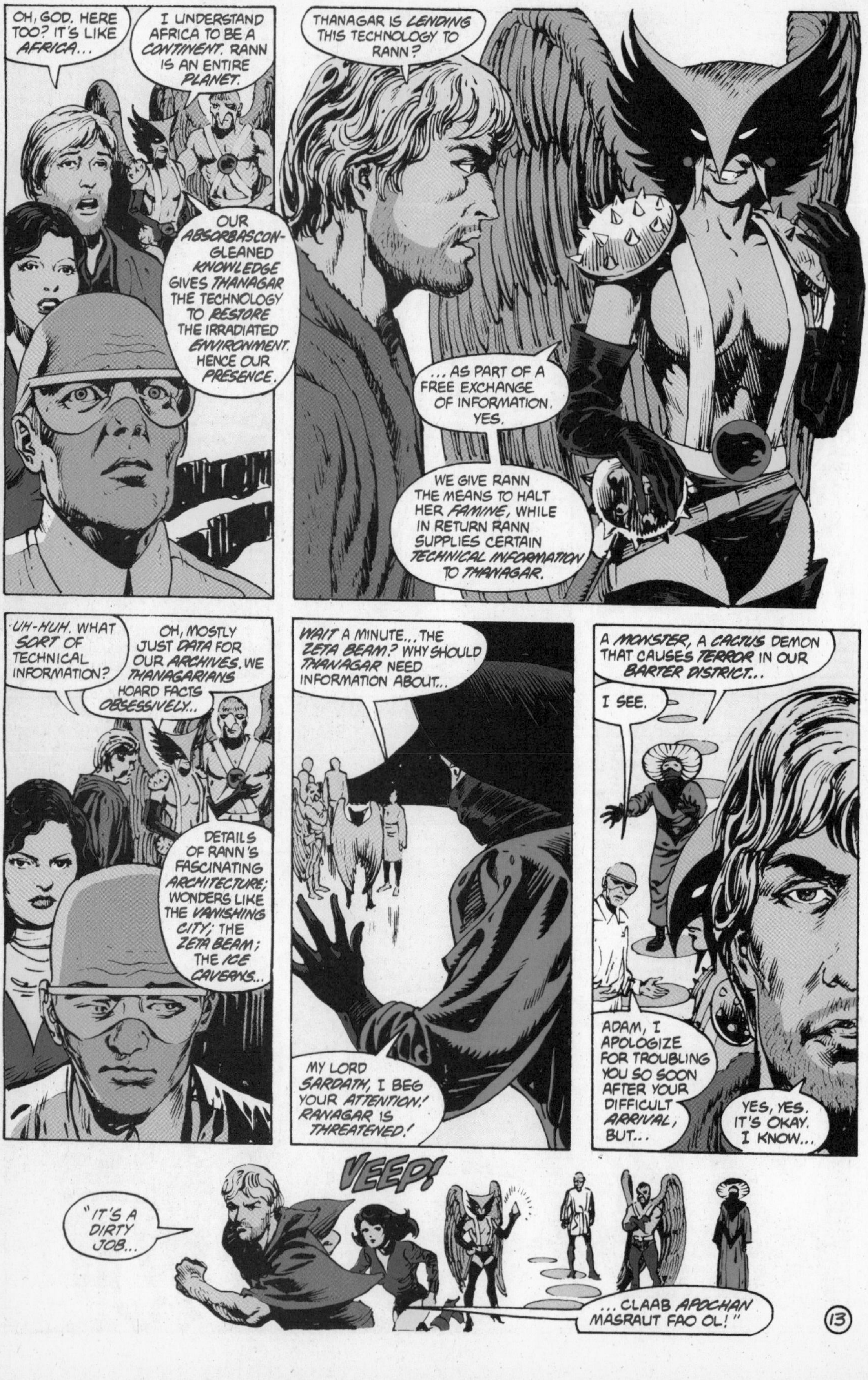
OH, GOD. HERE TOO? IT'S LIKE AFRICA...
I UNDERSTAND AFRICA TO BE A CONTINENT. RANN IS AN ENTIRE PLANET.
OUR ABSORBASCON-GLEANED KNOWLEDGE GIVES THANAGAR THE TECHNOLOGY TO RESTORE THE IRRADIATED ENVIRONMENT. HENCE OUR PRESENCE.
THANAGAR IS LENDING THIS TECHNOLOGY TO RANN?
...AS PART OF A FREE EXCHANGE OF INFORMATION. YES.
WE GIVE RANN THE MEANS TO HALT HER FAMINE, WHILE IN RETURN RANN SUPPLIES CERTAIN TECHNICAL INFORMATION TO THANAGAR.
UH-HUH. WHAT SORT OF TECHNICAL INFORMATION?
OH, MOSTLY JUST DATA FOR OUR ARCHIVES. WE THANAGARIANS HOARD FACTS OBSESSIVELY...
DETAILS OF RANN'S FASCINATING ARCHITECTURE; WONDERS LIKE THE VANISHING CITY; THE ZETA BEAM; THE ICE CAVERNS...
WAIT A MINUTE... THE ZETA BEAM? WHY SHOULD THANAGAR NEED INFORMATION ABOUT...
MY LORD SARDATH, I BEG YOUR ATTENTION! RANAGAR IS THREATENED!
A MONSTER, A CACTUS DEMON THAT CAUSES TERROR IN OUR BARTER DISTRICT...
I SEE.
ADAM, I APOLOGIZE FOR TROUBLING YOU SO SOON AFTER YOUR DIFFICULT ARRIVAL, BUT...
YES, YES. IT'S OKAY. I KNOW...
"IT'S A DIRTY JOB...
VEEP!
...CLAAB APOCHAN MASRAUT FAO OL!"
13

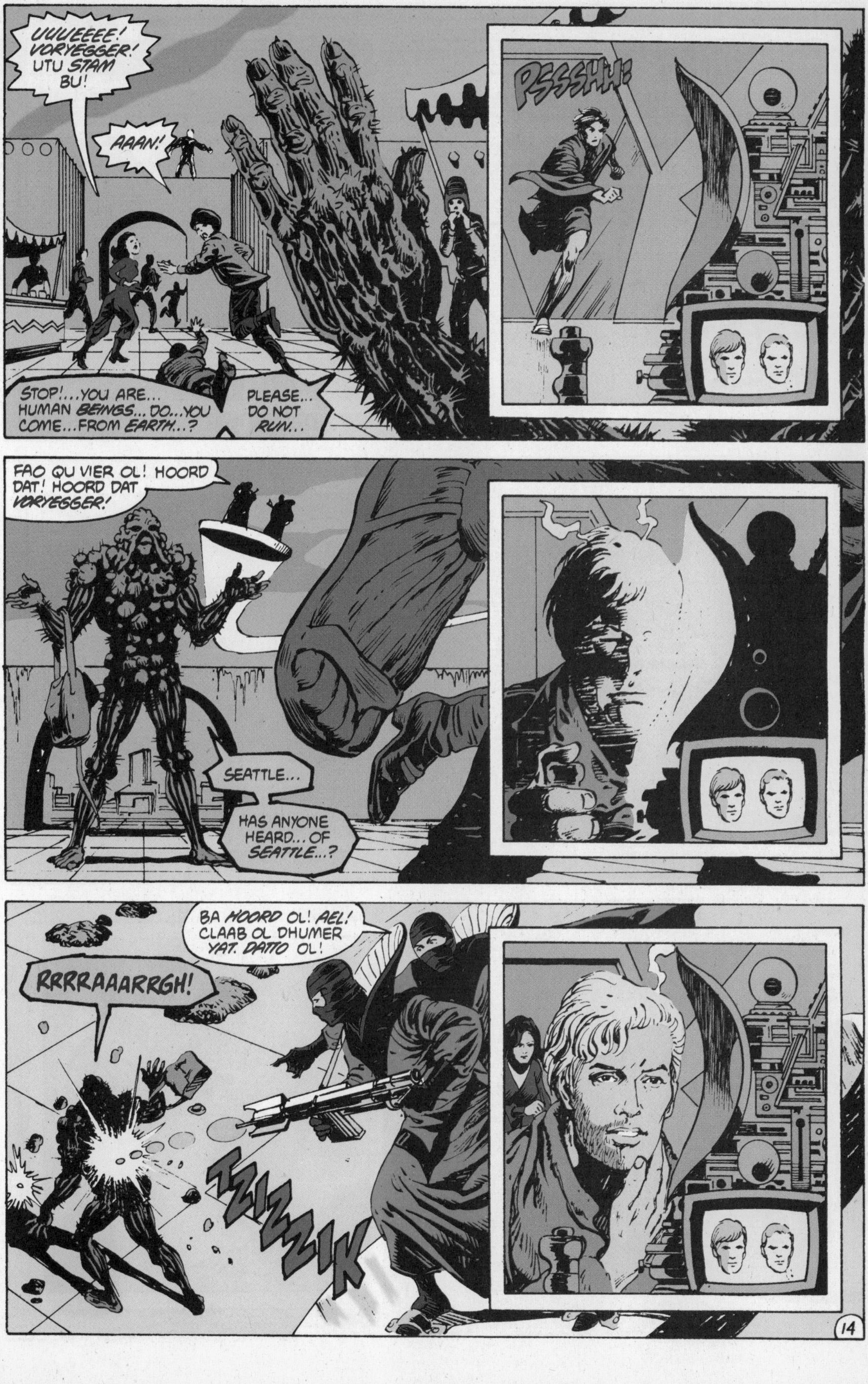
UUUEEEE! VORYEGGER! UTU STAM BU!
AAAN!
PSSSHH!
STOP!...YOU ARE... HUMAN BEINGS...DO...YOU COME...FROM EARTH...?
PLEASE... DO NOT RUN...
FAO QU VIER OL! HOORD DAT! HOORD DAT VORYEGGER!
SEATTLE...
HAS ANYONE HEARD...OF SEATTLE...?
BA HOORD OL! AEL! CLAAB OL DHUMER YAT. DATTO OL!
RRRRAAARRGH!
TZIZZIK
14

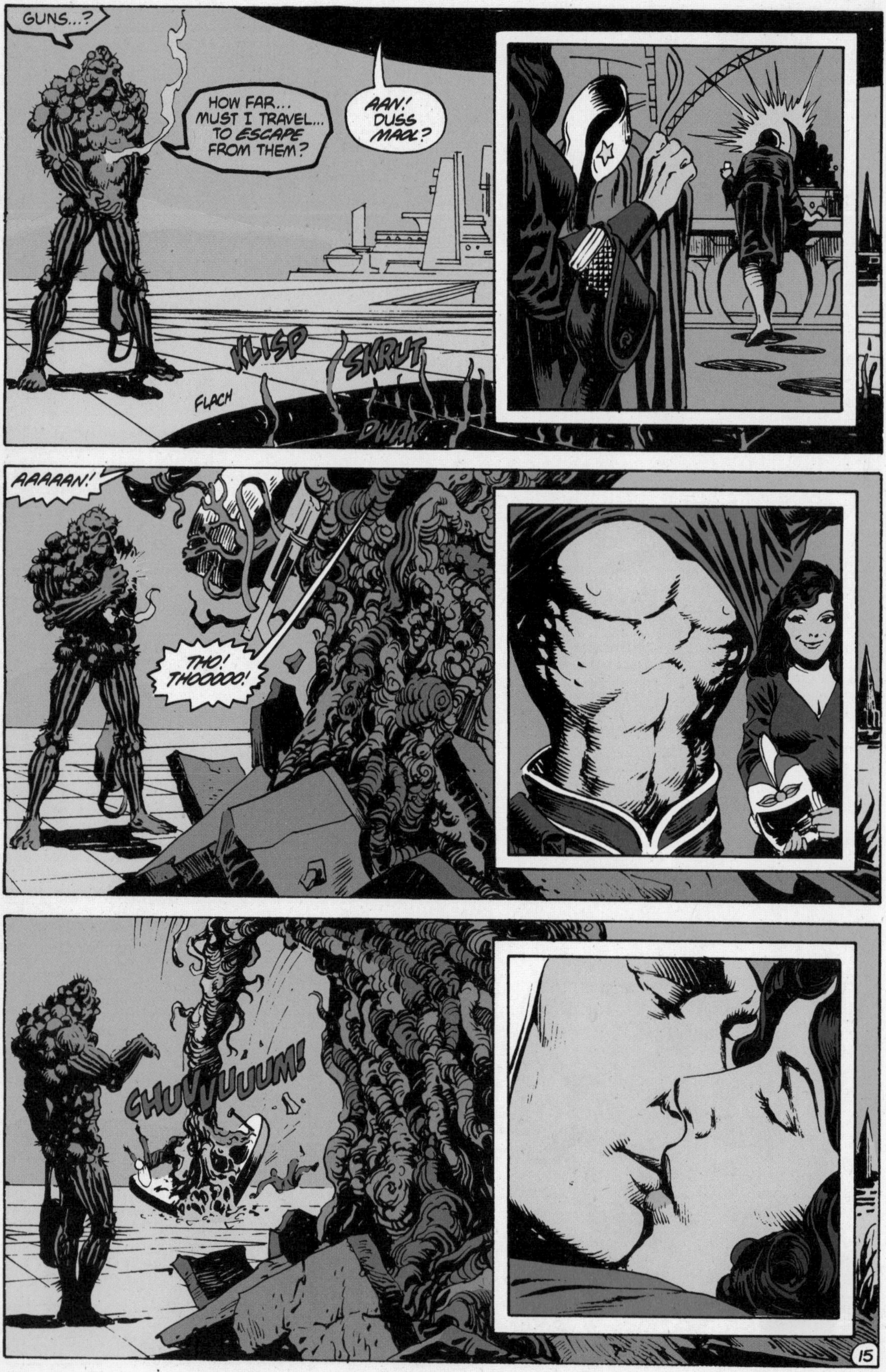
GUNS...?
HOW FAR... MUST I TRAVEL... TO *ESCAPE* FROM THEM?
AAN! DUSS MAOL?
KLISP
SKRUT
FLACH
DWAK
AAAAAN!
THO! THOOOOO!
CHUVVUUUM!
15

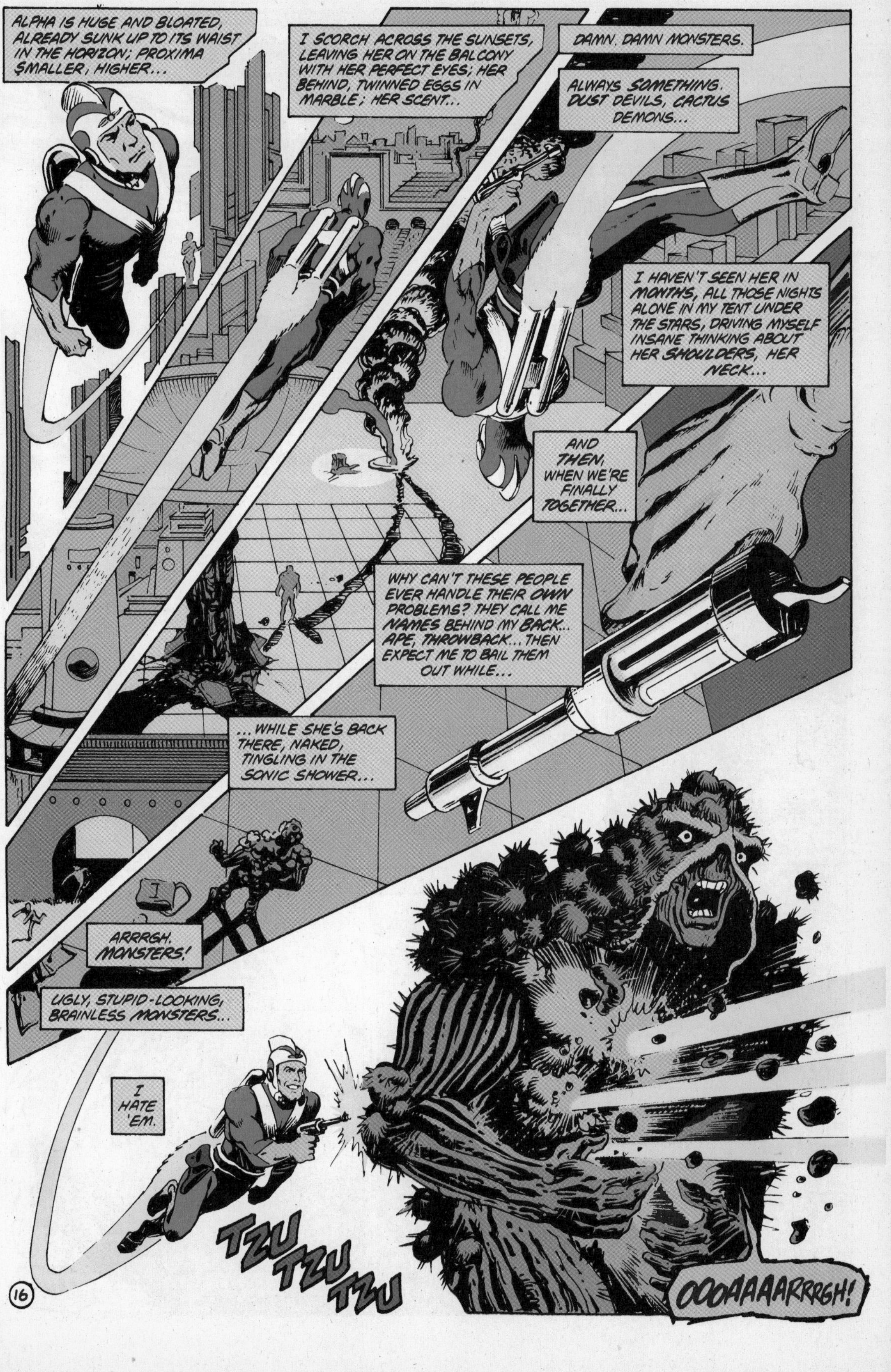
ALPHA IS HUGE AND BLOATED, ALREADY SUNK UP TO ITS WAIST IN THE HORIZON; PROXIMA SMALLER, HIGHER...
I SCORCH ACROSS THE SUNSETS, LEAVING HER ON THE BALCONY WITH HER PERFECT EYES; HER BEHIND, TWINNED EGGS IN MARBLE; HER SCENT...
DAMN. DAMN MONSTERS.
ALWAYS SOMETHING. DUST DEVILS, CACTUS DEMONS...
I HAVEN'T SEEN HER IN MONTHS, ALL THOSE NIGHTS ALONE IN MY TENT UNDER THE STARS, DRIVING MYSELF INSANE THINKING ABOUT HER SHOULDERS, HER NECK...
AND THEN, WHEN WE'RE FINALLY TOGETHER...
WHY CAN'T THESE PEOPLE EVER HANDLE THEIR OWN PROBLEMS? THEY CALL ME NAMES BEHIND MY BACK... APE, THROWBACK... THEN EXPECT ME TO BAIL THEM OUT WHILE...
...WHILE SHE'S BACK THERE, NAKED, TINGLING IN THE SONIC SHOWER...
ARRRGH. MONSTERS!
UGLY, STUPID-LOOKING, BRAINLESS MONSTERS...
I HATE 'EM.
TZU TZU TZU TZU
OOOAAAARRRGH!
16

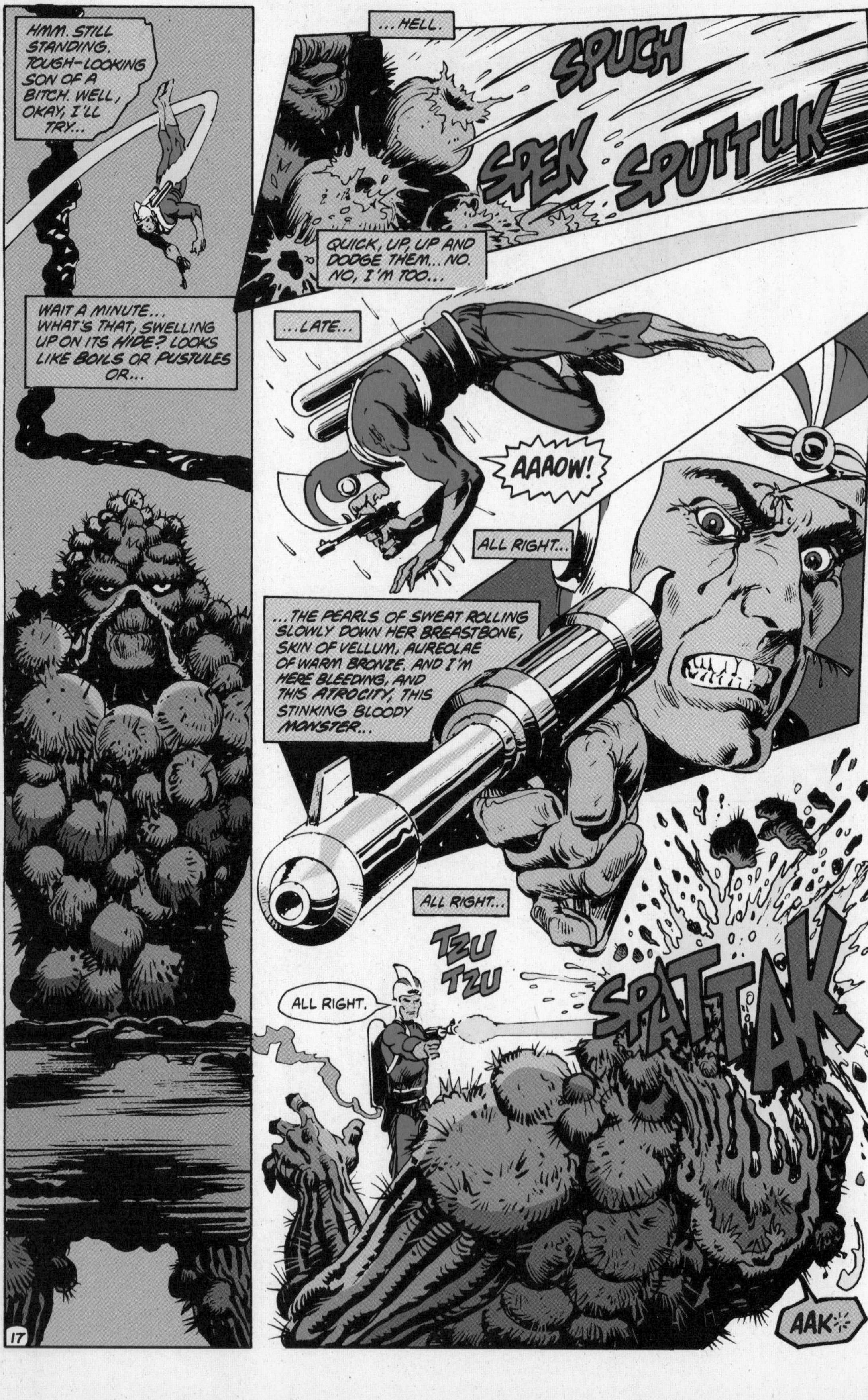
HMM. STILL STANDING. TOUGH-LOOKING SON OF A BITCH. WELL, OKAY, I'LL TRY...
WAIT A MINUTE... WHAT'S THAT, SWELLING UP ON ITS HIDE? LOOKS LIKE BOILS OR PUSTULES OR...
...HELL.
SPUCH
SPEK
SPUTTUK
QUICK, UP, UP AND DODGE THEM... NO. NO, I'M TOO...
...LATE...
AAAOW!
ALL RIGHT...
...THE PEARLS OF SWEAT ROLLING SLOWLY DOWN HER BREASTBONE, SKIN OF VELLUM, AUREOLAE OF WARM BRONZE. AND I'M HERE BLEEDING, AND THIS ATROCITY, THIS STINKING BLOODY MONSTER...
ALL RIGHT...
TZU TZU
ALL RIGHT.
SPATTAK
AAK
17

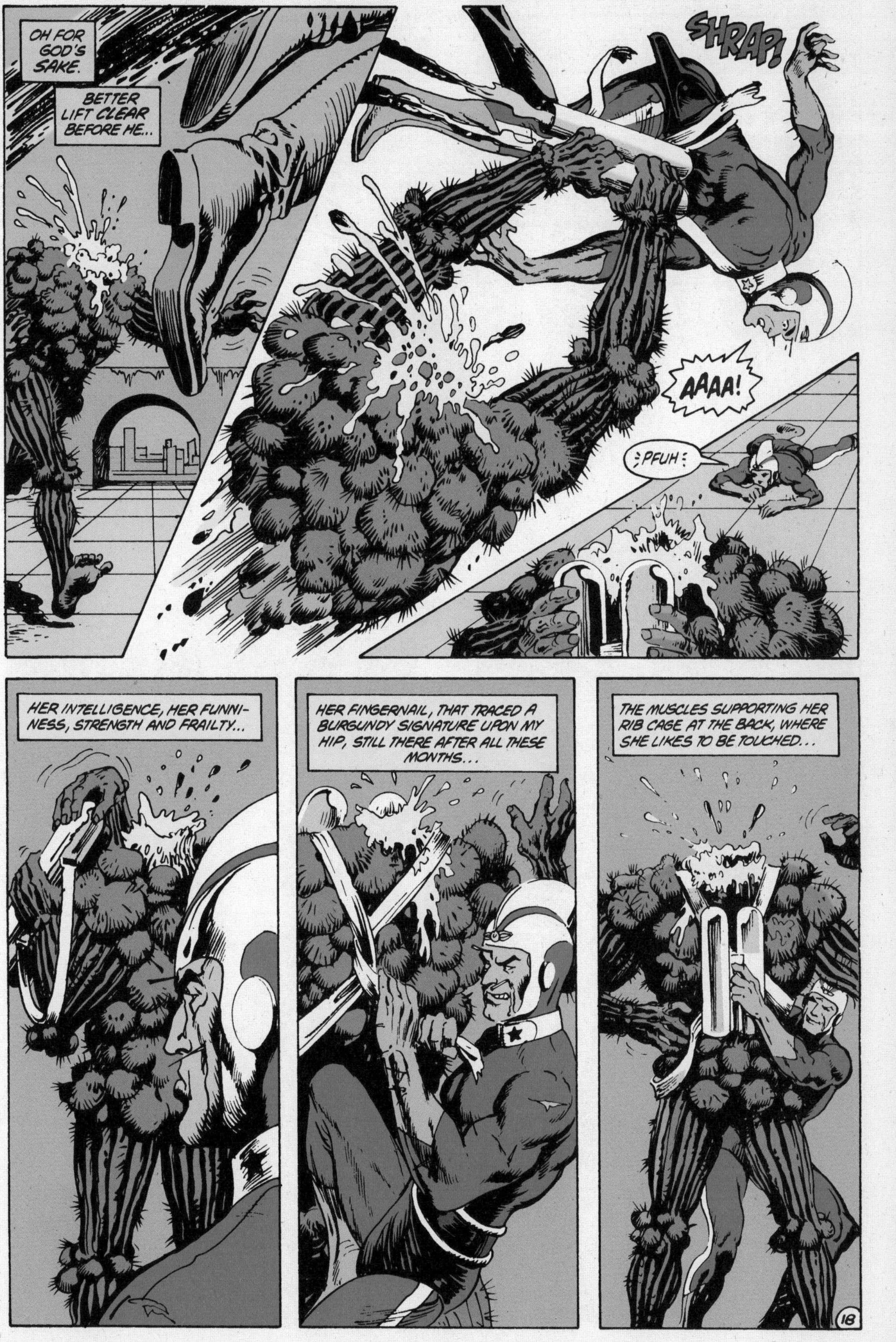
OH FOR GOD'S SAKE.
BETTER LIFT CLEAR BEFORE HE...
SHRAP!
AAAA!
PFUH
HER INTELLIGENCE, HER FUNNINESS, STRENGTH AND FRAILTY...
HER FINGERNAIL, THAT TRACED A BURGUNDY SIGNATURE UPON MY HIP, STILL THERE AFTER ALL THESE MONTHS...
THE MUSCLES SUPPORTING HER RIB CAGE AT THE BACK, WHERE SHE LIKES TO BE TOUCHED...
18

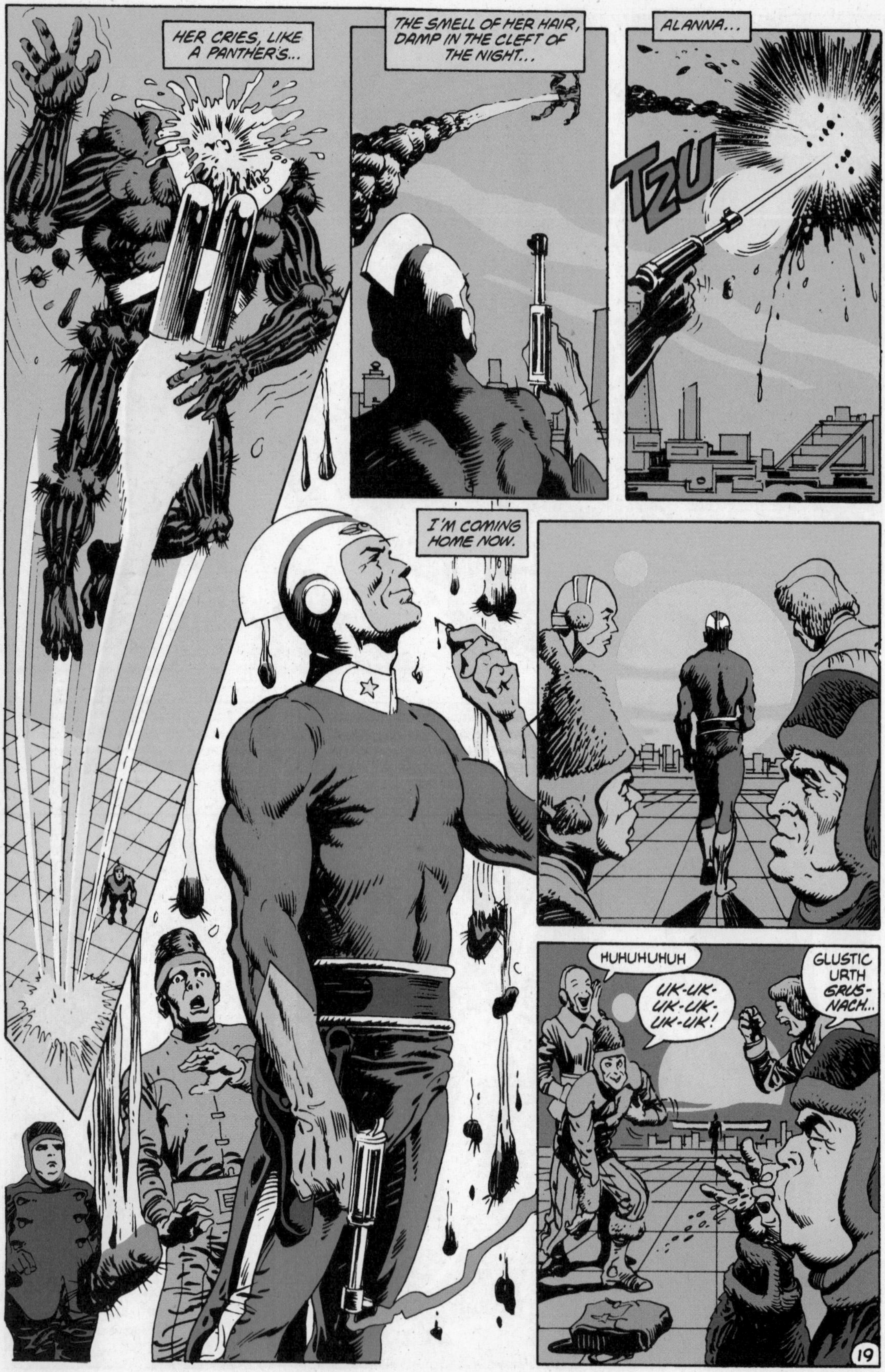
HER CRIES, LIKE A PANTHER'S...
THE SMELL OF HER HAIR, DAMP IN THE CLEFT OF THE NIGHT...
ALANNA...
TZU
I'M COMING HOME NOW.
HUHUHUHUH
UK-UK-UK-UK-UK-UK!
GLUSTIC URTH GRUS-NACH...
19

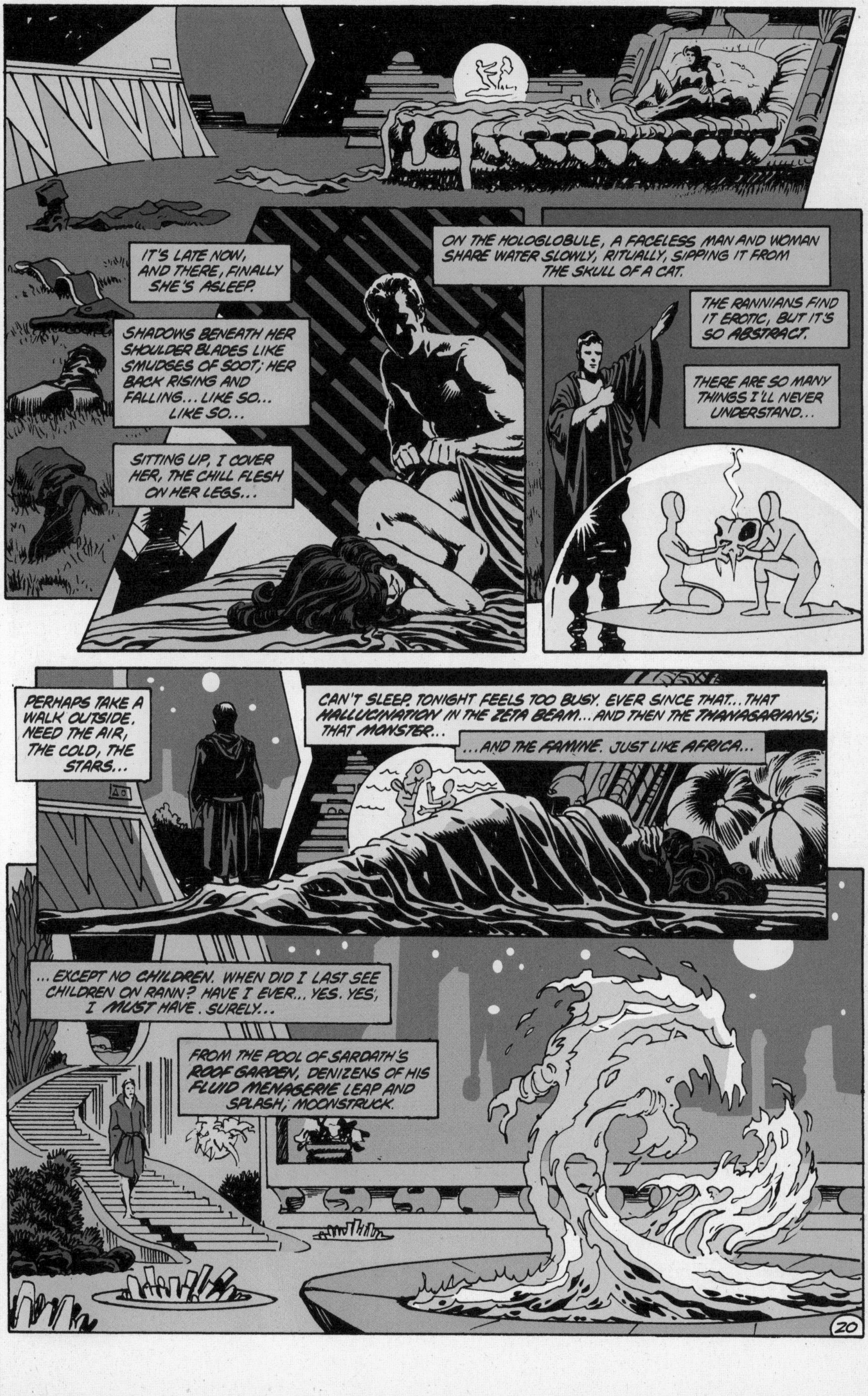
IT'S LATE NOW, AND THERE, FINALLY SHE'S ASLEEP.
SHADOWS BENEATH HER SHOULDER BLADES LIKE SMUDGES OF SOOT; HER BACK RISING AND FALLING... LIKE SO... LIKE SO...
SITTING UP, I COVER HER, THE CHILL FLESH ON HER LEGS...
ON THE HOLOGLOBULE, A FACELESS MAN AND WOMAN SHARE WATER SLOWLY, RITUALLY, SIPPING IT FROM THE SKULL OF A CAT.
THE RANNIANS FIND IT EROTIC, BUT IT'S SO ABSTRACT.
THERE ARE SO MANY THINGS I'LL NEVER UNDERSTAND...
PERHAPS TAKE A WALK OUTSIDE. NEED THE AIR, THE COLD, THE STARS...
CAN'T SLEEP. TONIGHT FEELS TOO BUSY. EVER SINCE THAT... THAT HALLUCINATION IN THE ZETA BEAM... AND THEN THE THANAGARIANS; THAT MONSTER...
...AND THE FAMINE. JUST LIKE AFRICA...
...EXCEPT NO CHILDREN. WHEN DID I LAST SEE CHILDREN ON RANN? HAVE I EVER... YES. YES; I MUST HAVE. SURELY...
FROM THE POOL OF SARDATH'S ROOF GARDEN, DENIZENS OF HIS FLUID MENAGERIE LEAP AND SPLASH; MOONSTRUCK.
20

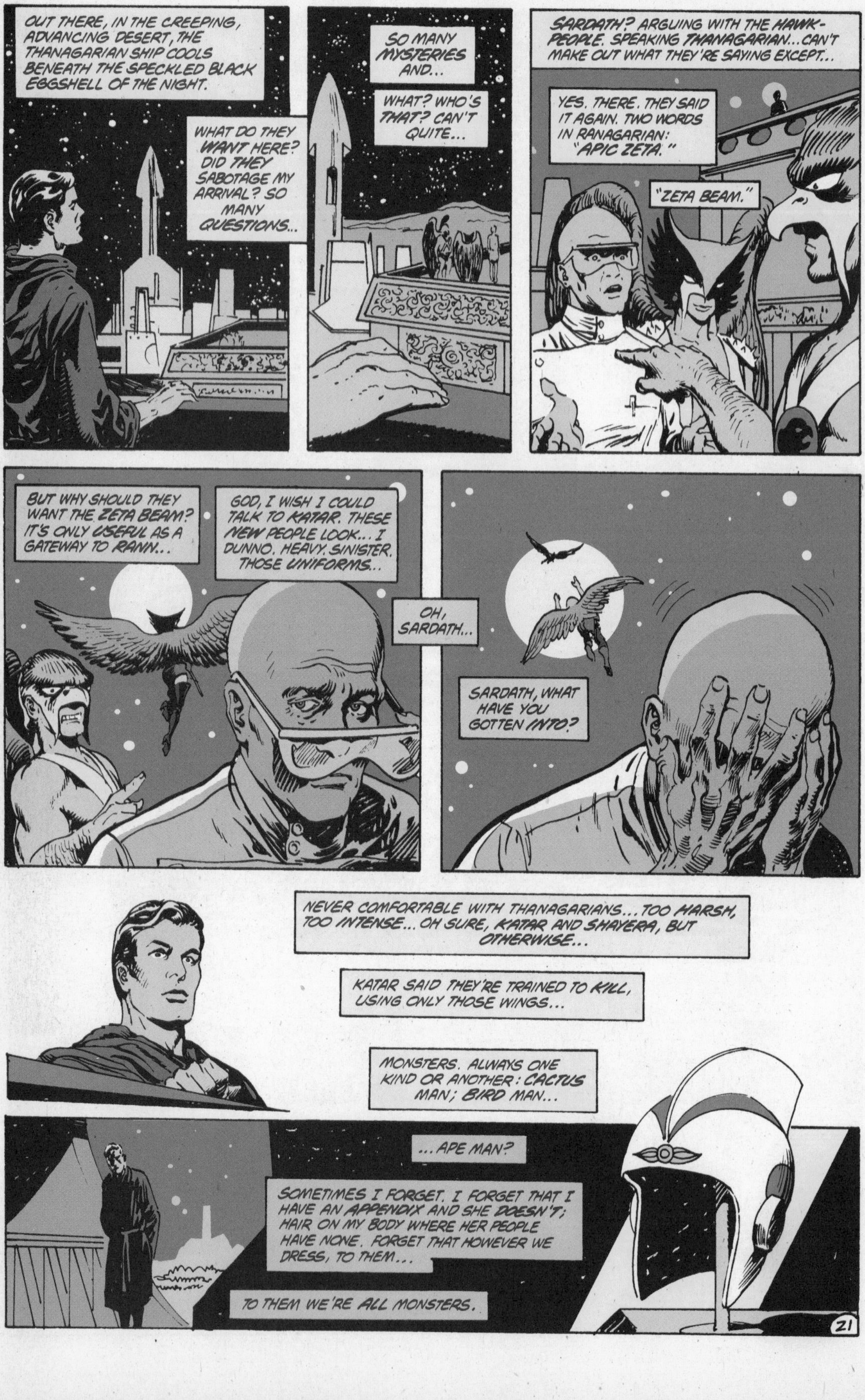
OUT THERE, IN THE CREEPING, ADVANCING DESERT, THE THANAGARIAN SHIP COOLS BENEATH THE SPECKLED BLACK EGGSHELL OF THE NIGHT.
WHAT DO THEY WANT HERE? DID THEY SABOTAGE MY ARRIVAL? SO MANY QUESTIONS...
SO MANY MYSTERIES AND...
WHAT? WHO'S THAT? CAN'T QUITE...
SARDATH? ARGUING WITH THE HAWK-PEOPLE. SPEAKING THANAGARIAN...CAN'T MAKE OUT WHAT THEY'RE SAYING EXCEPT...
YES. THERE. THEY SAID IT AGAIN. TWO WORDS IN RANAGARIAN: "APIC ZETA."
"ZETA BEAM."
BUT WHY SHOULD THEY WANT THE ZETA BEAM? IT'S ONLY USEFUL AS A GATEWAY TO RANN...
GOD, I WISH I COULD TALK TO KATAR. THESE NEW PEOPLE LOOK... I DUNNO. HEAVY. SINISTER. THOSE UNIFORMS...
OH, SARDATH...
SARDATH, WHAT HAVE YOU GOTTEN INTO?
NEVER COMFORTABLE WITH THANAGARIANS... TOO HARSH, TOO INTENSE... OH SURE, KATAR AND SHAYERA, BUT OTHERWISE...
KATAR SAID THEY'RE TRAINED TO KILL, USING ONLY THOSE WINGS...
MONSTERS. ALWAYS ONE KIND OR ANOTHER: CACTUS MAN; BIRD MAN...
...APE MAN?
SOMETIMES I FORGET. I FORGET THAT I HAVE AN APPENDIX AND SHE DOESN'T; HAIR ON MY BODY WHERE HER PEOPLE HAVE NONE. FORGET THAT HOWEVER WE DRESS, TO THEM...
TO THEM WE'RE ALL MONSTERS.
21

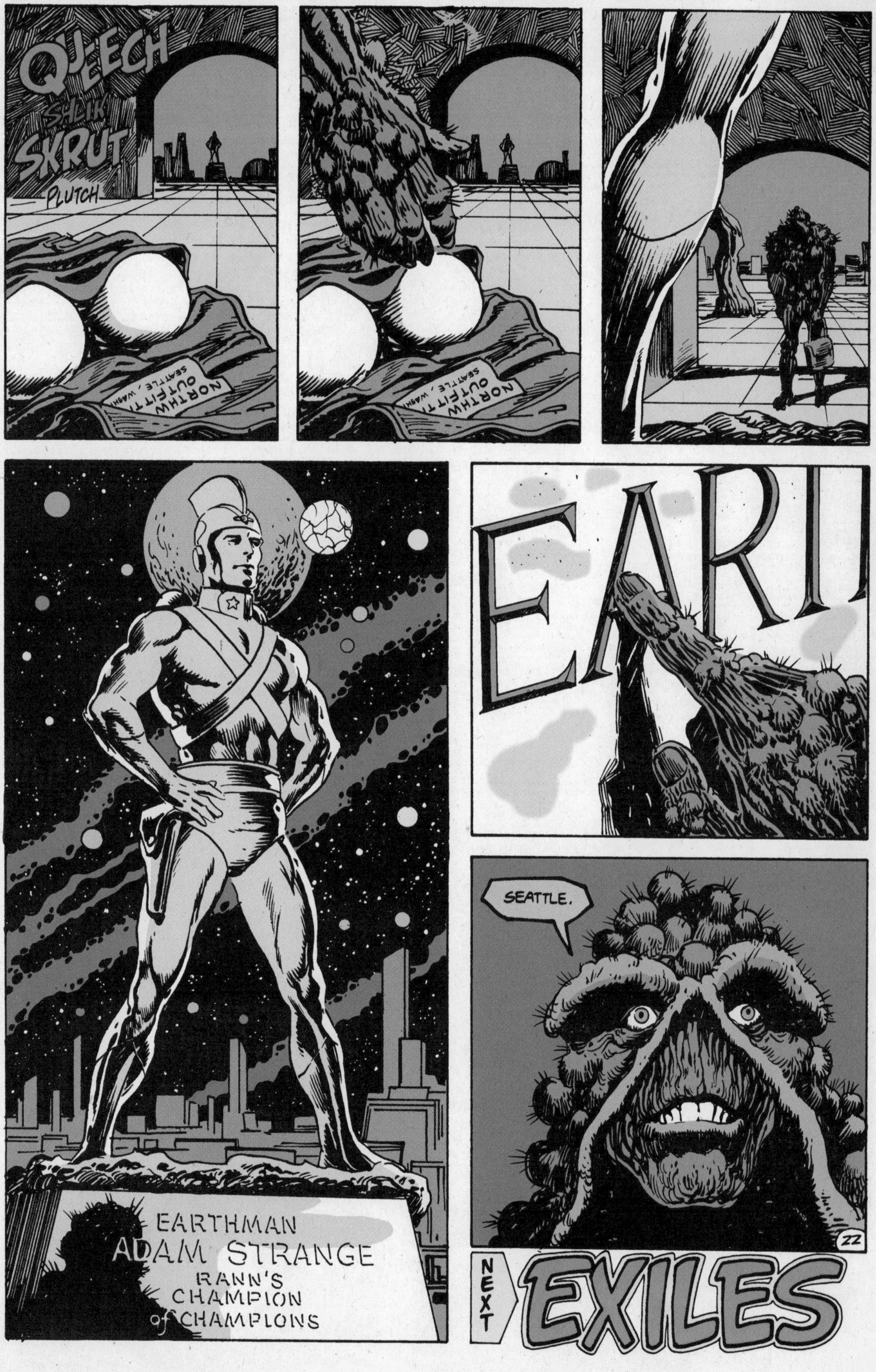
QUEECH
SHLIK
SKRUT
PLUTCH
NORTHW OUTFITT SEATTLE, WASH
NORTHW OUTFITT SEATTLE, WASH
EARTHMAN
ADAM STRANGE
RANN'S
CHAMPION
of CHAMPIONS
SEATTLE.
22
NEXT
EXILES

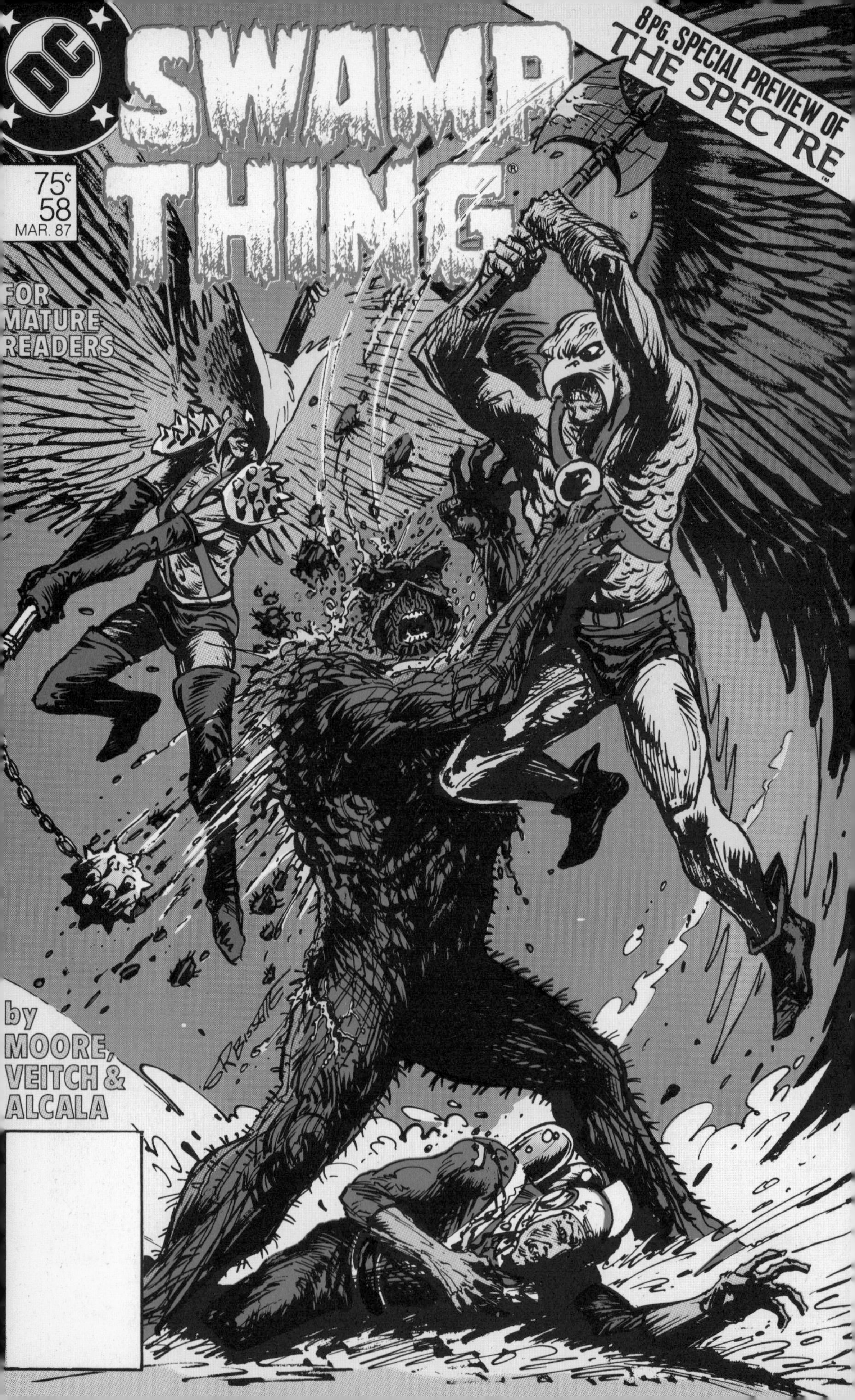
DC
SWAMP THING®
75¢
58
MAR. 87
8PG. SPECIAL PREVIEW OF
THE SPECTRE™
FOR MATURE READERS
by MOORE, VEITCH & ALCALA

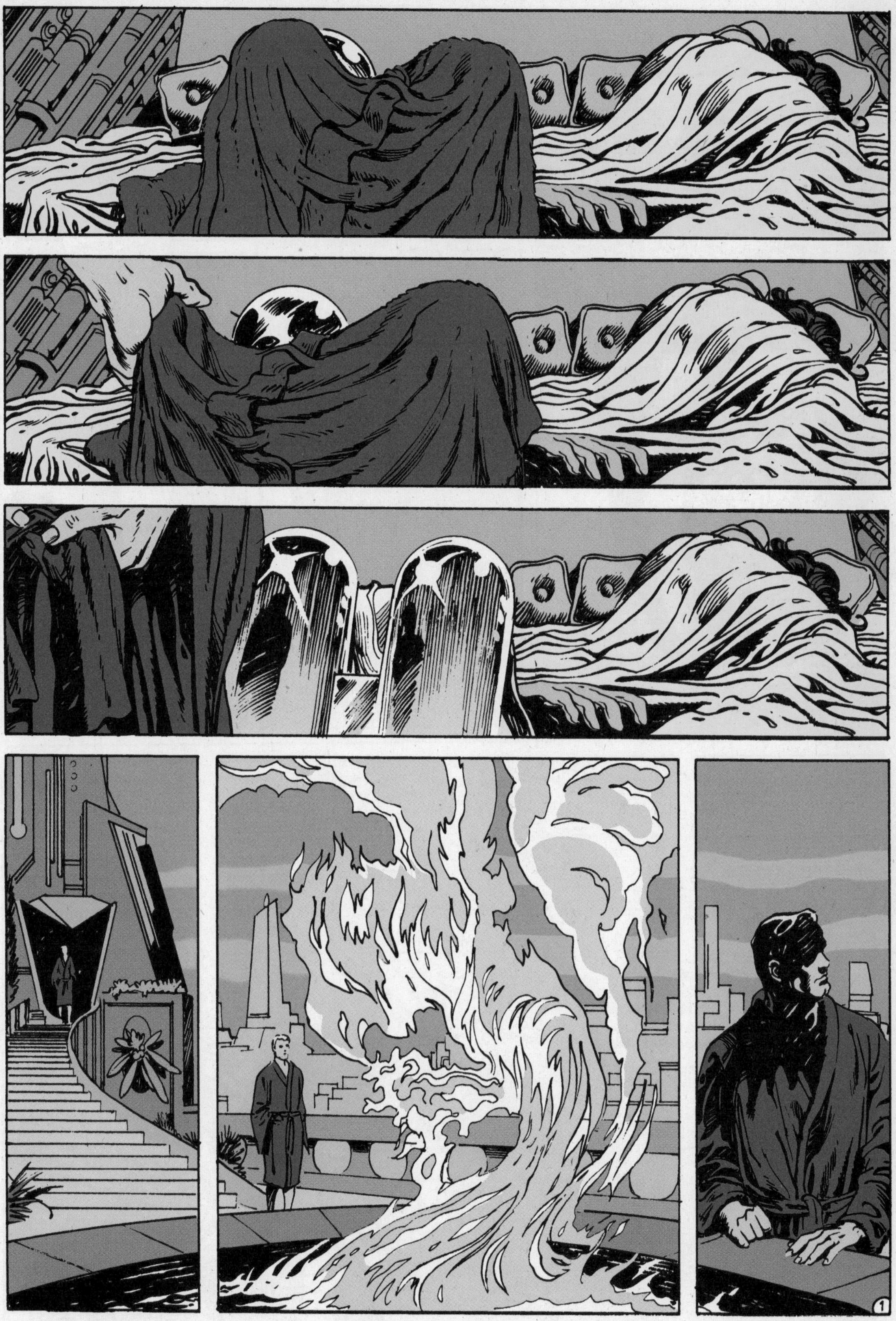
1

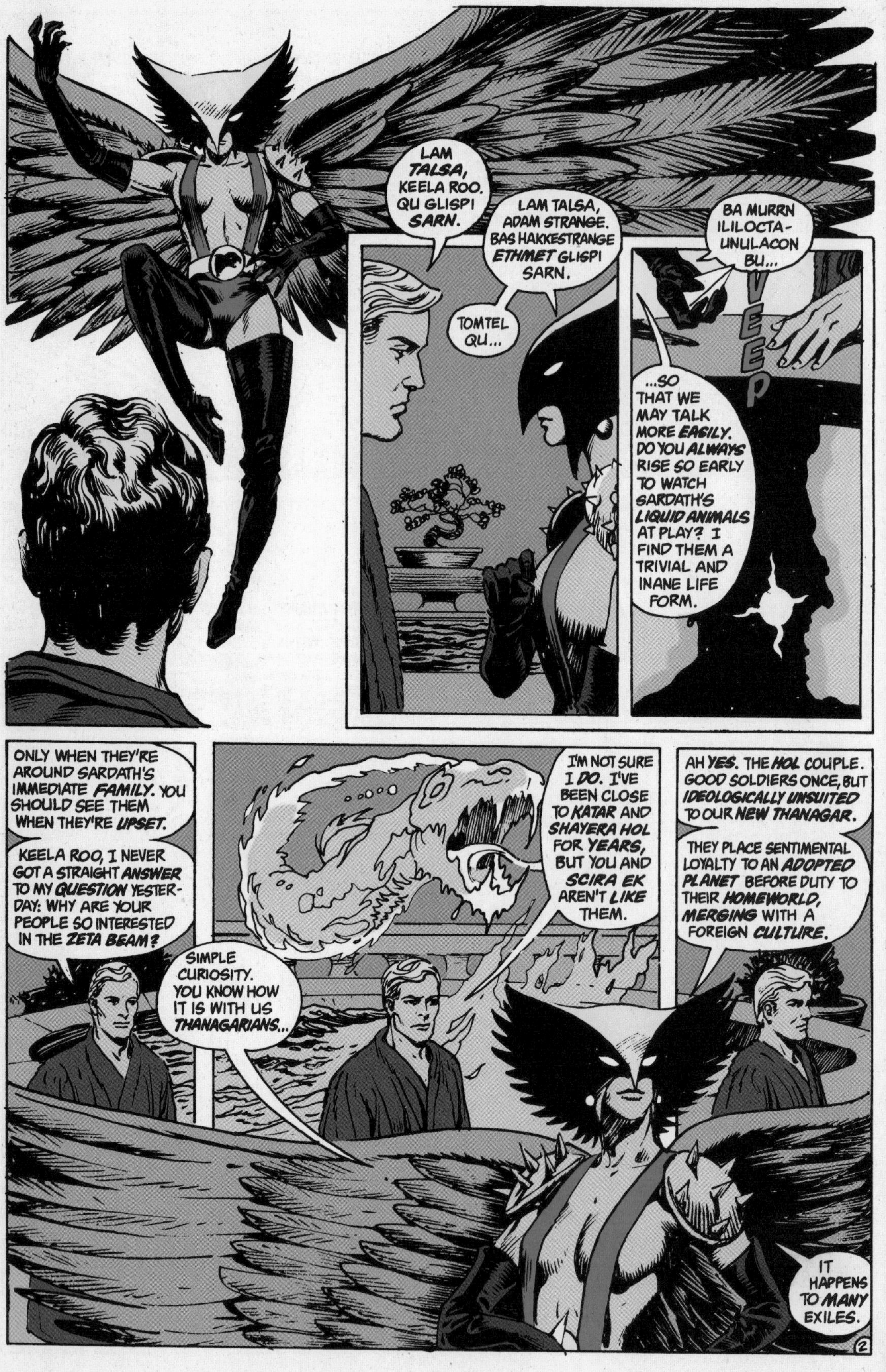
LAM TALSA, KEELA ROO. QU GLISPI SARN.
LAM TALSA, ADAM STRANGE. BAS HAKKESTRANGE ETHMET GLISPI SARN.
TOMTEL QU...
BA MURRN ILILOCTA-UNULACON BU...
VEEP
...SO THAT WE MAY TALK MORE EASILY. DO YOU ALWAYS RISE SO EARLY TO WATCH SARDATH'S LIQUID ANIMALS AT PLAY? I FIND THEM A TRIVIAL AND INANE LIFE FORM.
ONLY WHEN THEY'RE AROUND SARDATH'S IMMEDIATE FAMILY. YOU SHOULD SEE THEM WHEN THEY'RE UPSET.
KEELA ROO, I NEVER GOT A STRAIGHT ANSWER TO MY QUESTION YESTER-DAY: WHY ARE YOUR PEOPLE SO INTERESTED IN THE ZETA BEAM?
SIMPLE CURIOSITY. YOU KNOW HOW IT IS WITH US THANAGARIANS...
I'M NOT SURE I DO. I'VE BEEN CLOSE TO KATAR AND SHAYERA HOL FOR YEARS, BUT YOU AND SCIRA EK AREN'T LIKE THEM.
AH YES. THE HOL COUPLE. GOOD SOLDIERS ONCE, BUT IDEOLOGICALLY UNSUITED TO OUR NEW THANAGAR.
THEY PLACE SENTIMENTAL LOYALTY TO AN ADOPTED PLANET BEFORE DUTY TO THEIR HOMEWORLD, MERGING WITH A FOREIGN CULTURE.
IT HAPPENS TO MANY EXILES.
2

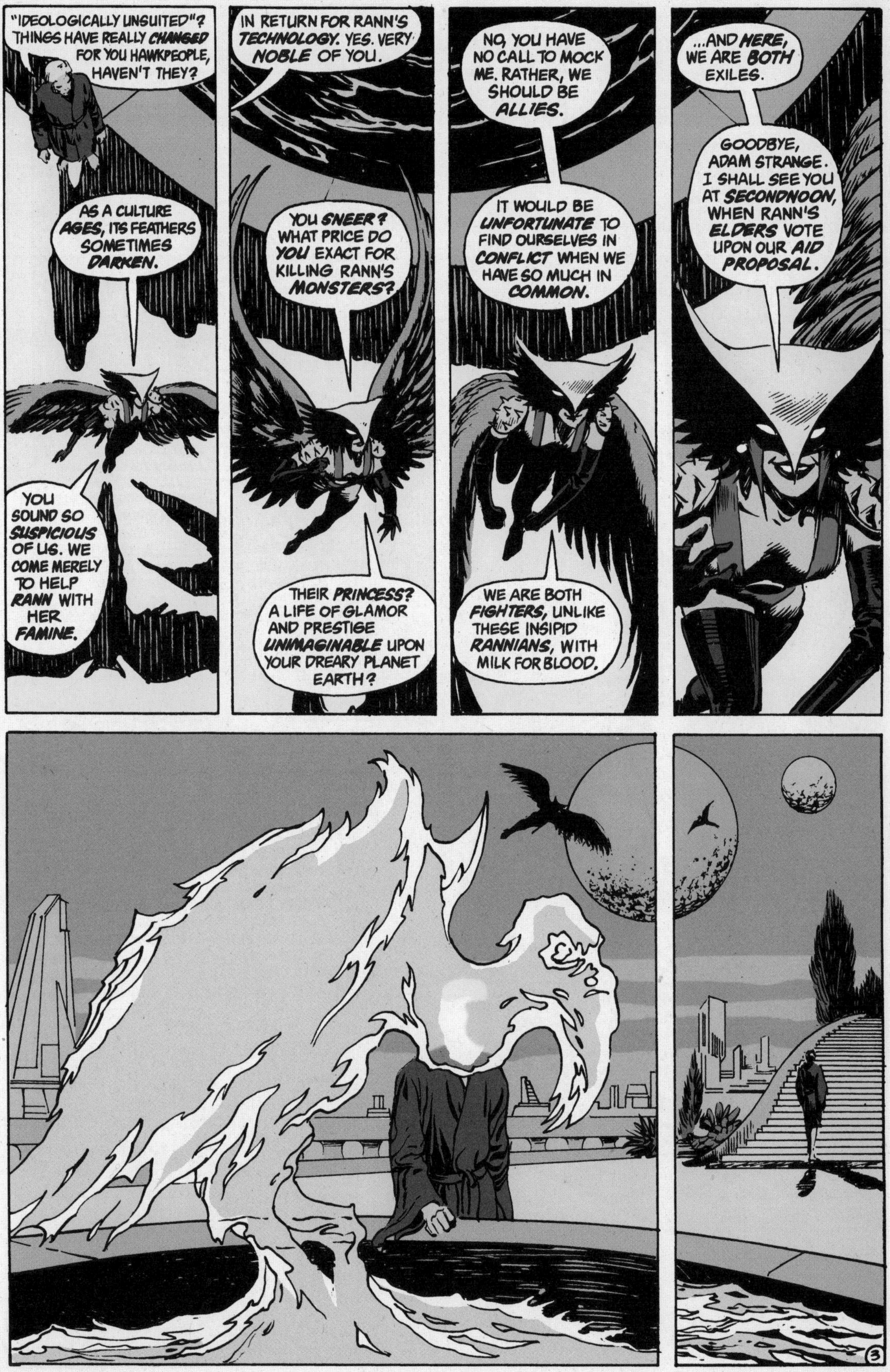
"IDEOLOGICALLY UNSUITED"? THINGS HAVE REALLY CHANGED FOR YOU HAWKPEOPLE, HAVEN'T THEY?
AS A CULTURE AGES, ITS FEATHERS SOMETIMES DARKEN.
YOU SOUND SO SUSPICIOUS OF US. WE COME MERELY TO HELP RANN WITH HER FAMINE.
IN RETURN FOR RANN'S TECHNOLOGY. YES. VERY NOBLE OF YOU.
YOU SNEER? WHAT PRICE DO YOU EXACT FOR KILLING RANN'S MONSTERS?
THEIR PRINCESS? A LIFE OF GLAMOR AND PRESTIGE UNIMAGINABLE UPON YOUR DREARY PLANET EARTH?
NO, YOU HAVE NO CALL TO MOCK ME. RATHER, WE SHOULD BE ALLIES.
IT WOULD BE UNFORTUNATE TO FIND OURSELVES IN CONFLICT WHEN WE HAVE SO MUCH IN COMMON.
WE ARE BOTH FIGHTERS, UNLIKE THESE INSIPID RANNIANS, WITH MILK FOR BLOOD.
...AND HERE, WE ARE BOTH EXILES.
GOODBYE, ADAM STRANGE. I SHALL SEE YOU AT SECONDNOON, WHEN RANN'S ELDERS VOTE UPON OUR AID PROPOSAL.
3

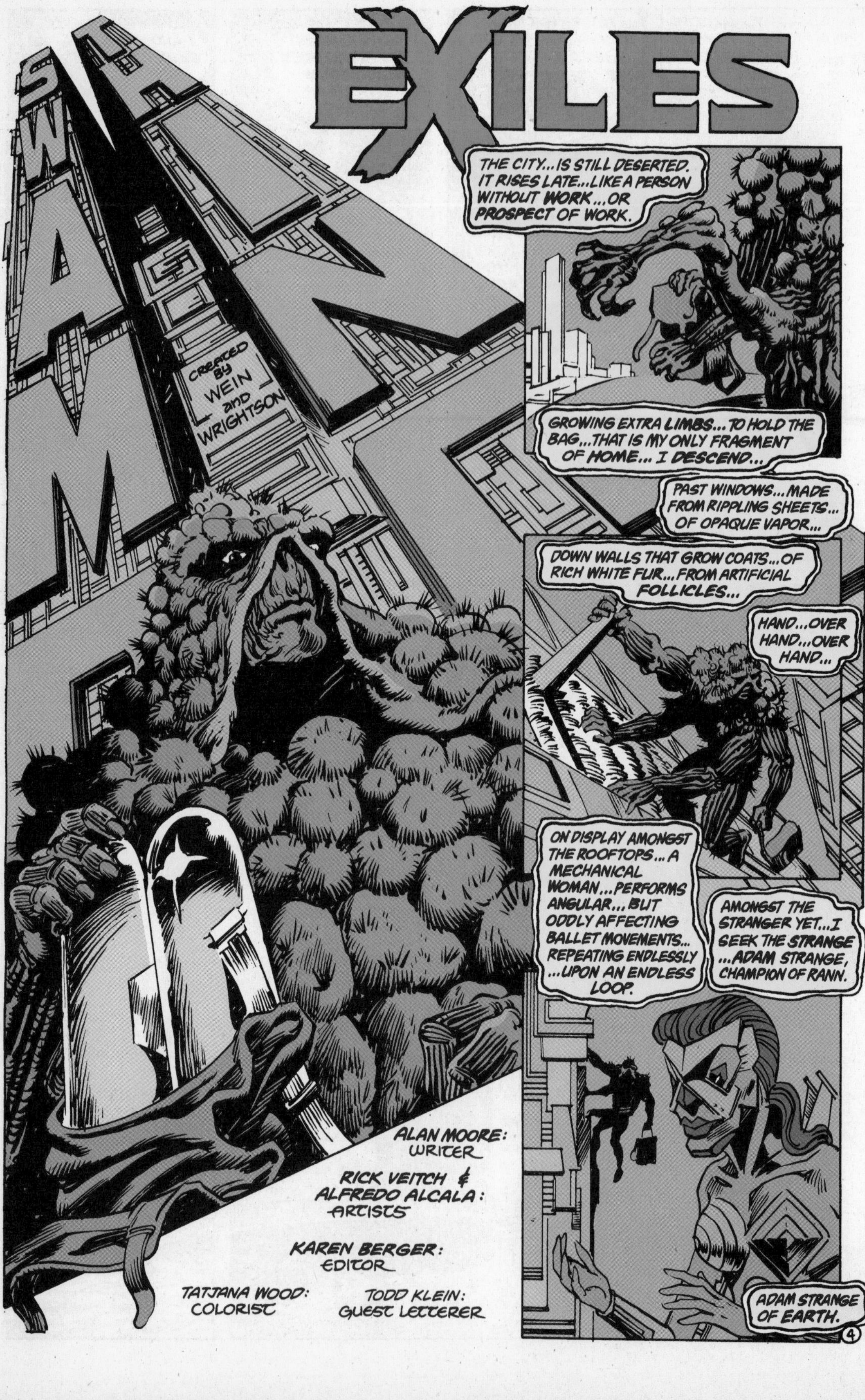
SWAMP THING
EXILES
CREATED BY WEIN and WRIGHTSON
THE CITY... IS STILL DESERTED. IT RISES LATE... LIKE A PERSON WITHOUT WORK... OR PROSPECT OF WORK.
GROWING EXTRA LIMBS... TO HOLD THE BAG... THAT IS MY ONLY FRAGMENT OF HOME... I DESCEND...
PAST WINDOWS... MADE FROM RIPPLING SHEETS... OF OPAQUE VAPOR...
DOWN WALLS THAT GROW COATS... OF RICH WHITE FUR... FROM ARTIFICIAL FOLLICLES...
HAND... OVER HAND... OVER HAND...
ON DISPLAY AMONGST THE ROOFTOPS... A MECHANICAL WOMAN... PERFORMS ANGULAR... BUT ODDLY AFFECTING BALLET MOVEMENTS... REPEATING ENDLESSLY ...UPON AN ENDLESS LOOP.
AMONGST THE STRANGER YET... I SEEK THE STRANGE ...ADAM STRANGE, CHAMPION OF RANN.
ADAM STRANGE OF EARTH.
ALAN MOORE: WRITER
RICK VEITCH & ALFREDO ALCALA: ARTISTS
KAREN BERGER: EDITOR
TATJANA WOOD: COLORIST
TODD KLEIN: GUEST LETTERER
4

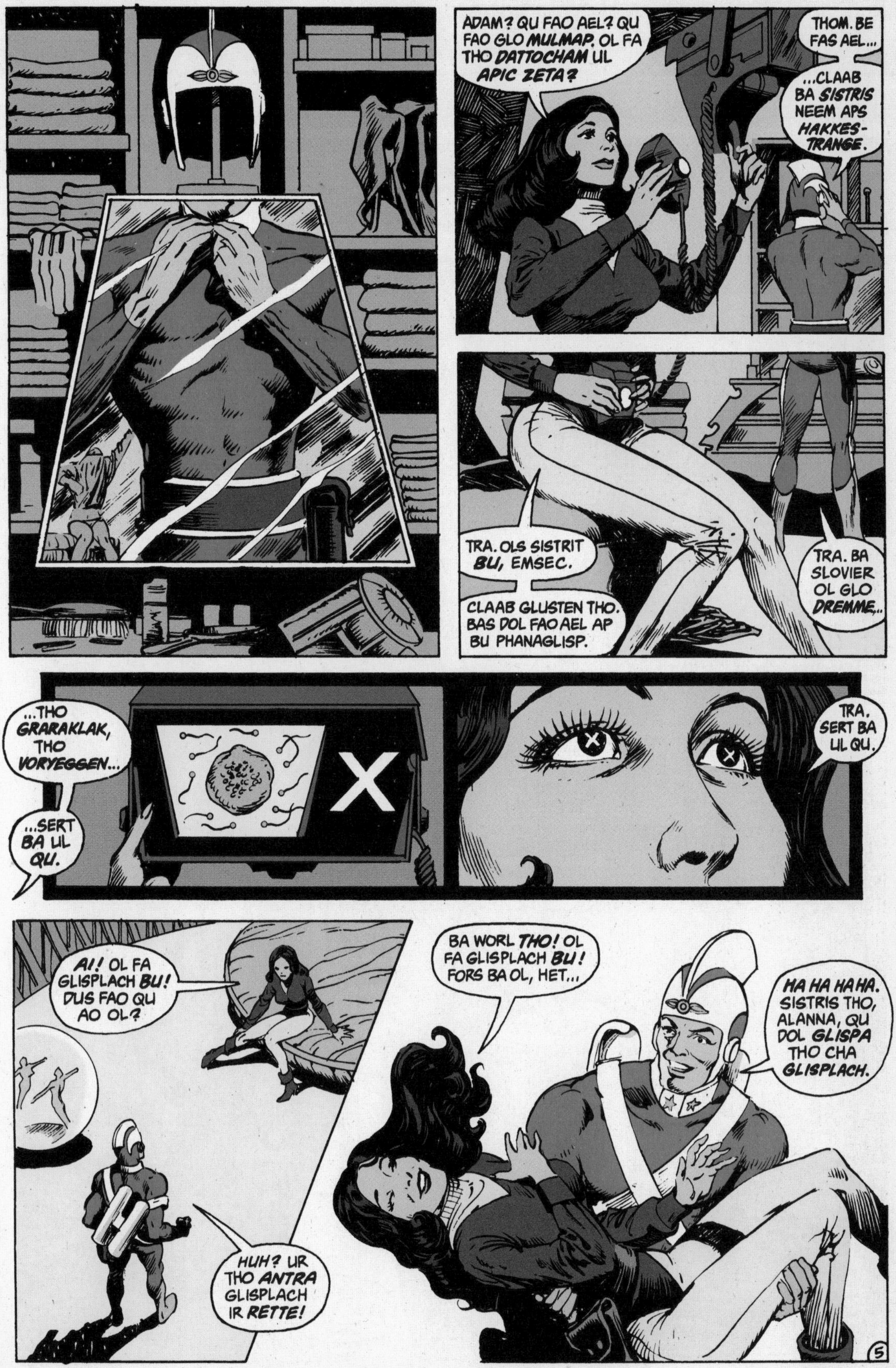
ADAM? QU FAO AEL? QU FAO GLO MULMAP. OL FA THO DATTOCHAM UL APIC ZETA?
THOM. BE FAS AEL...
...CLAAB BA SISTRIS NEEM APS HAKKES-TRANGE.
TRA. OLS SISTRIT BU, EMSEC.
CLAAB GLUSTEN THO. BAS DOL FAO AEL AP BU PHANAGLISP.
TRA. BA SLOVIER OL GLO DREMME...
...THO GRARAKLAK, THO VORYEGGEN...
...SERT BA UL QU.
TRA, SERT BA UL QU.
AI! OL FA GLISPLACH BU! DUS FAO QU AO OL?
HUH? UR THO ANTRA GLISPLACH IR RETTE!
BA WORL THO! OL FA GLISPLACH BU! FORS BA OL, HET...
HA HA HA HA. SISTRIS THO, ALANNA, QU DOL GLISPA THO CHA GLISPLACH.
5

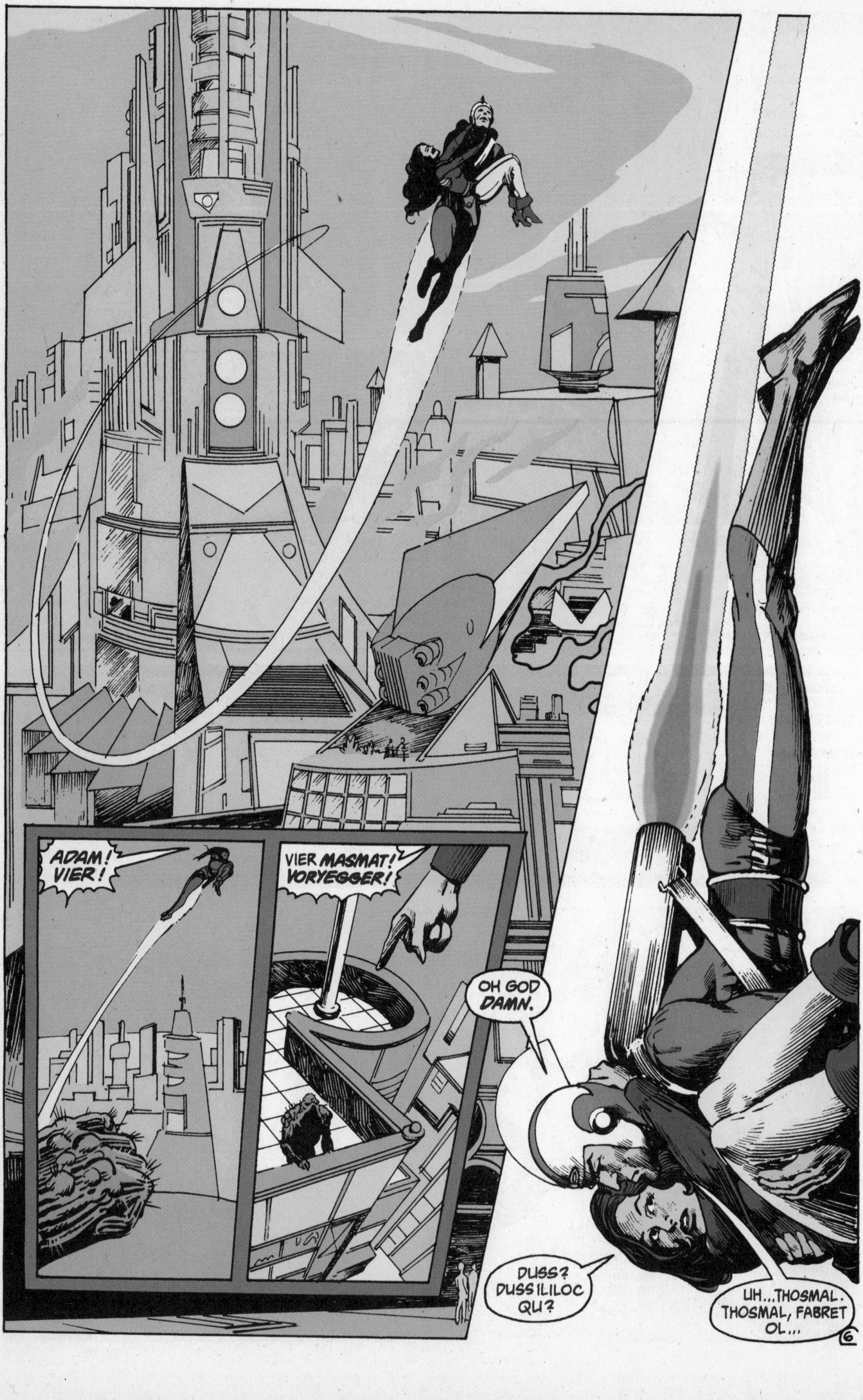
ADAM! VIER!
VIER MASMAT! VORYEGGER!
OH GOD DAMN.
DUSS? DUSSILILOC QU?
UH...THOSMAL. THOSMAL, FABRET OL...
6

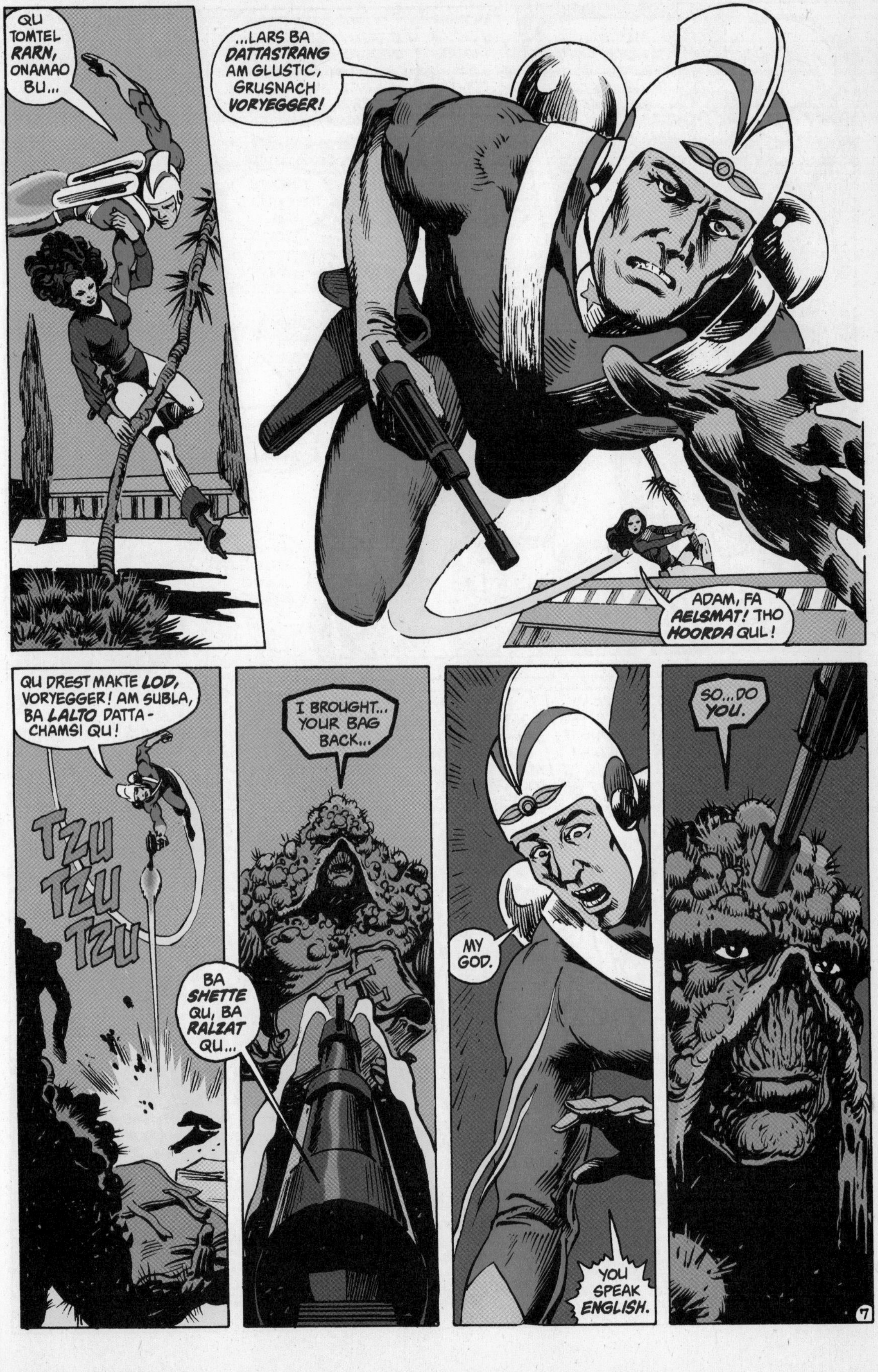
QU TOMTEL RARN, ONAMAO BU...
...LARS BA DATTASTRANG AM GLUSTIC, GRUSNACH VORYEGGER!
ADAM, FA AELSMAT! THO HOORDA QUL!
QU DREST MAKTE LOD, VORYEGGER! AM SUBLA, BA LALTO DATTA-CHAMSI QU!
TZU TZU TZU
BA SHETTE QU, BA RALZAT QU...
I BROUGHT... YOUR BAG BACK...
MY GOD.
YOU SPEAK ENGLISH.
SO...DO YOU.
7

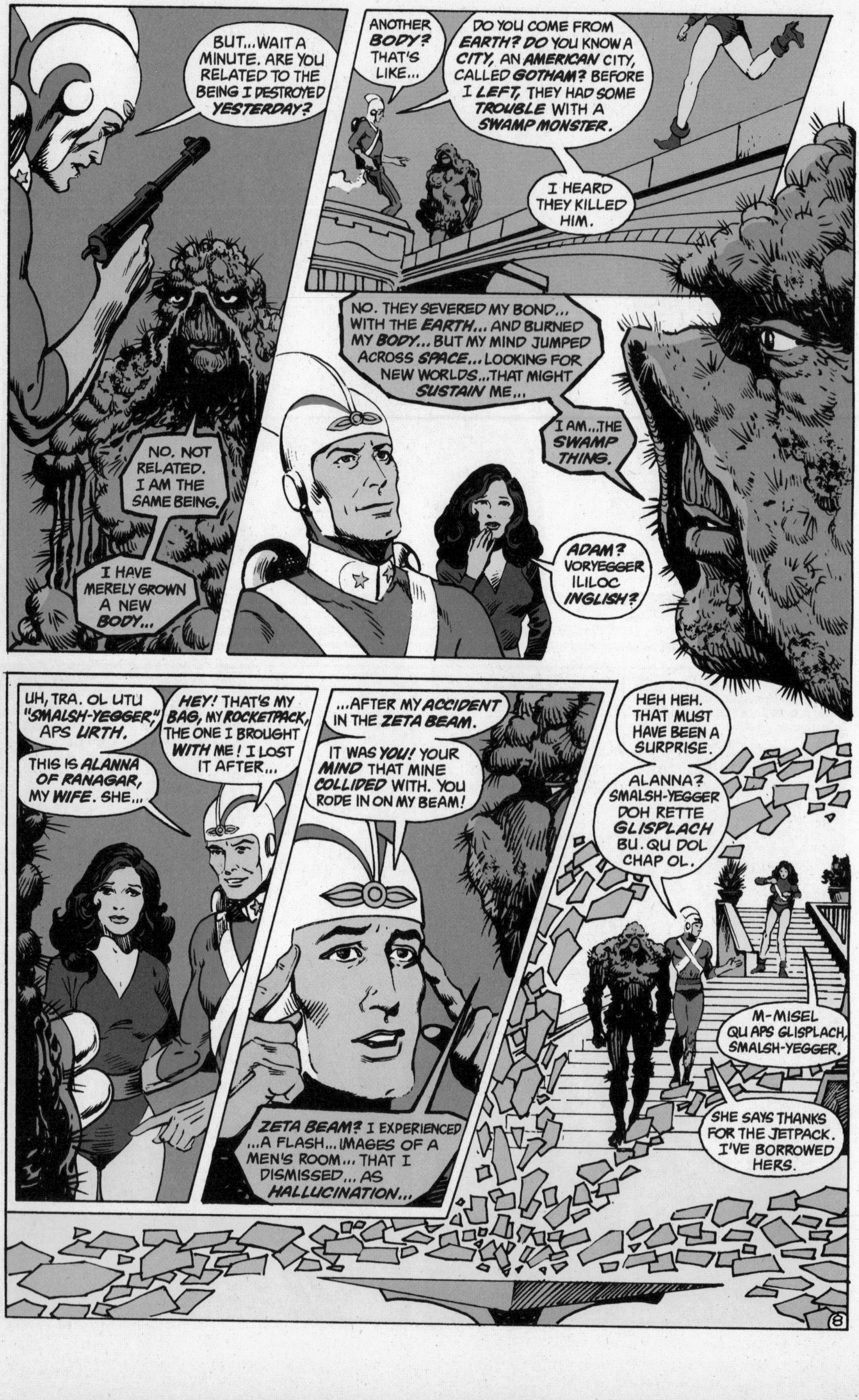
BUT...WAIT A MINUTE. ARE YOU RELATED TO THE BEING I DESTROYED YESTERDAY?
NO. NOT RELATED. I AM THE SAME BEING.
I HAVE MERELY GROWN A NEW BODY...
ANOTHER BODY? THAT'S LIKE...
DO YOU COME FROM EARTH? DO YOU KNOW A CITY, AN AMERICAN CITY, CALLED GOTHAM? BEFORE I LEFT, THEY HAD SOME TROUBLE WITH A SWAMP MONSTER.
I HEARD THEY KILLED HIM.
NO. THEY SEVERED MY BOND... WITH THE EARTH... AND BURNED MY BODY... BUT MY MIND JUMPED ACROSS SPACE... LOOKING FOR NEW WORLDS...THAT MIGHT SUSTAIN ME...
I AM...THE SWAMP THING.
ADAM? VORYEGGER ILILOC INGLISH?
UH, TRA. OL UTU "SMALSH-YEGGER," APS URTH.
THIS IS ALANNA OF RANAGAR, MY WIFE. SHE...
HEY! THAT'S MY BAG, MY ROCKETPACK, THE ONE I BROUGHT WITH ME! I LOST IT AFTER...
...AFTER MY ACCIDENT IN THE ZETA BEAM.
IT WAS YOU! YOUR MIND THAT MINE COLLIDED WITH. YOU RODE IN ON MY BEAM!
ZETA BEAM? I EXPERIENCED ...A FLASH... IMAGES OF A MEN'S ROOM... THAT I DISMISSED... AS HALLUCINATION...
HEH HEH. THAT MUST HAVE BEEN A SURPRISE.
ALANNA? SMALSH-YEGGER DOH RETTE GLISPLACH BU. QU DOL CHAP OL.
M-MISEL QU APS GLISPLACH, SMALSH-YEGGER.
SHE SAYS THANKS FOR THE JETPACK. I'VE BORROWED HERS.
8

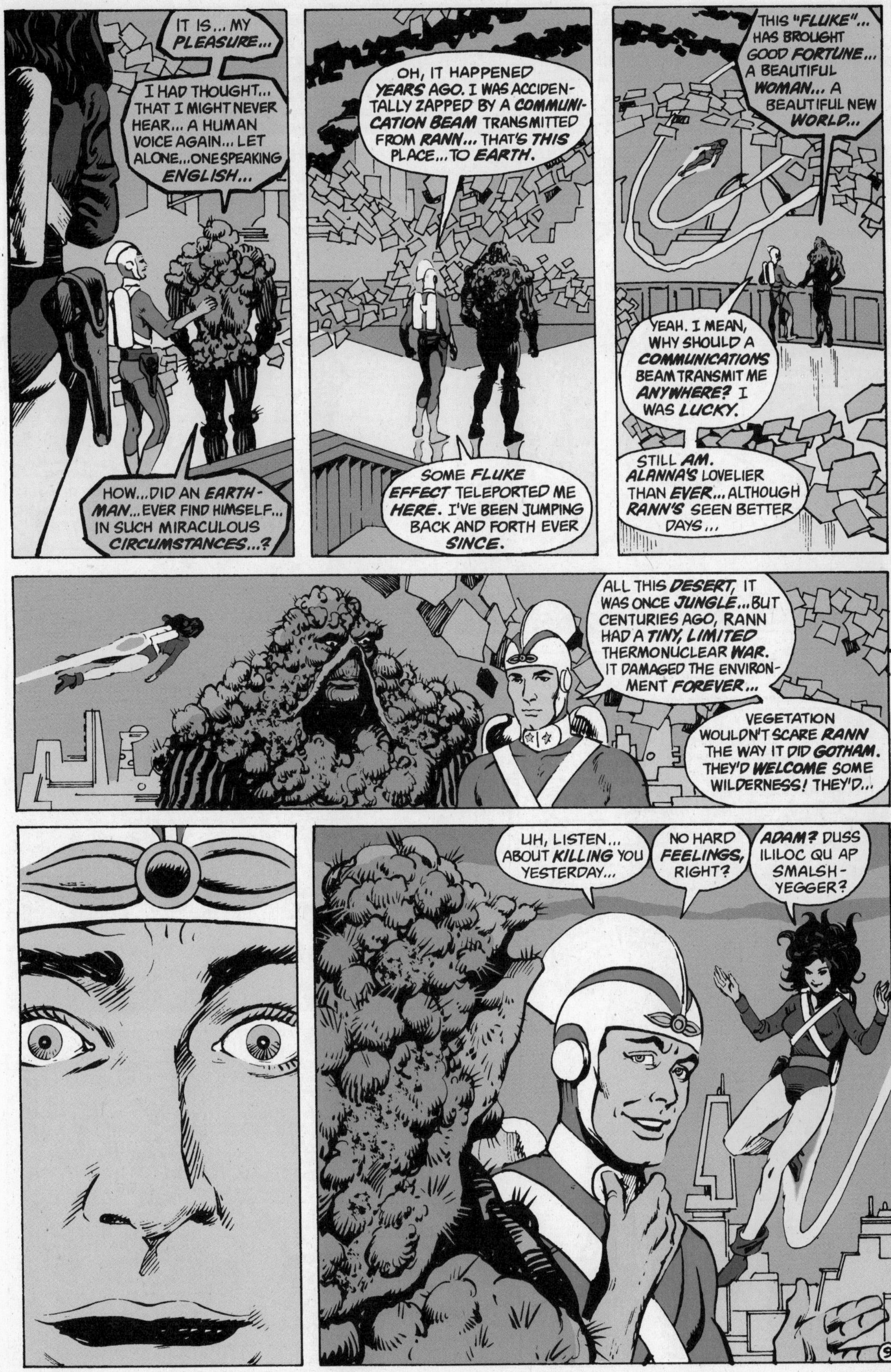

IT IS... MY PLEASURE...
I HAD THOUGHT... THAT I MIGHT NEVER HEAR... A HUMAN VOICE AGAIN... LET ALONE...ONE SPEAKING ENGLISH...
HOW...DID AN EARTH-MAN... EVER FIND HIMSELF... IN SUCH MIRACULOUS CIRCUMSTANCES...?
OH, IT HAPPENED YEARS AGO. I WAS ACCIDENTALLY ZAPPED BY A COMMUNICATION BEAM TRANSMITTED FROM RANN... THAT'S THIS PLACE... TO EARTH.
SOME FLUKE EFFECT TELEPORTED ME HERE. I'VE BEEN JUMPING BACK AND FORTH EVER SINCE.
THIS "FLUKE"... HAS BROUGHT GOOD FORTUNE... A BEAUTIFUL WOMAN... A BEAUTIFUL NEW WORLD...
YEAH. I MEAN, WHY SHOULD A COMMUNICATIONS BEAM TRANSMIT ME ANYWHERE? I WAS LUCKY.
STILL AM. ALANNA'S LOVELIER THAN EVER... ALTHOUGH RANN'S SEEN BETTER DAYS...
ALL THIS DESERT, IT WAS ONCE JUNGLE... BUT CENTURIES AGO, RANN HAD A TINY, LIMITED THERMONUCLEAR WAR. IT DAMAGED THE ENVIRONMENT FOREVER...
VEGETATION WOULDN'T SCARE RANN THE WAY IT DID GOTHAM. THEY'D WELCOME SOME WILDERNESS! THEY'D...
UH, LISTEN... ABOUT KILLING YOU YESTERDAY...
NO HARD FEELINGS, RIGHT?
ADAM? DUSS ILILOC QU AP SMALSH-YEGGER?
9

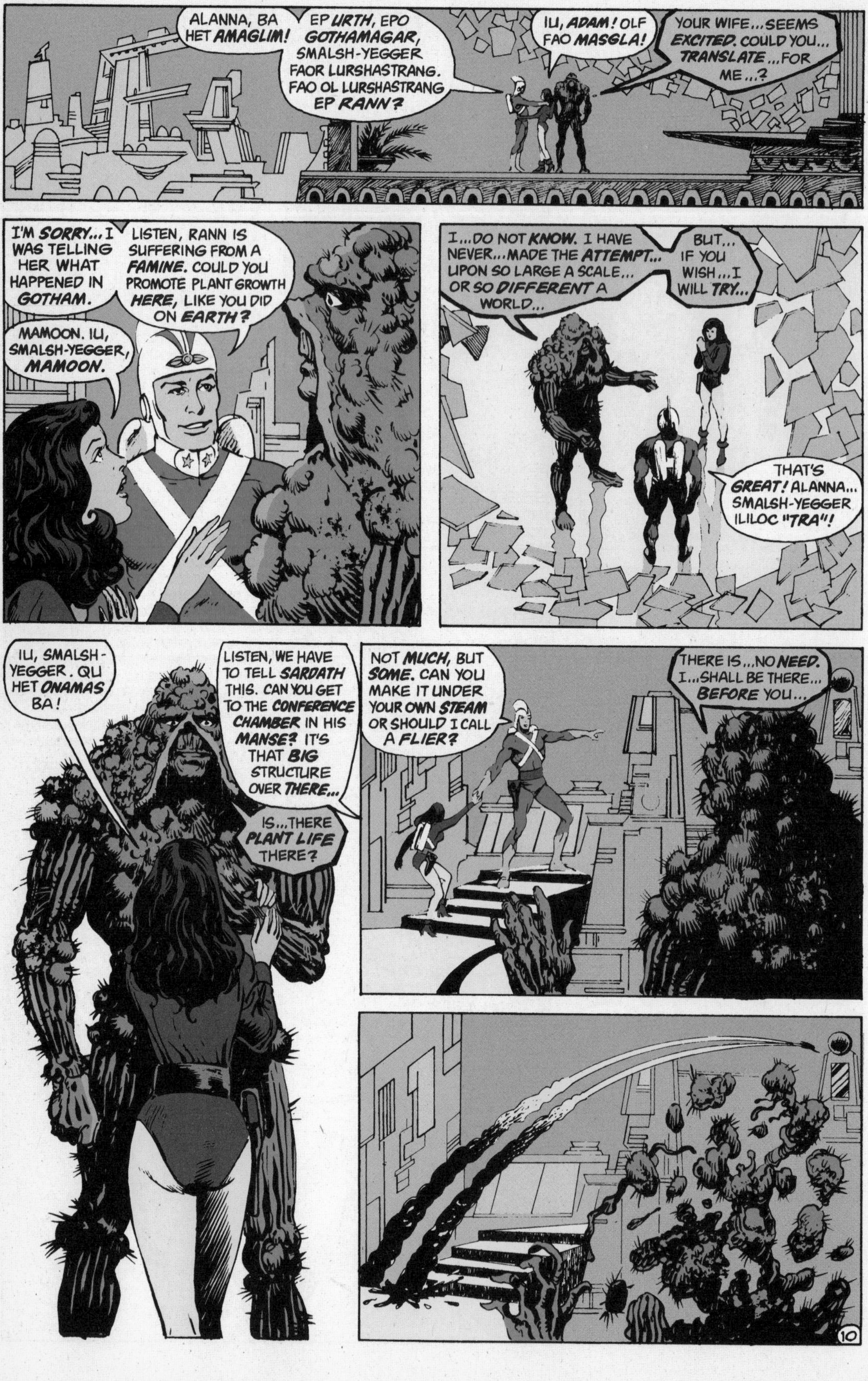
ALANNA, BA HET AMAGLIM!
EP URTH, EPO GOTHAMAGAR, SMALSH-YEGGER FAOR LURSHASTRANG. FAO OL LURSHASTRANG EP RANN?
IU, ADAM! OLF FAO MASGLA!
YOUR WIFE...SEEMS EXCITED. COULD YOU... TRANSLATE...FOR ME...?
I'M SORRY...I WAS TELLING HER WHAT HAPPENED IN GOTHAM.
LISTEN, RANN IS SUFFERING FROM A FAMINE. COULD YOU PROMOTE PLANT GROWTH HERE, LIKE YOU DID ON EARTH?
MAMOON. IU, SMALSH-YEGGER, MAMOON.
I...DO NOT KNOW. I HAVE NEVER...MADE THE ATTEMPT... UPON SO LARGE A SCALE... OR SO DIFFERENT A WORLD...
BUT... IF YOU WISH...I WILL TRY...
THAT'S GREAT! ALANNA... SMALSH-YEGGER ILILOC "TRA"!
IU, SMALSH-YEGGER. QU HET ONAMAS BA!
LISTEN, WE HAVE TO TELL SARDATH THIS. CAN YOU GET TO THE CONFERENCE CHAMBER IN HIS MANSE? IT'S THAT BIG STRUCTURE OVER THERE...
IS...THERE PLANT LIFE THERE?
NOT MUCH, BUT SOME. CAN YOU MAKE IT UNDER YOUR OWN STEAM OR SHOULD I CALL A FLIER?
THERE IS...NO NEED. I...SHALL BE THERE... BEFORE YOU...
10

IT TAKES ME *LONGER*...TO LOCATE SUITABLE *SUBSTANCE*... THAN I HAD *ANTICIPATED*...AND MY *ARRIVAL*... IN THE *CONFERENCE CHAMBER*...COINCIDES WITH THAT OF *STRANGE*...AND HIS ALIEN *BRIDE*...

THERE IS SO LITTLE... VEGETATION HERE...

I MEET *SARDATH*...CHIEF SCIENTIST...OF *RANAGAR CITY*. HE DISPLAYS...DRY, REPTILIAN *INTEREST*... AS STRANGE TELLS HIM...OF MY WAR WITH *GOTHAM*...

ABOUT US... SIT RANN'S *OTHER* TECHNOCRATS... SIMILAR ENOUGH...TO BE HIS *BROTHERS*... WERE THEY NOT...SO *NUMEROUS*...

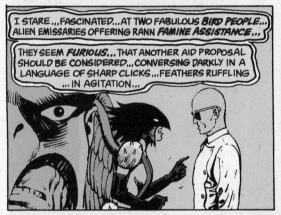

I STARE...FASCINATED...AT TWO FABULOUS *BIRD PEOPLE*... ALIEN EMISSARIES OFFERING RANN *FAMINE ASSISTANCE*...

THEY SEEM *FURIOUS*...THAT ANOTHER AID PROPOSAL SHOULD BE CONSIDERED...CONVERSING DARKLY IN A LANGUAGE OF SHARP CLICKS...FEATHERS RUFFLING ...IN AGITATION...

FINALLY, RANAGAR'S ELDERS *VOTE*... SPEAKING WITH ONE VOICE... ALBEIT *MULTIPLE TRACKED*...

THEY CHOOSE ME. SARDATH SHAKES MY HAND... BEFORE A SCREEN UPON WHICH ...PEOPLE DIE FAMILIAR DEATHS... BENEATH UNFAMILIAR *SUNS*...

OFFENDED BY THIS SEEMING *REJECTION*...THE BLACK LEATHER BIRDS...MARCH ABRUPTLY FROM THE CONFERENCE CHAMBER... BLACK WINGTIPS BRUSHING THE CHAMBER FLOOR... EACH STEP A CONTEMPTUOUS *HISS*...

SARDATH TELLS ME...I MAY INSPECT THE DESERT TONIGHT...IF I WISH...

DARKNESS COMES...UNFAMILIAR CONSTELLATIONS FADING INTO VIEW...LIKE DEVELOPING PHOTOGRAPHS...AND STRANGE POINTS OUT *SOL*.

IT LOOKS... LIKE ALL THE *OTHERS*...

HE LEADS ME...TO RANAGAR'S *MARGINS*...TO THE DESERT'S EDGE... WHENCE...I CONTINUE *ALONE*...

11

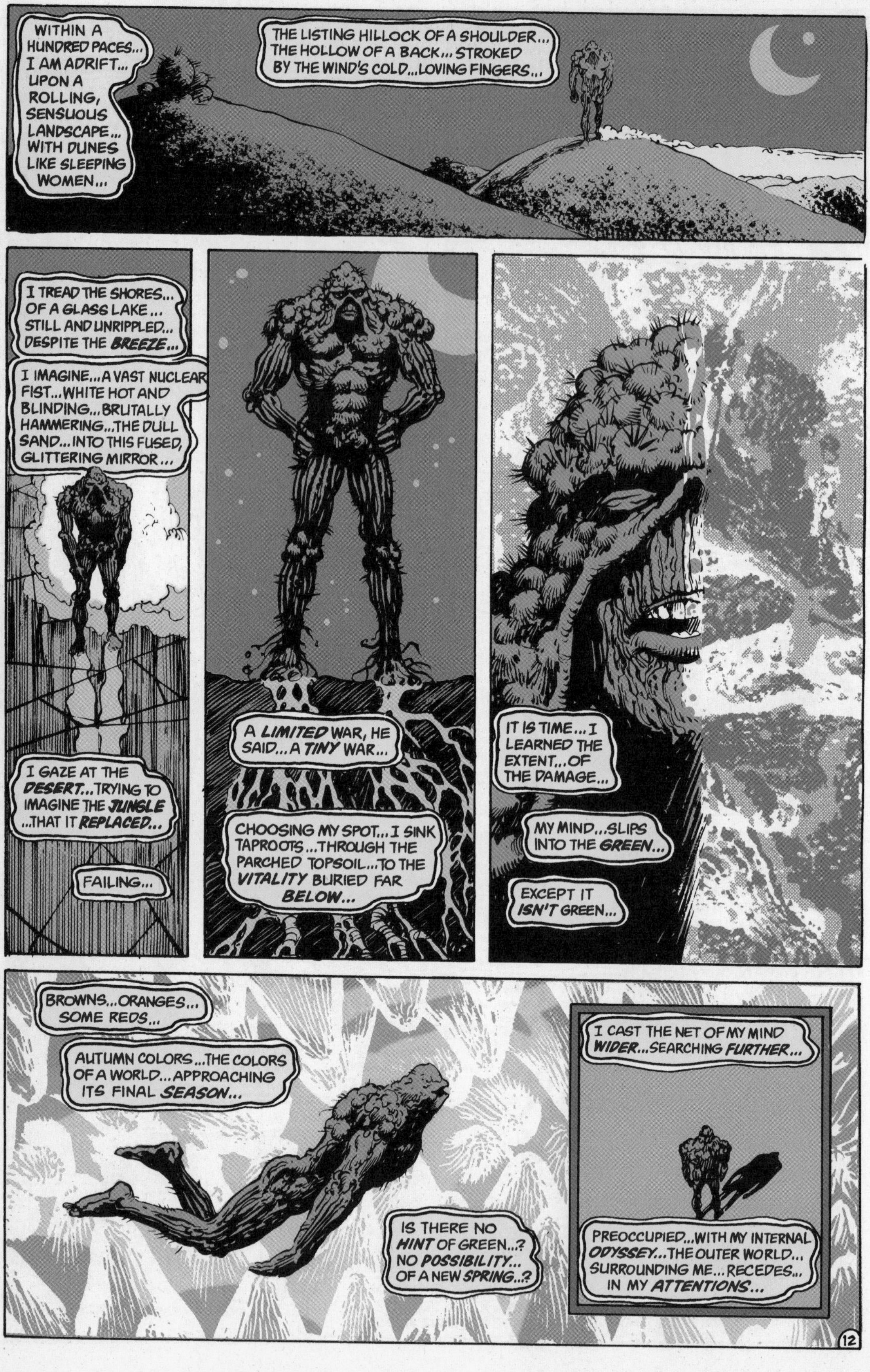
WITHIN A HUNDRED PACES... I AM ADRIFT... UPON A ROLLING, SENSUOUS LANDSCAPE... WITH DUNES LIKE SLEEPING WOMEN...
THE LISTING HILLOCK OF A SHOULDER... THE HOLLOW OF A BACK... STROKED BY THE WIND'S COLD... LOVING FINGERS...
I TREAD THE SHORES... OF A GLASS LAKE... STILL AND UNRIPPLED... DESPITE THE BREEZE...
I IMAGINE... A VAST NUCLEAR FIST... WHITE HOT AND BLINDING... BRUTALLY HAMMERING... THE DULL SAND... INTO THIS FUSED, GLITTERING MIRROR...
I GAZE AT THE DESERT... TRYING TO IMAGINE THE JUNGLE ...THAT IT REPLACED...
FAILING...
A LIMITED WAR, HE SAID... A TINY WAR...
CHOOSING MY SPOT... I SINK TAPROOTS... THROUGH THE PARCHED TOPSOIL... TO THE VITALITY BURIED FAR BELOW...
IT IS TIME... I LEARNED THE EXTENT... OF THE DAMAGE...
MY MIND... SLIPS INTO THE GREEN...
EXCEPT IT ISN'T GREEN...
BROWNS... ORANGES... SOME REDS...
AUTUMN COLORS... THE COLORS OF A WORLD... APPROACHING ITS FINAL SEASON...
IS THERE NO HINT OF GREEN...? NO POSSIBILITY... OF A NEW SPRING...?
I CAST THE NET OF MY MIND WIDER... SEARCHING FURTHER...
PREOCCUPIED... WITH MY INTERNAL ODYSSEY... THE OUTER WORLD... SURROUNDING ME... RECEDES... IN MY ATTENTIONS...
12

SOMEWHERE FAR, FAR BELOW... WHERE THE RADIATION DID NOT *PENETRATE*...THERE MUST YET BE *LIFE*...

SOME STILL-FERTILE STRATA...THAT REMAIN UNTOUCHED...BY THAT BLAZING *HAND*...OR ITS POISONOUS *SHADOW*...

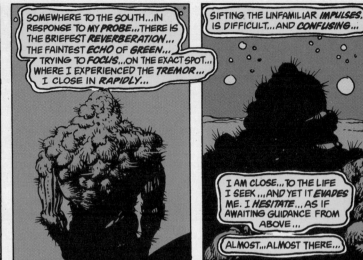

SOMEWHERE TO THE SOUTH...IN RESPONSE TO MY *PROBE*...THERE IS THE BRIEFEST *REVERBERATION*... THE FAINTEST *ECHO* OF *GREEN*... TRYING TO *FOCUS*...ON THE EXACT SPOT... WHERE I EXPERIENCED THE *TREMOR*... I CLOSE IN *RAPIDLY*...

SIFTING THE UNFAMILIAR *IMPULSES*... IS DIFFICULT...AND *CONFUSING*...

I AM CLOSE...TO THE LIFE I SEEK...AND YET IT *EVADES* ME. I *HESITATE*...AS IF AWAITING GUIDANCE FROM ABOVE...

ALMOST...ALMOST THERE...

CHOK!

⑬

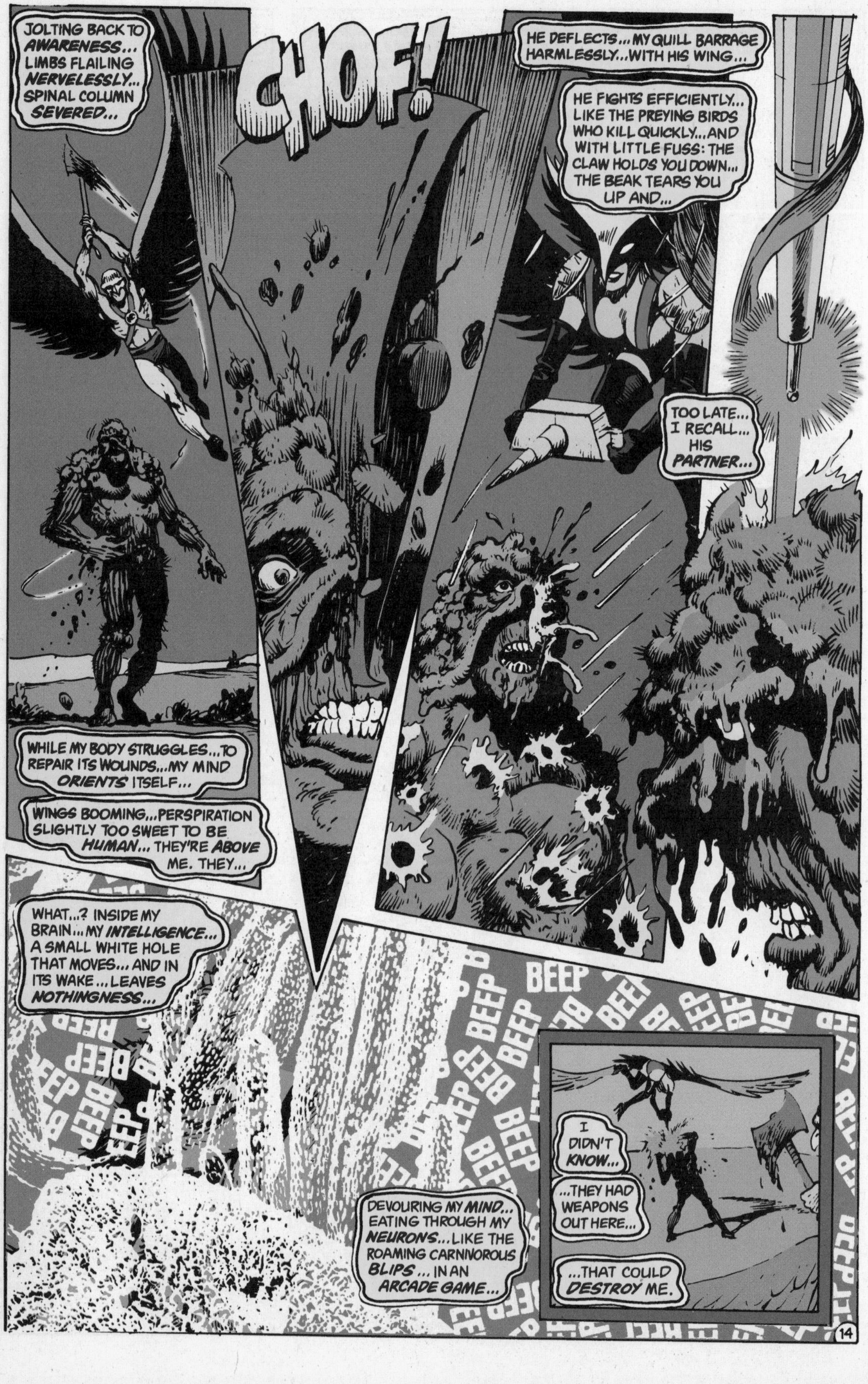
JOLTING BACK TO AWARENESS... LIMBS FLAILING NERVELESSLY... SPINAL COLUMN SEVERED...
CHOF!
HE DEFLECTS... MY QUILL BARRAGE HARMLESSLY... WITH HIS WING...
HE FIGHTS EFFICIENTLY... LIKE THE PREYING BIRDS WHO KILL QUICKLY... AND WITH LITTLE FUSS: THE CLAW HOLDS YOU DOWN... THE BEAK TEARS YOU UP AND...
TOO LATE... I RECALL... HIS PARTNER...
WHILE MY BODY STRUGGLES... TO REPAIR ITS WOUNDS... MY MIND ORIENTS ITSELF...
WINGS BOOMING... PERSPIRATION SLIGHTLY TOO SWEET TO BE HUMAN... THEY'RE ABOVE ME. THEY...
WHAT...? INSIDE MY BRAIN... MY INTELLIGENCE... A SMALL WHITE HOLE THAT MOVES... AND IN ITS WAKE... LEAVES NOTHINGNESS...
BEEP
DEVOURING MY MIND... EATING THROUGH MY NEURONS... LIKE THE ROAMING CARNIVOROUS BLIPS... IN AN ARCADE GAME...
I DIDN'T KNOW...
...THEY HAD WEAPONS OUT HERE...
...THAT COULD DESTROY ME.
14

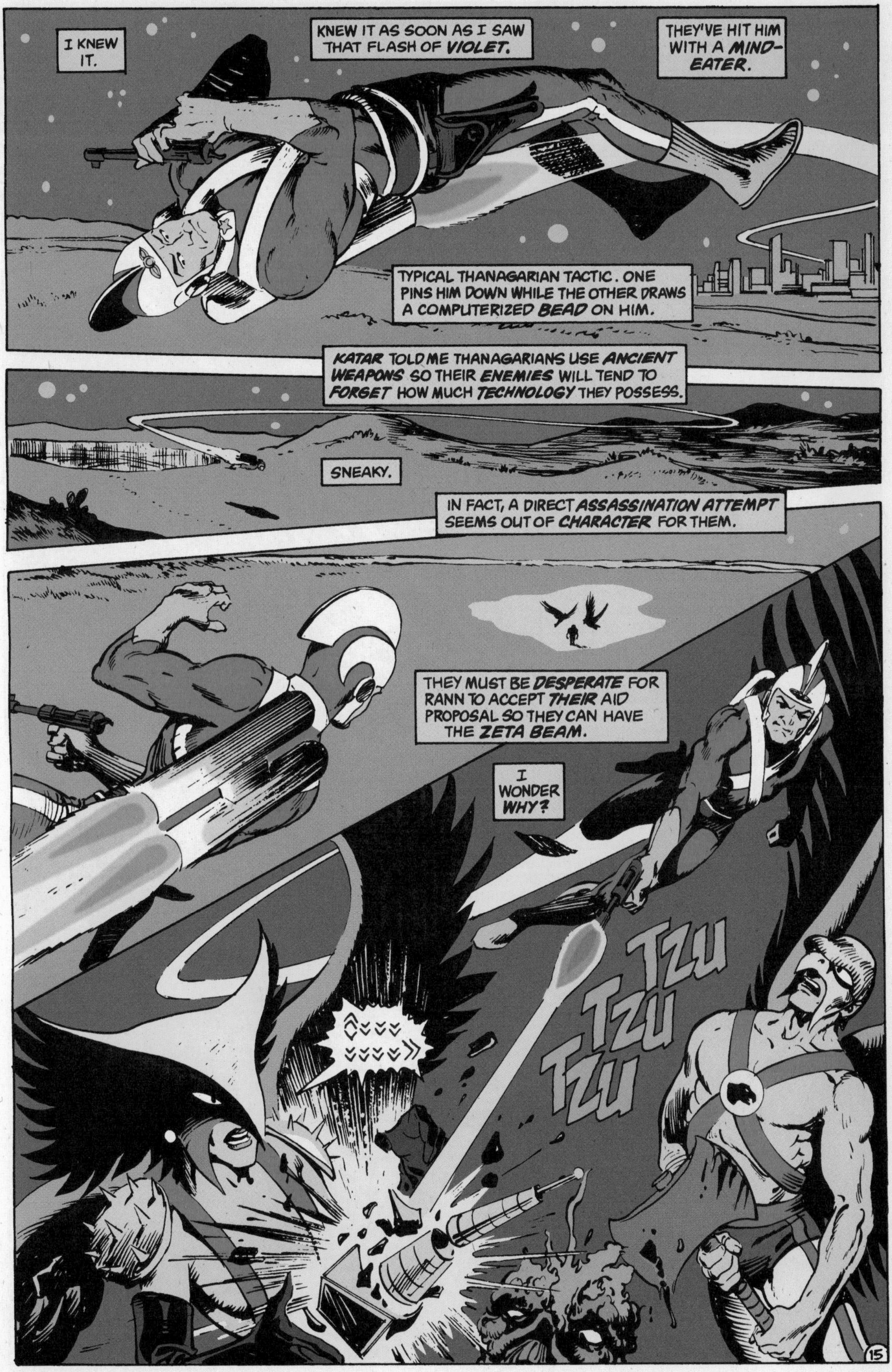
I KNEW IT.
KNEW IT AS SOON AS I SAW THAT FLASH OF VIOLET.
THEY'VE HIT HIM WITH A MIND-EATER.
TYPICAL THANAGARIAN TACTIC. ONE PINS HIM DOWN WHILE THE OTHER DRAWS A COMPUTERIZED BEAD ON HIM.
KATAR TOLD ME THANAGARIANS USE ANCIENT WEAPONS SO THEIR ENEMIES WILL TEND TO FORGET HOW MUCH TECHNOLOGY THEY POSSESS.
SNEAKY.
IN FACT, A DIRECT ASSASSINATION ATTEMPT SEEMS OUT OF CHARACTER FOR THEM.
THEY MUST BE DESPERATE FOR RANN TO ACCEPT THEIR AID PROPOSAL SO THEY CAN HAVE THE ZETA BEAM.
I WONDER WHY?
TZU TZU TZU TZU
15

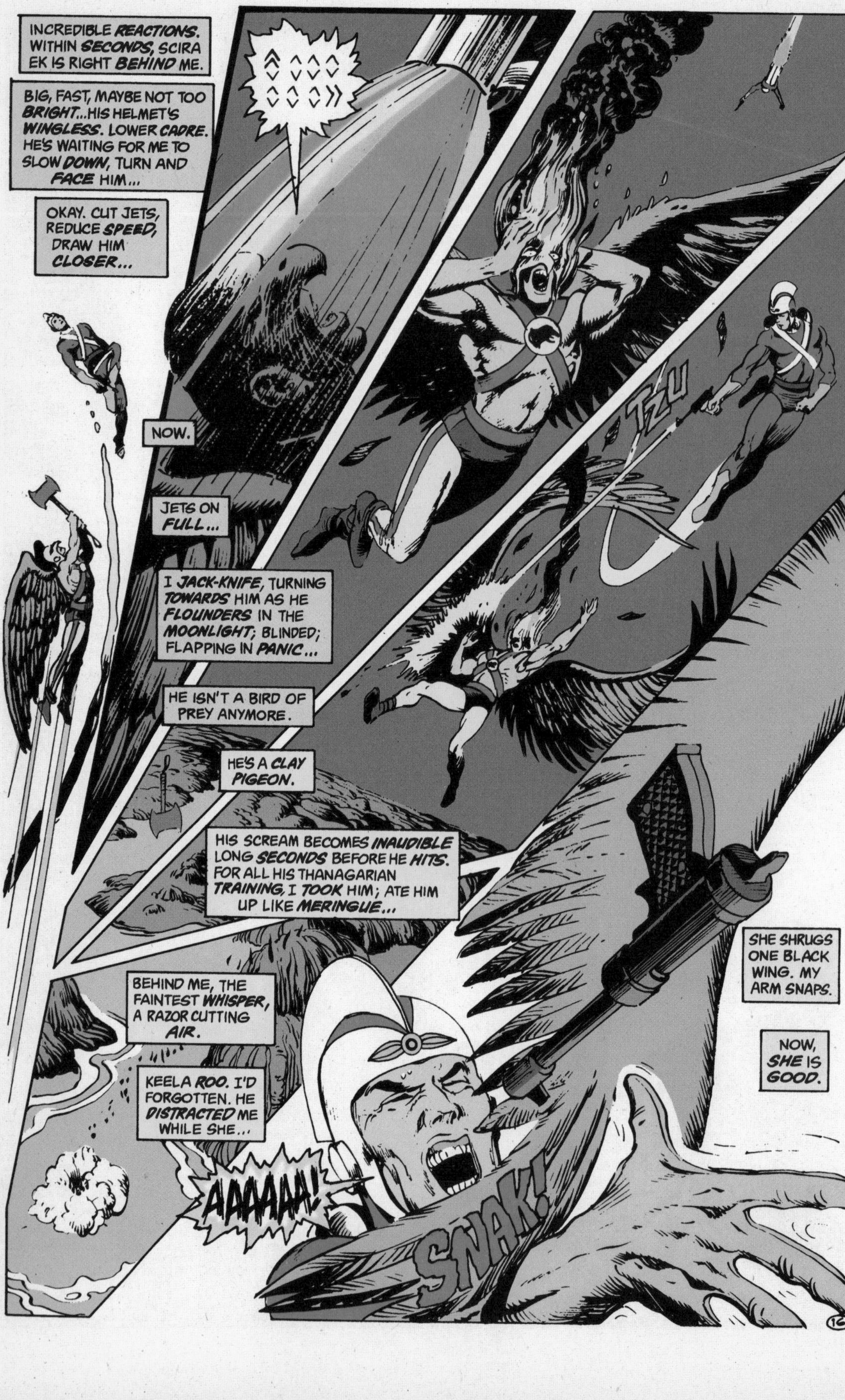
INCREDIBLE REACTIONS. WITHIN SECONDS, SCIRA EK IS RIGHT BEHIND ME.
BIG, FAST, MAYBE NOT TOO BRIGHT...HIS HELMET'S WINGLESS. LOWER CADRE. HE'S WAITING FOR ME TO SLOW DOWN, TURN AND FACE HIM...
OKAY. CUT JETS, REDUCE SPEED, DRAW HIM CLOSER...
NOW.
JETS ON FULL...
I JACK-KNIFE, TURNING TOWARDS HIM AS HE FLOUNDERS IN THE MOONLIGHT; BLINDED; FLAPPING IN PANIC...
TZU
HE ISN'T A BIRD OF PREY ANYMORE.
HE'S A CLAY PIGEON.
HIS SCREAM BECOMES INAUDIBLE LONG SECONDS BEFORE HE HITS. FOR ALL HIS THANAGARIAN TRAINING, I TOOK HIM; ATE HIM UP LIKE MERINGUE...
BEHIND ME, THE FAINTEST WHISPER, A RAZOR CUTTING AIR.
KEELA ROO. I'D FORGOTTEN. HE DISTRACTED ME WHILE SHE...
SHE SHRUGS ONE BLACK WING. MY ARM SNAPS.
NOW, SHE IS GOOD.
AAAAAA!
SNAK!
16

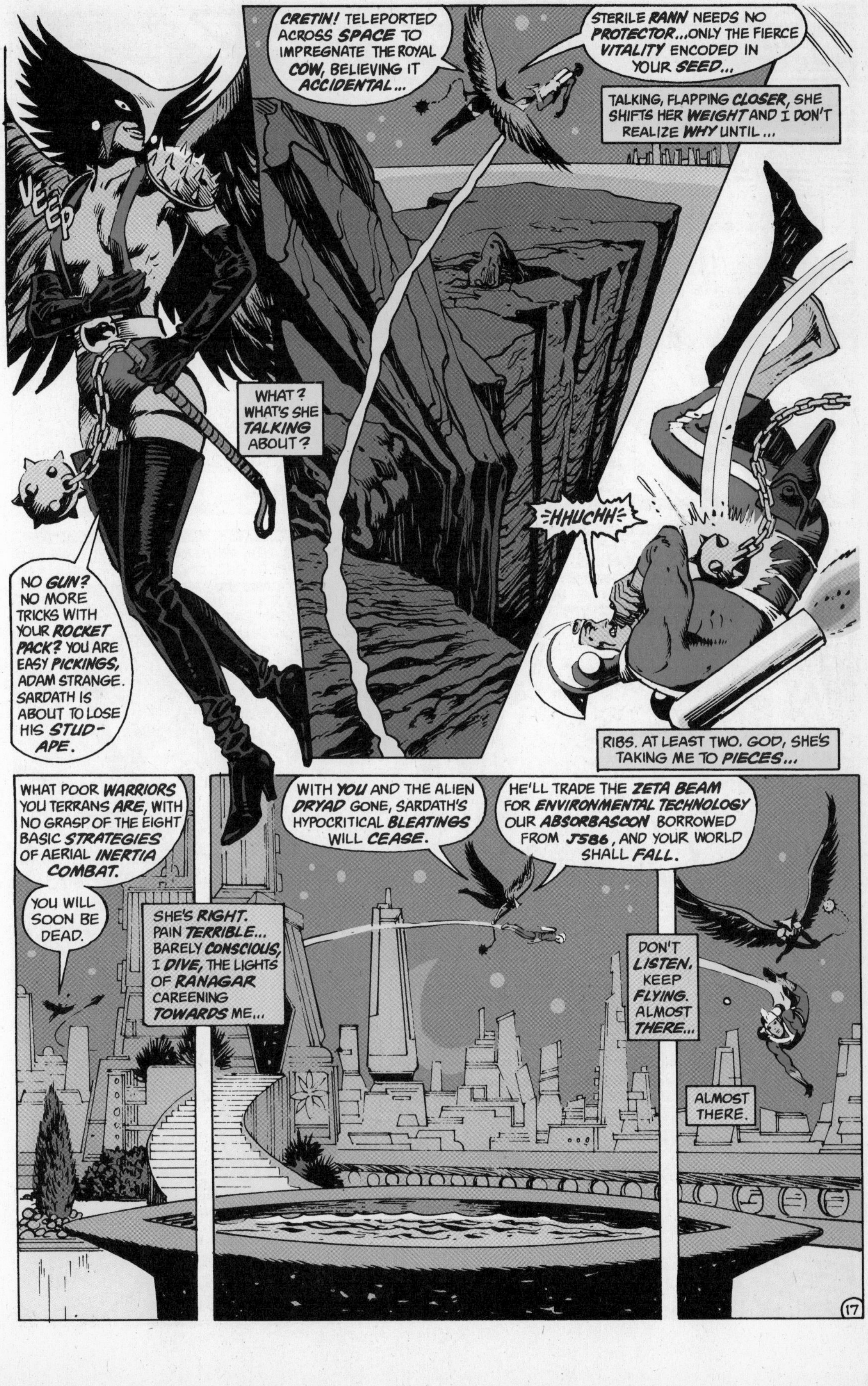
VEEP
CRETIN! TELEPORTED ACROSS SPACE TO IMPREGNATE THE ROYAL COW, BELIEVING IT ACCIDENTAL...
STERILE RANN NEEDS NO PROTECTOR...ONLY THE FIERCE VITALITY ENCODED IN YOUR SEED...
TALKING, FLAPPING CLOSER, SHE SHIFTS HER WEIGHT AND I DON'T REALIZE WHY UNTIL...
WHAT? WHAT'S SHE TALKING ABOUT?
HHUCHH
NO GUN? NO MORE TRICKS WITH YOUR ROCKET PACK? YOU ARE EASY PICKINGS, ADAM STRANGE. SARDATH IS ABOUT TO LOSE HIS STUD-APE.
RIBS. AT LEAST TWO. GOD, SHE'S TAKING ME TO PIECES...
WHAT POOR WARRIORS YOU TERRANS ARE, WITH NO GRASP OF THE EIGHT BASIC STRATEGIES OF AERIAL INERTIA COMBAT.
YOU WILL SOON BE DEAD.
SHE'S RIGHT. PAIN TERRIBLE... BARELY CONSCIOUS, I DIVE, THE LIGHTS OF RANAGAR CAREENING TOWARDS ME...
WITH YOU AND THE ALIEN DRYAD GONE, SARDATH'S HYPOCRITICAL BLEATINGS WILL CEASE.
HE'LL TRADE THE ZETA BEAM FOR ENVIRONMENTAL TECHNOLOGY OUR ABSORBASCON BORROWED FROM J586, AND YOUR WORLD SHALL FALL.
DON'T LISTEN. KEEP FLYING. ALMOST THERE...
ALMOST THERE.
17

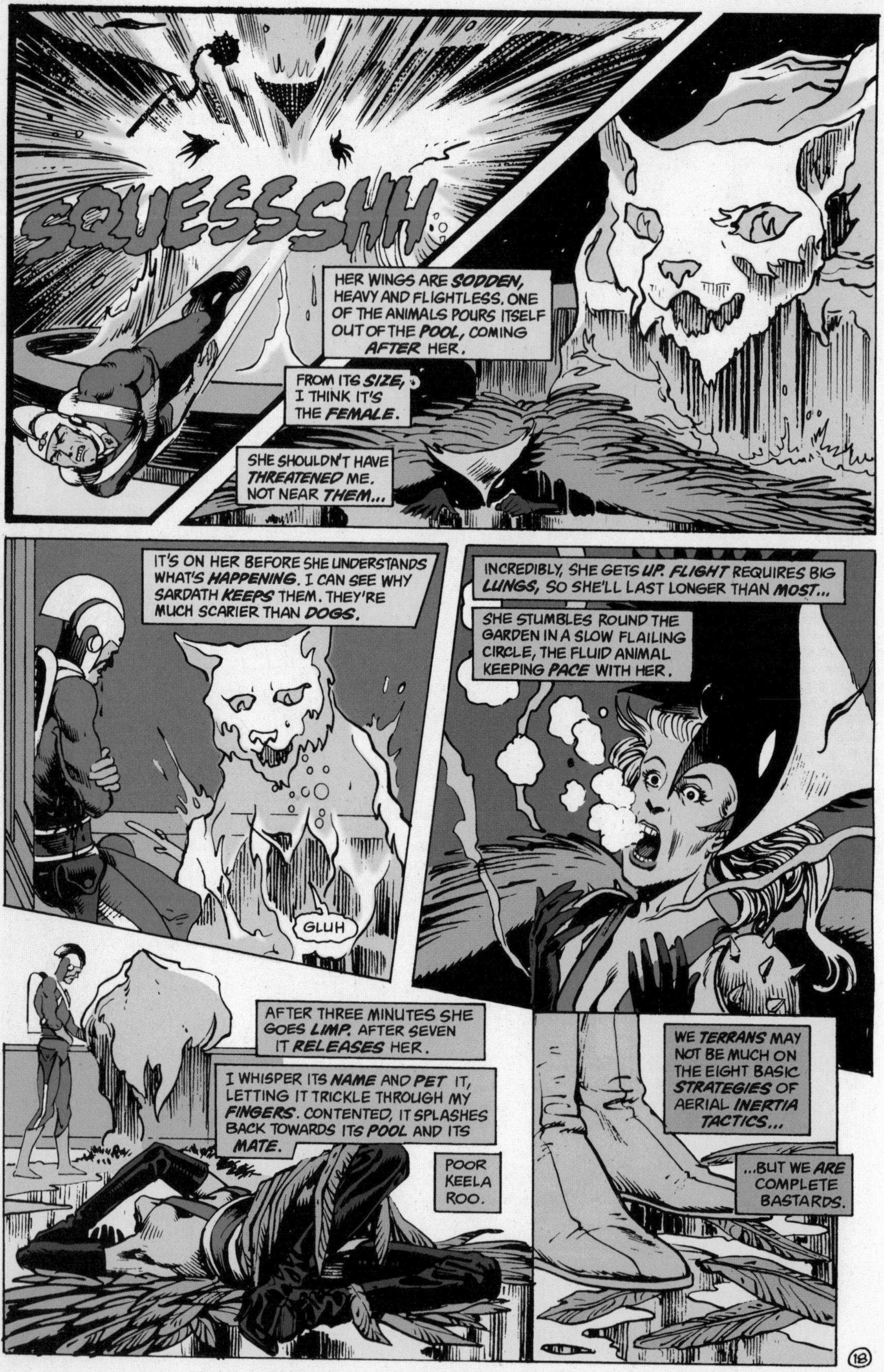
SQUESSSHH
HER WINGS ARE SODDEN, HEAVY AND FLIGHTLESS. ONE OF THE ANIMALS POURS ITSELF OUT OF THE POOL, COMING AFTER HER.
FROM ITS SIZE, I THINK IT'S THE FEMALE.
SHE SHOULDN'T HAVE THREATENED ME. NOT NEAR THEM...
IT'S ON HER BEFORE SHE UNDERSTANDS WHAT'S HAPPENING. I CAN SEE WHY SARDATH KEEPS THEM. THEY'RE MUCH SCARIER THAN DOGS.
GLUH
INCREDIBLY, SHE GETS UP. FLIGHT REQUIRES BIG LUNGS, SO SHE'LL LAST LONGER THAN MOST...
SHE STUMBLES ROUND THE GARDEN IN A SLOW FLAILING CIRCLE, THE FLUID ANIMAL KEEPING PACE WITH HER.
AFTER THREE MINUTES SHE GOES LIMP. AFTER SEVEN IT RELEASES HER.
I WHISPER ITS NAME AND PET IT, LETTING IT TRICKLE THROUGH MY FINGERS. CONTENTED, IT SPLASHES BACK TOWARDS ITS POOL AND ITS MATE.
POOR KEELA ROO.
WE TERRANS MAY NOT BE MUCH ON THE EIGHT BASIC STRATEGIES OF AERIAL INERTIA TACTICS...
...BUT WE ARE COMPLETE BASTARDS.
18

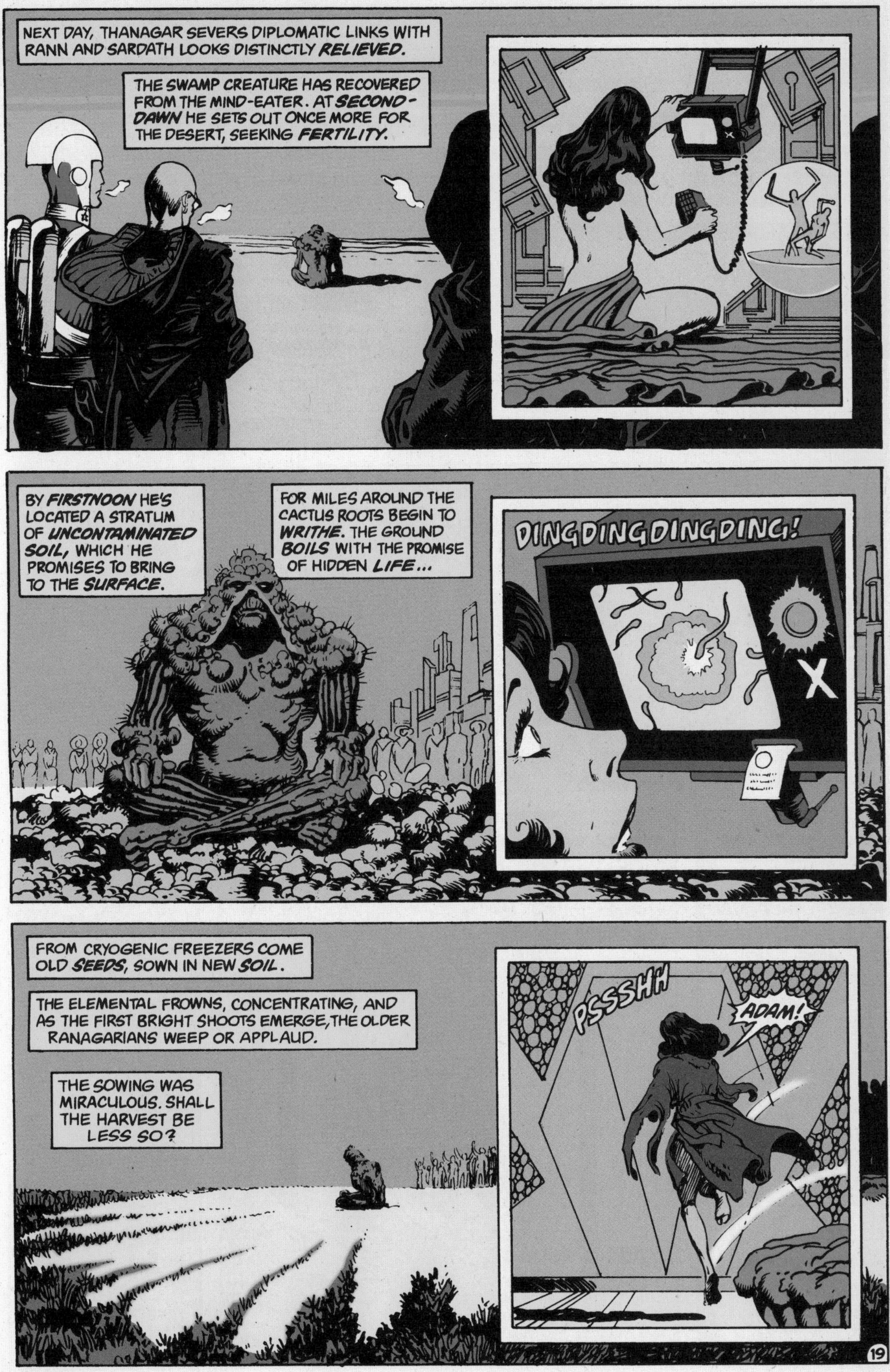
NEXT DAY, THANAGAR SEVERS DIPLOMATIC LINKS WITH RANN AND SARDATH LOOKS DISTINCTLY RELIEVED.
THE SWAMP CREATURE HAS RECOVERED FROM THE MIND-EATER. AT SECOND-DAWN HE SETS OUT ONCE MORE FOR THE DESERT, SEEKING FERTILITY.
BY FIRSTNOON HE'S LOCATED A STRATUM OF UNCONTAMINATED SOIL, WHICH HE PROMISES TO BRING TO THE SURFACE.
FOR MILES AROUND THE CACTUS ROOTS BEGIN TO WRITHE. THE GROUND BOILS WITH THE PROMISE OF HIDDEN LIFE...
DINGDINGDINGDING!
FROM CRYOGENIC FREEZERS COME OLD SEEDS, SOWN IN NEW SOIL.
THE ELEMENTAL FROWNS, CONCENTRATING, AND AS THE FIRST BRIGHT SHOOTS EMERGE, THE OLDER RANAGARIANS WEEP OR APPLAUD.
THE SOWING WAS MIRACULOUS. SHALL THE HARVEST BE LESS SO?
PSSSHH
ADAM!
19

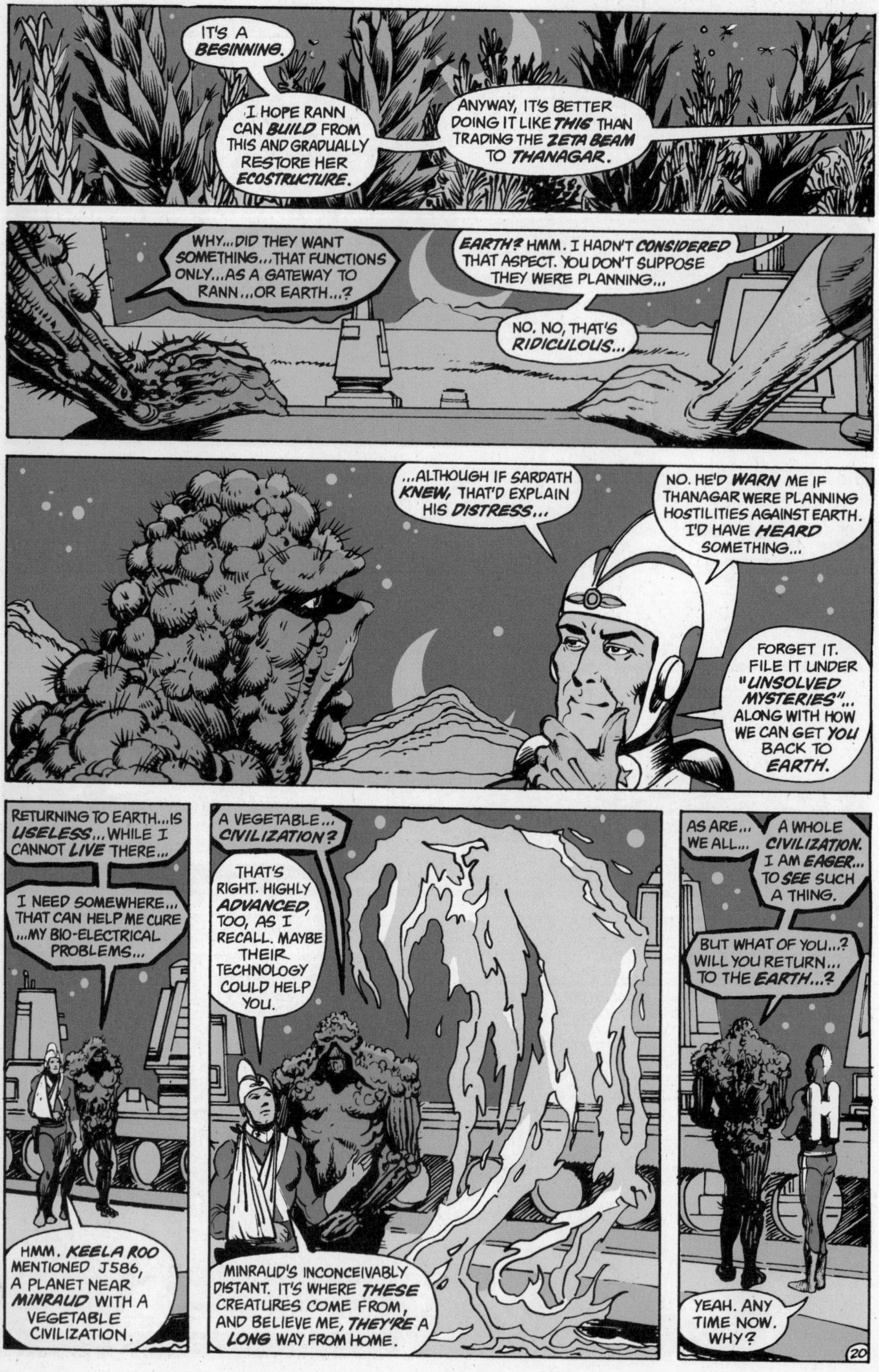
IT'S A BEGINNING.
I HOPE RANN CAN BUILD FROM THIS AND GRADUALLY RESTORE HER ECOSTRUCTURE.
ANYWAY, IT'S BETTER DOING IT LIKE THIS THAN TRADING THE ZETA BEAM TO THANAGAR.
WHY...DID THEY WANT SOMETHING...THAT FUNCTIONS ONLY...AS A GATEWAY TO RANN...OR EARTH...?
EARTH? HMM. I HADN'T CONSIDERED THAT ASPECT. YOU DON'T SUPPOSE THEY WERE PLANNING...
NO. NO, THAT'S RIDICULOUS...
...ALTHOUGH IF SARDATH KNEW, THAT'D EXPLAIN HIS DISTRESS...
NO. HE'D WARN ME IF THANAGAR WERE PLANNING HOSTILITIES AGAINST EARTH. I'D HAVE HEARD SOMETHING...
FORGET IT. FILE IT UNDER "UNSOLVED MYSTERIES"... ALONG WITH HOW WE CAN GET YOU BACK TO EARTH.
RETURNING TO EARTH...IS USELESS...WHILE I CANNOT LIVE THERE...
I NEED SOMEWHERE... THAT CAN HELP ME CURE ...MY BIO-ELECTRICAL PROBLEMS...
HMM. KEELA ROO MENTIONED J586, A PLANET NEAR MINRAUD WITH A VEGETABLE CIVILIZATION.
A VEGETABLE... CIVILIZATION?
THAT'S RIGHT. HIGHLY ADVANCED, TOO, AS I RECALL. MAYBE THEIR TECHNOLOGY COULD HELP YOU.
MINRAUD'S INCONCEIVABLY DISTANT. IT'S WHERE THESE CREATURES COME FROM, AND BELIEVE ME, THEY'RE A LONG WAY FROM HOME.
AS ARE... WE ALL...
A WHOLE CIVILIZATION. I AM EAGER... TO SEE SUCH A THING.
BUT WHAT OF YOU...? WILL YOU RETURN... TO THE EARTH...?
YEAH. ANY TIME NOW. WHY?
20

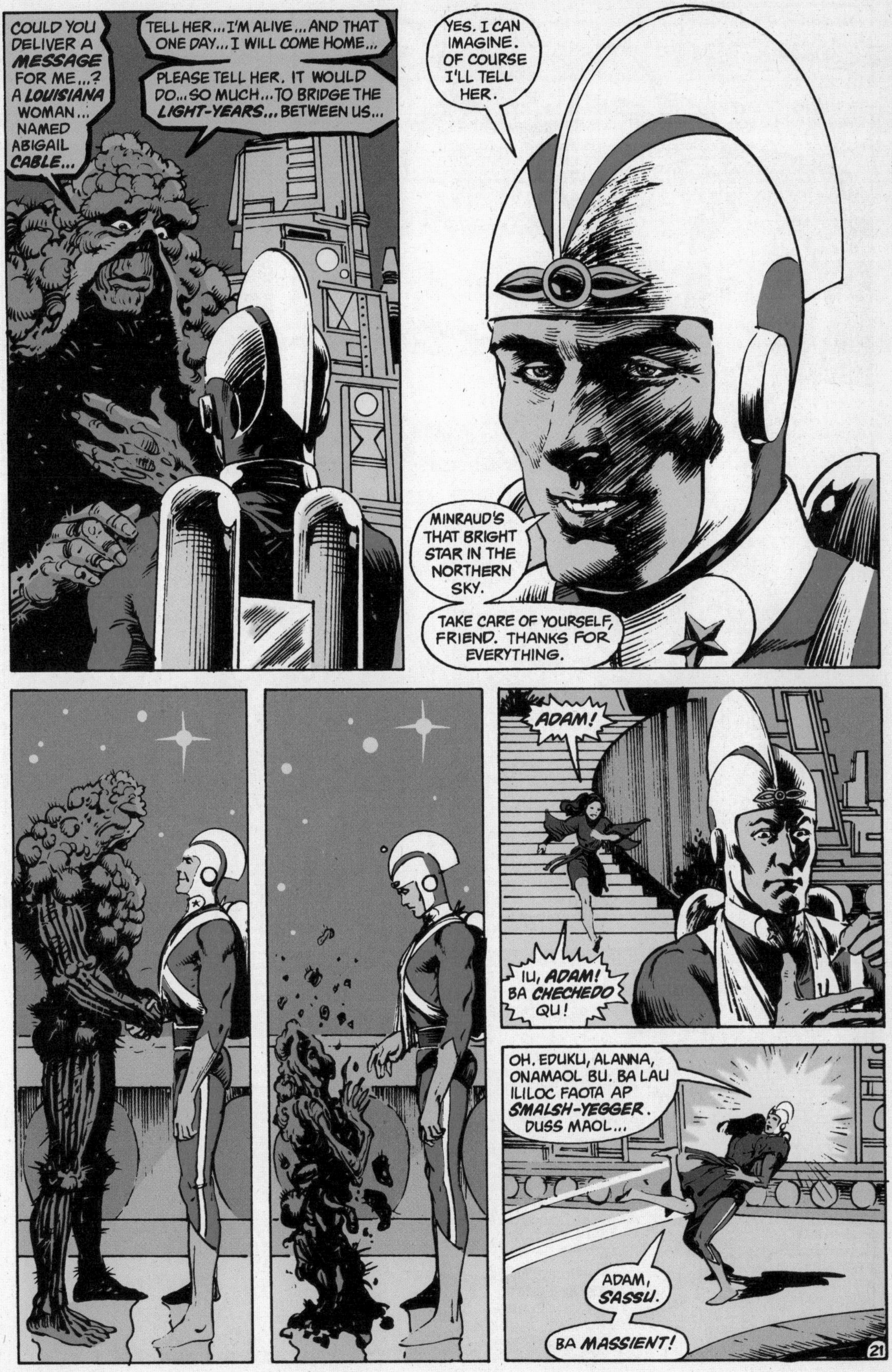
COULD YOU DELIVER A MESSAGE FOR ME...? A LOUISIANA WOMAN... NAMED ABIGAIL CABLE...
TELL HER...I'M ALIVE...AND THAT ONE DAY...I WILL COME HOME...
PLEASE TELL HER. IT WOULD DO...SO MUCH...TO BRIDGE THE LIGHT-YEARS...BETWEEN US...
YES. I CAN IMAGINE. OF COURSE I'LL TELL HER.
MINRAUD'S THAT BRIGHT STAR IN THE NORTHERN SKY.
TAKE CARE OF YOURSELF, FRIEND. THANKS FOR EVERYTHING.
ADAM!
IU, ADAM! BA CHECHEDO QU!
OH, EDUKU, ALANNA, ONAMAOL BU. BA LAU ILILOC FAOTA AP SMALSH-YEGGER. DUSS MAOL...
ADAM, SASSU.
BA MASSIENT!
21

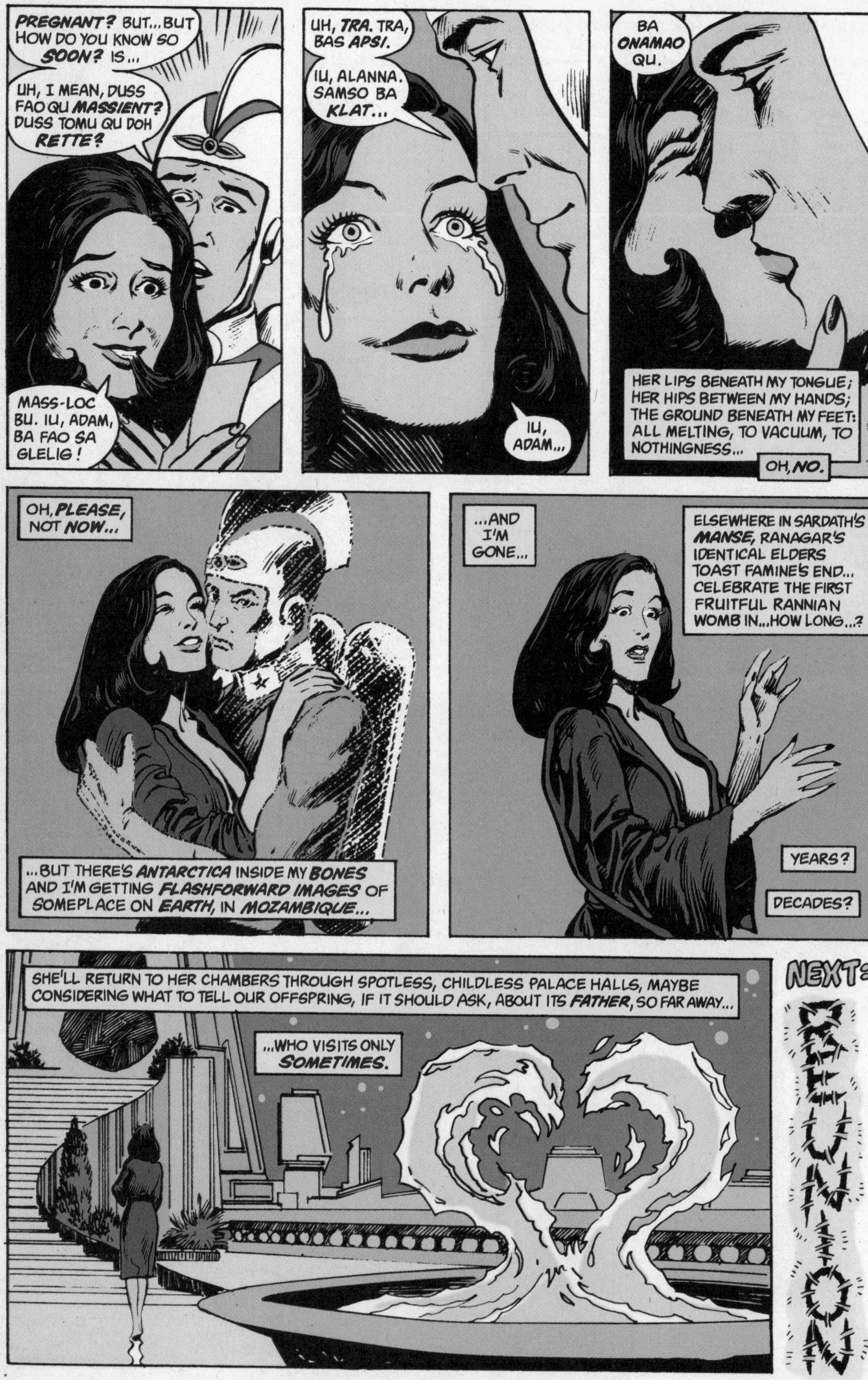
PREGNANT? BUT...BUT HOW DO YOU KNOW SO SOON? IS...
UH, I MEAN, DUSS FAO QU MASSIENT? DUSS TOMU QU DOH RETTE?
MASS-LOC BU. IU, ADAM, BA FAO SA GLELIG!
UH, TRA. TRA, BAS APSI.
IU, ALANNA. SAMSO BA KLAT...
IU, ADAM...
BA ONAMAO QU.
HER LIPS BENEATH MY TONGUE; HER HIPS BETWEEN MY HANDS; THE GROUND BENEATH MY FEET: ALL MELTING, TO VACUUM, TO NOTHINGNESS...
OH, NO.
OH, PLEASE, NOT NOW...
...BUT THERE'S ANTARCTICA INSIDE MY BONES AND I'M GETTING FLASHFORWARD IMAGES OF SOMEPLACE ON EARTH, IN MOZAMBIQUE...
...AND I'M GONE...
ELSEWHERE IN SARDATH'S MANSE, RANAGAR'S IDENTICAL ELDERS TOAST FAMINE'S END... CELEBRATE THE FIRST FRUITFUL RANNIAN WOMB IN...HOW LONG...?
YEARS?
DECADES?
SHE'LL RETURN TO HER CHAMBERS THROUGH SPOTLESS, CHILDLESS PALACE HALLS, MAYBE CONSIDERING WHAT TO TELL OUR OFFSPRING, IF IT SHOULD ASK, ABOUT ITS FATHER, SO FAR AWAY...
...WHO VISITS ONLY SOMETIMES.
NEXT:
REUNION

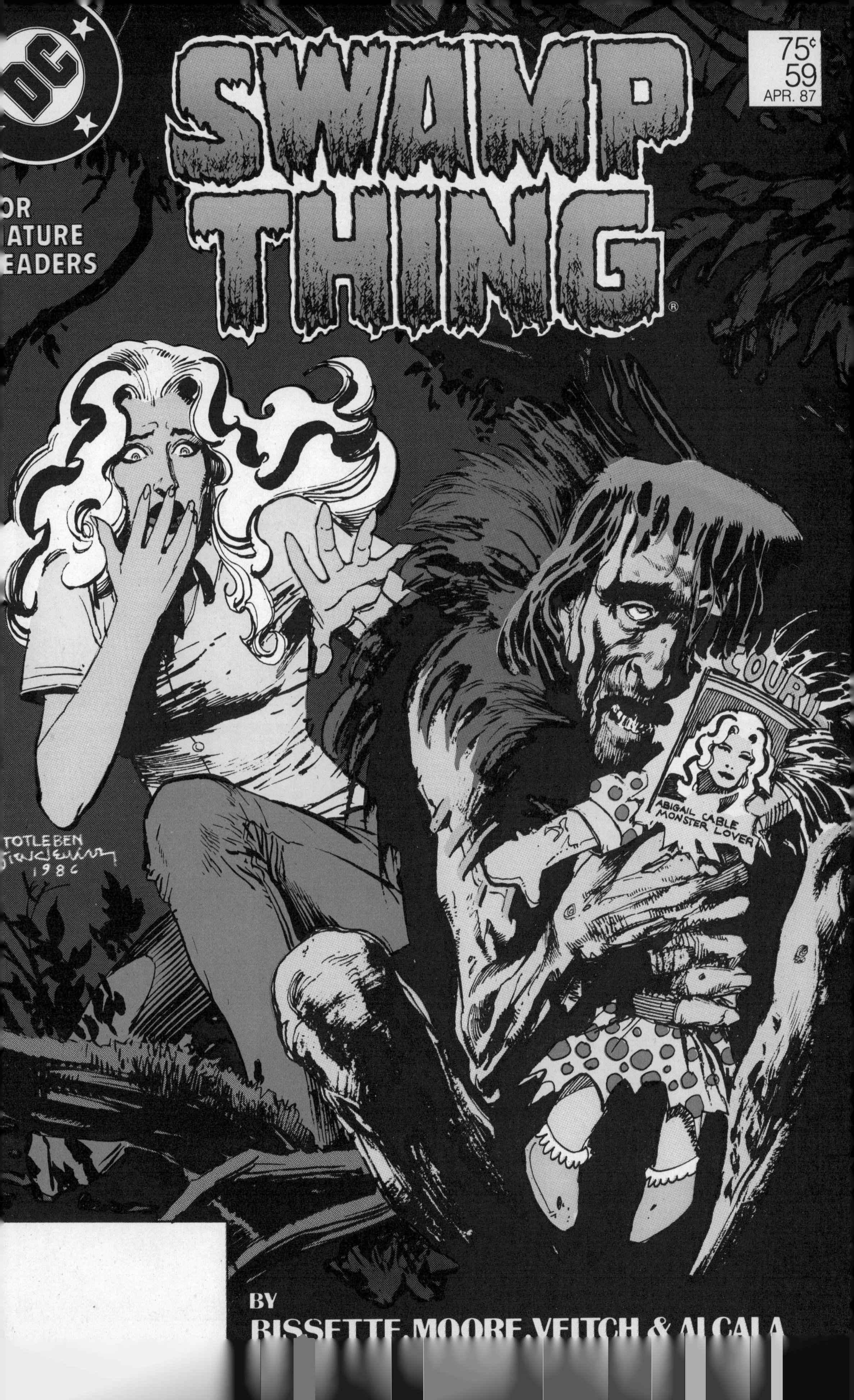
DC
SWAMP THING
75¢
59
APR. 87
OR
IATURE
EADERS
TOTLEBEN
1986
ABIGAIL CABLE
MONSTER LOVER
BY
BISSETTE, MOORE, VEITCH & ALCALA

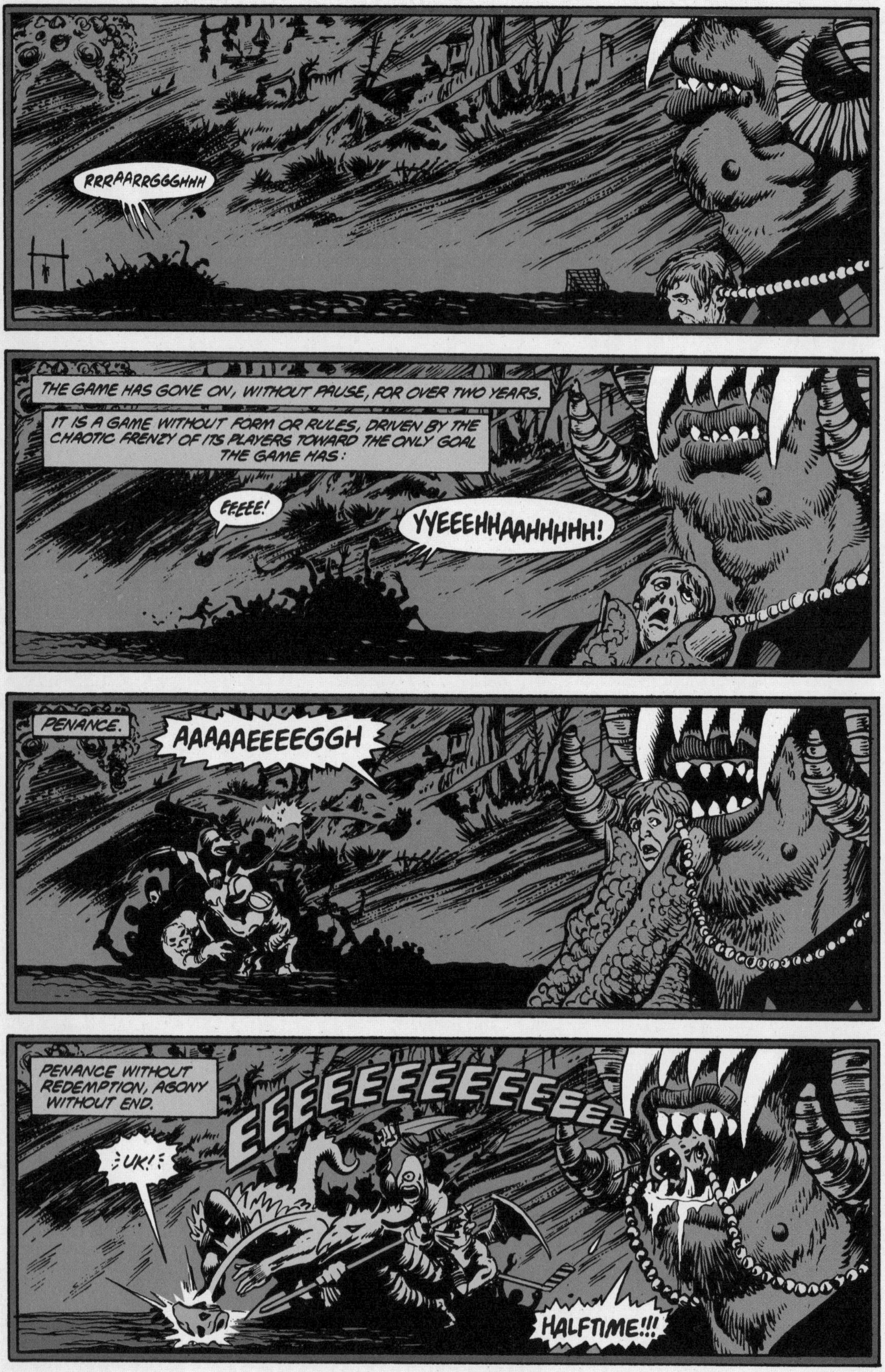
RRRAARRGGGHHH
THE GAME HAS GONE ON, WITHOUT PAUSE, FOR OVER TWO YEARS.
IT IS A GAME WITHOUT FORM OR RULES, DRIVEN BY THE CHAOTIC FRENZY OF ITS PLAYERS TOWARD THE ONLY GOAL THE GAME HAS:
EEEEE!
YYEEEHHAAHHHHH!
PENANCE.
AAAAAEEEEGGH
PENANCE WITHOUT REDEMPTION, AGONY WITHOUT END.
EEEEEEEEEEEEE
UK!
HALFTIME!!!

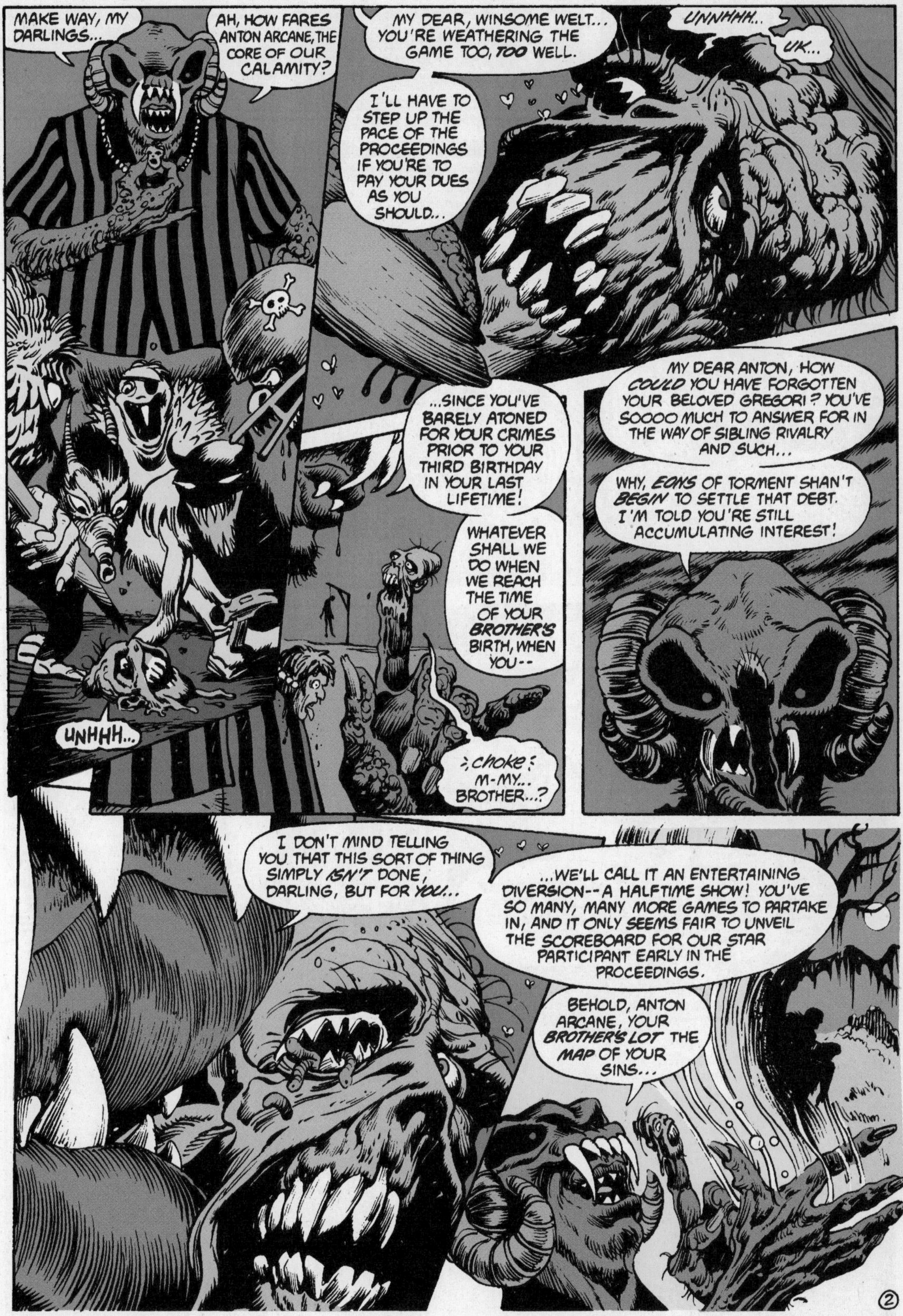
MAKE WAY, MY DARLINGS...
AH, HOW FARES ANTON ARCANE, THE CORE OF OUR CALAMITY?
MY DEAR, WINSOME WELT... YOU'RE WEATHERING THE GAME TOO, TOO WELL.
I'LL HAVE TO STEP UP THE PACE OF THE PROCEEDINGS IF YOU'RE TO PAY YOUR DUES AS YOU SHOULD...
UNNHHH...
UK...
...SINCE YOU'VE BARELY ATONED FOR YOUR CRIMES PRIOR TO YOUR THIRD BIRTHDAY IN YOUR LAST LIFETIME!
WHATEVER SHALL WE DO WHEN WE REACH THE TIME OF YOUR BROTHER'S BIRTH, WHEN YOU--
UNHHH...
choke M-MY... BROTHER...?
MY DEAR ANTON, HOW COULD YOU HAVE FORGOTTEN YOUR BELOVED GREGORI? YOU'VE SOOOO MUCH TO ANSWER FOR IN THE WAY OF SIBLING RIVALRY AND SUCH...
WHY, EONS OF TORMENT SHAN'T BEGIN TO SETTLE THAT DEBT. I'M TOLD YOU'RE STILL ACCUMULATING INTEREST!
I DON'T MIND TELLING YOU THAT THIS SORT OF THING SIMPLY ISN'T DONE, DARLING, BUT FOR YOU...
...WE'LL CALL IT AN ENTERTAINING DIVERSION-- A HALFTIME SHOW! YOU'VE SO MANY, MANY MORE GAMES TO PARTAKE IN, AND IT ONLY SEEMS FAIR TO UNVEIL THE SCOREBOARD FOR OUR STAR PARTICIPANT EARLY IN THE PROCEEDINGS.
BEHOLD, ANTON ARCANE, YOUR BROTHER'S LOT THE MAP OF YOUR SINS...
2

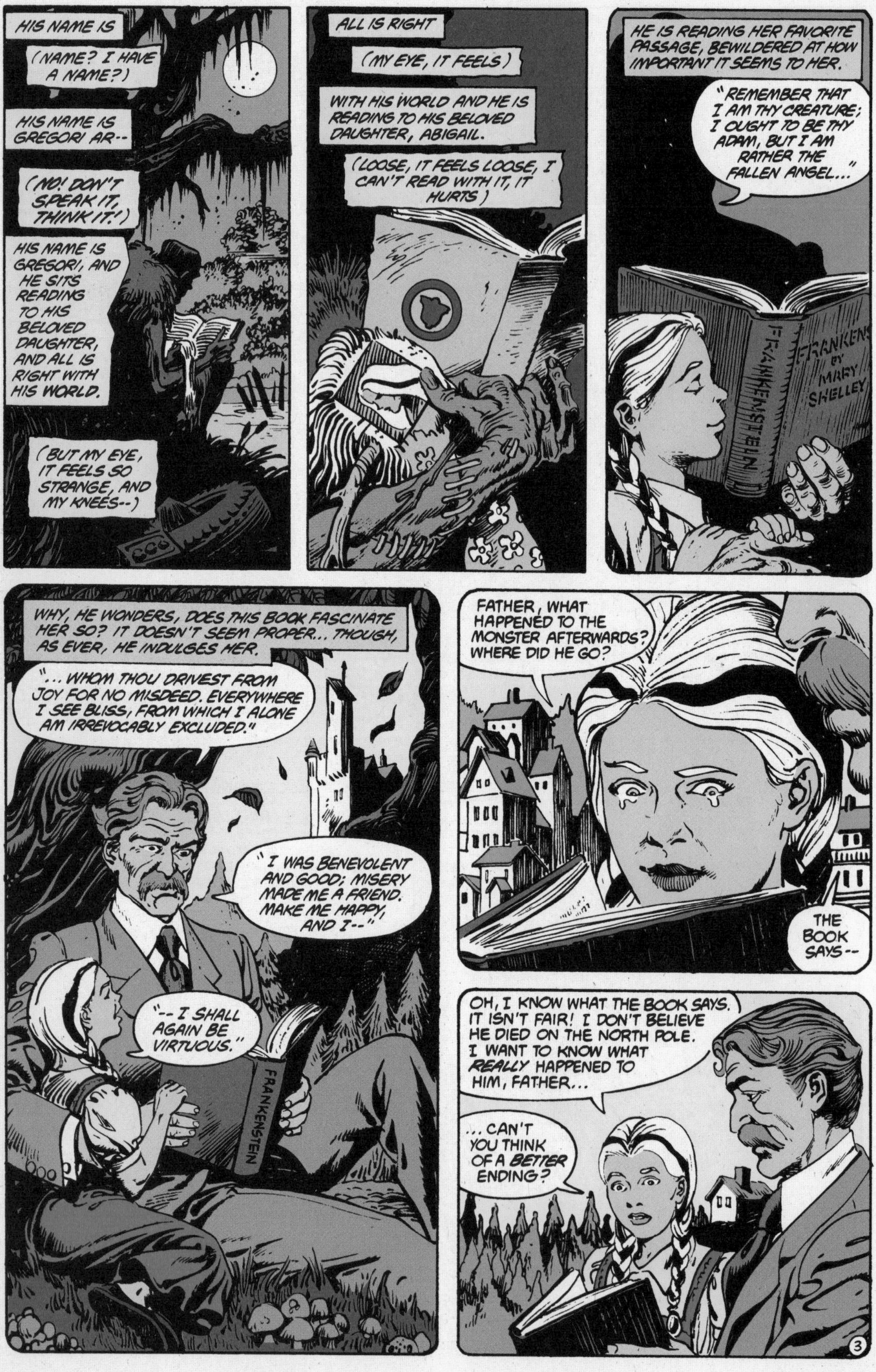
HIS NAME IS
(NAME? I HAVE A NAME?)
HIS NAME IS GREGORI AR--
(NO! DON'T SPEAK IT, THINK IT!)
HIS NAME IS GREGORI, AND HE SITS READING TO HIS BELOVED DAUGHTER, AND ALL IS RIGHT WITH HIS WORLD.
(BUT MY EYE, IT FEELS SO STRANGE, AND MY KNEES--)
ALL IS RIGHT
(MY EYE, IT FEELS)
WITH HIS WORLD AND HE IS READING TO HIS BELOVED DAUGHTER, ABIGAIL.
(LOOSE, IT FEELS LOOSE, I CAN'T READ WITH IT, IT HURTS)
HE IS READING HER FAVORITE PASSAGE, BEWILDERED AT HOW IMPORTANT IT SEEMS TO HER.
"REMEMBER THAT I AM THY CREATURE; I OUGHT TO BE THY ADAM, BUT I AM RATHER THE FALLEN ANGEL..."
FRANKENSTEIN
FRANKENS BY MARY SHELLEY
WHY, HE WONDERS, DOES THIS BOOK FASCINATE HER SO? IT DOESN'T SEEM PROPER... THOUGH, AS EVER, HE INDULGES HER.
"...WHOM THOU DRIVEST FROM JOY FOR NO MISDEED. EVERYWHERE I SEE BLISS, FROM WHICH I ALONE AM IRREVOCABLY EXCLUDED."
"I WAS BENEVOLENT AND GOOD; MISERY MADE ME A FRIEND. MAKE ME HAPPY, AND I--"
"--I SHALL AGAIN BE VIRTUOUS."
FRANKENSTEIN
FATHER, WHAT HAPPENED TO THE MONSTER AFTERWARDS? WHERE DID HE GO?
THE BOOK SAYS--
OH, I KNOW WHAT THE BOOK SAYS. IT ISN'T FAIR! I DON'T BELIEVE HE DIED ON THE NORTH POLE. I WANT TO KNOW WHAT *REALLY* HAPPENED TO HIM, FATHER...
...CAN'T YOU THINK OF A *BETTER* ENDING?
3

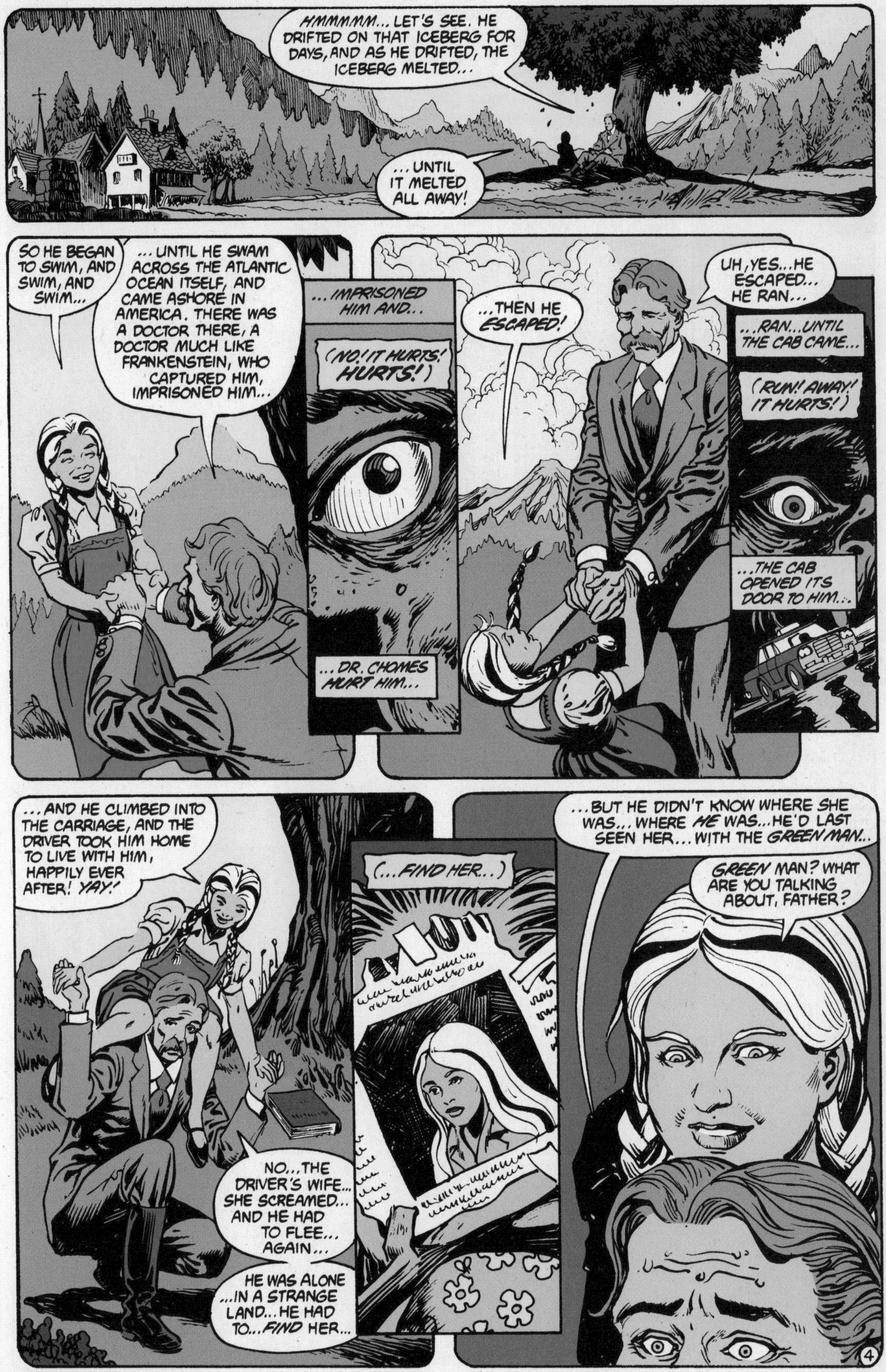
HMMMMM... LET'S SEE. HE DRIFTED ON THAT ICEBERG FOR DAYS, AND AS HE DRIFTED, THE ICEBERG MELTED...
...UNTIL IT MELTED ALL AWAY!
SO HE BEGAN TO SWIM, AND SWIM, AND SWIM...
...UNTIL HE SWAM ACROSS THE ATLANTIC OCEAN ITSELF, AND CAME ASHORE IN AMERICA. THERE WAS A DOCTOR THERE, A DOCTOR MUCH LIKE FRANKENSTEIN, WHO CAPTURED HIM, IMPRISONED HIM...
...IMPRISONED HIM AND...
(NO! IT HURTS! HURTS!)
...DR. CHOMES HURT HIM...
...THEN HE ESCAPED!
UH, YES... HE ESCAPED... HE RAN...
...RAN... UNTIL THE CAB CAME...
(RUN! AWAY! IT HURTS!)
...THE CAB OPENED ITS DOOR TO HIM...
...AND HE CLIMBED INTO THE CARRIAGE, AND THE DRIVER TOOK HIM HOME TO LIVE WITH HIM, HAPPILY EVER AFTER! YAY!
NO... THE DRIVER'S WIFE... SHE SCREAMED... AND HE HAD TO FLEE... AGAIN...
HE WAS ALONE ...IN A STRANGE LAND... HE HAD TO... FIND HER...
(...FIND HER...)
...BUT HE DIDN'T KNOW WHERE SHE WAS... WHERE HE WAS... HE'D LAST SEEN HER... WITH THE GREEN MAN...
GREEN MAN? WHAT ARE YOU TALKING ABOUT, FATHER?
4

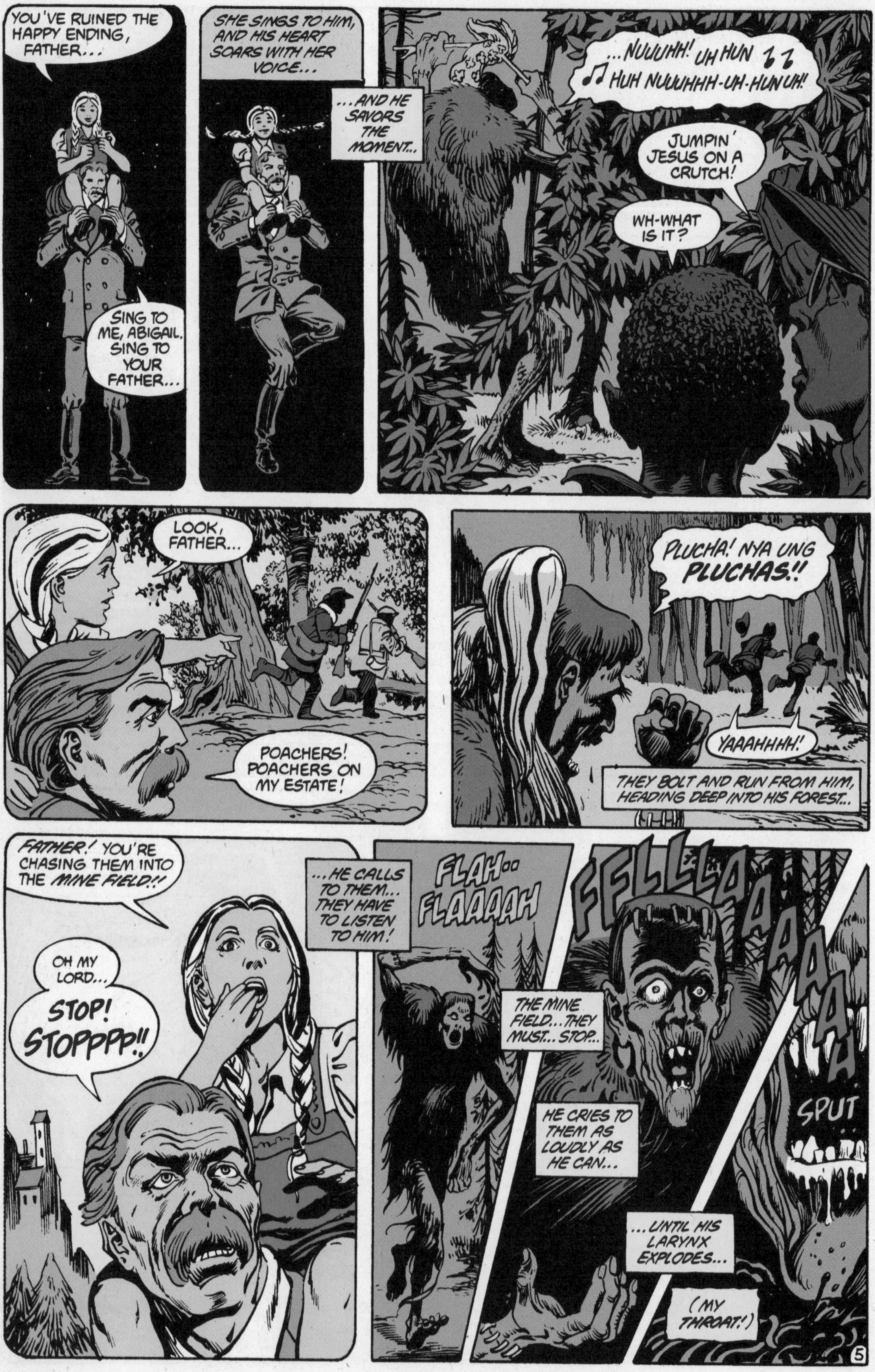
YOU'VE RUINED THE HAPPY ENDING, FATHER...
SING TO ME, ABIGAIL. SING TO YOUR FATHER...
SHE SINGS TO HIM, AND HIS HEART SOARS WITH HER VOICE...
...AND HE SAVORS THE MOMENT...
...NUUUHH! UH HUN HUH NUUUHHH-UH-HUNUH!
JUMPIN' JESUS ON A CRUTCH!
WH-WHAT IS IT?
LOOK, FATHER...
POACHERS! POACHERS ON MY ESTATE!
PLUCHA! NYA UNG PLUCHAS!!
YAAAHHHH!
THEY BOLT AND RUN FROM HIM, HEADING DEEP INTO HIS FOREST...
FATHER! YOU'RE CHASING THEM INTO THE MINE FIELD!!
OH MY LORD... STOP! STOPPPP!!
...HE CALLS TO THEM... THEY HAVE TO LISTEN TO HIM!
FLAH-- FLAAAAH
THE MINE FIELD... THEY MUST... STOP...
HE CRIES TO THEM AS LOUDLY AS HE CAN...
FFLLLAAAAAAA
SPUT
...UNTIL HIS LARYNX EXPLODES...
(MY THROAT!)
5

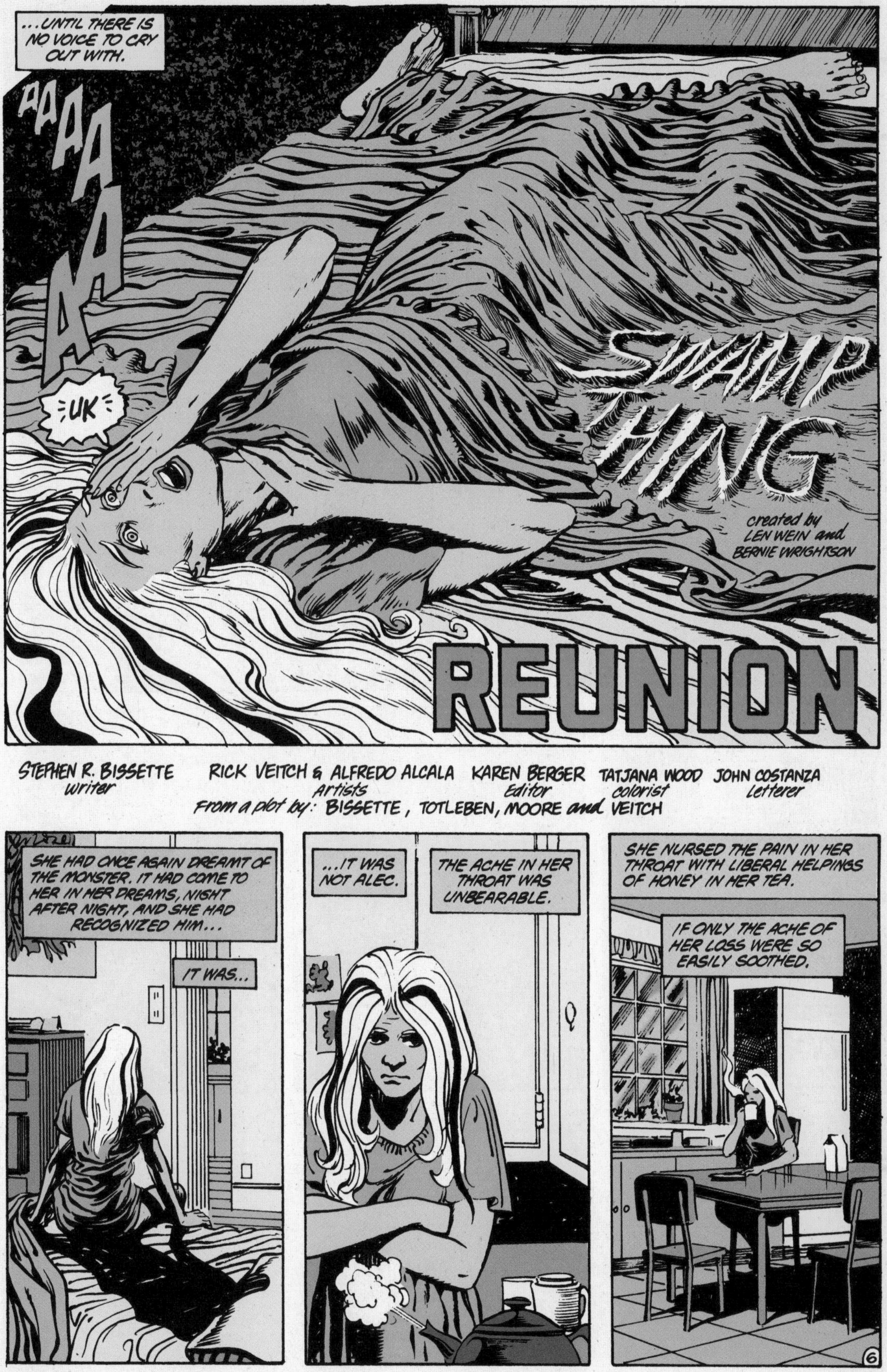
...UNTIL THERE IS NO VOICE TO CRY OUT WITH.
AAAAAAA
UK
SWAMP THING
created by LEN WEIN and BERNIE WRIGHTSON
REUNION
STEPHEN R. BISSETTE writer
RICK VEITCH & ALFREDO ALCALA Artists
KAREN BERGER Editor
TATJANA WOOD colorist
JOHN COSTANZA Letterer
From a plot by: BISSETTE, TOTLEBEN, MOORE and VEITCH
SHE HAD ONCE AGAIN DREAMT OF THE MONSTER. IT HAD COME TO HER IN HER DREAMS, NIGHT AFTER NIGHT, AND SHE HAD RECOGNIZED HIM...
IT WAS...
...IT WAS NOT ALEC.
THE ACHE IN HER THROAT WAS UNBEARABLE.
SHE NURSED THE PAIN IN HER THROAT WITH LIBERAL HELPINGS OF HONEY IN HER TEA.
IF ONLY THE ACHE OF HER LOSS WERE SO EASILY SOOTHED.
6

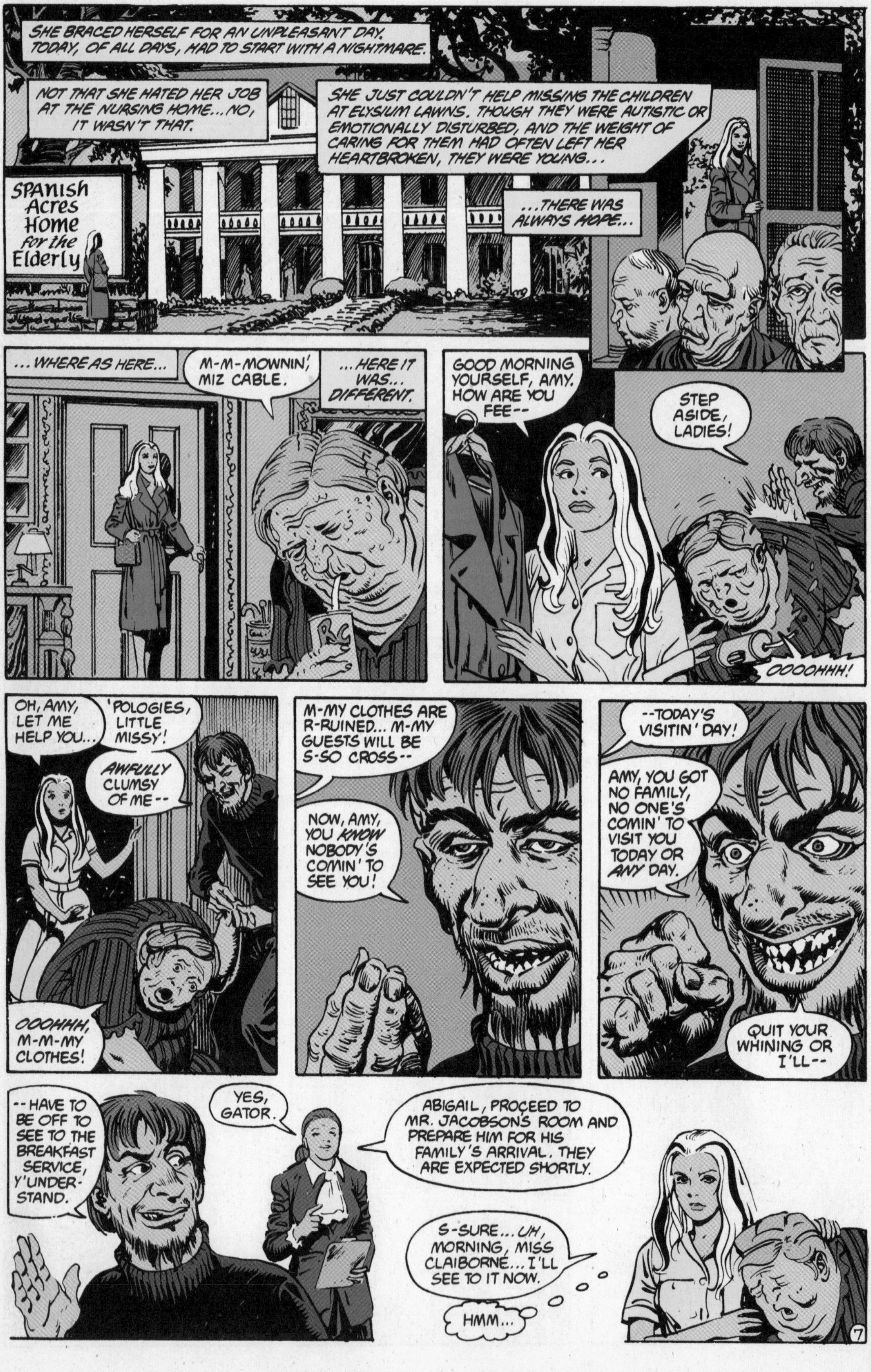
SHE BRACED HERSELF FOR AN UNPLEASANT DAY. TODAY, OF ALL DAYS, HAD TO START WITH A NIGHTMARE.
NOT THAT SHE HATED HER JOB AT THE NURSING HOME... NO, IT WASN'T THAT.
SHE JUST COULDN'T HELP MISSING THE CHILDREN AT ELYSIUM LAWNS. THOUGH THEY WERE AUTISTIC OR EMOTIONALLY DISTURBED, AND THE WEIGHT OF CARING FOR THEM HAD OFTEN LEFT HER HEARTBROKEN, THEY WERE YOUNG...
Spanish Acres Home for the Elderly
...THERE WAS ALWAYS HOPE...
...WHERE AS HERE...
M-M-MOWNIN', MIZ CABLE.
...HERE IT WAS... DIFFERENT.
GOOD MORNING YOURSELF, AMY. HOW ARE YOU FEE--
STEP ASIDE, LADIES!
OOOOHHH!
OH, AMY, LET ME HELP YOU...
'POLOGIES, LITTLE MISSY!
AWFULLY CLUMSY OF ME--
OOOHHH, M-M-MY CLOTHES!
M-MY CLOTHES ARE R-RUINED... M-MY GUESTS WILL BE S-SO CROSS--
NOW, AMY, YOU KNOW NOBODY'S COMIN' TO SEE YOU!
--TODAY'S VISITIN' DAY!
AMY, YOU GOT NO FAMILY, NO ONE'S COMIN' TO VISIT YOU TODAY OR ANY DAY.
QUIT YOUR WHINING OR I'LL--
--HAVE TO BE OFF TO SEE TO THE BREAKFAST SERVICE, Y'UNDER-STAND.
YES, GATOR.
ABIGAIL, PROCEED TO MR. JACOBSON'S ROOM AND PREPARE HIM FOR HIS FAMILY'S ARRIVAL. THEY ARE EXPECTED SHORTLY.
S-SURE... UH, MORNING, MISS CLAIBORNE... I'LL SEE TO IT NOW.
HMM...
7

ABIGAIL, COULD YOU ALSO SEE TO AMY'S ATTIRE. YOU REALLY MUST BE MORE CAREFUL, AMY.

♪ As I walk this levee 'round, I'm lookin' for that bully, an' he must be found... ♪

HE HAD TO FIND HER

(FIND HER)

BUT IT WAS SO HARD TO CONCENTRATE, SO HARD TO

(SEE, HARD TO SEE, MY EYE FEELS)

KEEP TRACK OF WHAT HE HAD TO DO

(LOOSE, IT HURTS)

THEY HAD DARED TO COME INTO HIS OWN HOME WITH TALK OF TAKING ABIGAIL AWAY FROM HIM... SHE HAD RUN AWAY CRYING... HE COULD HEAR HER STILL...

(M-MY THROAT, TASTING BLOOD)

EVER SINCE ABIGAIL'S MOTHER HAD DIED, HE HAD DONE HIS BEST TO GIVE HER A PROPER HOME. BUT HIS WORK TOOK HIM AWAY OFTEN, AND HIS BROTHER, HIS MEDDLING BROTHER--

--HIS BROTHER AN--

(DON'T DARE SPEAK IT! I HAVE NO BROTHER!!)

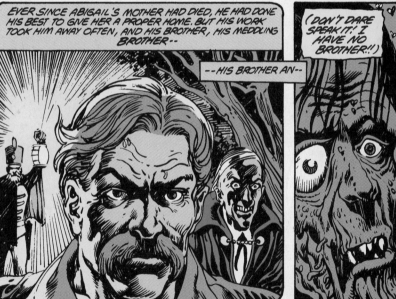

-- HAD MADE AN ISSUE OF IT TOO OFTEN... THE AUTHORITIES HAD COME, AND THERE HAD BEEN HARSH WORDS--

(BLOOD IN MY THROAT)

--AND ABIGAIL RAN CRYING... HE MUST FIND HER...

:SOB:

OH, ABIGAIL...

SHE MUST BE

(FOUND HER!)

FOUND...

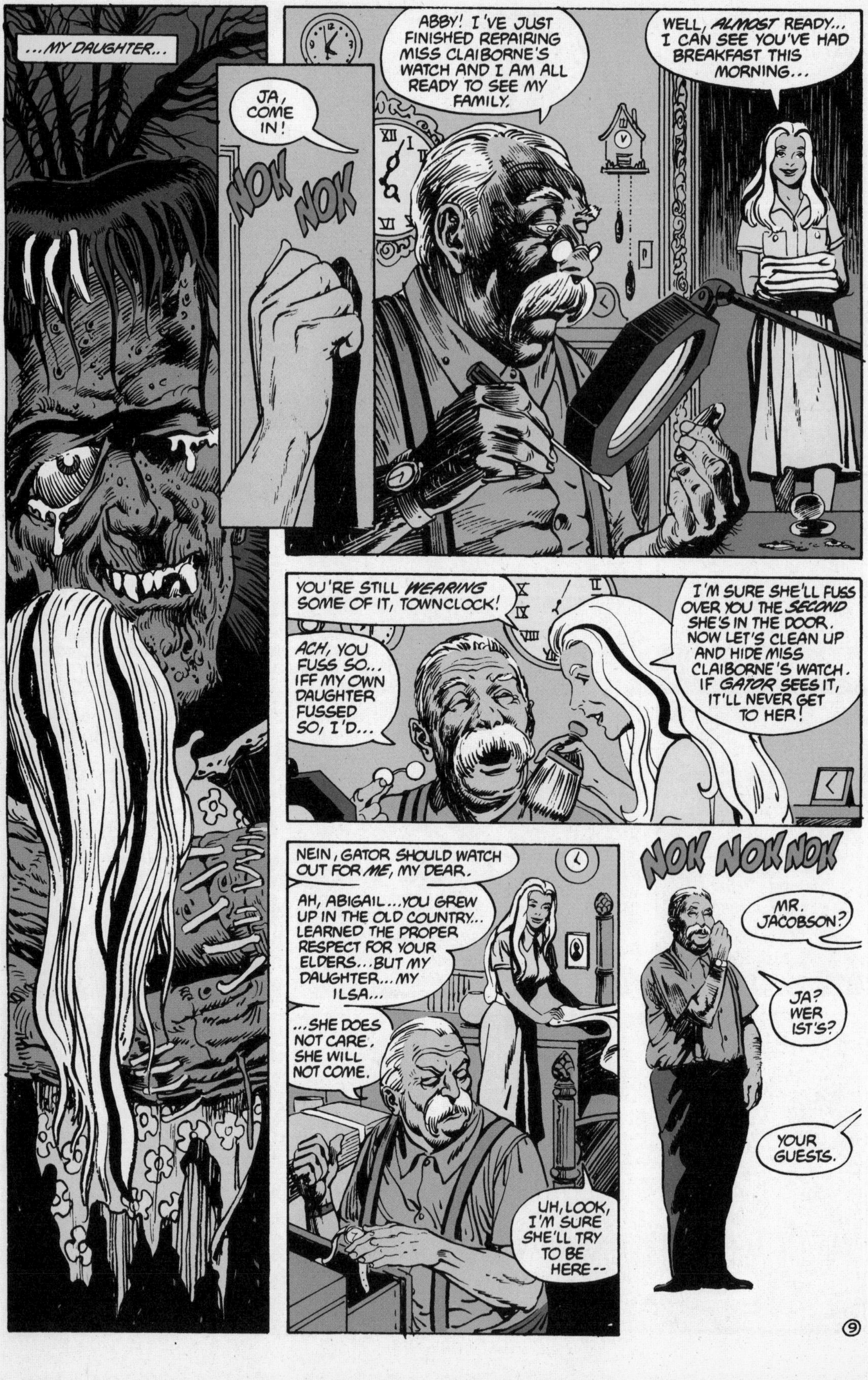
...MY DAUGHTER...
NOK NOK
JA, COME IN!
ABBY! I'VE JUST FINISHED REPAIRING MISS CLAIBORNE'S WATCH AND I AM ALL READY TO SEE MY FAMILY.
WELL, ALMOST READY... I CAN SEE YOU'VE HAD BREAKFAST THIS MORNING...
YOU'RE STILL WEARING SOME OF IT, TOWNCLOCK!
ACH, YOU FUSS SO... IFF MY OWN DAUGHTER FUSSED SO, I'D...
I'M SURE SHE'LL FUSS OVER YOU THE SECOND SHE'S IN THE DOOR. NOW LET'S CLEAN UP AND HIDE MISS CLAIBORNE'S WATCH. IF GATOR SEES IT, IT'LL NEVER GET TO HER!
NEIN, GATOR SHOULD WATCH OUT FOR ME, MY DEAR.
AH, ABIGAIL...YOU GREW UP IN THE OLD COUNTRY... LEARNED THE PROPER RESPECT FOR YOUR ELDERS...BUT MY DAUGHTER... MY ILSA...
...SHE DOES NOT CARE. SHE WILL NOT COME.
UH, LOOK, I'M SURE SHE'LL TRY TO BE HERE--
NOK NOK NOK
MR. JACOBSON?
JA? WER IST'S?
YOUR GUESTS.
9

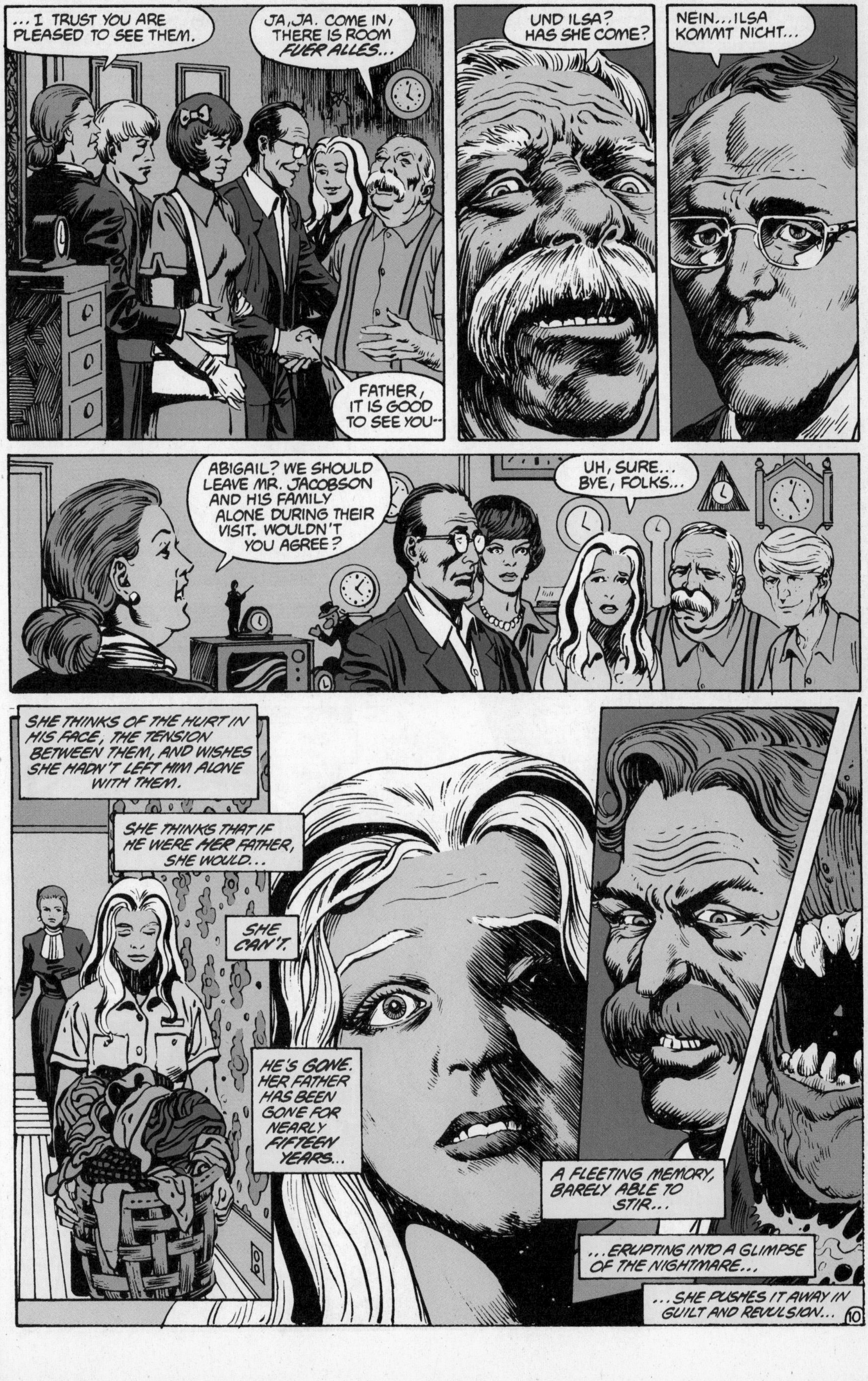
...I TRUST YOU ARE PLEASED TO SEE THEM.
JA, JA. COME IN, THERE IS ROOM FUER ALLES...
FATHER, IT IS GOOD TO SEE YOU--
UND ILSA? HAS SHE COME?
NEIN...ILSA KOMMT NICHT...
ABIGAIL? WE SHOULD LEAVE MR. JACOBSON AND HIS FAMILY ALONE DURING THEIR VISIT. WOULDN'T YOU AGREE?
UH, SURE... BYE, FOLKS...
SHE THINKS OF THE HURT IN HIS FACE, THE TENSION BETWEEN THEM, AND WISHES SHE HADN'T LEFT HIM ALONE WITH THEM.
SHE THINKS THAT IF HE WERE HER FATHER, SHE WOULD...
SHE CAN'T.
HE'S GONE. HER FATHER HAS BEEN GONE FOR NEARLY FIFTEEN YEARS...
A FLEETING MEMORY, BARELY ABLE TO STIR...
...ERUPTING INTO A GLIMPSE OF THE NIGHTMARE...
...SHE PUSHES IT AWAY IN GUILT AND REVULSION...
10

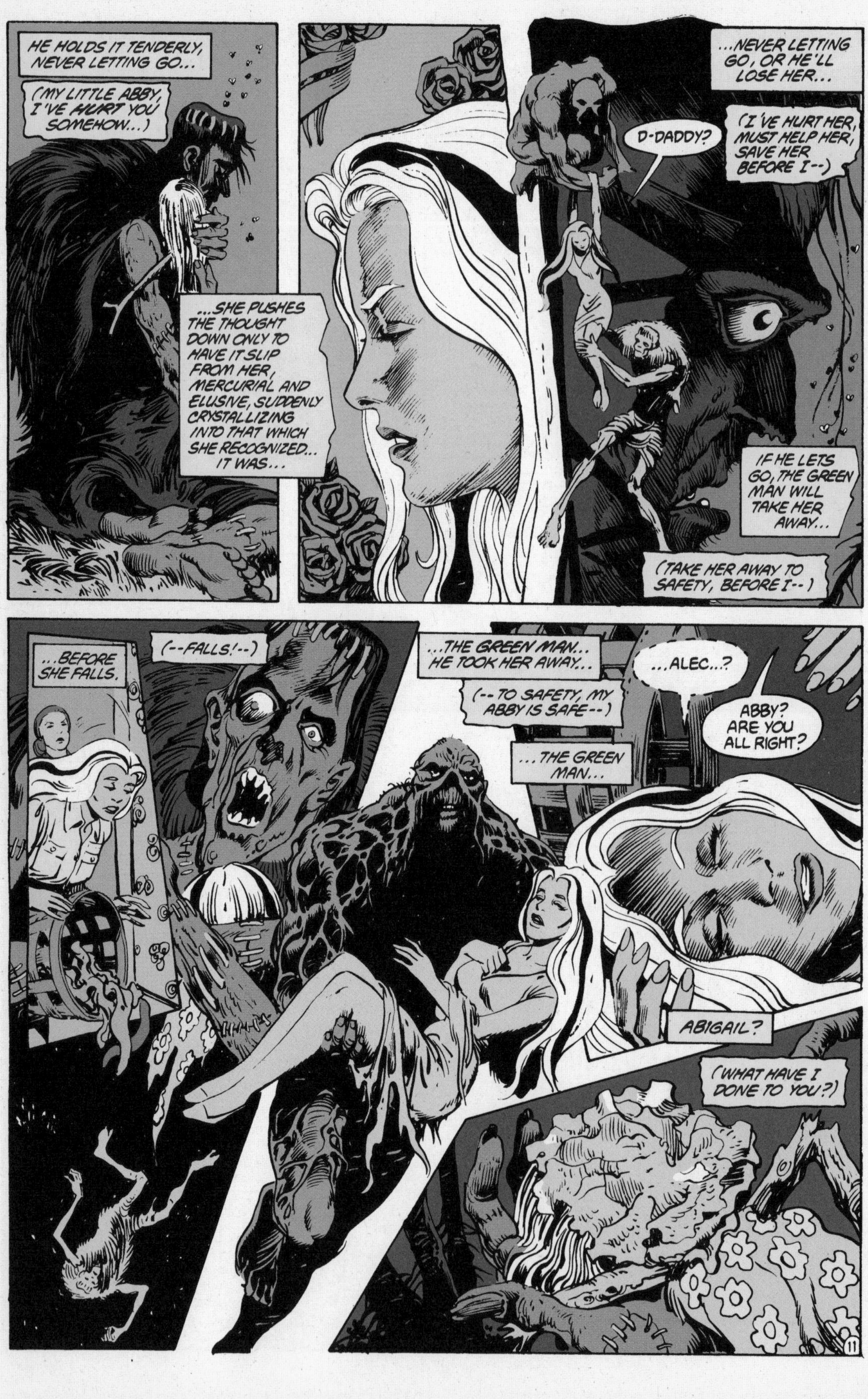
HE HOLDS IT TENDERLY, NEVER LETTING GO...
(MY LITTLE ABBY, I'VE HURT YOU SOMEHOW...)
...SHE PUSHES THE THOUGHT DOWN ONLY TO HAVE IT SLIP FROM HER, MERCURIAL AND ELUSIVE, SUDDENLY CRYSTALLIZING INTO THAT WHICH SHE RECOGNIZED... IT WAS...
...NEVER LETTING GO, OR HE'LL LOSE HER...
D-DADDY?
(I'VE HURT HER, MUST HELP HER, SAVE HER BEFORE I--)
IF HE LETS GO, THE GREEN MAN WILL TAKE HER AWAY...
(TAKE HER AWAY TO SAFETY, BEFORE I--)
...BEFORE SHE FALLS.
(--FALLS!--)
...THE GREEN MAN... HE TOOK HER AWAY...
(--TO SAFETY, MY ABBY IS SAFE--)
...THE GREEN MAN...
...ALEC...?
ABBY? ARE YOU ALL RIGHT?
ABIGAIL?
(WHAT HAVE I DONE TO YOU?)
11

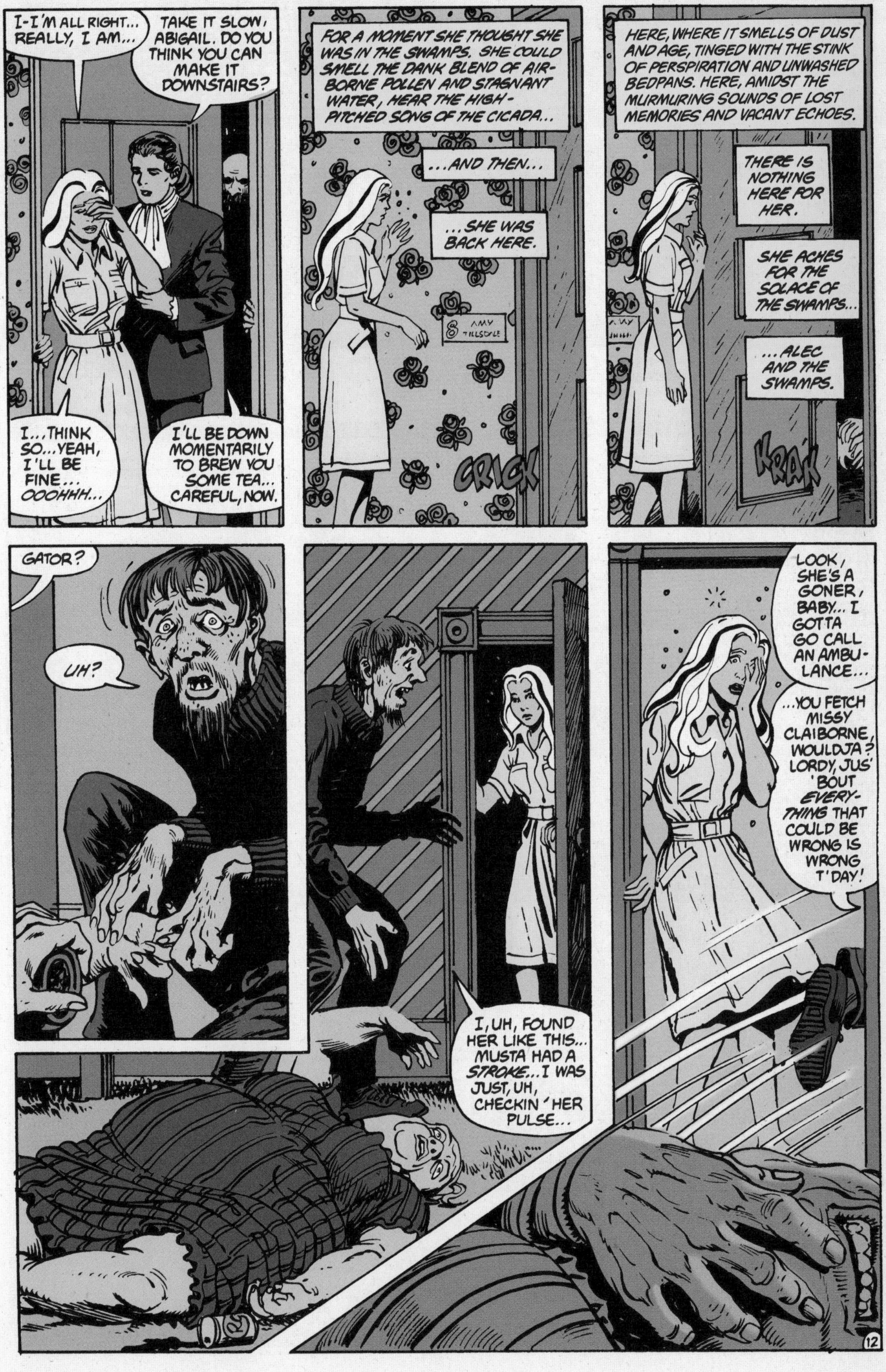
I-I'M ALL RIGHT... REALLY, I AM...
TAKE IT SLOW, ABIGAIL. DO YOU THINK YOU CAN MAKE IT DOWNSTAIRS?
I...THINK SO...YEAH, I'LL BE FINE... OOOHHH...
I'LL BE DOWN MOMENTARILY TO BREW YOU SOME TEA... CAREFUL, NOW.
FOR A MOMENT SHE THOUGHT SHE WAS IN THE SWAMPS. SHE COULD SMELL THE DANK BLEND OF AIRBORNE POLLEN AND STAGNANT WATER, HEAR THE HIGH-PITCHED SONG OF THE CICADA...
...AND THEN...
...SHE WAS BACK HERE.
AMY TILLSDALE
CRICK
HERE, WHERE IT SMELLS OF DUST AND AGE, TINGED WITH THE STINK OF PERSPIRATION AND UNWASHED BEDPANS. HERE, AMIDST THE MURMURING SOUNDS OF LOST MEMORIES AND VACANT ECHOES.
THERE IS NOTHING HERE FOR HER.
SHE ACHES FOR THE SOLACE OF THE SWAMPS...
...ALEC AND THE SWAMPS.
KRAK
GATOR?
UH?
I, UH, FOUND HER LIKE THIS... MUSTA HAD A STROKE... I WAS JUST, UH, CHECKIN' HER PULSE...
LOOK, SHE'S A GONER, BABY... I GOTTA GO CALL AN AMBULANCE...
...YOU FETCH MISSY CLAIBORNE, WOULDJA? LORDY, JUS' 'BOUT EVERYTHING THAT COULD BE WRONG IS WRONG T'DAY!
12

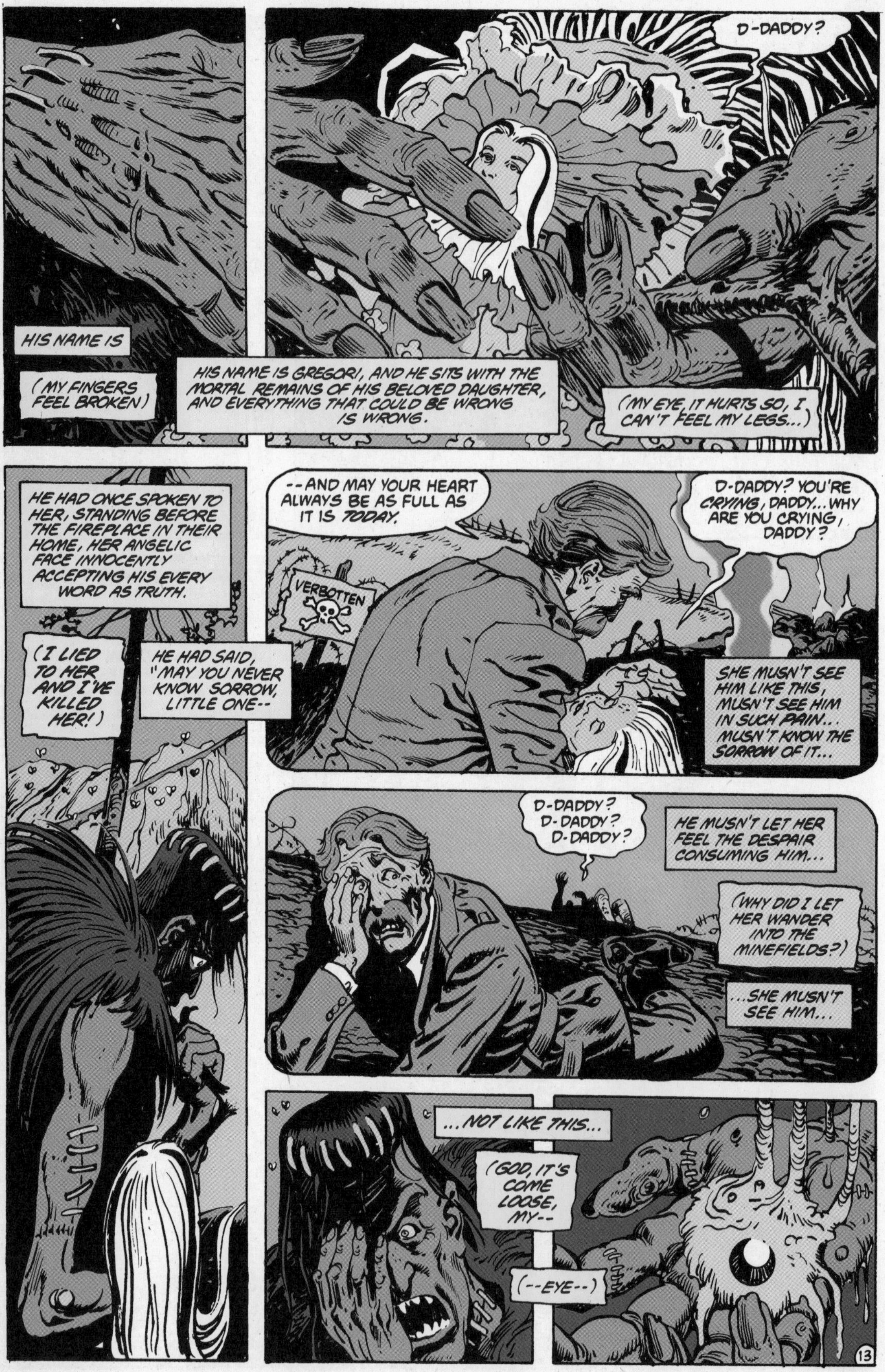
HIS NAME IS
(MY FINGERS FEEL BROKEN)
D-DADDY?
HIS NAME IS GREGORI, AND HE SITS WITH THE MORTAL REMAINS OF HIS BELOVED DAUGHTER, AND EVERYTHING THAT COULD BE WRONG IS WRONG.
(MY EYE, IT HURTS SO, I CAN'T FEEL MY LEGS...)
HE HAD ONCE SPOKEN TO HER, STANDING BEFORE THE FIREPLACE IN THEIR HOME, HER ANGELIC FACE INNOCENTLY ACCEPTING HIS EVERY WORD AS TRUTH.
(I LIED TO HER AND I'VE KILLED HER!)
HE HAD SAID, "MAY YOU NEVER KNOW SORROW, LITTLE ONE--
--AND MAY YOUR HEART ALWAYS BE AS FULL AS IT IS TODAY.
VERBOTTEN
D-DADDY? YOU'RE CRYING, DADDY... WHY ARE YOU CRYING, DADDY?
SHE MUSN'T SEE HIM LIKE THIS, MUSN'T SEE HIM IN SUCH PAIN... MUSN'T KNOW THE SORROW OF IT...
D-DADDY? D-DADDY? D-DADDY?
HE MUSN'T LET HER FEEL THE DESPAIR CONSUMING HIM...
(WHY DID I LET HER WANDER INTO THE MINEFIELDS?)
...SHE MUSN'T SEE HIM...
...NOT LIKE THIS...
(GOD, IT'S COME LOOSE, MY--
(--EYE--)
13

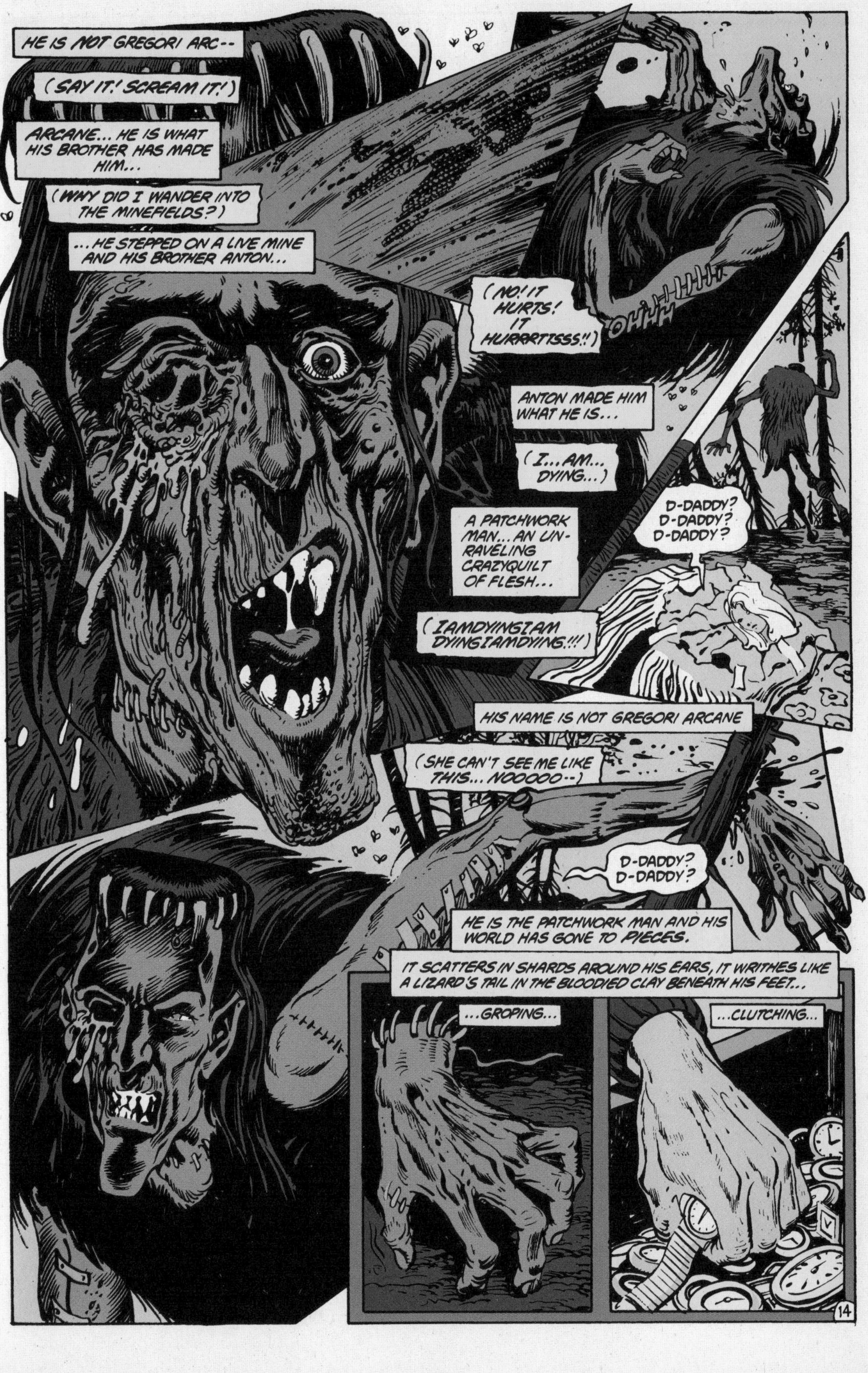
HE IS NOT GREGORI ARC--
(SAY IT! SCREAM IT!)
ARCANE... HE IS WHAT HIS BROTHER HAS MADE HIM...
(WHY DID I WANDER INTO THE MINEFIELDS?)
...HE STEPPED ON A LIVE MINE AND HIS BROTHER ANTON...
(NO! IT HURTS! IT HURRRTSSS!!)
OHHH
ANTON MADE HIM WHAT HE IS...
(I...AM... DYING...)
A PATCHWORK MAN... AN UN-RAVELING CRAZYQUILT OF FLESH...
D-DADDY? D-DADDY? D-DADDY?
(IAMDYINGIAM DYINGIAMDYING!!!)
HIS NAME IS NOT GREGORI ARCANE
(SHE CAN'T SEE ME LIKE THIS... NOOOOO--)
D-DADDY? D-DADDY?
HE IS THE PATCHWORK MAN AND HIS WORLD HAS GONE TO PIECES.
IT SCATTERS IN SHARDS AROUND HIS EARS, IT WRITHES LIKE A LIZARD'S TAIL IN THE BLOODIED CLAY BENEATH HIS FEET...
...GROPING...
...CLUTCHING...
14

...REACHING OUT...

AMY'S DEAD, I'M AFRAID. A HEART ATTACK... SORRY TO SAY, IT'S AN ALL TOO COMMON EVENT HERE.

OH, GOD... HOW DO YOU STAND IT? I DON'T KNOW IF I--

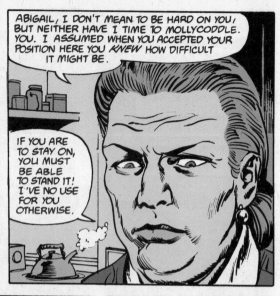

ABIGAIL, I DON'T MEAN TO BE HARD ON YOU, BUT NEITHER HAVE I TIME TO MOLLYCODDLE YOU. I ASSUMED WHEN YOU ACCEPTED YOUR POSITION HERE YOU *KNEW* HOW DIFFICULT IT MIGHT BE.

IF YOU ARE TO STAY ON, YOU MUST BE ABLE TO STAND IT! I'VE NO USE FOR YOU OTHERWISE.

YOU DON'T SEEM TO LIKE THE PATIENTS, AS IF IT WERE THEIR FAULT THEY ARE OLD AND NEED ATTENTION. IT'S EASY TO GET ALONG WITH THE LIKES OF TOWNCLOCK, BUT THAT ISN'T ENOUGH...

THEY *ALL* NEED CARE AND ACCEPTANCE.

I-IT'S HARD, WITH ALL THAT'S HAPPENED... LIZ LIVING WITH ME, SHE'S PRACTICALLY AN INVALID HERS--

I KNOW WHAT YOU'VE BEEN THROUGH, THOUGH IT'S REALLY NO BUSINESS OF MINE. YOU'VE WORKED WITH AUTISTIC CHILDREN, AND WHEN DEANNA FRENCH GAVE SUCH GOOD REFERENCES, I'D HOPED--

IT'S *DIFFERENT* HERE!

IT'S NOT LIKE WORKING WITH CHILDREN AT *ALL!* THESE PEOPLE--

"*THESE PEOPLE*"-- PEOPLE LIKE YOUR PARENTS, PERHAPS? YOUR FATHER? WOULD YOU BE ABLE TO ACCEPT AND CARE FOR *HIM*, ABIGAIL?

TAKE THE REST OF THE DAY OFF, ABIGAIL, AND THINK ABOUT WHAT YOU WANT TO DO.

I...

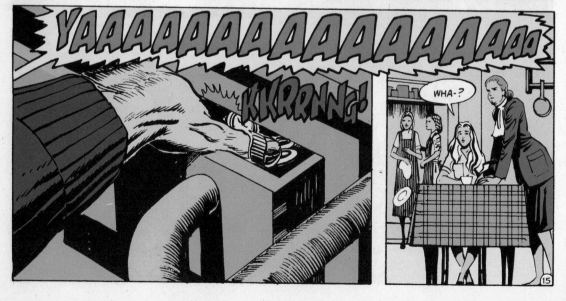

YAAAAAAAAAAAAAAAAAAAAAa

KKRRNNG!

WHA-?

⑮

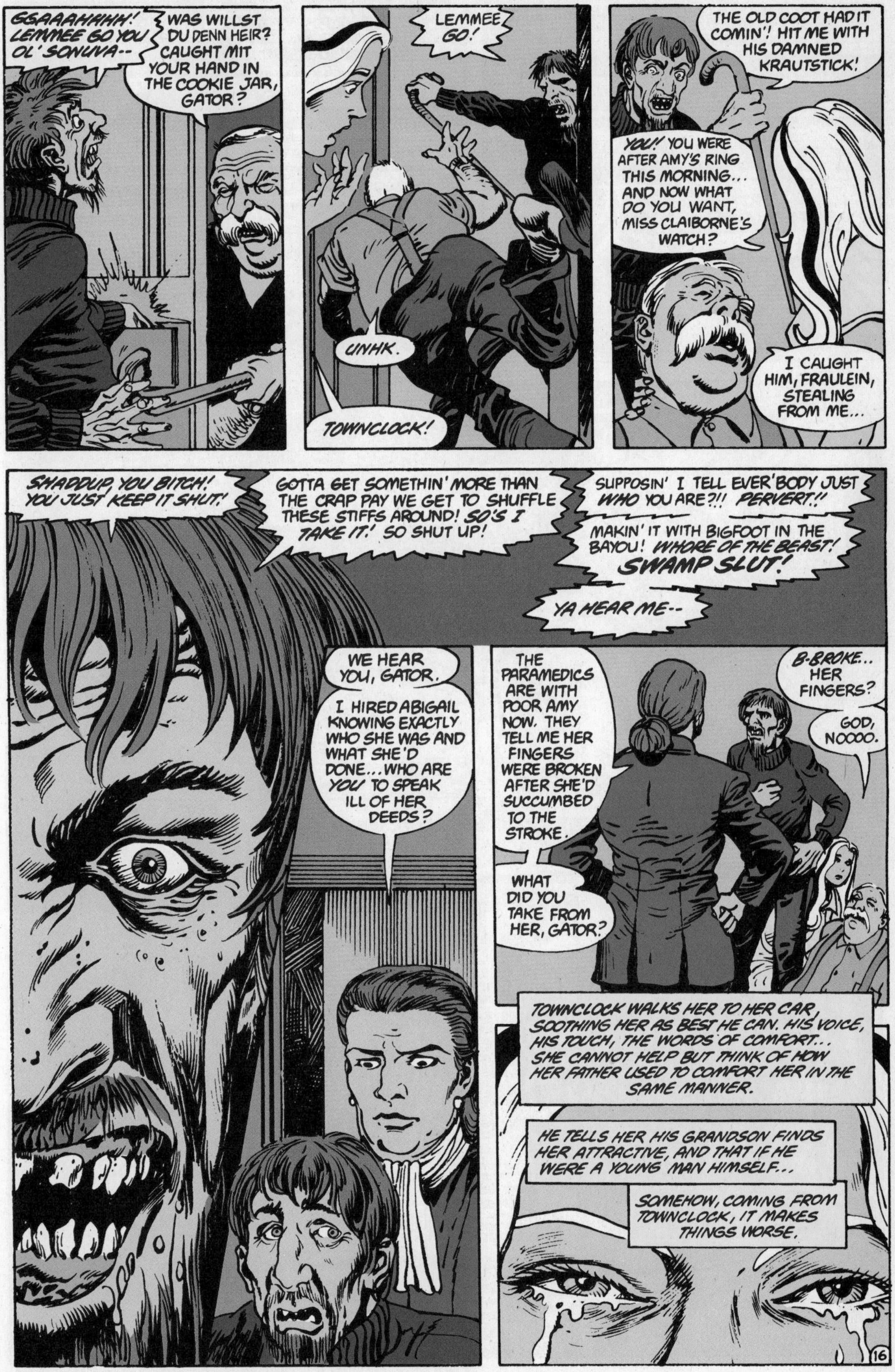
GGAAAHHHH! LEMMEE GO YOU OL' SONUVA--
WAS WILLST DU DENN HEIR? CAUGHT MIT YOUR HAND IN THE COOKIE JAR, GATOR?
LEMMEE GO!
UNHK.
TOWNCLOCK!
THE OLD COOT HAD IT COMIN'! HIT ME WITH HIS DAMNED KRAUTSTICK!
YOU! YOU WERE AFTER AMY'S RING THIS MORNING... AND NOW WHAT DO YOU WANT, MISS CLAIBORNE'S WATCH?
I CAUGHT HIM, FRAULEIN, STEALING FROM ME...
SHADDUP, YOU BITCH! YOU JUST KEEP IT SHUT!
GOTTA GET SOMETHIN' MORE THAN THE CRAP PAY WE GET TO SHUFFLE THESE STIFFS AROUND! SO'S I TAKE IT! SO SHUT UP!
SUPPOSIN' I TELL EVER'BODY JUST WHO YOU ARE?!! PERVERT!!
MAKIN' IT WITH BIGFOOT IN THE BAYOU! WHORE OF THE BEAST! SWAMP SLUT!
YA HEAR ME--
WE HEAR YOU, GATOR.
I HIRED ABIGAIL KNOWING EXACTLY WHO SHE WAS AND WHAT SHE'D DONE... WHO ARE YOU TO SPEAK ILL OF HER DEEDS?
THE PARAMEDICS ARE WITH POOR AMY NOW. THEY TELL ME HER FINGERS WERE BROKEN AFTER SHE'D SUCCUMBED TO THE STROKE.
B-BROKE... HER FINGERS?
GOD, NOOOO.
WHAT DID YOU TAKE FROM HER, GATOR?
TOWNCLOCK WALKS HER TO HER CAR, SOOTHING HER AS BEST HE CAN. HIS VOICE, HIS TOUCH, THE WORDS OF COMFORT... SHE CANNOT HELP BUT THINK OF HOW HER FATHER USED TO COMFORT HER IN THE SAME MANNER.
HE TELLS HER HIS GRANDSON FINDS HER ATTRACTIVE, AND THAT IF HE WERE A YOUNG MAN HIMSELF...
SOMEHOW, COMING FROM TOWNCLOCK, IT MAKES THINGS WORSE.
16

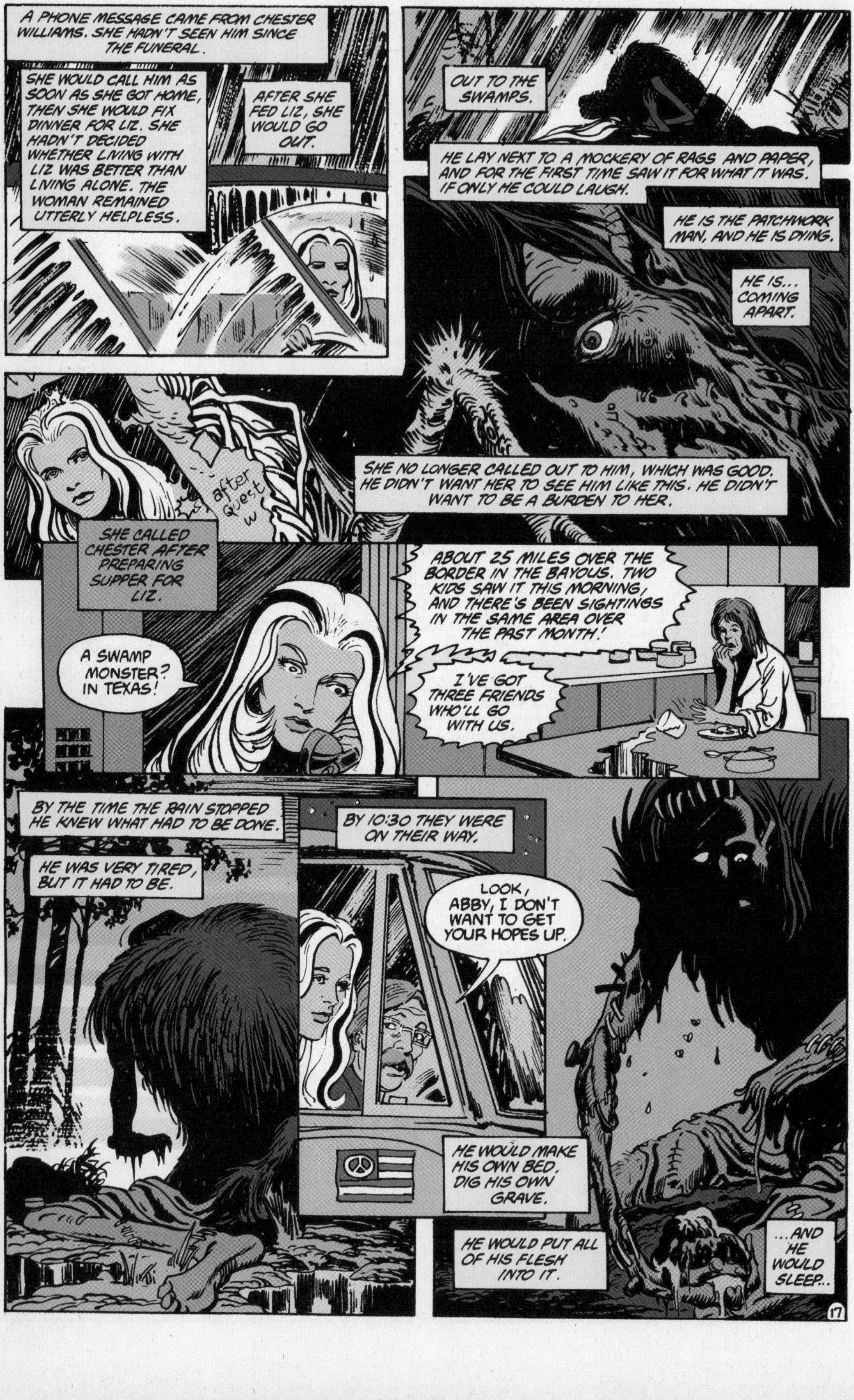
A PHONE MESSAGE CAME FROM CHESTER WILLIAMS. SHE HADN'T SEEN HIM SINCE THE FUNERAL.
SHE WOULD CALL HIM AS SOON AS SHE GOT HOME, THEN SHE WOULD FIX DINNER FOR LIZ. SHE HADN'T DECIDED WHETHER LIVING WITH LIZ WAS BETTER THAN LIVING ALONE. THE WOMAN REMAINED UTTERLY HELPLESS.
AFTER SHE FED LIZ, SHE WOULD GO OUT.
OUT TO THE SWAMPS.
HE LAY NEXT TO A MOCKERY OF RAGS AND PAPER, AND FOR THE FIRST TIME SAW IT FOR WHAT IT WAS. IF ONLY HE COULD LAUGH.
HE IS THE PATCHWORK MAN, AND HE IS DYING.
HE IS... COMING APART.
SHE NO LONGER CALLED OUT TO HIM, WHICH WAS GOOD. HE DIDN'T WANT HER TO SEE HIM LIKE THIS. HE DIDN'T WANT TO BE A BURDEN TO HER.
after Quest w
SHE CALLED CHESTER AFTER PREPARING SUPPER FOR LIZ.
A SWAMP MONSTER? IN TEXAS!
ABOUT 25 MILES OVER THE BORDER IN THE BAYOUS. TWO KIDS SAW IT THIS MORNING, AND THERE'S BEEN SIGHTINGS IN THE SAME AREA OVER THE PAST MONTH!
I'VE GOT THREE FRIENDS WHO'LL GO WITH US.
BY THE TIME THE RAIN STOPPED HE KNEW WHAT HAD TO BE DONE.
HE WAS VERY TIRED, BUT IT HAD TO BE.
BY 10:30 THEY WERE ON THEIR WAY.
LOOK, ABBY, I DON'T WANT TO GET YOUR HOPES UP.
HE WOULD MAKE HIS OWN BED, DIG HIS OWN GRAVE.
HE WOULD PUT ALL OF HIS FLESH INTO IT.
...AND HE WOULD SLEEP...
17

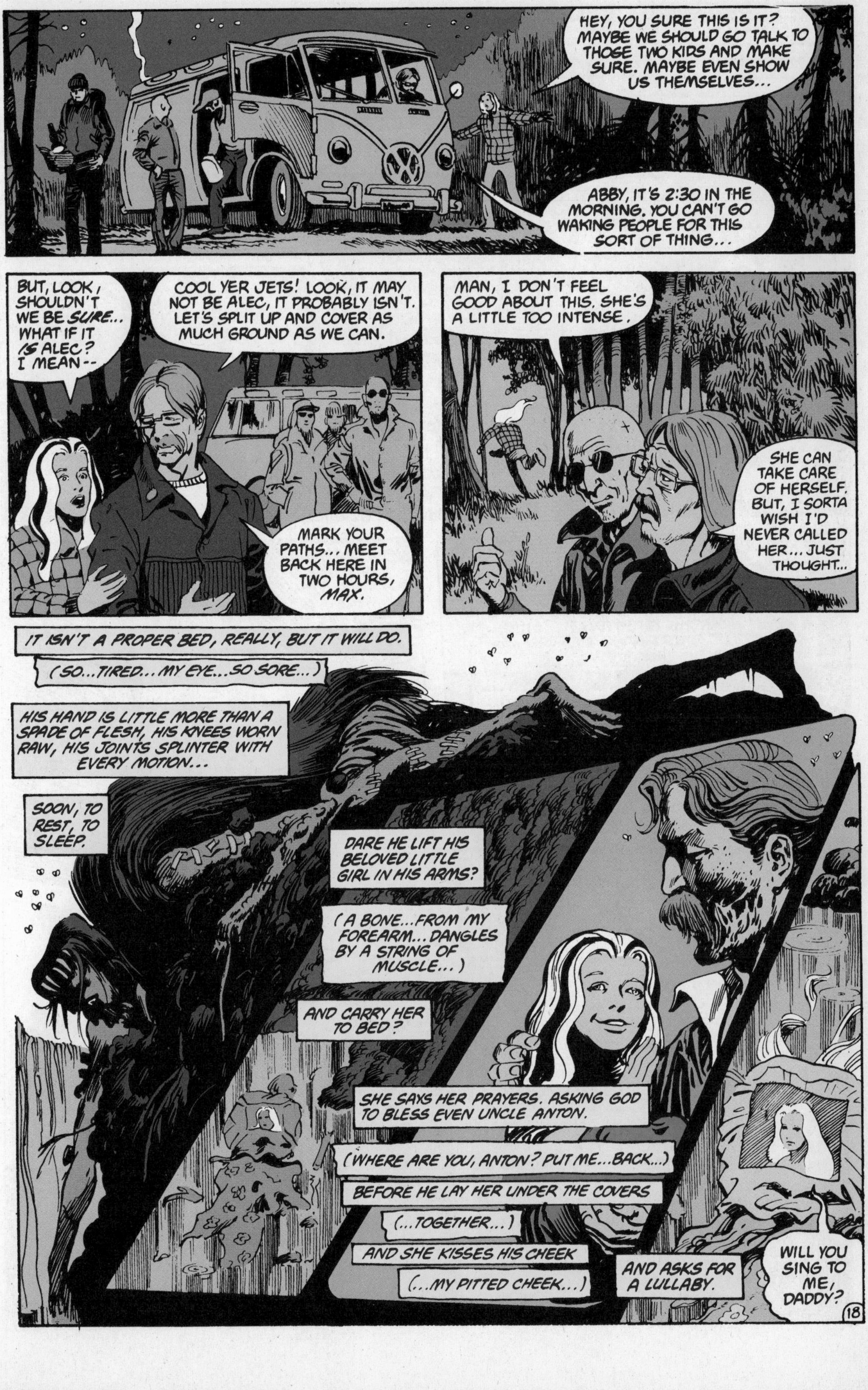
HEY, YOU SURE THIS IS IT? MAYBE WE SHOULD GO TALK TO THOSE TWO KIDS AND MAKE SURE. MAYBE EVEN SHOW US THEMSELVES...
ABBY, IT'S 2:30 IN THE MORNING. YOU CAN'T GO WAKING PEOPLE FOR THIS SORT OF THING...
BUT, LOOK, SHOULDN'T WE BE SURE... WHAT IF IT IS ALEC? I MEAN--
COOL YER JETS! LOOK, IT MAY NOT BE ALEC, IT PROBABLY ISN'T. LET'S SPLIT UP AND COVER AS MUCH GROUND AS WE CAN.
MARK YOUR PATHS... MEET BACK HERE IN TWO HOURS, MAX.
MAN, I DON'T FEEL GOOD ABOUT THIS. SHE'S A LITTLE TOO INTENSE.
SHE CAN TAKE CARE OF HERSELF. BUT, I SORTA WISH I'D NEVER CALLED HER... JUST THOUGHT...
IT ISN'T A PROPER BED, REALLY, BUT IT WILL DO.
(SO...TIRED...MY EYE...SO SORE...)
HIS HAND IS LITTLE MORE THAN A SPADE OF FLESH, HIS KNEES WORN RAW, HIS JOINTS SPLINTER WITH EVERY MOTION...
SOON, TO REST, TO SLEEP.
DARE HE LIFT HIS BELOVED LITTLE GIRL IN HIS ARMS?
(A BONE...FROM MY FOREARM... DANGLES BY A STRING OF MUSCLE...)
AND CARRY HER TO BED?
SHE SAYS HER PRAYERS. ASKING GOD TO BLESS EVEN UNCLE ANTON.
(WHERE ARE YOU, ANTON? PUT ME...BACK...)
BEFORE HE LAY HER UNDER THE COVERS
(...TOGETHER...)
AND SHE KISSES HIS CHEEK
(...MY PITTED CHEEK...)
AND ASKS FOR A LULLABY.
WILL YOU SING TO ME, DADDY?
18

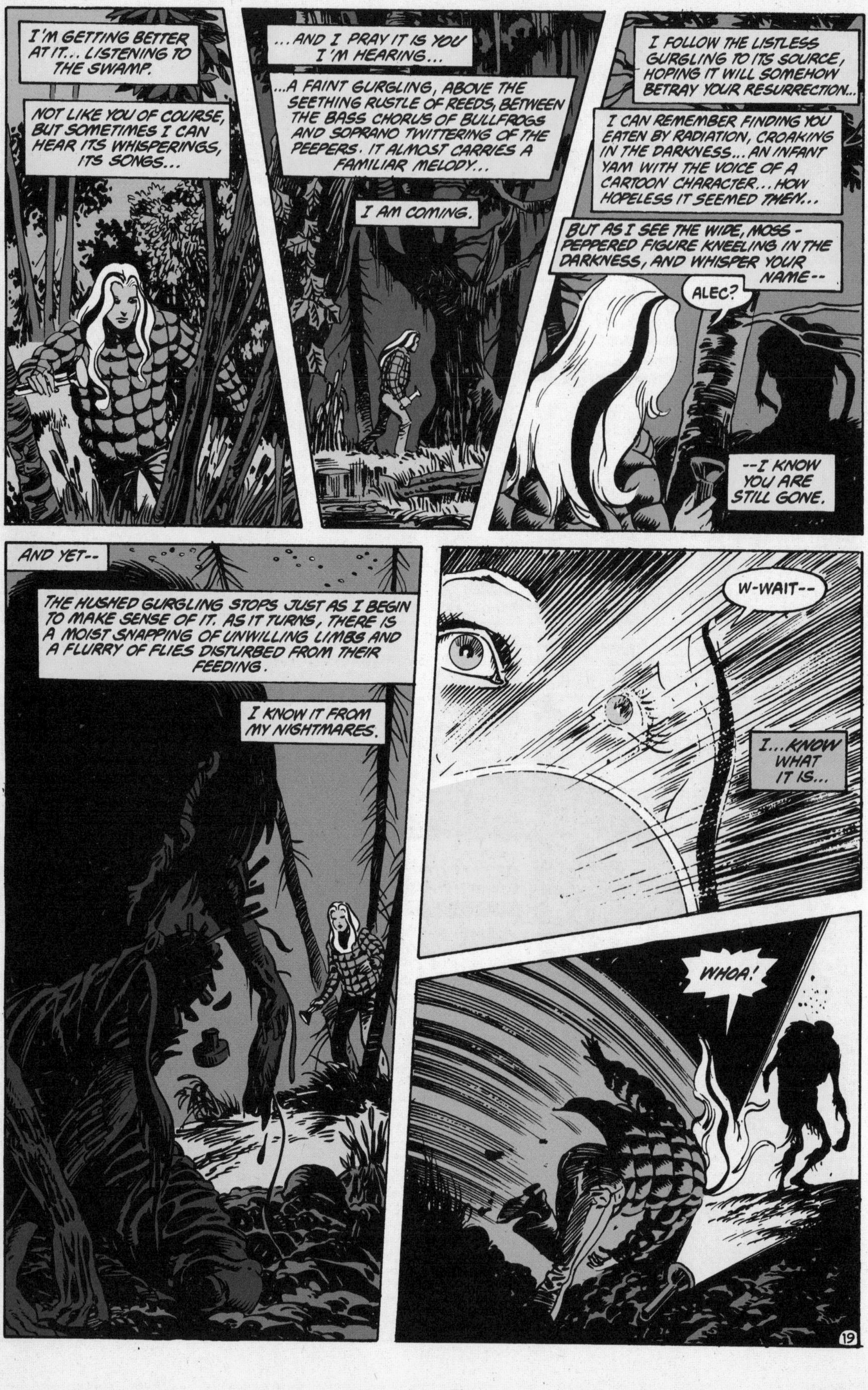
I'M GETTING BETTER AT IT... LISTENING TO THE SWAMP.
NOT LIKE YOU OF COURSE, BUT SOMETIMES I CAN HEAR ITS WHISPERINGS, ITS SONGS...
...AND I PRAY IT IS YOU I'M HEARING...
...A FAINT GURGLING, ABOVE THE SEETHING RUSTLE OF REEDS, BETWEEN THE BASS CHORUS OF BULLFROGS AND SOPRANO TWITTERING OF THE PEEPERS. IT ALMOST CARRIES A FAMILIAR MELODY...
I AM COMING.
I FOLLOW THE LISTLESS GURGLING TO ITS SOURCE, HOPING IT WILL SOMEHOW BETRAY YOUR RESURRECTION...
I CAN REMEMBER FINDING YOU EATEN BY RADIATION, CROAKING IN THE DARKNESS... AN INFANT YAM WITH THE VOICE OF A CARTOON CHARACTER... HOW HOPELESS IT SEEMED THEN...
BUT AS I SEE THE WIDE, MOSS-PEPPERED FIGURE KNEELING IN THE DARKNESS, AND WHISPER YOUR NAME--
ALEC?
--I KNOW YOU ARE STILL GONE.
AND YET--
THE HUSHED GURGLING STOPS JUST AS I BEGIN TO MAKE SENSE OF IT. AS IT TURNS, THERE IS A MOIST SNAPPING OF UNWILLING LIMBS AND A FLURRY OF FLIES DISTURBED FROM THEIR FEEDING.
I KNOW IT FROM MY NIGHTMARES.
W-WAIT--
I...KNOW WHAT IT IS...
WHOA!
19

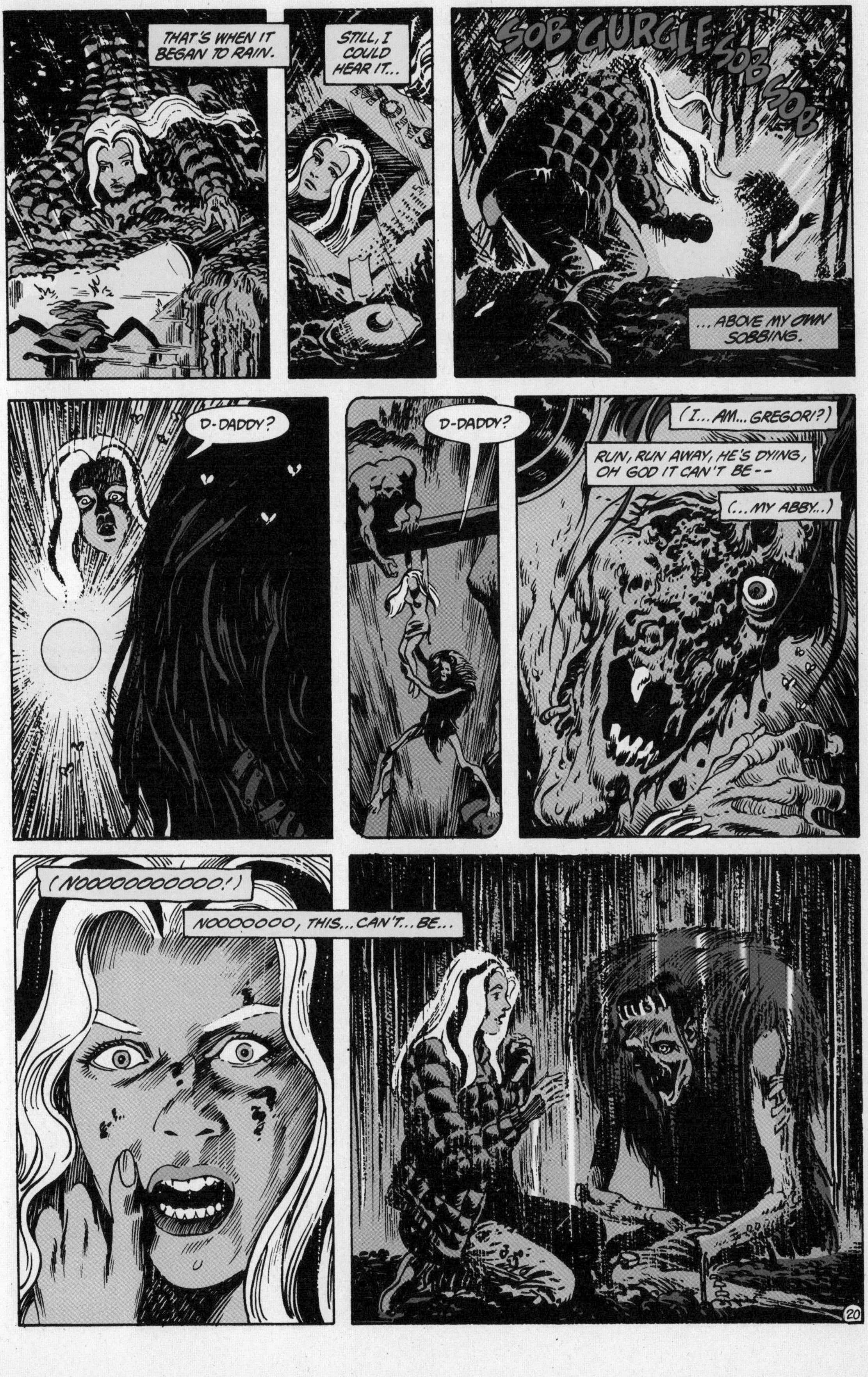
THAT'S WHEN IT BEGAN TO RAIN.
STILL, I COULD HEAR IT...
SOB GURGLE SOB SOB SOB
...ABOVE MY OWN SOBBING.
D-DADDY?
D-DADDY?
(I... AM... GREGORI?)
RUN, RUN AWAY, HE'S DYING, OH GOD IT CAN'T BE--
(...MY ABBY...)
(NOOOOOOOOOOO!)
NOOOOOOO, THIS... CAN'T... BE...
20

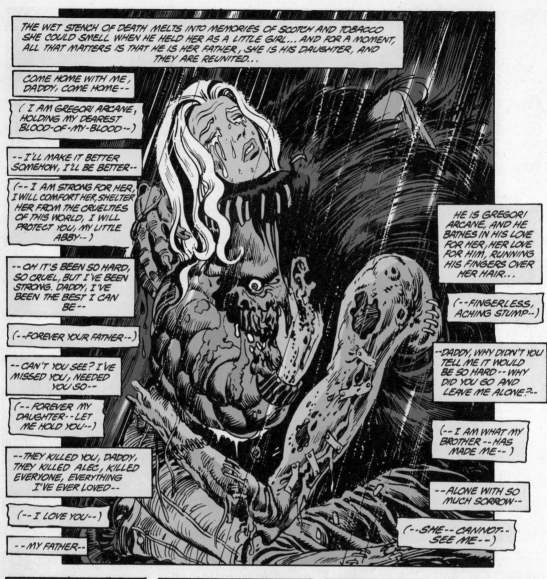

THE WET STENCH OF DEATH MELTS INTO MEMORIES OF SCOTCH AND TOBACCO SHE COULD SMELL WHEN HE HELD HER AS A LITTLE GIRL... AND FOR A MOMENT, ALL THAT MATTERS IS THAT HE IS HER FATHER, SHE IS HIS DAUGHTER, AND THEY ARE REUNITED...

COME HOME WITH ME, DADDY, COME HOME--

(I AM GREGORI ARCANE, HOLDING MY DEAREST BLOOD-OF-MY-BLOOD--)

--I'LL MAKE IT BETTER SOMEHOW, I'LL BE BETTER--

(-- I AM STRONG FOR HER, I WILL COMFORT HER, SHELTER HER FROM THE CRUELTIES OF THIS WORLD, I WILL PROTECT YOU, MY LITTLE ABBY--)

--OH IT'S BEEN SO HARD, SO CRUEL, BUT I'VE BEEN STRONG. DADDY, I'VE BEEN THE BEST I CAN BE--

(--FOREVER YOUR FATHER--)

--CAN'T YOU SEE? I'VE MISSED YOU, NEEDED YOU SO--

(-- FOREVER MY DAUGHTER -- LET ME HOLD YOU--)

--THEY KILLED YOU, DADDY, THEY KILLED ALEC, KILLED EVERYONE, EVERYTHING I'VE EVER LOVED--

(-- I LOVE YOU--)

--MY FATHER--

HE IS GREGORI ARCANE, AND HE BATHES IN HIS LOVE FOR HER, HER LOVE FOR HIM, RUNNING HIS FINGERS OVER HER HAIR...

(--FINGERLESS, ACHING STUMP--)

--DADDY, WHY DIDN'T YOU TELL ME IT WOULD BE SO HARD -- WHY DID YOU GO AND LEAVE ME ALONE?--

(-- I AM WHAT MY BROTHER -- HAS MADE ME--)

--ALONE WITH SO MUCH SORROW--

(--SHE--CANNOT-- SEE ME--)

(--LIKE THIS--)

RRRRIIIIP

SHE KNEELS IN THE TORRENTIAL RAINS, REELING, BEFORE CRYING OUT AND FOLLOWING HIM...

SHE SEES HIS LEG GIVE WAY, AND A FLEETING GLIMPSE OF A SPINDLY FIGURE; ITS HEAD IMPOSSIBLY AKIMBO, BEFORE LOSING HIM IN THE DOWNPOUR...

THEN IT BEGAN TO HAIL...

21

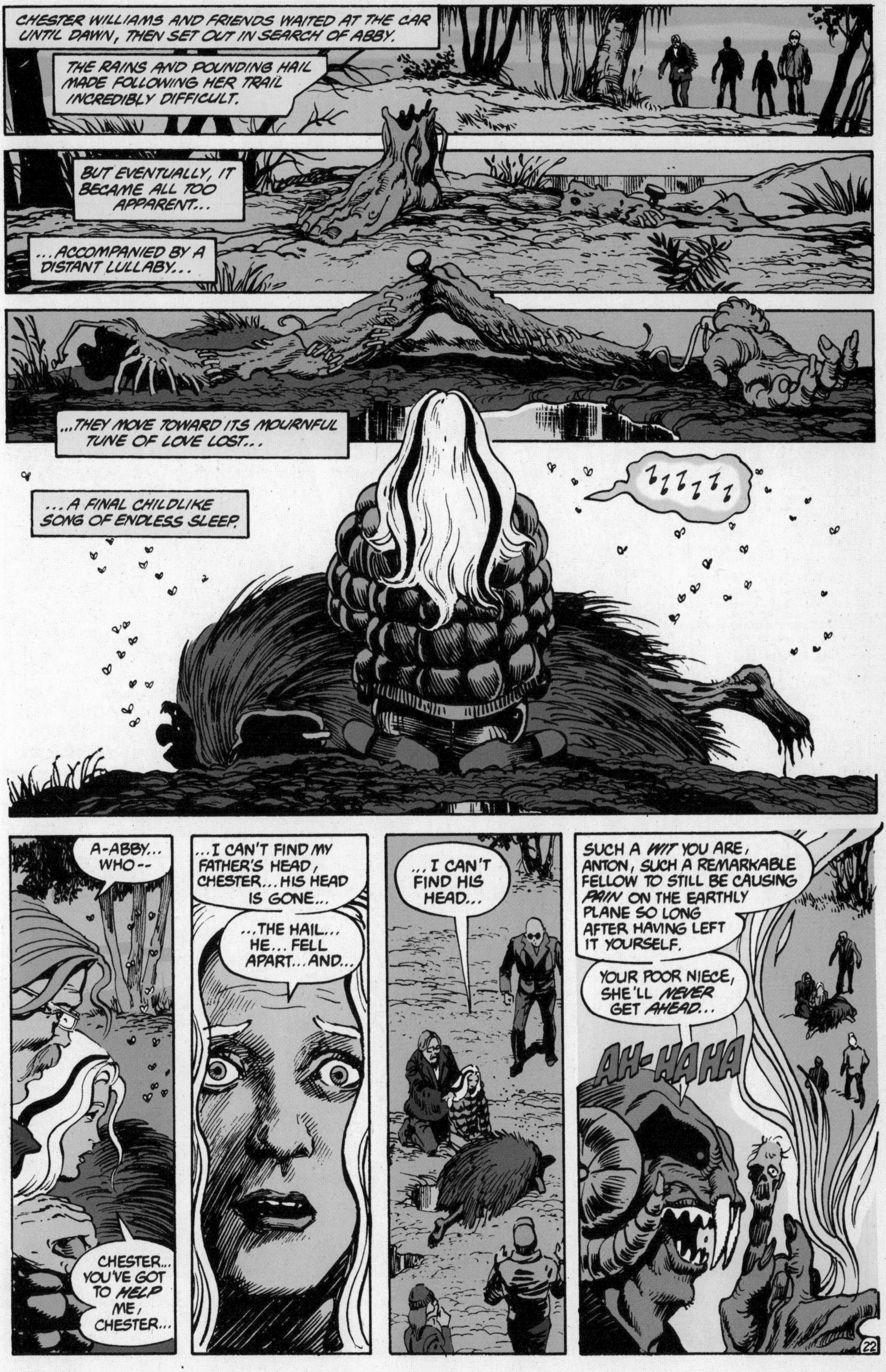
CHESTER WILLIAMS AND FRIENDS WAITED AT THE CAR UNTIL DAWN, THEN SET OUT IN SEARCH OF ABBY.
THE RAINS AND POUNDING HAIL MADE FOLLOWING HER TRAIL INCREDIBLY DIFFICULT.
BUT EVENTUALLY, IT BECAME ALL TOO APPARENT...
...ACCOMPANIED BY A DISTANT LULLABY...
...THEY MOVE TOWARD ITS MOURNFUL TUNE OF LOVE LOST...
...A FINAL CHILDLIKE SONG OF ENDLESS SLEEP.
A-ABBY... WHO--
CHESTER... YOU'VE GOT TO HELP ME, CHESTER...
...I CAN'T FIND MY FATHER'S HEAD, CHESTER... HIS HEAD IS GONE...
...THE HAIL... HE... FELL APART... AND...
...I CAN'T FIND HIS HEAD...
SUCH A WIT YOU ARE, ANTON, SUCH A REMARKABLE FELLOW TO STILL BE CAUSING PAIN ON THE EARTHLY PLANE SO LONG AFTER HAVING LEFT IT YOURSELF.
YOUR POOR NIECE, SHE'LL NEVER GET AHEAD...
AH-HAHA
22

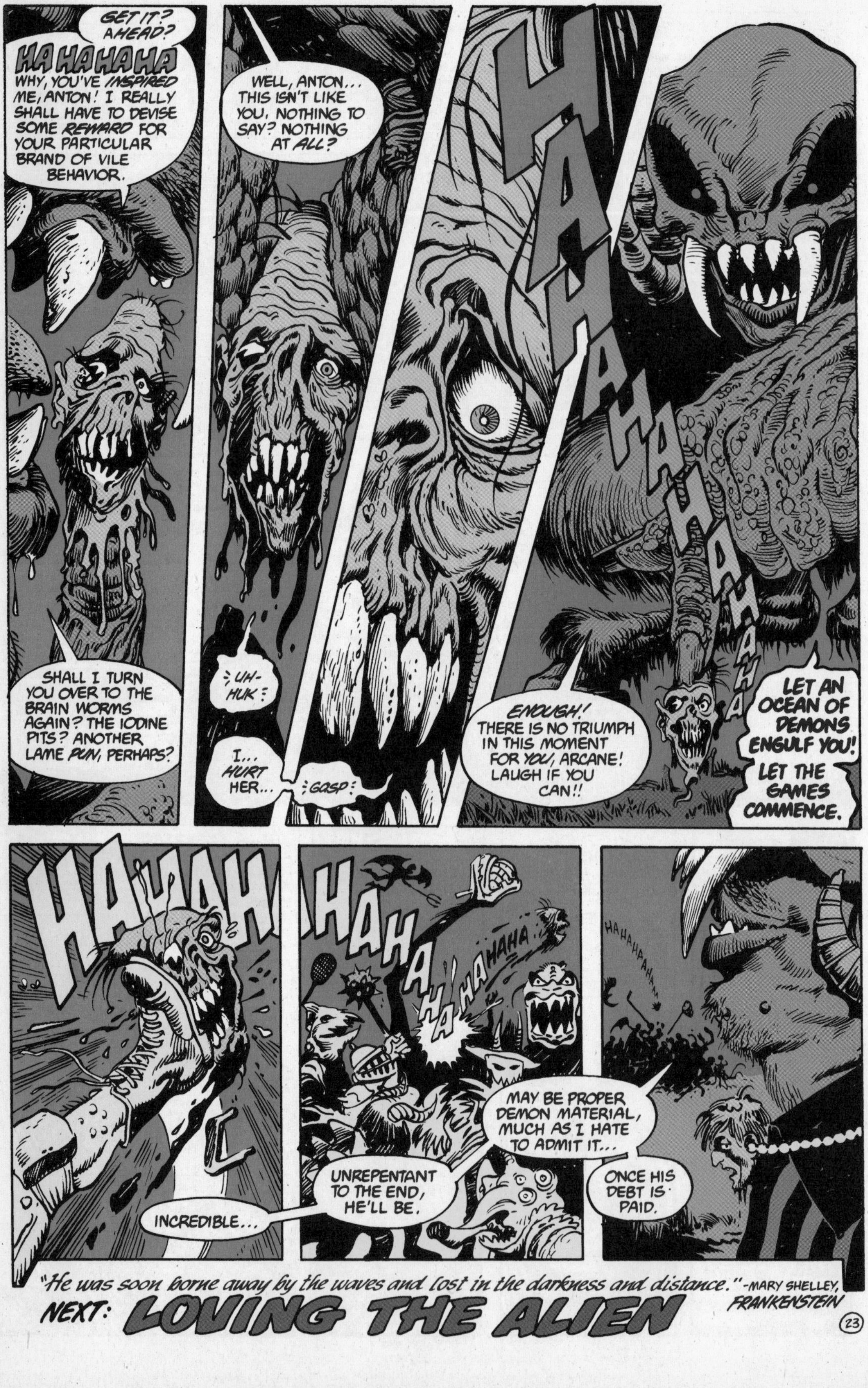
GET IT? AHEAD?
HA HA HA HA HA
WHY, YOU'VE INSPIRED ME, ANTON! I REALLY SHALL HAVE TO DEVISE SOME REWARD FOR YOUR PARTICULAR BRAND OF VILE BEHAVIOR.
SHALL I TURN YOU OVER TO THE BRAIN WORMS AGAIN? THE IODINE PITS? ANOTHER LAME PUN, PERHAPS?
WELL, ANTON... THIS ISN'T LIKE YOU. NOTHING TO SAY? NOTHING AT ALL?
UH-HUK
I... HURT HER...
GASP
HAHAHAHAHAHAHAHAHA
ENOUGH! THERE IS NO TRIUMPH IN THIS MOMENT FOR YOU, ARCANE! LAUGH IF YOU CAN!!
LET AN OCEAN OF DEMONS ENGULF YOU! LET THE GAMES COMMENCE.
HAHAHAHAHAHAHAHA
HAHAHAHA
INCREDIBLE...
UNREPENTANT TO THE END, HE'LL BE.
MAY BE PROPER DEMON MATERIAL, MUCH AS I HATE TO ADMIT IT...
HAHAHAHAHAHA
ONCE HIS DEBT IS PAID.
"He was soon borne away by the waves and lost in the darkness and distance." -MARY SHELLEY, FRANKENSTEIN
NEXT: LOVING THE ALIEN
23

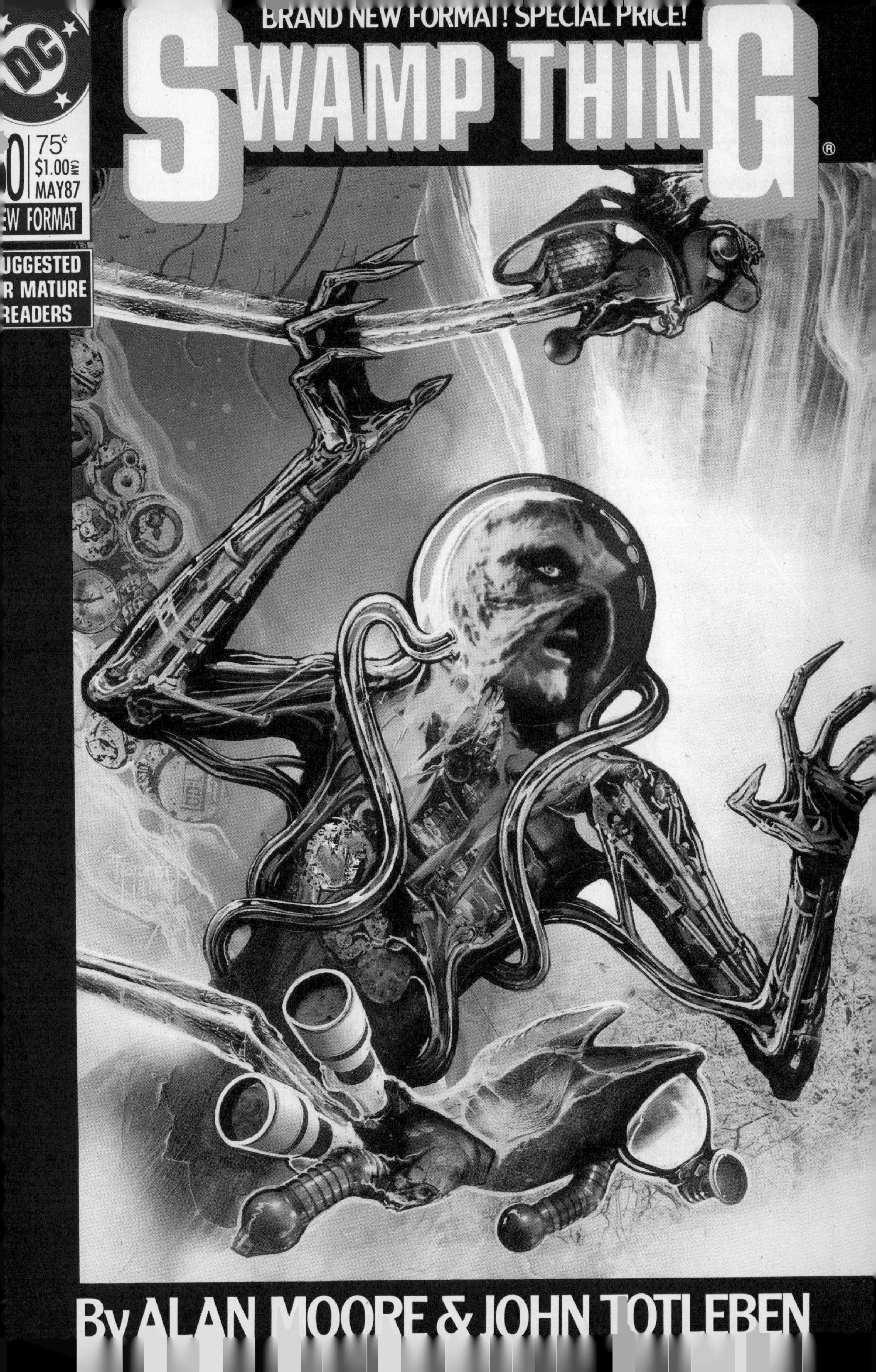
BRAND NEW FORMAT! SPECIAL PRICE!
SWAMP THING
0
75¢
$1.00 CAN
MAY87
EW FORMAT
UGGESTED
R MATURE
READERS
By ALAN MOORE & JOHN TOTLEBEN

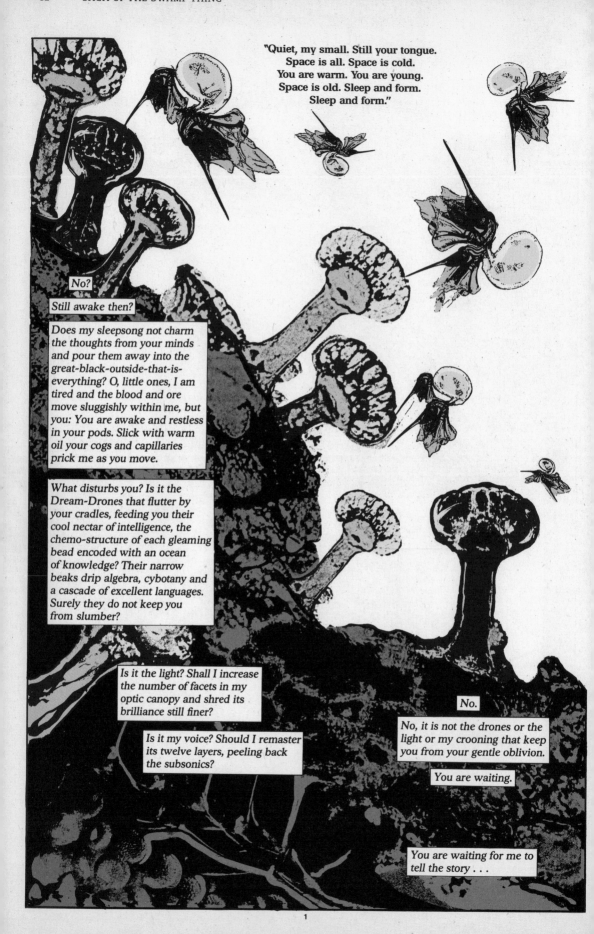

"Quiet, my small. Still your tongue.
Space is all. Space is cold.
You are warm. You are young.
Space is old. Sleep and form.
Sleep and form."

No?

Still awake then?

*Does my sleepsong not charm
the thoughts from your minds
and pour them away into the
great-black-outside-that-is-
everything? O, little ones, I am
tired and the blood and ore
move sluggishly within me, but
you: You are awake and restless
in your pods. Slick with warm
oil your cogs and capillaries
prick me as you move.*

*What disturbs you? Is it the
Dream-Drones that flutter by
your cradles, feeding you their
cool nectar of intelligence, the
chemo-structure of each gleaming
bead encoded with an ocean
of knowledge? Their narrow
beaks drip algebra, cybotany and
a cascade of excellent languages.
Surely they do not keep you
from slumber?*

*Is it the light? Shall I increase
the number of facets in my
optic canopy and shred its
brilliance still finer?*

No.

*No, it is not the drones or the
light or my crooning that keep
you from your gentle oblivion.*

*Is it my voice? Should I remaster
its twelve layers, peeling back
the subsonics?*

You are waiting.

*You are waiting for me to
tell the story . . .*

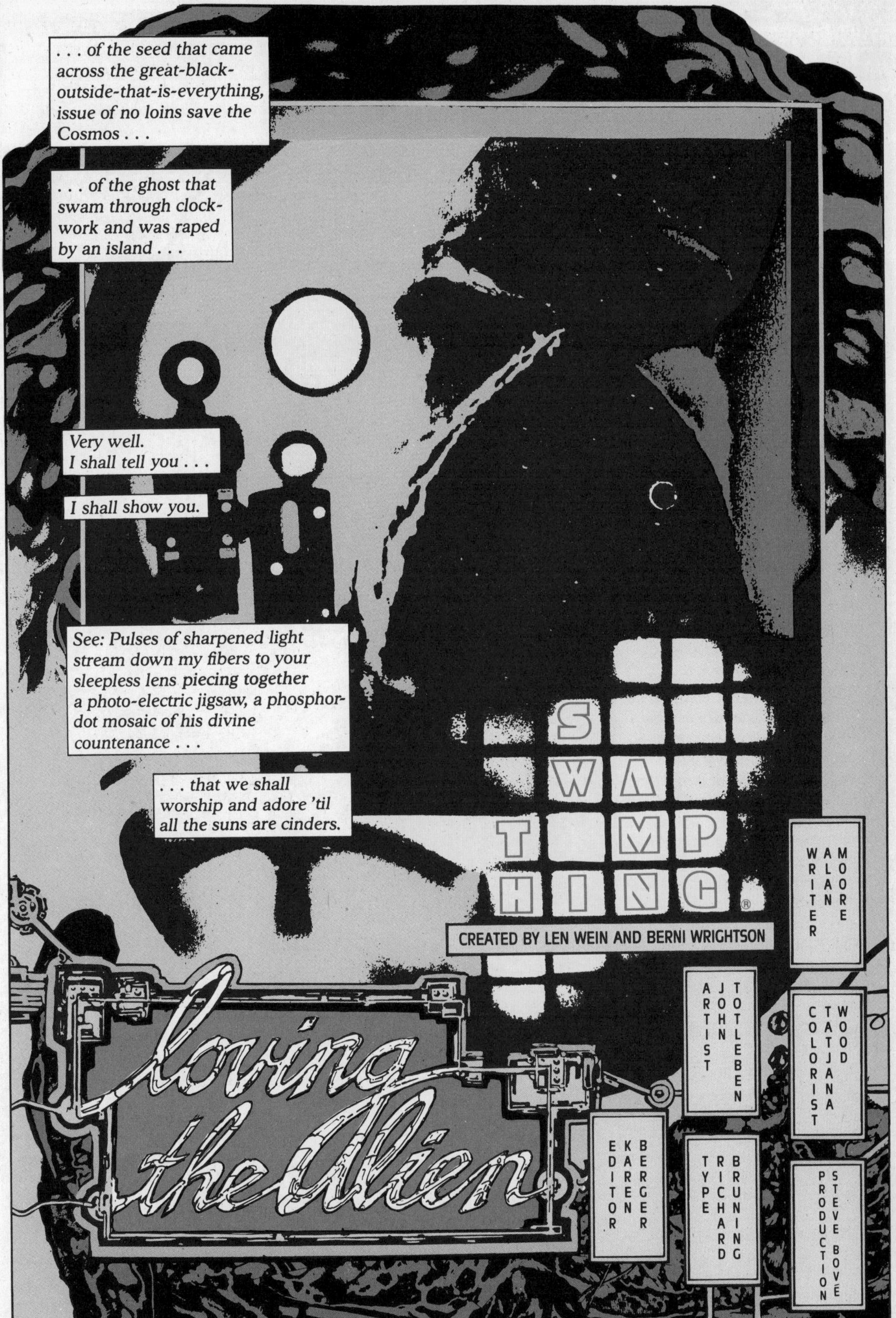
. . . of the seed that came across the great-black-outside-that-is-everything, issue of no loins save the Cosmos . . .
. . . of the ghost that swam through clock-work and was raped by an island . . .
Very well. I shall tell you . . .
I shall show you.
See: Pulses of sharpened light stream down my fibers to your sleepless lens piecing together a photo-electric jigsaw, a phosphor-dot mosaic of his divine countenance . . .
. . . that we shall worship and adore 'til all the suns are cinders.
SWAMP THING®
CREATED BY LEN WEIN AND BERNI WRIGHTSON
loving the Alien
WRITER ALAN MOORE
ARTIST JOHN TOTLEBEN
COLORIST TATJANA WOOD
EDITOR KAREN BERGER
TYPE RICHARD BRUNING
PRODUCTION STEVE BOVÉ

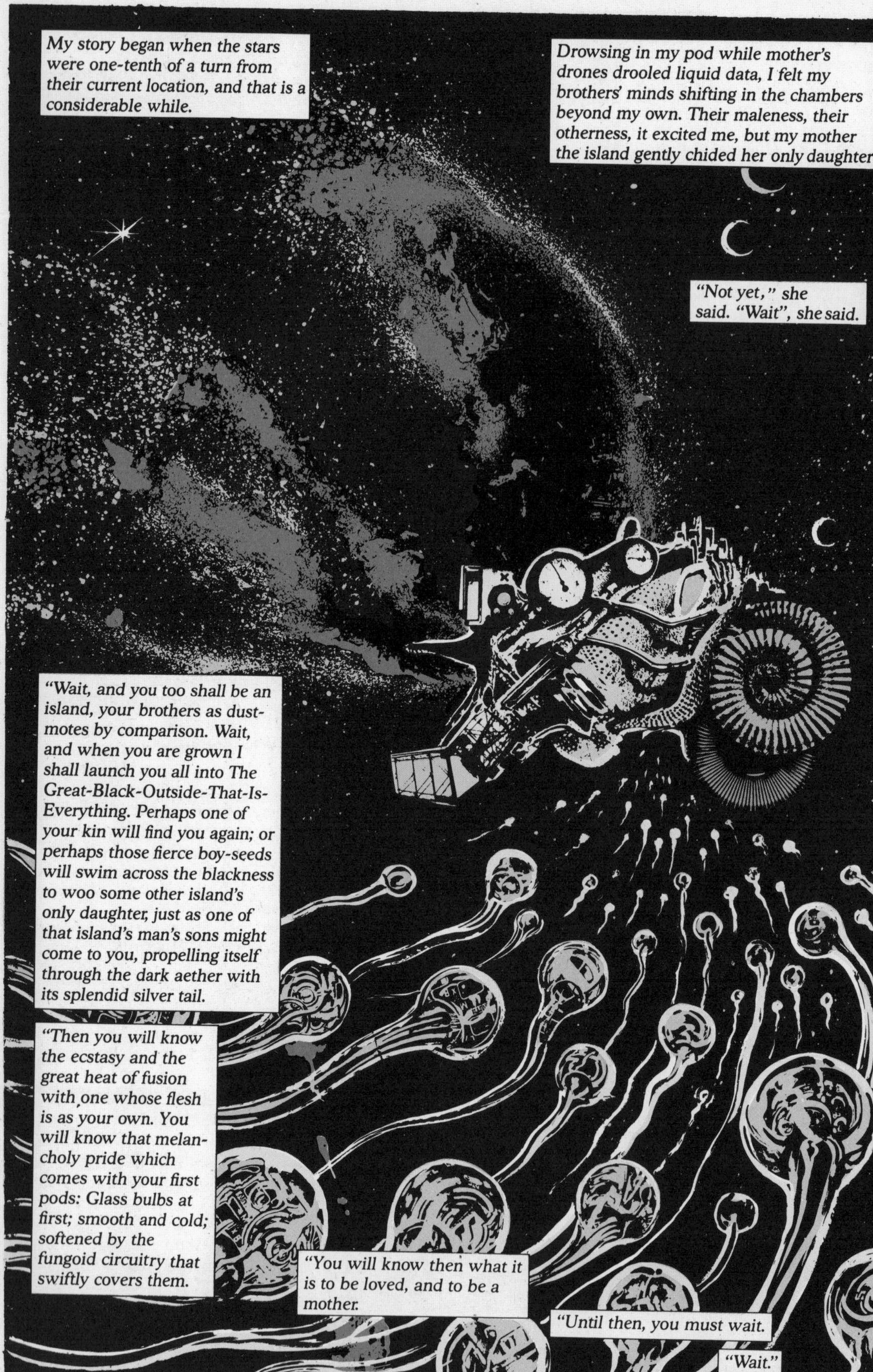
My story began when the stars were one-tenth of a turn from their current location, and that is a considerable while.
Drowsing in my pod while mother's drones drooled liquid data, I felt my brothers' minds shifting in the chambers beyond my own. Their maleness, their otherness, it excited me, but my mother the island gently chided her only daughter:
"Not yet," she said. "Wait", she said.
"Wait, and you too shall be an island, your brothers as dust-motes by comparison. Wait, and when you are grown I shall launch you all into The Great-Black-Outside-That-Is-Everything. Perhaps one of your kin will find you again; or perhaps those fierce boy-seeds will swim across the blackness to woo some other island's only daughter, just as one of that island's man's sons might come to you, propelling itself through the dark aether with its splendid silver tail.
"Then you will know the ecstasy and the great heat of fusion with one whose flesh is as your own. You will know that melancholy pride which comes with your first pods: Glass bulbs at first; smooth and cold; softened by the fungoid circuitry that swiftly covers them.
"You will know then what it is to be loved, and to be a mother.
"Until then, you must wait.
"Wait."

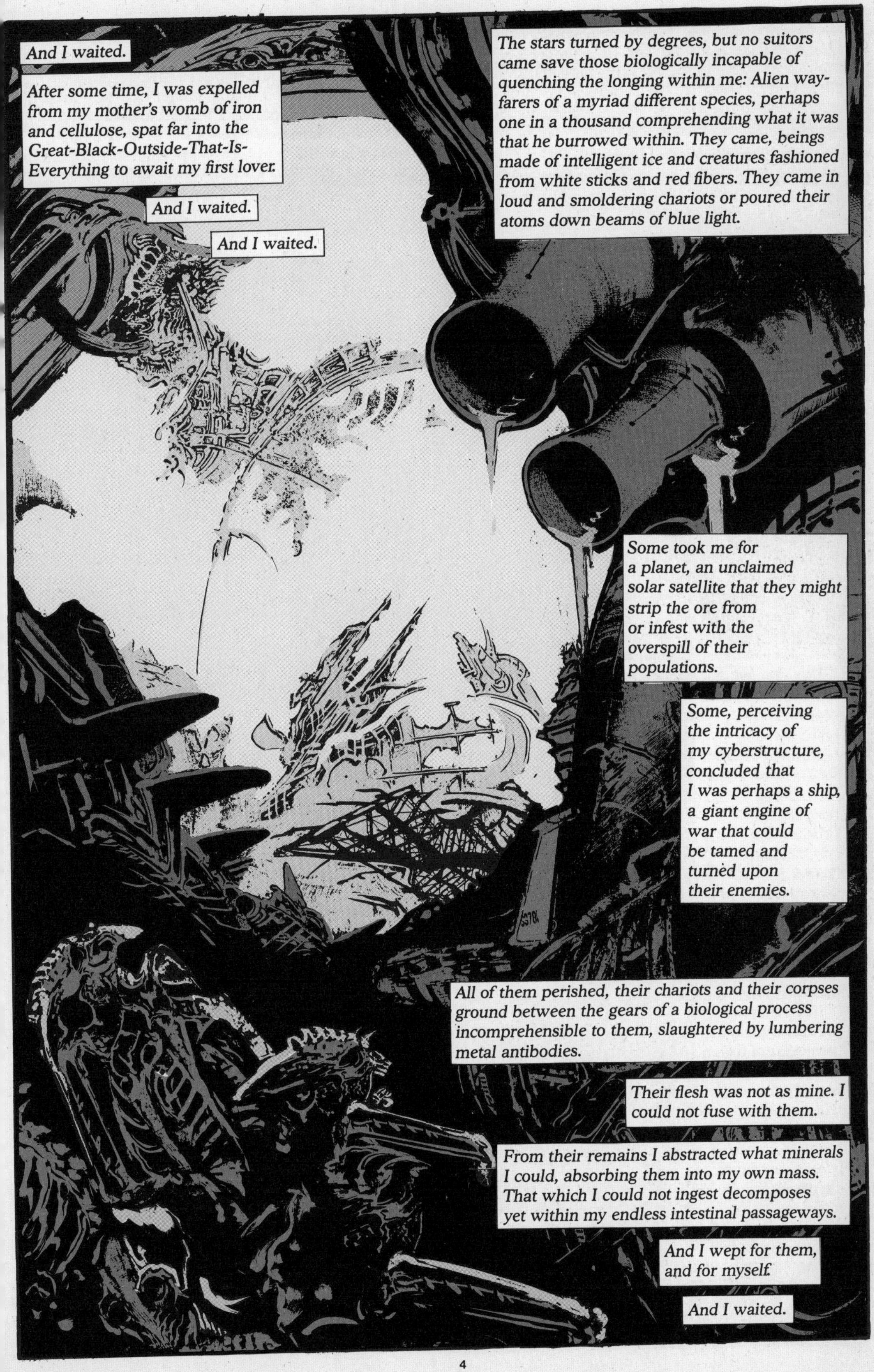
And I waited.
After some time, I was expelled from my mother's womb of iron and cellulose, spat far into the Great-Black-Outside-That-Is-Everything to await my first lover.
And I waited.
And I waited.
The stars turned by degrees, but no suitors came save those biologically incapable of quenching the longing within me: Alien wayfarers of a myriad different species, perhaps one in a thousand comprehending what it was that he burrowed within. They came, beings made of intelligent ice and creatures fashioned from white sticks and red fibers. They came in loud and smoldering chariots or poured their atoms down beams of blue light.
Some took me for a planet, an unclaimed solar satellite that they might strip the ore from or infest with the overspill of their populations.
Some, perceiving the intricacy of my cyberstructure, concluded that I was perhaps a ship, a giant engine of war that could be tamed and turned upon their enemies.
All of them perished, their chariots and their corpses ground between the gears of a biological process incomprehensible to them, slaughtered by lumbering metal antibodies.
Their flesh was not as mine. I could not fuse with them.
From their remains I abstracted what minerals I could, absorbing them into my own mass. That which I could not ingest decomposes yet within my endless intestinal passageways.
And I wept for them, and for myself.
And I waited.

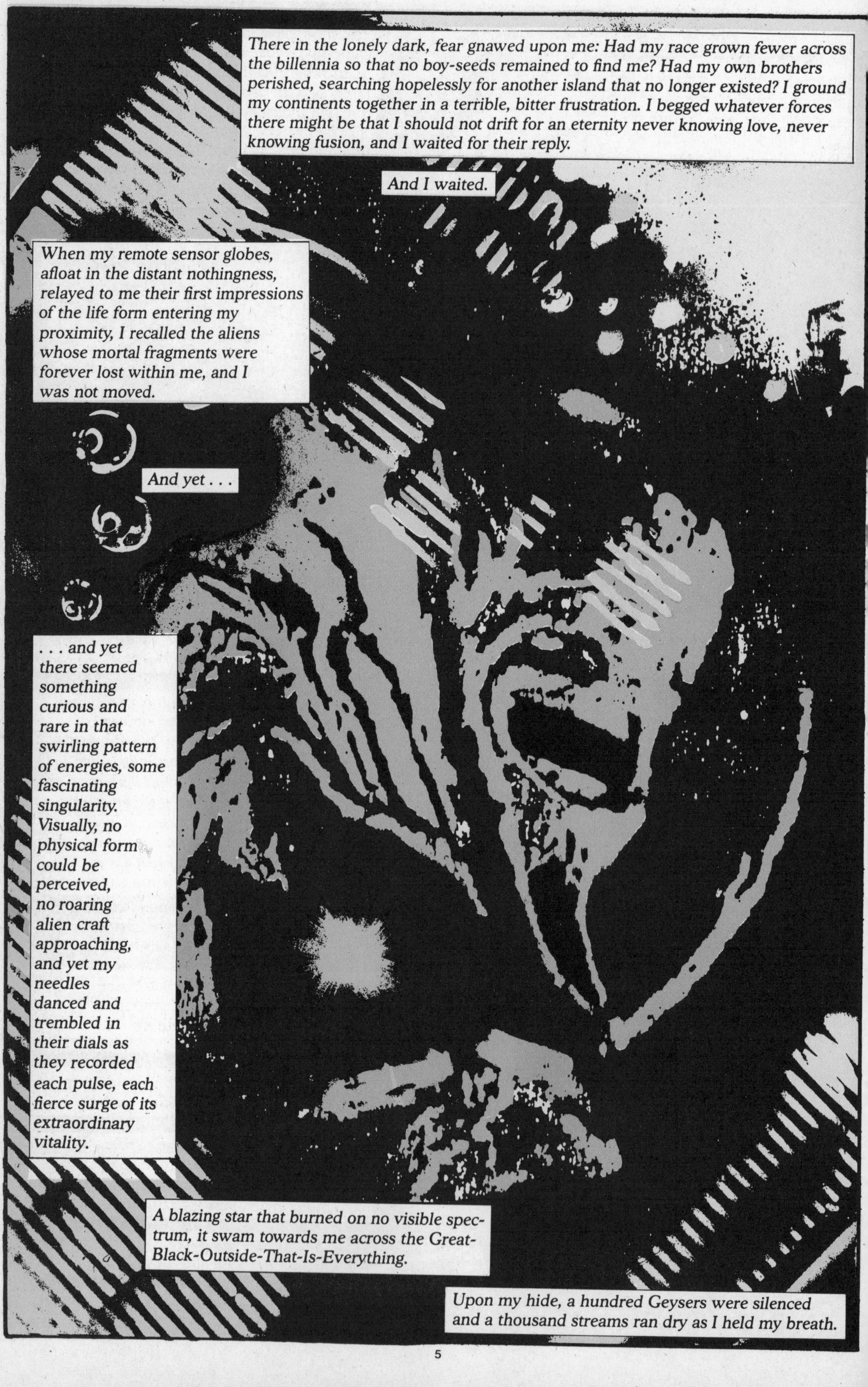
There in the lonely dark, fear gnawed upon me: Had my race grown fewer across the billennia so that no boy-seeds remained to find me? Had my own brothers perished, searching hopelessly for another island that no longer existed? I ground my continents together in a terrible, bitter frustration. I begged whatever forces there might be that I should not drift for an eternity never knowing love, never knowing fusion, and I waited for their reply.
And I waited.
When my remote sensor globes, afloat in the distant nothingness, relayed to me their first impressions of the life form entering my proximity, I recalled the aliens whose mortal fragments were forever lost within me, and I was not moved.
And yet . . .
. . . and yet there seemed something curious and rare in that swirling pattern of energies, some fascinating singularity. Visually, no physical form could be perceived, no roaring alien craft approaching, and yet my needles danced and trembled in their dials as they recorded each pulse, each fierce surge of its extraordinary vitality.
A blazing star that burned on no visible spectrum, it swam towards me across the Great-Black-Outside-That-Is-Everything.
Upon my hide, a hundred Geysers were silenced and a thousand streams ran dry as I held my breath.

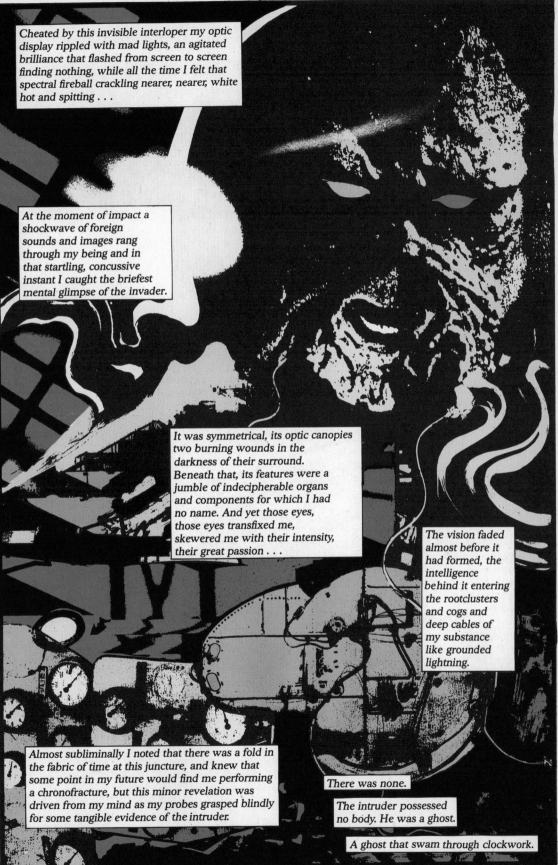

Cheated by this invisible interloper my optic display rippled with mad lights, an agitated brilliance that flashed from screen to screen finding nothing, while all the time I felt that spectral fireball crackling nearer, nearer, white hot and spitting . . .

At the moment of impact a shockwave of foreign sounds and images rang through my being and in that startling, concussive instant I caught the briefest mental glimpse of the invader.

It was symmetrical, its optic canopies two burning wounds in the darkness of their surround. Beneath that, its features were a jumble of indecipherable organs and components for which I had no name. And yet those eyes, those eyes transfixed me, skewered me with their intensity, their great passion . . .

The vision faded almost before it had formed, the intelligence behind it entering the rootclusters and cogs and deep cables of my substance like grounded lightning.

Almost subliminally I noted that there was a fold in the fabric of time at this juncture, and knew that some point in my future would find me performing a chronofracture, but this minor revelation was driven from my mind as my probes grasped blindly for some tangible evidence of the intruder.

There was none.

The intruder possessed no body. He was a ghost.

A ghost that swam through clockwork.

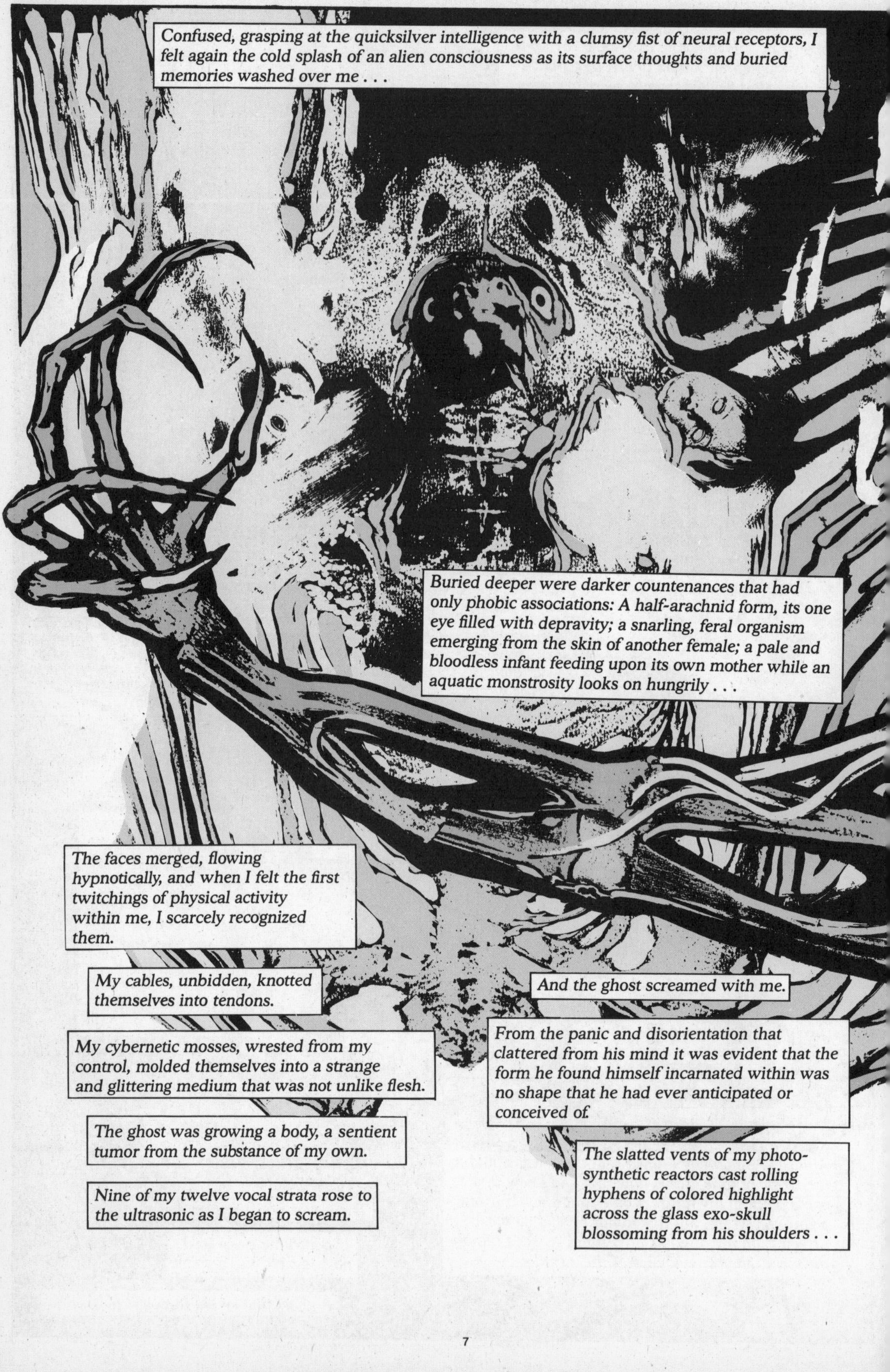
Confused, grasping at the quicksilver intelligence with a clumsy fist of neural receptors, I felt again the cold splash of an alien consciousness as its surface thoughts and buried memories washed over me . . .
Buried deeper were darker countenances that had only phobic associations: A half-arachnid form, its one eye filled with depravity; a snarling, feral organism emerging from the skin of another female; a pale and bloodless infant feeding upon its own mother while an aquatic monstrosity looks on hungrily . . .
The faces merged, flowing hypnotically, and when I felt the first twitchings of physical activity within me, I scarcely recognized them.
My cables, unbidden, knotted themselves into tendons.
My cybernetic mosses, wrested from my control, molded themselves into a strange and glittering medium that was not unlike flesh.
The ghost was growing a body, a sentient tumor from the substance of my own.
Nine of my twelve vocal strata rose to the ultrasonic as I began to scream.
And the ghost screamed with me.
From the panic and disorientation that clattered from his mind it was evident that the form he found himself incarnated within was no shape that he had ever anticipated or conceived of.
The slatted vents of my photo-synthetic reactors cast rolling hyphens of colored highlight across the glass exo-skull blossoming from his shoulders . . .
7

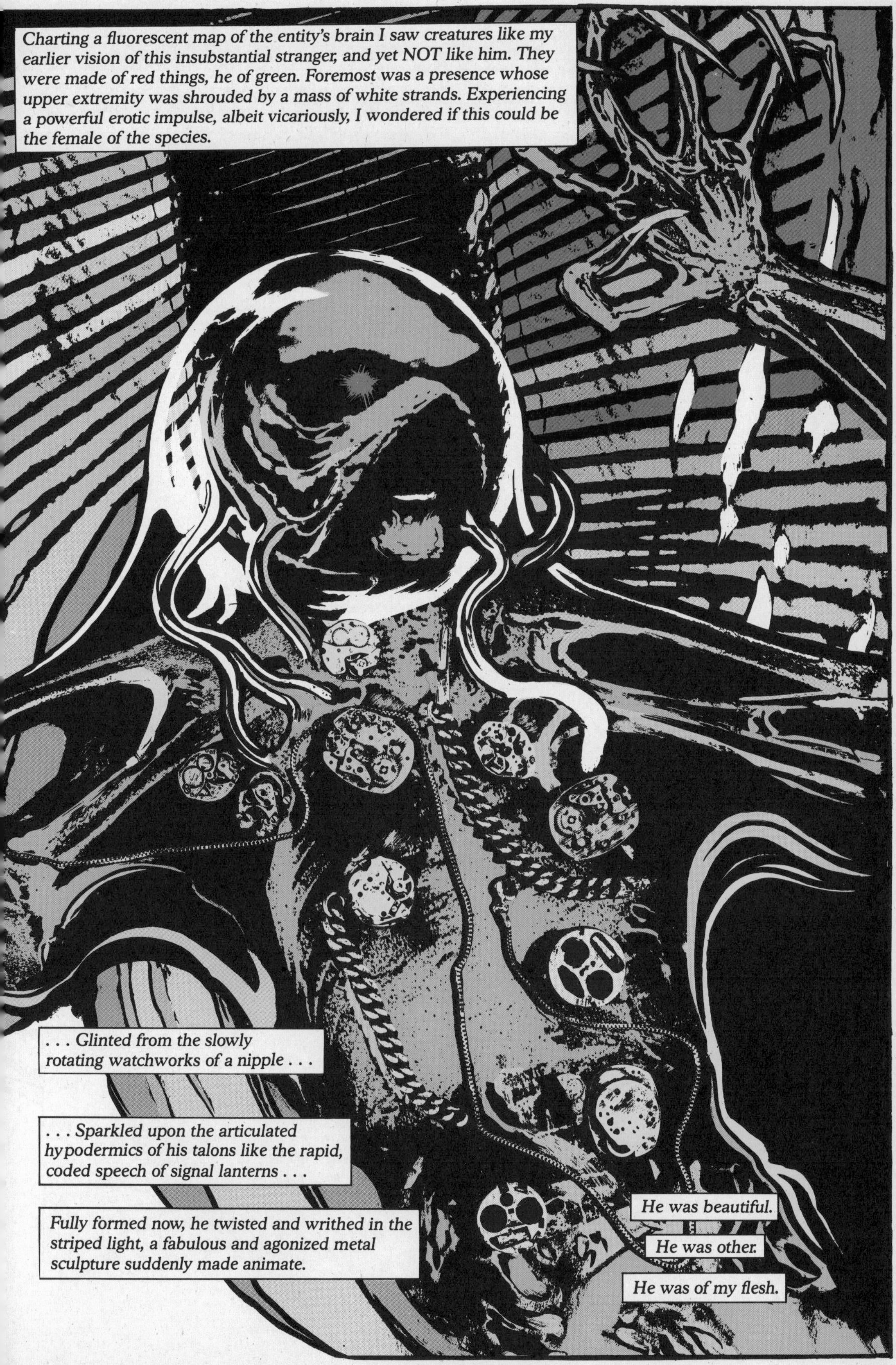
Charting a fluorescent map of the entity's brain I saw creatures like my earlier vision of this insubstantial stranger, and yet NOT like him. They were made of red things, he of green. Foremost was a presence whose upper extremity was shrouded by a mass of white strands. Experiencing a powerful erotic impulse, albeit vicariously, I wondered if this could be the female of the species.
. . . Glinted from the slowly rotating watchworks of a nipple . . .
. . . Sparkled upon the articulated hypodermics of his talons like the rapid, coded speech of signal lanterns . . .
Fully formed now, he twisted and writhed in the striped light, a fabulous and agonized metal sculpture suddenly made animate.
He was beautiful.
He was other.
He was of my flesh.

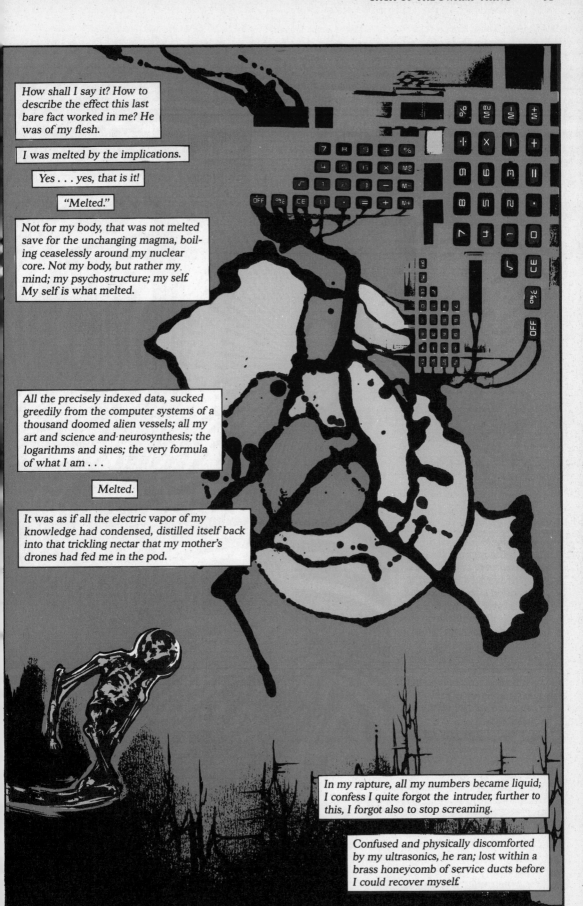

How shall I say it? How to describe the effect this last bare fact worked in me? He was of my flesh.

I was melted by the implications.

Yes . . . yes, that is it!

"Melted."

Not for my body, that was not melted save for the unchanging magma, boiling ceaselessly around my nuclear core. Not my body, but rather my mind; my psychostructure; my self. My self is what melted.

All the precisely indexed data, sucked greedily from the computer systems of a thousand doomed alien vessels; all my art and science and neurosynthesis; the logarithms and sines; the very formula of what I am . . .

Melted.

It was as if all the electric vapor of my knowledge had condensed, distilled itself back into that trickling nectar that my mother's drones had fed me in the pod.

In my rapture, all my numbers became liquid; I confess I quite forgot the intruder, further to this, I forgot also to stop screaming.

Confused and physically discomforted by my ultrasonics, he ran; lost within a brass honeycomb of service ducts before I could recover myself.

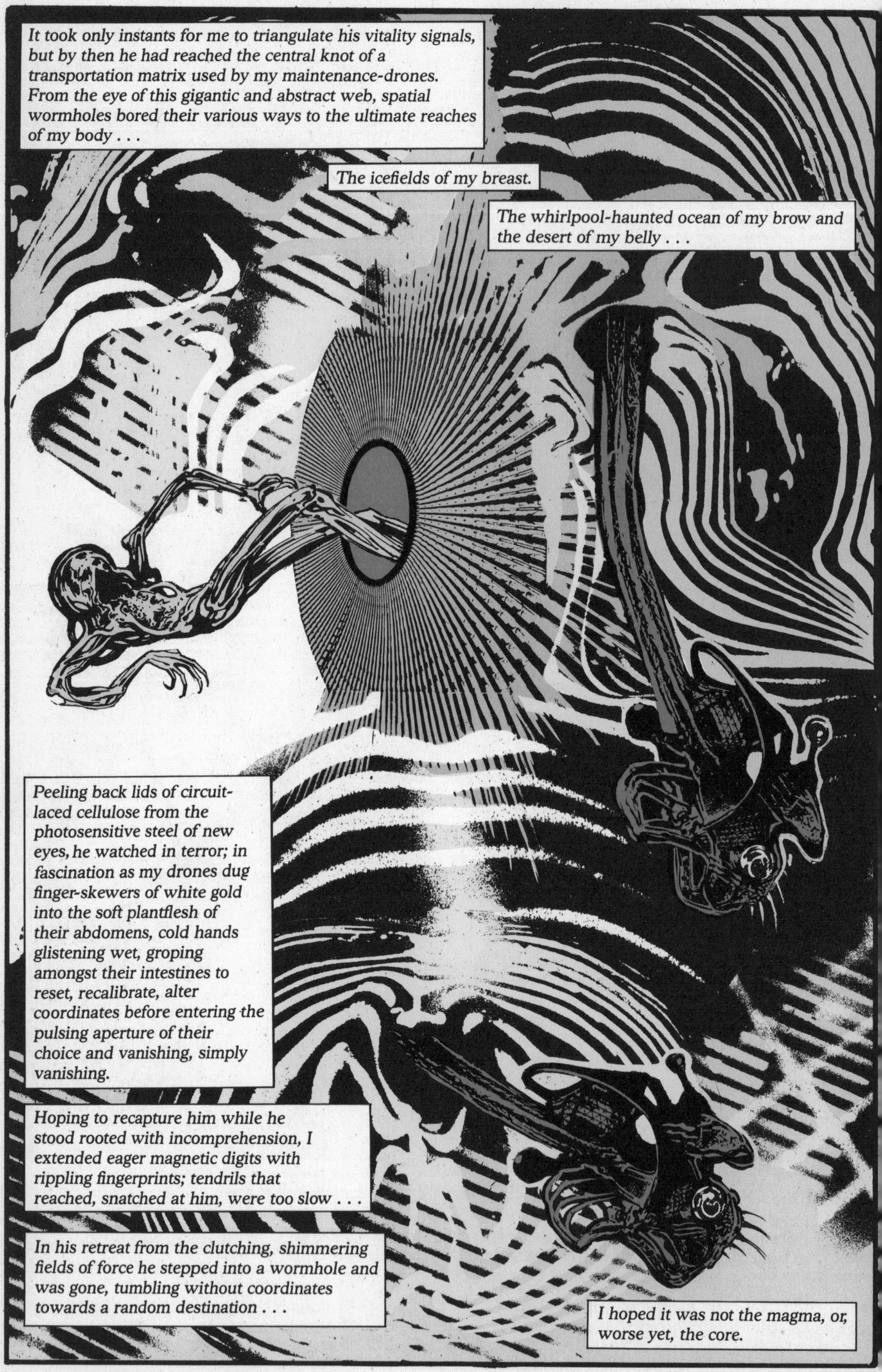
It took only instants for me to triangulate his vitality signals, but by then he had reached the central knot of a transportation matrix used by my maintenance-drones. From the eye of this gigantic and abstract web, spatial wormholes bored their various ways to the ultimate reaches of my body . . .
The icefields of my breast.
The whirlpool-haunted ocean of my brow and the desert of my belly . . .
Peeling back lids of circuit-laced cellulose from the photosensitive steel of new eyes, he watched in terror; in fascination as my drones dug finger-skewers of white gold into the soft plantflesh of their abdomens, cold hands glistening wet, groping amongst their intestines to reset, recalibrate, alter coordinates before entering the pulsing aperture of their choice and vanishing, simply vanishing.
Hoping to recapture him while he stood rooted with incomprehension, I extended eager magnetic digits with rippling fingerprints; tendrils that reached, snatched at him, were too slow . . .
In his retreat from the clutching, shimmering fields of force he stepped into a wormhole and was gone, tumbling without coordinates towards a random destination . . .
I hoped it was not the magma, or, worse yet, the core.

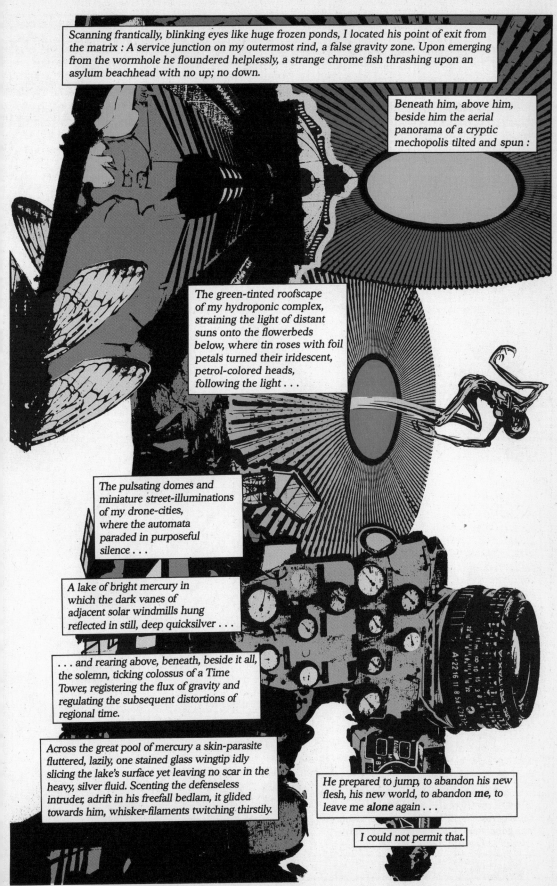

Scanning frantically, blinking eyes like huge frozen ponds, I located his point of exit from the matrix : A service junction on my outermost rind, a false gravity zone. Upon emerging from the wormhole he floundered helplessly, a strange chrome fish thrashing upon an asylum beachhead with no up; no down.

Beneath him, above him, beside him the aerial panorama of a cryptic mechopolis tilted and spun :

The green-tinted roofscape of my hydroponic complex, straining the light of distant suns onto the flowerbeds below, where tin roses with foil petals turned their iridescent, petrol-colored heads, following the light . . .

The pulsating domes and miniature street-illuminations of my drone-cities, where the automata paraded in purposeful silence . . .

A lake of bright mercury in which the dark vanes of adjacent solar windmills hung reflected in still, deep quicksilver . . .

. . . and rearing above, beneath, beside it all, the solemn, ticking colossus of a Time Tower, registering the flux of gravity and regulating the subsequent distortions of regional time.

Across the great pool of mercury a skin-parasite fluttered, lazily, one stained glass wingtip idly slicing the lake's surface yet leaving no scar in the heavy, silver fluid. Scenting the defenseless intruder, adrift in his freefall bedlam, it glided towards him, whisker-filaments twitching thirstily.

He prepared to jump, to abandon his new flesh, his new world, to abandon me, to leave me alone again . . .

I could not permit that.

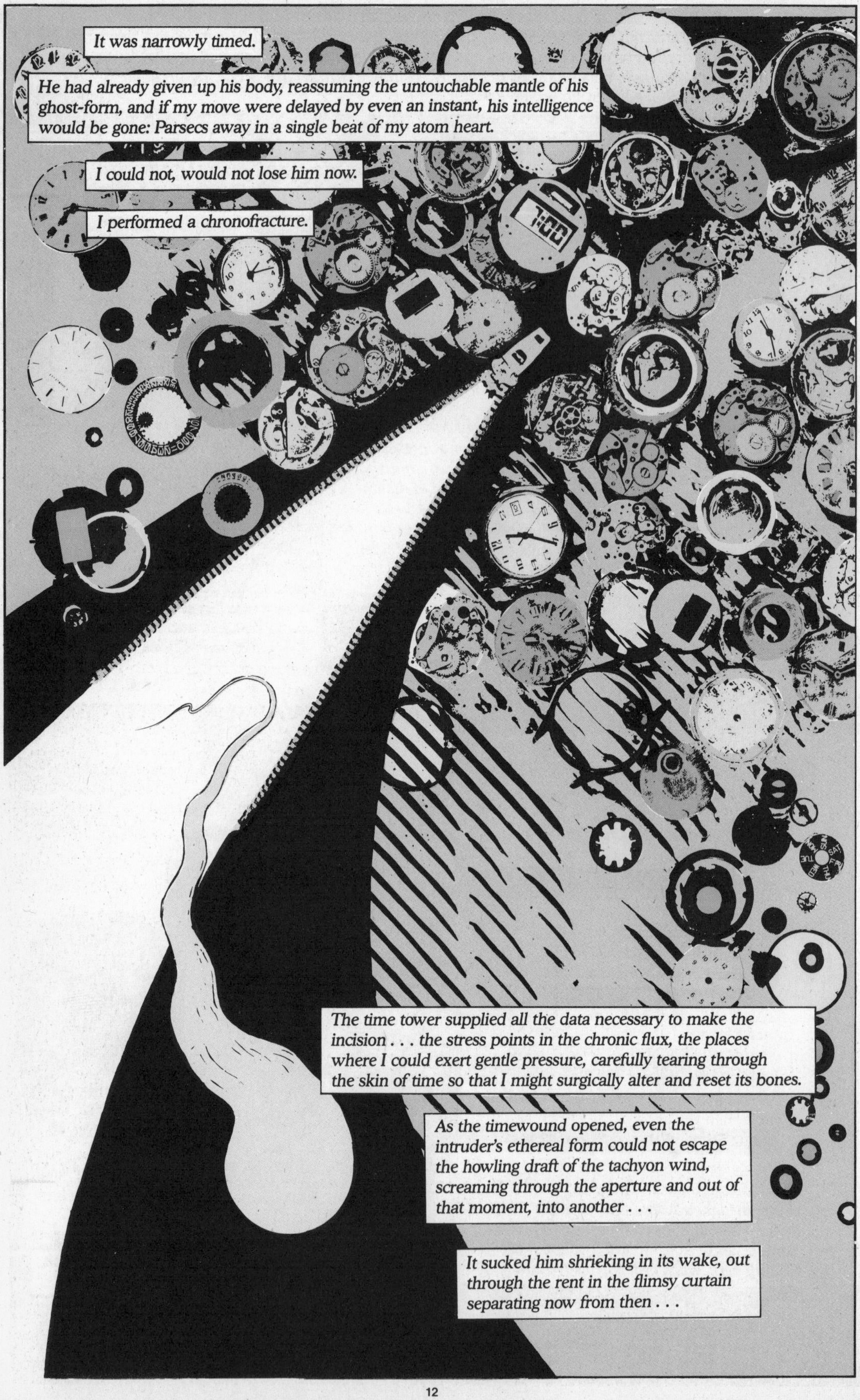
It was narrowly timed.
He had already given up his body, reassuming the untouchable mantle of his ghost-form, and if my move were delayed by even an instant, his intelligence would be gone: Parsecs away in a single beat of my atom heart.
I could not, would not lose him now.
I performed a chronofracture.
The time tower supplied all the data necessary to make the incision . . . the stress points in the chronic flux, the places where I could exert gentle pressure, carefully tearing through the skin of time so that I might surgically alter and reset its bones.
As the timewound opened, even the intruder's ethereal form could not escape the howling draft of the tachyon wind, screaming through the aperture and out of that moment, into another . . .
It sucked him shrieking in its wake, out through the rent in the flimsy curtain separating now from then . . .

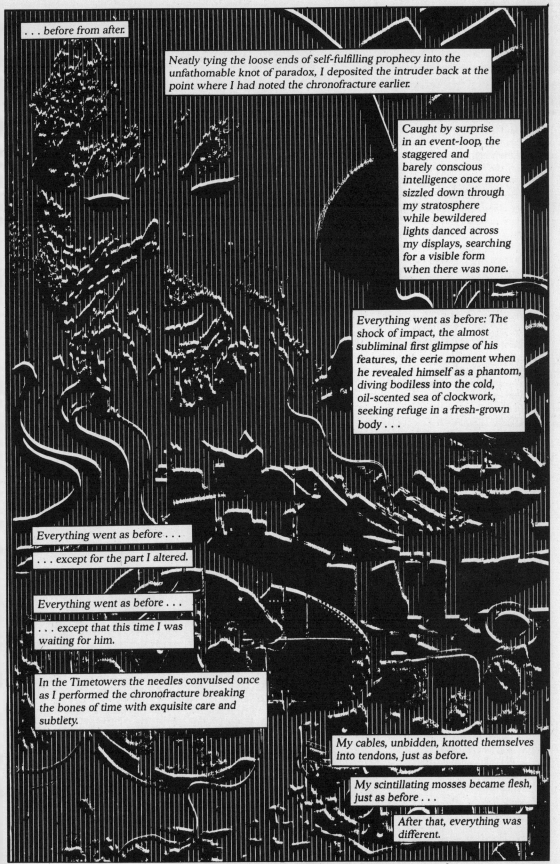

. . . before from after.

Neatly tying the loose ends of self-fulfilling prophecy into the unfathomable knot of paradox, I deposited the intruder back at the point where I had noted the chronofracture earlier.

Caught by surprise in an event-loop, the staggered and barely conscious intelligence once more sizzled down through my stratosphere while bewildered lights danced across my displays, searching for a visible form when there was none.

Everything went as before: The shock of impact, the almost subliminal first glimpse of his features, the eerie moment when he revealed himself as a phantom, diving bodiless into the cold, oil-scented sea of clockwork, seeking refuge in a fresh-grown body . . .

Everything went as before . . .

. . . except for the part I altered.

Everything went as before . . .

. . . except that this time I was waiting for him.

In the Timetowers the needles convulsed once as I performed the chronofracture breaking the bones of time with exquisite care and subtlety.

My cables, unbidden, knotted themselves into tendons, just as before.

My scintillating mosses became flesh, just as before . . .

After that, everything was different.

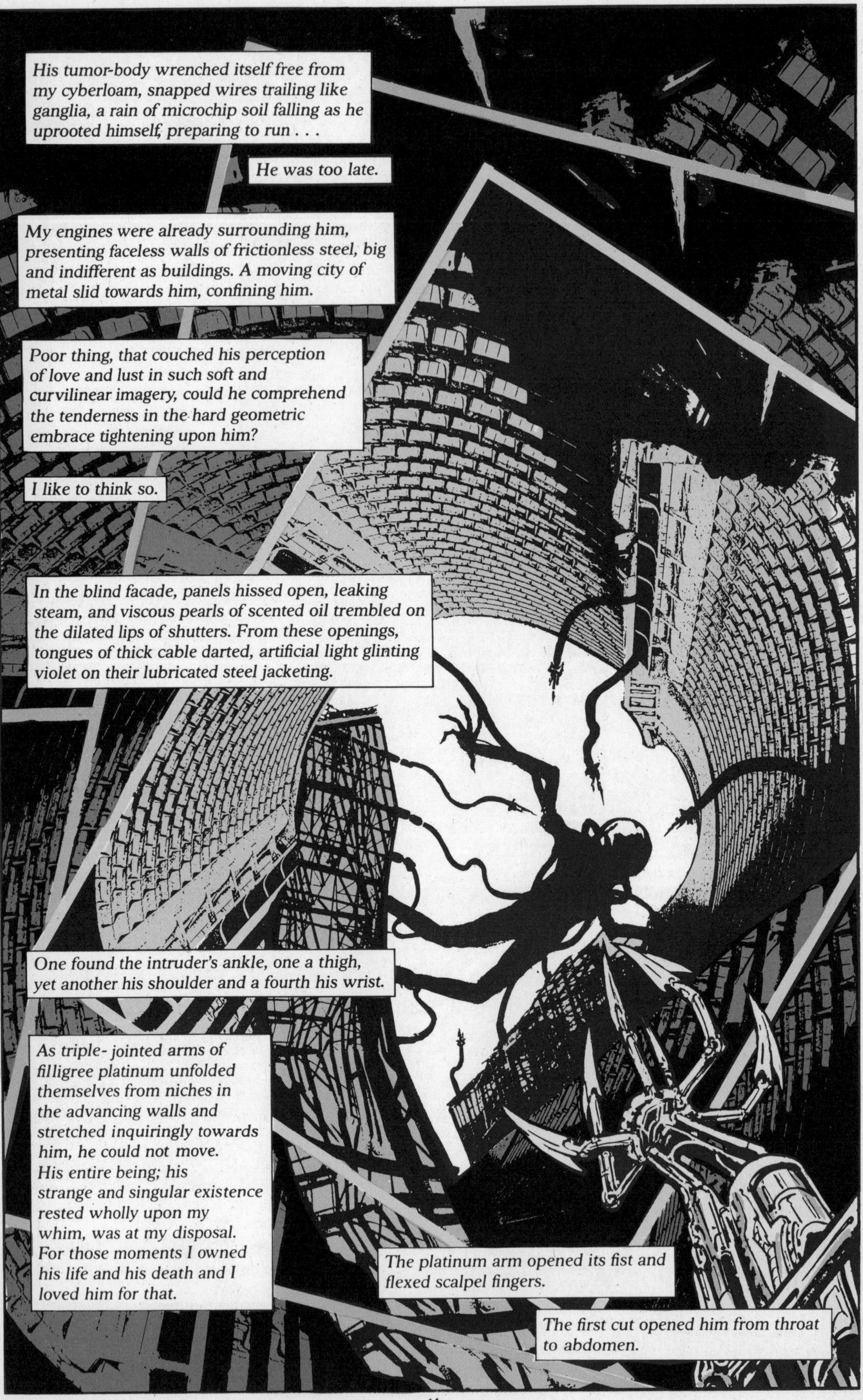
His tumor-body wrenched itself free from my cyberloam, snapped wires trailing like ganglia, a rain of microchip soil falling as he uprooted himself, preparing to run . . .
He was too late.
My engines were already surrounding him, presenting faceless walls of frictionless steel, big and indifferent as buildings. A moving city of metal slid towards him, confining him.
Poor thing, that couched his perception of love and lust in such soft and curvilinear imagery, could he comprehend the tenderness in the hard geometric embrace tightening upon him?
I like to think so.
In the blind facade, panels hissed open, leaking steam, and viscous pearls of scented oil trembled on the dilated lips of shutters. From these openings, tongues of thick cable darted, artificial light glinting violet on their lubricated steel jacketing.
One found the intruder's ankle, one a thigh, yet another his shoulder and a fourth his wrist.
As triple-jointed arms of filligree platinum unfolded themselves from niches in the advancing walls and stretched inquiringly towards him, he could not move. His entire being; his strange and singular existence rested wholly upon my whim, was at my disposal. For those moments I owned his life and his death and I loved him for that.
The platinum arm opened its fist and flexed scalpel fingers.
The first cut opened him from throat to abdomen.

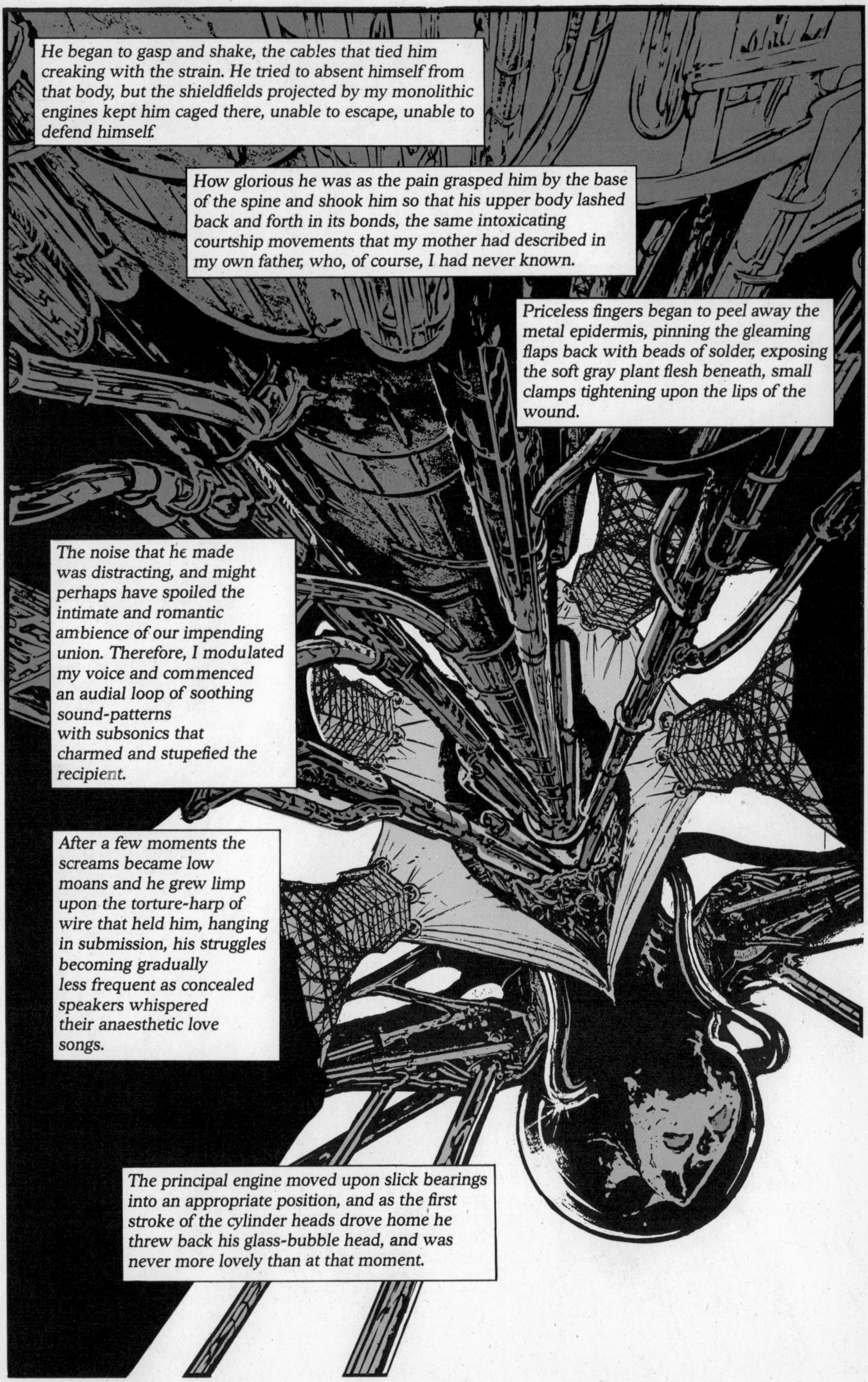
He began to gasp and shake, the cables that tied him creaking with the strain. He tried to absent himself from that body, but the shieldfields projected by my monolithic engines kept him caged there, unable to escape, unable to defend himself.
How glorious he was as the pain grasped him by the base of the spine and shook him so that his upper body lashed back and forth in its bonds, the same intoxicating courtship movements that my mother had described in my own father, who, of course, I had never known.
Priceless fingers began to peel away the metal epidermis, pinning the gleaming flaps back with beads of solder, exposing the soft gray plant flesh beneath, small clamps tightening upon the lips of the wound.
The noise that he made was distracting, and might perhaps have spoiled the intimate and romantic ambience of our impending union. Therefore, I modulated my voice and commenced an audial loop of soothing sound-patterns with subsonics that charmed and stupefied the recipient.
After a few moments the screams became low moans and he grew limp upon the torture-harp of wire that held him, hanging in submission, his struggles becoming gradually less frequent as concealed speakers whispered their anaesthetic love songs.
The principal engine moved upon slick bearings into an appropriate position, and as the first stroke of the cylinder heads drove home he threw back his glass-bubble head, and was never more lovely than at that moment.

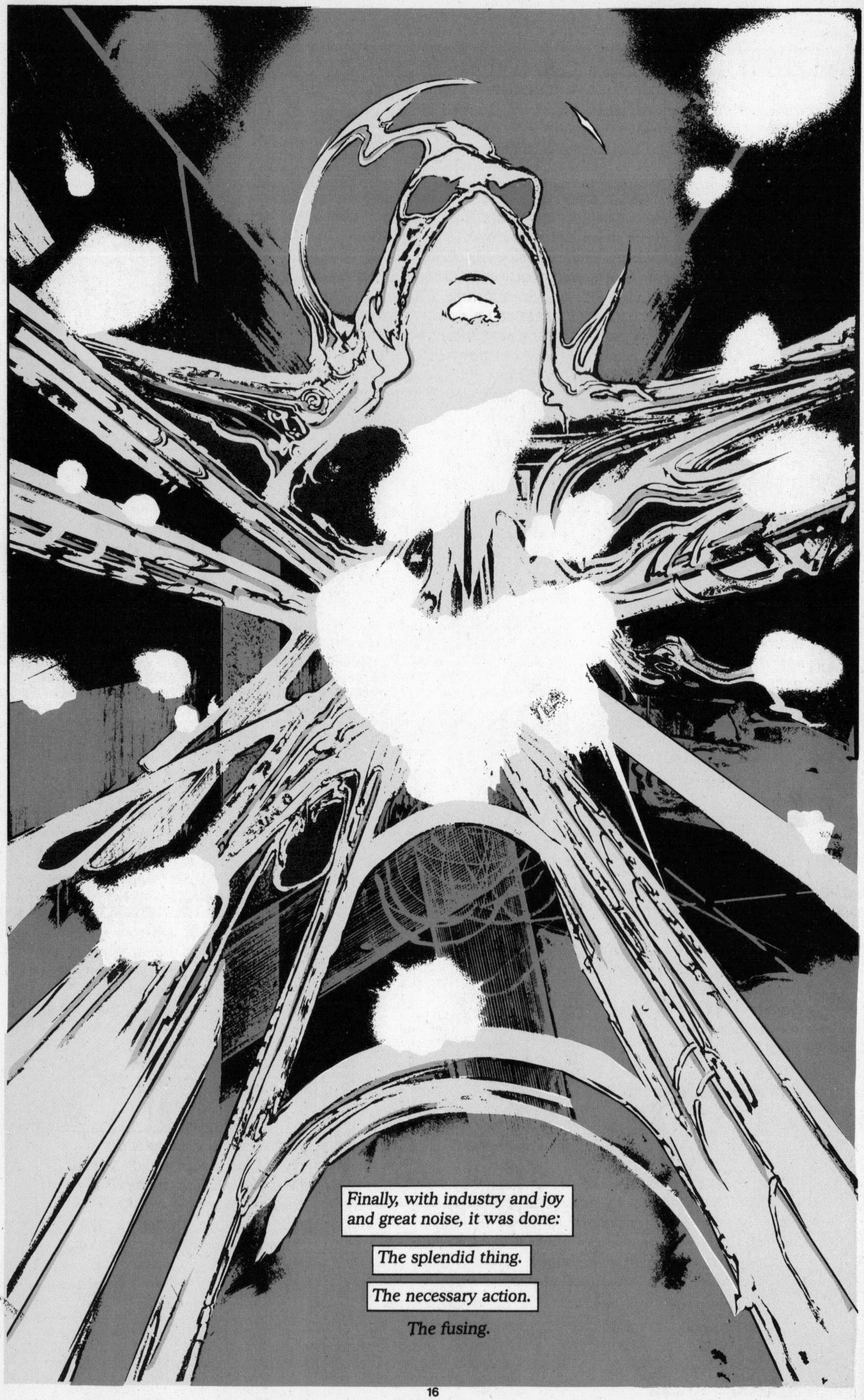
Finally, with industry and joy and great noise, it was done:
The splendid thing.
The necessary action.
The fusing.
16

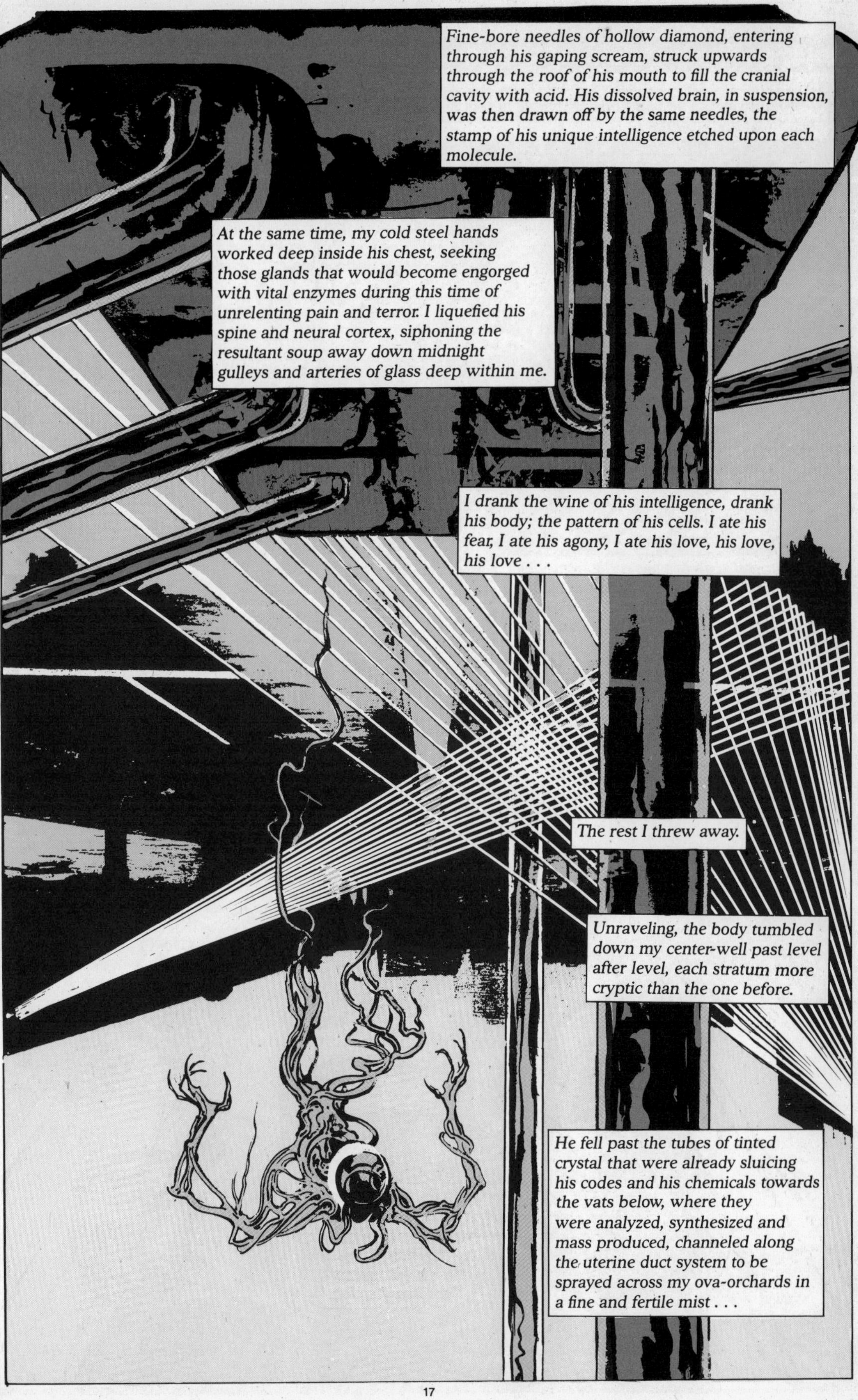
Fine-bore needles of hollow diamond, entering through his gaping scream, struck upwards through the roof of his mouth to fill the cranial cavity with acid. His dissolved brain, in suspension, was then drawn off by the same needles, the stamp of his unique intelligence etched upon each molecule.
At the same time, my cold steel hands worked deep inside his chest, seeking those glands that would become engorged with vital enzymes during this time of unrelenting pain and terror. I liquefied his spine and neural cortex, siphoning the resultant soup away down midnight gulleys and arteries of glass deep within me.
I drank the wine of his intelligence, drank his body; the pattern of his cells. I ate his fear, I ate his agony, I ate his love, his love, his love . . .
The rest I threw away.
Unraveling, the body tumbled down my center-well past level after level, each stratum more cryptic than the one before.
He fell past the tubes of tinted crystal that were already sluicing his codes and his chemicals towards the vats below, where they were analyzed, synthesized and mass produced, channeled along the uterine duct system to be sprayed across my ova-orchards in a fine and fertile mist . . .

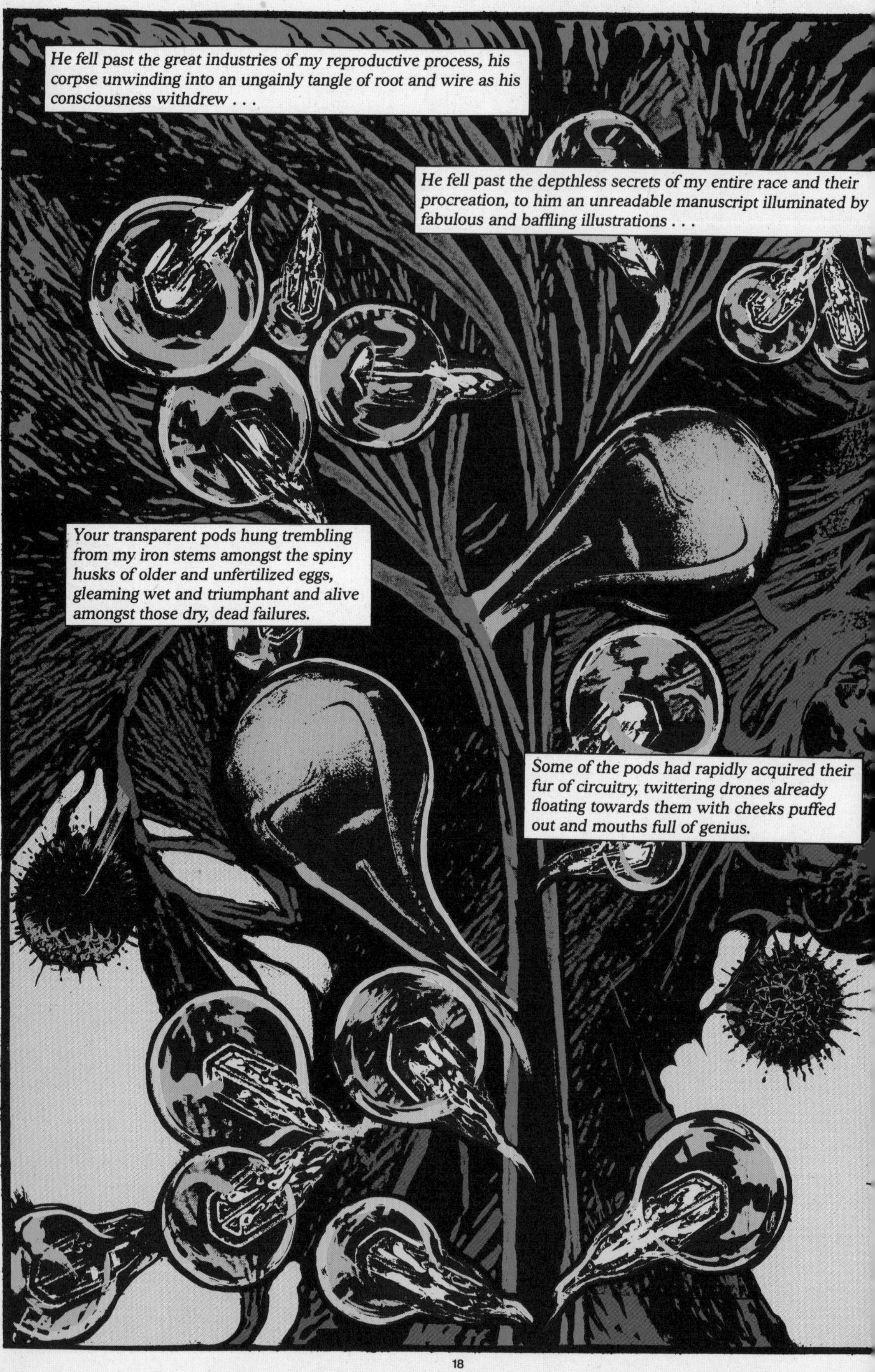
He fell past the great industries of my reproductive process, his corpse unwinding into an ungainly tangle of root and wire as his consciousness withdrew . . .
He fell past the depthless secrets of my entire race and their procreation, to him an unreadable manuscript illuminated by fabulous and baffling illustrations . . .
Your transparent pods hung trembling from my iron stems amongst the spiny husks of older and unfertilized eggs, gleaming wet and triumphant and alive amongst those dry, dead failures.
Some of the pods had rapidly acquired their fur of circuitry, twittering drones already floating towards them with cheeks puffed out and mouths full of genius.

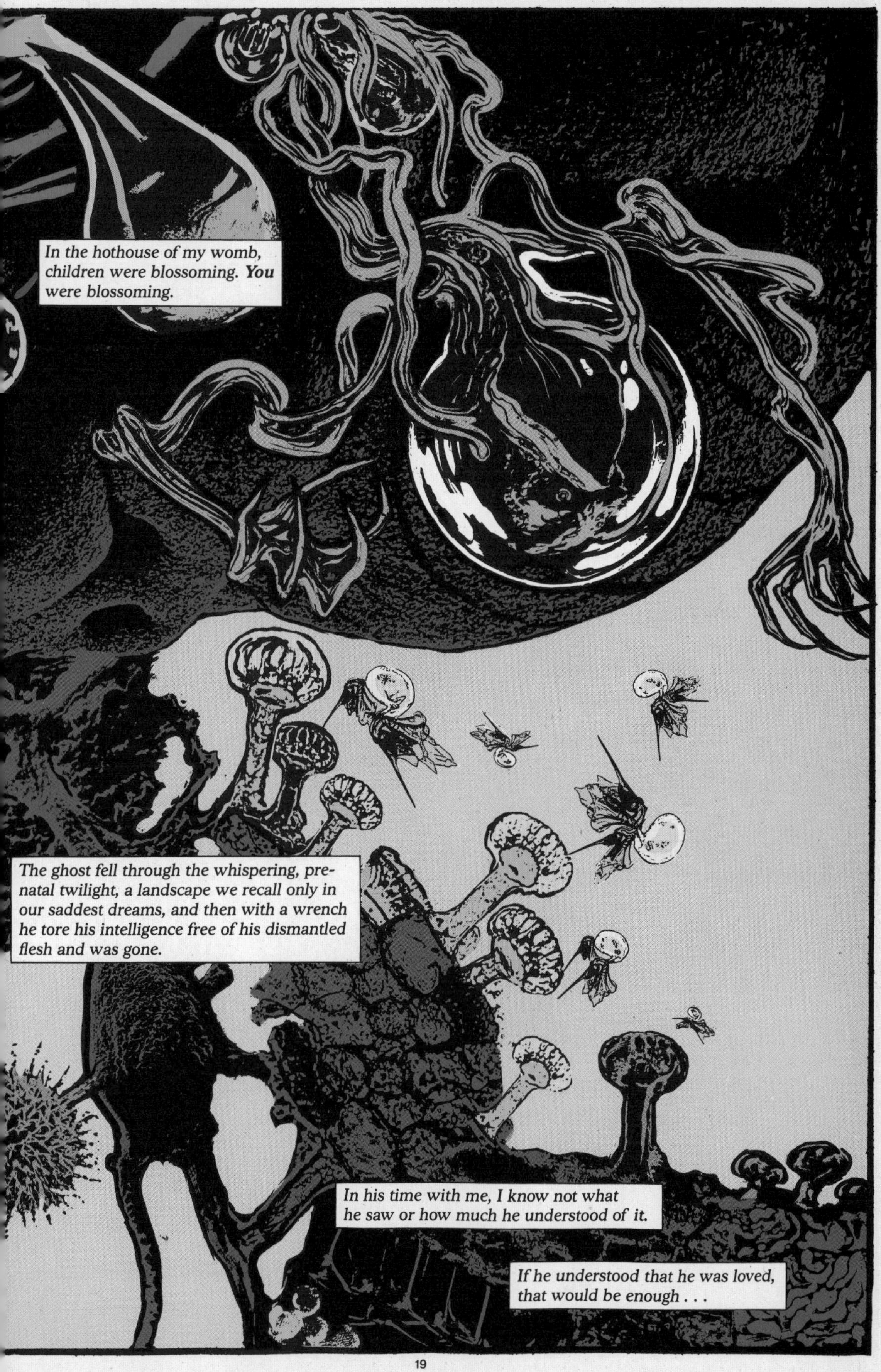
In the hothouse of my womb, children were blossoming. ***You*** were blossoming.
The ghost fell through the whispering, pre-natal twilight, a landscape we recall only in our saddest dreams, and then with a wrench he tore his intelligence free of his dismantled flesh and was gone.
In his time with me, I know not what he saw or how much he understood of it.
If he understood that he was loved, that would be enough . . .

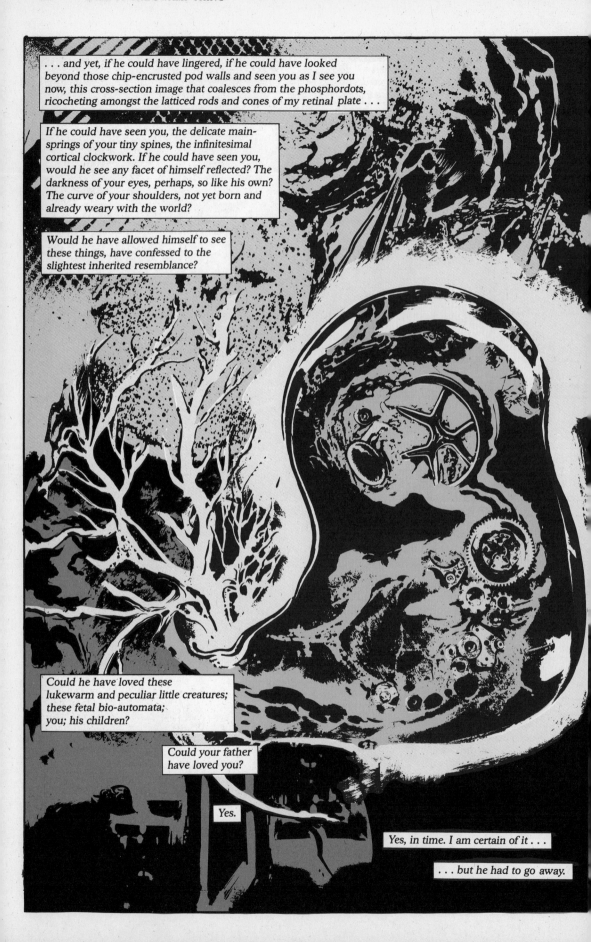

... and yet, if he could have lingered, if he could have looked beyond those chip-encrusted pod walls and seen you as I see you now, this cross-section image that coalesces from the phosphordots, ricocheting amongst the latticed rods and cones of my retinal plate ...

If he could have seen you, the delicate main-springs of your tiny spines, the infinitesimal cortical clockwork. If he could have seen you, would he see any facet of himself reflected? The darkness of your eyes, perhaps, so like his own? The curve of your shoulders, not yet born and already weary with the world?

Would he have allowed himself to see these things, have confessed to the slightest inherited resemblance?

Could he have loved these lukewarm and peculiar little creatures; these fetal bio-automata; you; his children?

Could your father have loved you?

Yes.

Yes, in time. I am certain of it ...

... but he had to go away.

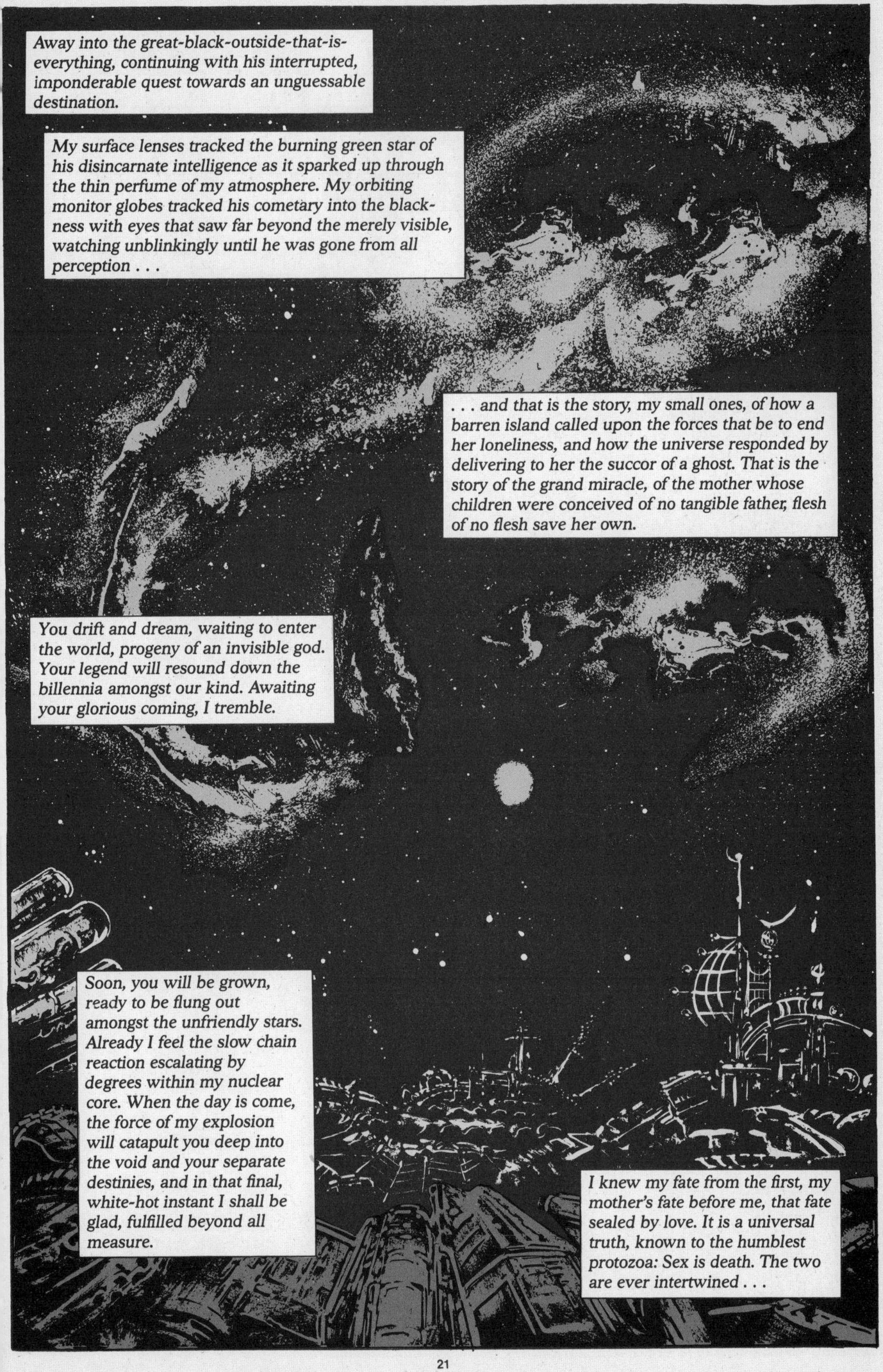
Away into the great-black-outside-that-is-everything, continuing with his interrupted, imponderable quest towards an unguessable destination.
My surface lenses tracked the burning green star of his disincarnate intelligence as it sparked up through the thin perfume of my atmosphere. My orbiting monitor globes tracked his cometary into the blackness with eyes that saw far beyond the merely visible, watching unblinkingly until he was gone from all perception . . .
. . . and that is the story, my small ones, of how a barren island called upon the forces that be to end her loneliness, and how the universe responded by delivering to her the succor of a ghost. That is the story of the grand miracle, of the mother whose children were conceived of no tangible father, flesh of no flesh save her own.
You drift and dream, waiting to enter the world, progeny of an invisible god. Your legend will resound down the billennia amongst our kind. Awaiting your glorious coming, I tremble.
Soon, you will be grown, ready to be flung out amongst the unfriendly stars. Already I feel the slow chain reaction escalating by degrees within my nuclear core. When the day is come, the force of my explosion will catapult you deep into the void and your separate destinies, and in that final, white-hot instant I shall be glad, fulfilled beyond all measure.
I knew my fate from the first, my mother's fate before me, that fate sealed by love. It is a universal truth, known to the humblest protozoa: Sex is death. The two are ever intertwined . . .

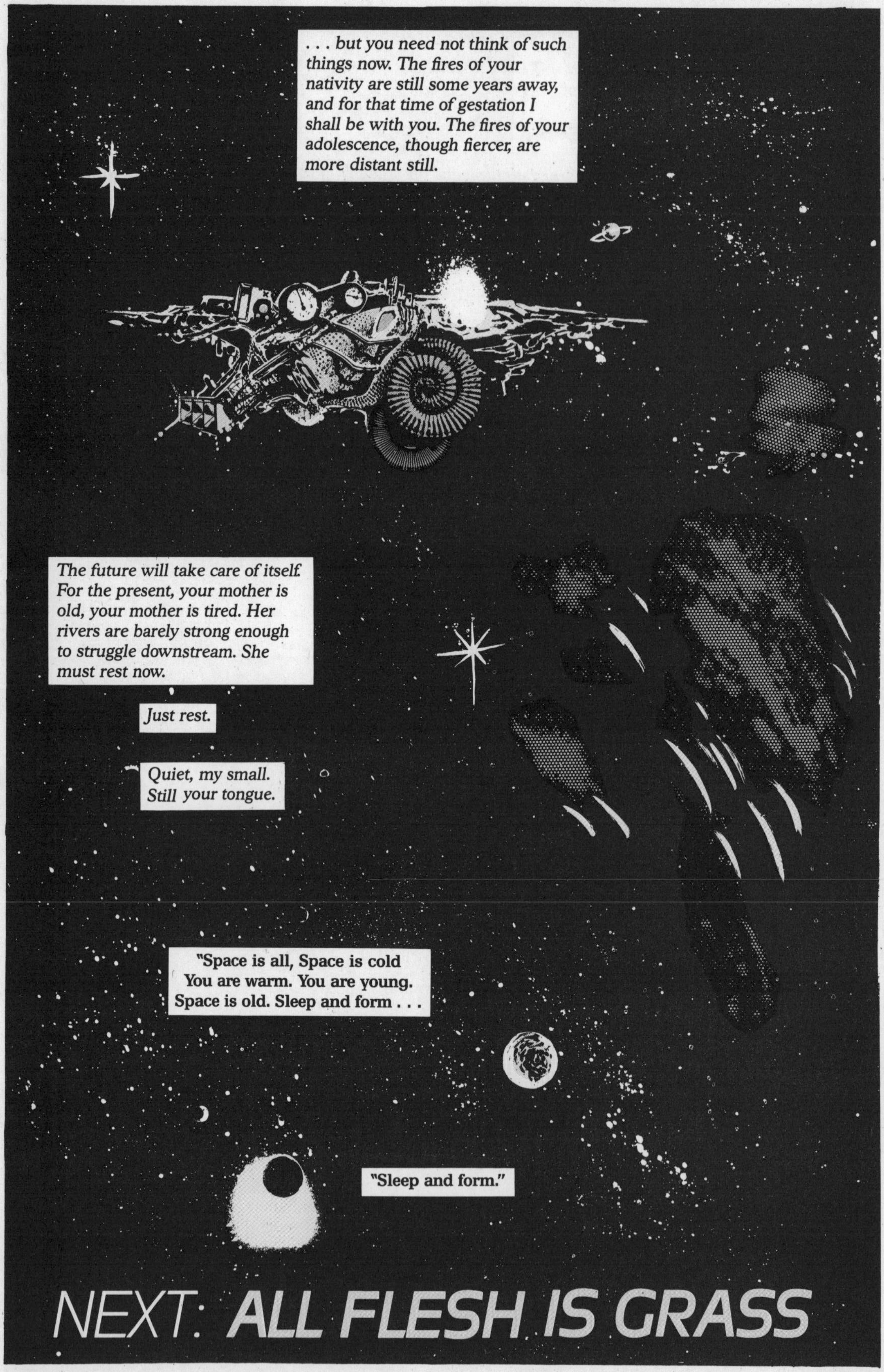
. . . but you need not think of such things now. The fires of your nativity are still some years away, and for that time of gestation I shall be with you. The fires of your adolescence, though fiercer, are more distant still.
The future will take care of itself. For the present, your mother is old, your mother is tired. Her rivers are barely strong enough to struggle downstream. She must rest now.
Just rest.
Quiet, my small. Still your tongue.
"Space is all, Space is cold You are warm. You are young. Space is old. Sleep and form . . .
"Sleep and form."
NEXT: ALL FLESH IS GRASS

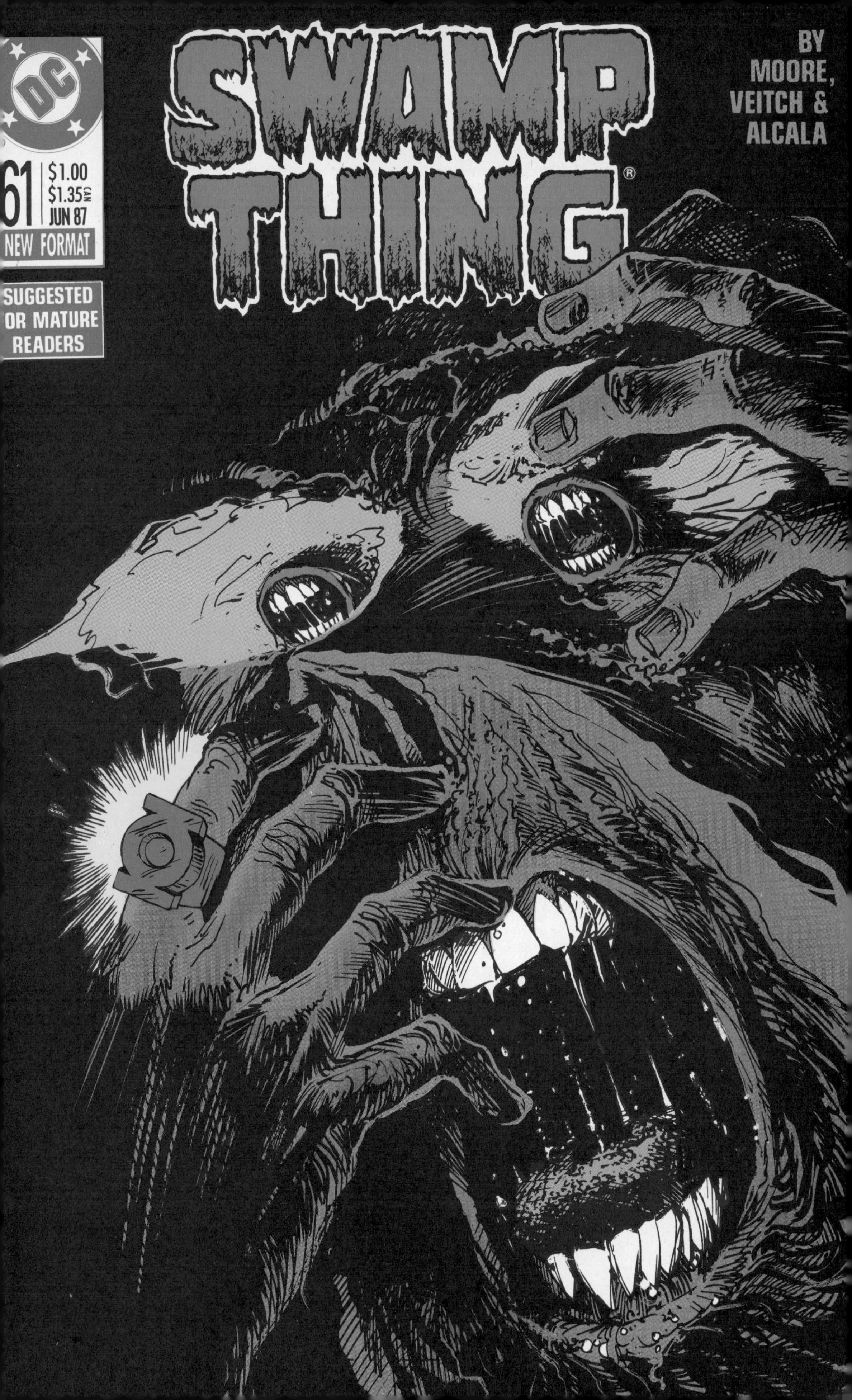
SWAMP THING®
BY MOORE, VEITCH & ALCALA
61 $1.00 $1.35 CAN JUN 87
NEW FORMAT
SUGGESTED FOR MATURE READERS

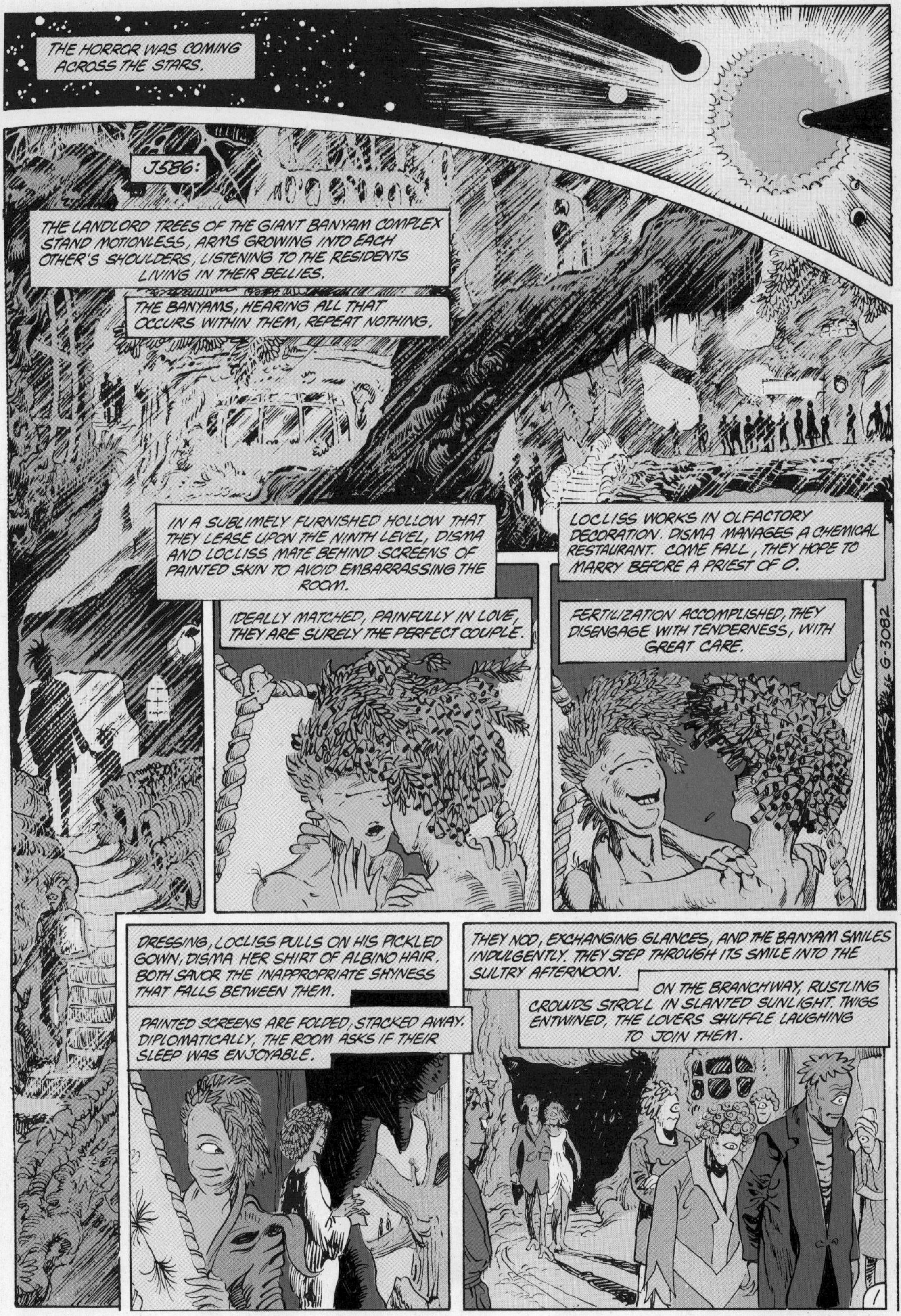
THE HORROR WAS COMING ACROSS THE STARS.
J586:
THE LANDLORD TREES OF THE GIANT BANYAM COMPLEX STAND MOTIONLESS, ARMS GROWING INTO EACH OTHER'S SHOULDERS, LISTENING TO THE RESIDENTS LIVING IN THEIR BELLIES.
THE BANYAMS, HEARING ALL THAT OCCURS WITHIN THEM, REPEAT NOTHING.
IN A SUBLIMELY FURNISHED HOLLOW THAT THEY LEASE UPON THE NINTH LEVEL, DISMA AND LOCLISS MATE BEHIND SCREENS OF PAINTED SKIN TO AVOID EMBARRASSING THE ROOM.
IDEALLY MATCHED, PAINFULLY IN LOVE, THEY ARE SURELY THE PERFECT COUPLE.
LOCLISS WORKS IN OLFACTORY DECORATION. DISMA MANAGES A CHEMICAL RESTAURANT. COME FALL, THEY HOPE TO MARRY BEFORE A PRIEST OF O.
FERTILIZATION ACCOMPLISHED, THEY DISENGAGE WITH TENDERNESS, WITH GREAT CARE.
G-3082
DRESSING, LOCLISS PULLS ON HIS PICKLED GOWN, DISMA HER SHIRT OF ALBINO HAIR. BOTH SAVOR THE INAPPROPRIATE SHYNESS THAT FALLS BETWEEN THEM.
PAINTED SCREENS ARE FOLDED, STACKED AWAY. DIPLOMATICALLY, THE ROOM ASKS IF THEIR SLEEP WAS ENJOYABLE.
THEY NOD, EXCHANGING GLANCES, AND THE BANYAM SMILES INDULGENTLY. THEY STEP THROUGH ITS SMILE INTO THE SULTRY AFTERNOON.
ON THE BRANCHWAY, RUSTLING CROWDS STROLL IN SLANTED SUNLIGHT. TWIGS ENTWINED, THE LOVERS SHUFFLE LAUGHING TO JOIN THEM.
1

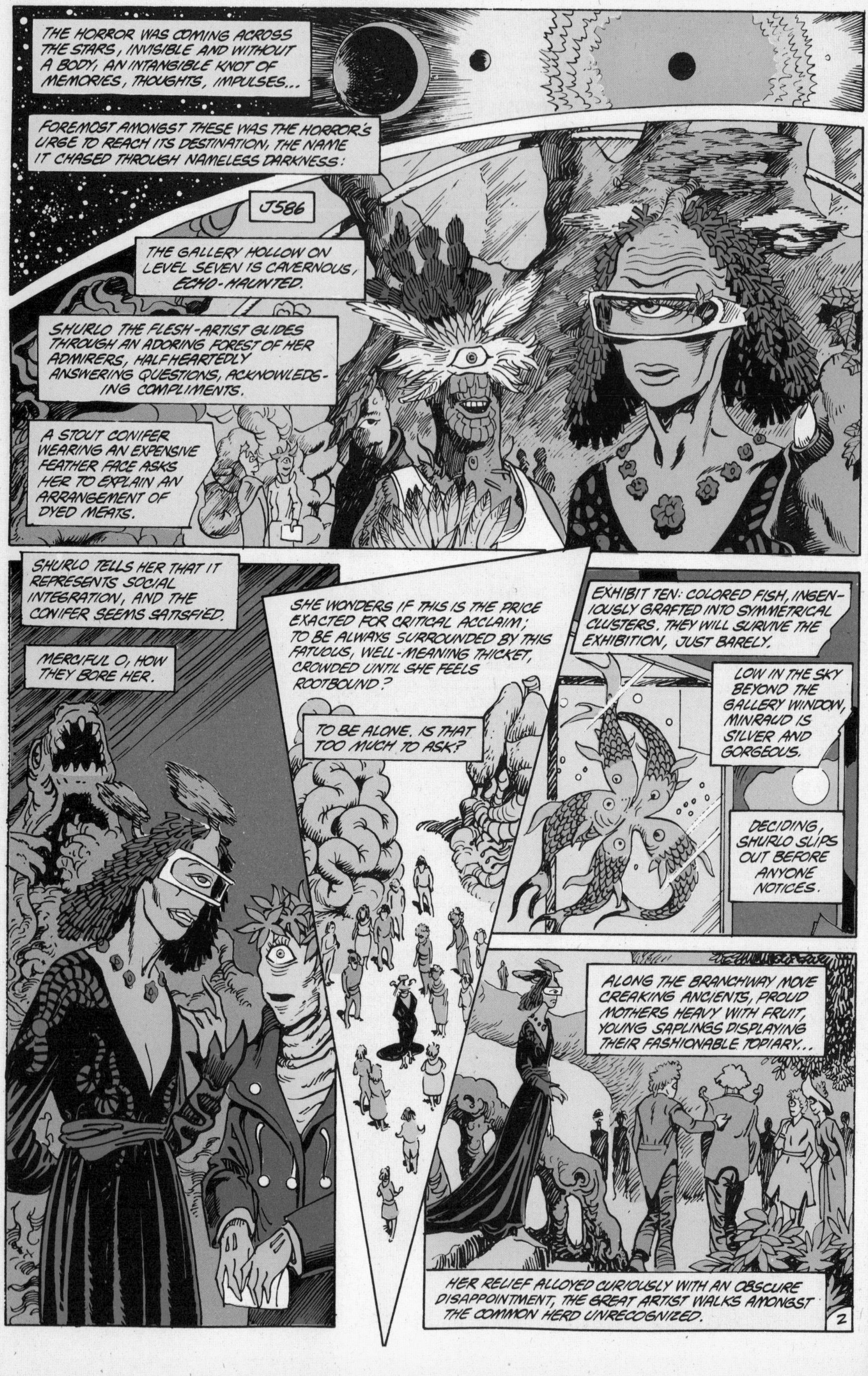
THE HORROR WAS COMING ACROSS THE STARS, INVISIBLE AND WITHOUT A BODY; AN INTANGIBLE KNOT OF MEMORIES, THOUGHTS, IMPULSES...
FOREMOST AMONGST THESE WAS THE HORROR'S URGE TO REACH ITS DESTINATION, THE NAME IT CHASED THROUGH NAMELESS DARKNESS:
J586
THE GALLERY HOLLOW ON LEVEL SEVEN IS CAVERNOUS, ECHO-HAUNTED.
SHURLO THE FLESH-ARTIST GLIDES THROUGH AN ADORING FOREST OF HER ADMIRERS, HALFHEARTEDLY ANSWERING QUESTIONS, ACKNOWLEDGING COMPLIMENTS.
A STOUT CONIFER WEARING AN EXPENSIVE FEATHER FACE ASKS HER TO EXPLAIN AN ARRANGEMENT OF DYED MEATS.
SHURLO TELLS HER THAT IT REPRESENTS SOCIAL INTEGRATION, AND THE CONIFER SEEMS SATISFIED.
MERCIFUL O, HOW THEY BORE HER.
SHE WONDERS IF THIS IS THE PRICE EXACTED FOR CRITICAL ACCLAIM; TO BE ALWAYS SURROUNDED BY THIS FATUOUS, WELL-MEANING THICKET, CROWDED UNTIL SHE FEELS ROOTBOUND?
TO BE ALONE. IS THAT TOO MUCH TO ASK?
EXHIBIT TEN: COLORED FISH, INGENIOUSLY GRAFTED INTO SYMMETRICAL CLUSTERS. THEY WILL SURVIVE THE EXHIBITION, JUST BARELY.
LOW IN THE SKY BEYOND THE GALLERY WINDOW, MINRAUD IS SILVER AND GORGEOUS.
DECIDING, SHURLO SLIPS OUT BEFORE ANYONE NOTICES.
ALONG THE BRANCHWAY MOVE CREAKING ANCIENTS, PROUD MOTHERS HEAVY WITH FRUIT, YOUNG SAPLINGS DISPLAYING THEIR FASHIONABLE TOPIARY...
HER RELIEF ALLOYED CURIOUSLY WITH AN OBSCURE DISAPPOINTMENT, THE GREAT ARTIST WALKS AMONGST THE COMMON HERD UNRECOGNIZED.
2

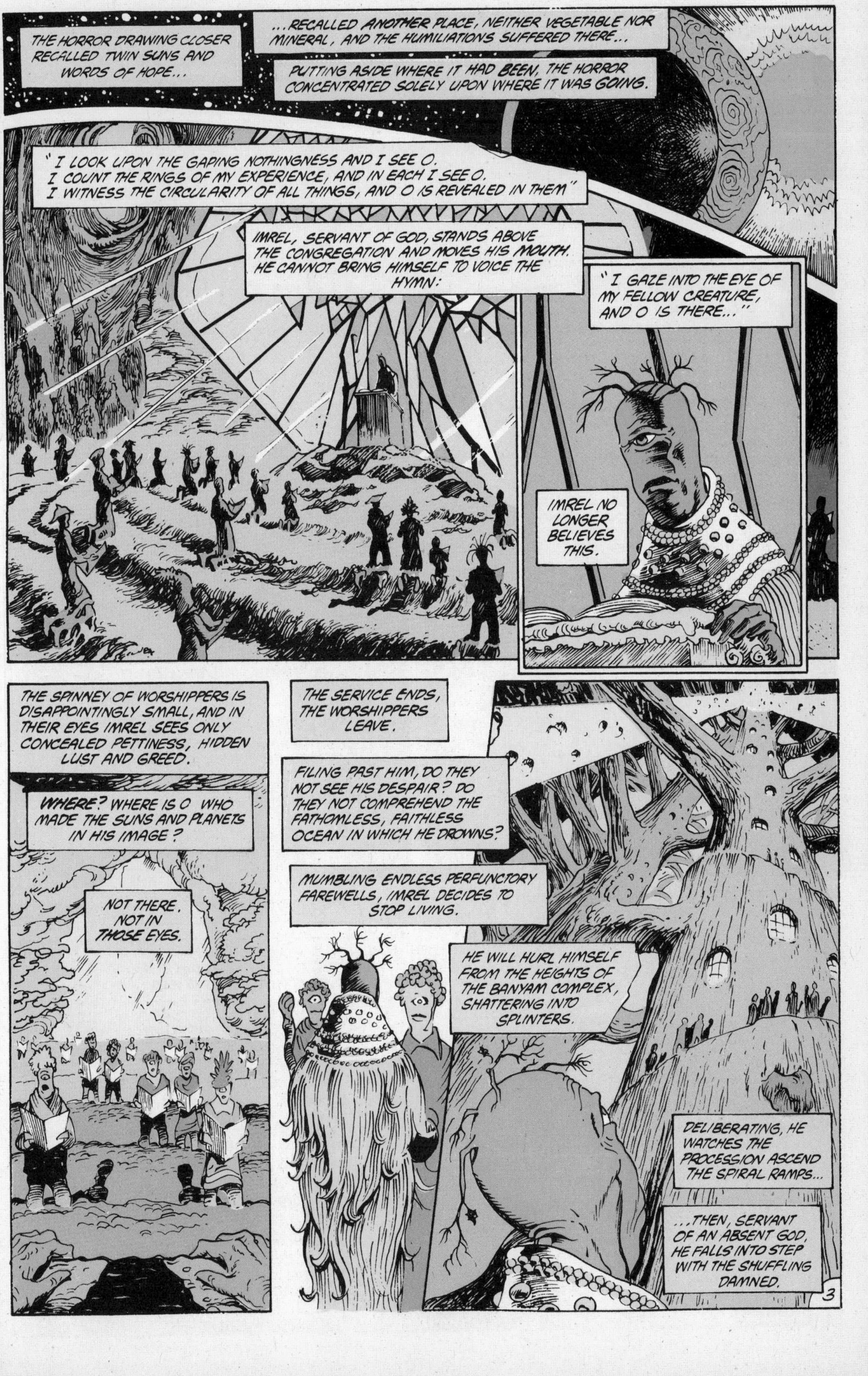
THE HORROR DRAWING CLOSER RECALLED TWIN SUNS AND WORDS OF HOPE...
...RECALLED ANOTHER PLACE, NEITHER VEGETABLE NOR MINERAL, AND THE HUMILIATIONS SUFFERED THERE...
PUTTING ASIDE WHERE IT HAD BEEN, THE HORROR CONCENTRATED SOLELY UPON WHERE IT WAS GOING.
"I LOOK UPON THE GAPING NOTHINGNESS AND I SEE O. I COUNT THE RINGS OF MY EXPERIENCE, AND IN EACH I SEE O. I WITNESS THE CIRCULARITY OF ALL THINGS, AND O IS REVEALED IN THEM"
IMREL, SERVANT OF GOD, STANDS ABOVE THE CONGREGATION AND MOVES HIS MOUTH. HE CANNOT BRING HIMSELF TO VOICE THE HYMN:
"I GAZE INTO THE EYE OF MY FELLOW CREATURE, AND O IS THERE..."
IMREL NO LONGER BELIEVES THIS.
THE SPINNEY OF WORSHIPPERS IS DISAPPOINTINGLY SMALL, AND IN THEIR EYES IMREL SEES ONLY CONCEALED PETTINESS, HIDDEN LUST AND GREED.
WHERE? WHERE IS O WHO MADE THE SUNS AND PLANETS IN HIS IMAGE?
NOT THERE. NOT IN THOSE EYES.
THE SERVICE ENDS, THE WORSHIPPERS LEAVE.
FILING PAST HIM, DO THEY NOT SEE HIS DESPAIR? DO THEY NOT COMPREHEND THE FATHOMLESS, FAITHLESS OCEAN IN WHICH HE DROWNS?
MUMBLING ENDLESS PERFUNCTORY FAREWELLS, IMREL DECIDES TO STOP LIVING.
HE WILL HURL HIMSELF FROM THE HEIGHTS OF THE BANYAM COMPLEX, SHATTERING INTO SPLINTERS.
DELIBERATING, HE WATCHES THE PROCESSION ASCEND THE SPIRAL RAMPS...
...THEN, SERVANT OF AN ABSENT GOD, HE FALLS INTO STEP WITH THE SHUFFLING DAMNED.
3

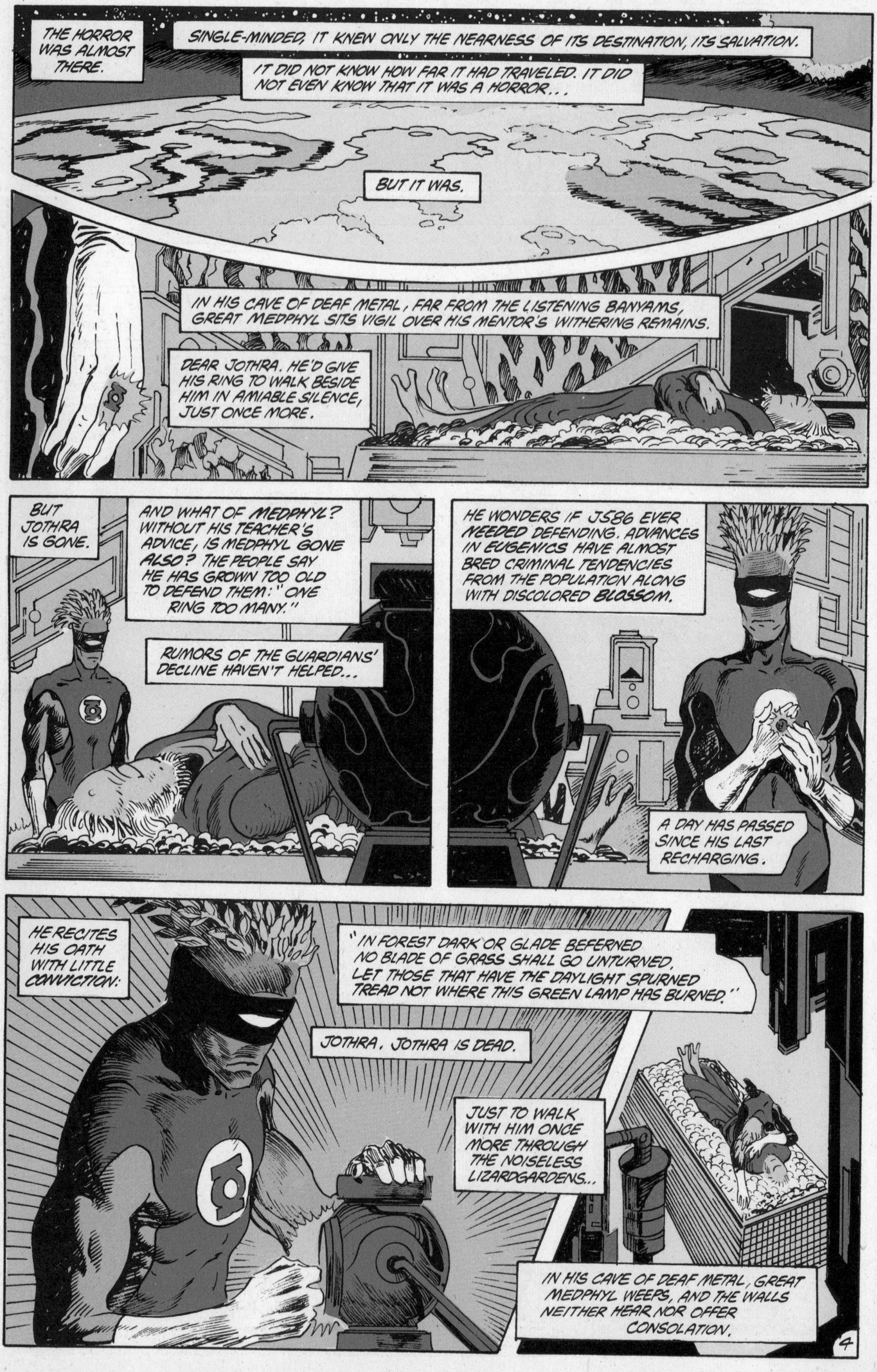
THE HORROR WAS ALMOST THERE.
SINGLE-MINDED, IT KNEW ONLY THE NEARNESS OF ITS DESTINATION, ITS SALVATION.
IT DID NOT KNOW HOW FAR IT HAD TRAVELED. IT DID NOT EVEN KNOW THAT IT WAS A HORROR...
BUT IT WAS.
IN HIS CAVE OF DEAF METAL, FAR FROM THE LISTENING BANYAMS, GREAT MEDPHYL SITS VIGIL OVER HIS MENTOR'S WITHERING REMAINS.
DEAR JOTHRA. HE'D GIVE HIS RING TO WALK BESIDE HIM IN AMIABLE SILENCE, JUST ONCE MORE.
BUT JOTHRA IS GONE.
AND WHAT OF MEDPHYL? WITHOUT HIS TEACHER'S ADVICE, IS MEDPHYL GONE ALSO? THE PEOPLE SAY HE HAS GROWN TOO OLD TO DEFEND THEM: "ONE RING TOO MANY."
RUMORS OF THE GUARDIANS' DECLINE HAVEN'T HELPED...
HE WONDERS IF J586 EVER NEEDED DEFENDING. ADVANCES IN EUGENICS HAVE ALMOST BRED CRIMINAL TENDENCIES FROM THE POPULATION ALONG WITH DISCOLORED BLOSSOM.
A DAY HAS PASSED SINCE HIS LAST RECHARGING.
HE RECITES HIS OATH WITH LITTLE CONVICTION:
"IN FOREST DARK OR GLADE BEFERNED NO BLADE OF GRASS SHALL GO UNTURNED, LET THOSE THAT HAVE THE DAYLIGHT SPURNED TREAD NOT WHERE THIS GREEN LAMP HAS BURNED."
JOTHRA. JOTHRA IS DEAD.
JUST TO WALK WITH HIM ONCE MORE THROUGH THE NOISELESS LIZARDGARDENS...
IN HIS CAVE OF DEAF METAL, GREAT MEDPHYL WEEPS, AND THE WALLS NEITHER HEAR NOR OFFER CONSOLATION.
4

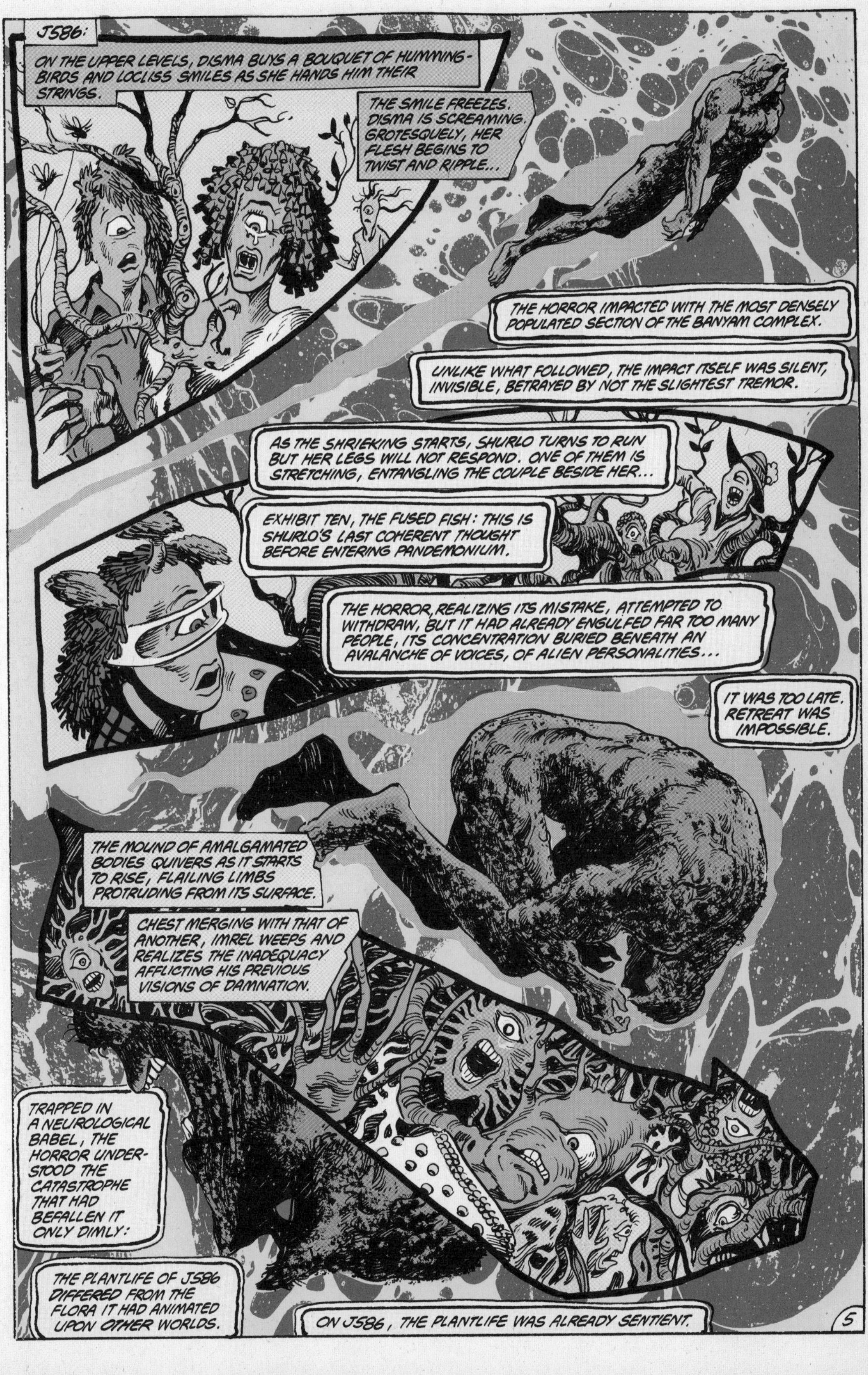
J586:
ON THE UPPER LEVELS, DISMA BUYS A BOUQUET OF HUMMING-BIRDS AND LOCLISS SMILES AS SHE HANDS HIM THEIR STRINGS.
THE SMILE FREEZES. DISMA IS SCREAMING. GROTESQUELY, HER FLESH BEGINS TO TWIST AND RIPPLE...
THE HORROR IMPACTED WITH THE MOST DENSELY POPULATED SECTION OF THE BANYAM COMPLEX.
UNLIKE WHAT FOLLOWED, THE IMPACT ITSELF WAS SILENT, INVISIBLE, BETRAYED BY NOT THE SLIGHTEST TREMOR.
AS THE SHRIEKING STARTS, SHURLO TURNS TO RUN BUT HER LEGS WILL NOT RESPOND. ONE OF THEM IS STRETCHING, ENTANGLING THE COUPLE BESIDE HER...
EXHIBIT TEN, THE FUSED FISH: THIS IS SHURLO'S LAST COHERENT THOUGHT BEFORE ENTERING PANDEMONIUM.
THE HORROR, REALIZING ITS MISTAKE, ATTEMPTED TO WITHDRAW, BUT IT HAD ALREADY ENGULFED FAR TOO MANY PEOPLE, ITS CONCENTRATION BURIED BENEATH AN AVALANCHE OF VOICES, OF ALIEN PERSONALITIES...
IT WAS TOO LATE. RETREAT WAS IMPOSSIBLE.
THE MOUND OF AMALGAMATED BODIES QUIVERS AS IT STARTS TO RISE, FLAILING LIMBS PROTRUDING FROM ITS SURFACE.
CHEST MERGING WITH THAT OF ANOTHER, IMREL WEEPS AND REALIZES THE INADEQUACY AFFLICTING HIS PREVIOUS VISIONS OF DAMNATION.
TRAPPED IN A NEUROLOGICAL BABEL, THE HORROR UNDER-STOOD THE CATASTROPHE THAT HAD BEFALLEN IT ONLY DIMLY:
THE PLANTLIFE OF J586 DIFFERED FROM THE FLORA IT HAD ANIMATED UPON OTHER WORLDS.
ON J586, THE PLANTLIFE WAS ALREADY SENTIENT.
5

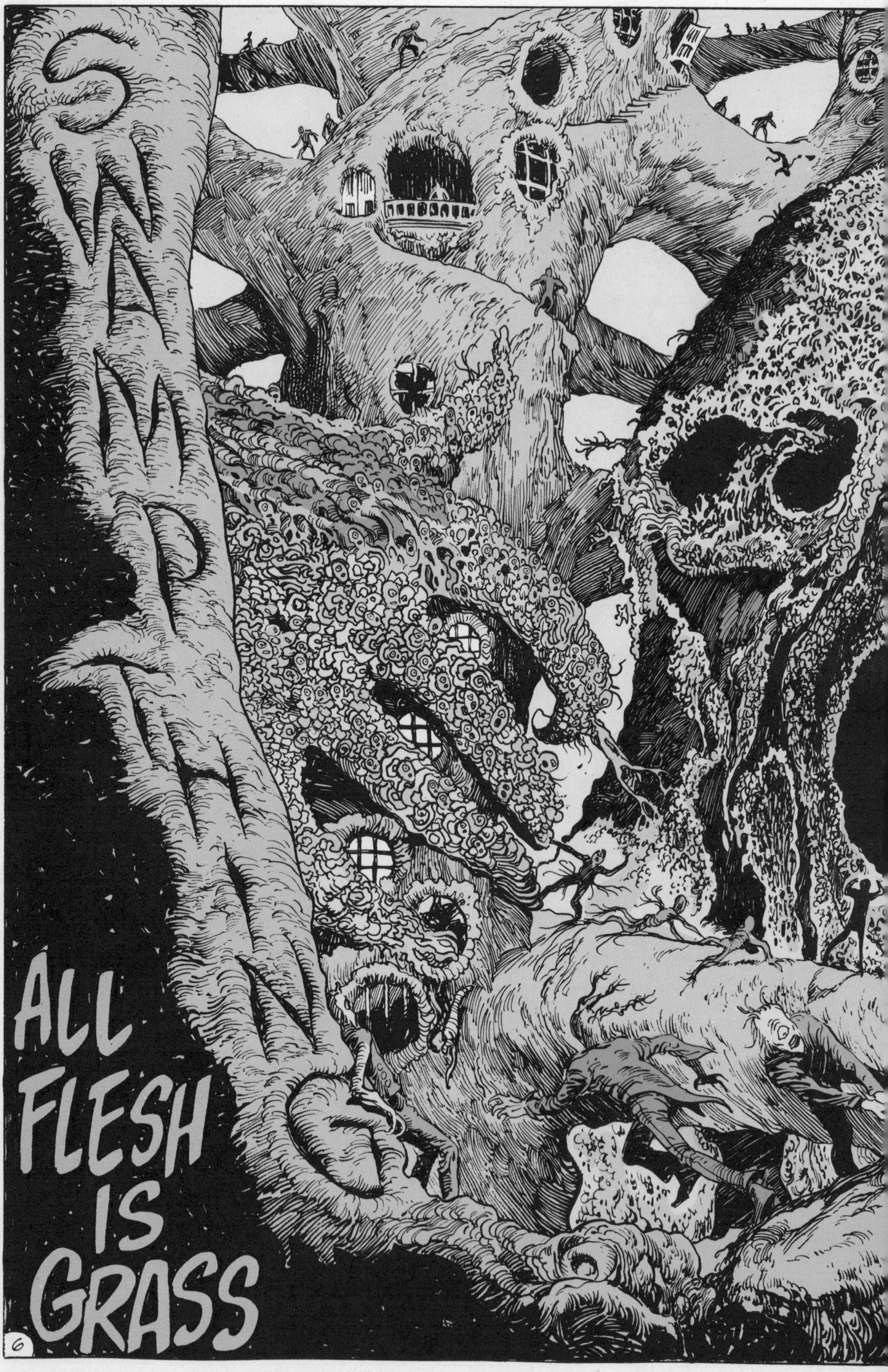
SWAMP THING
ALL FLESH IS GRASS
6

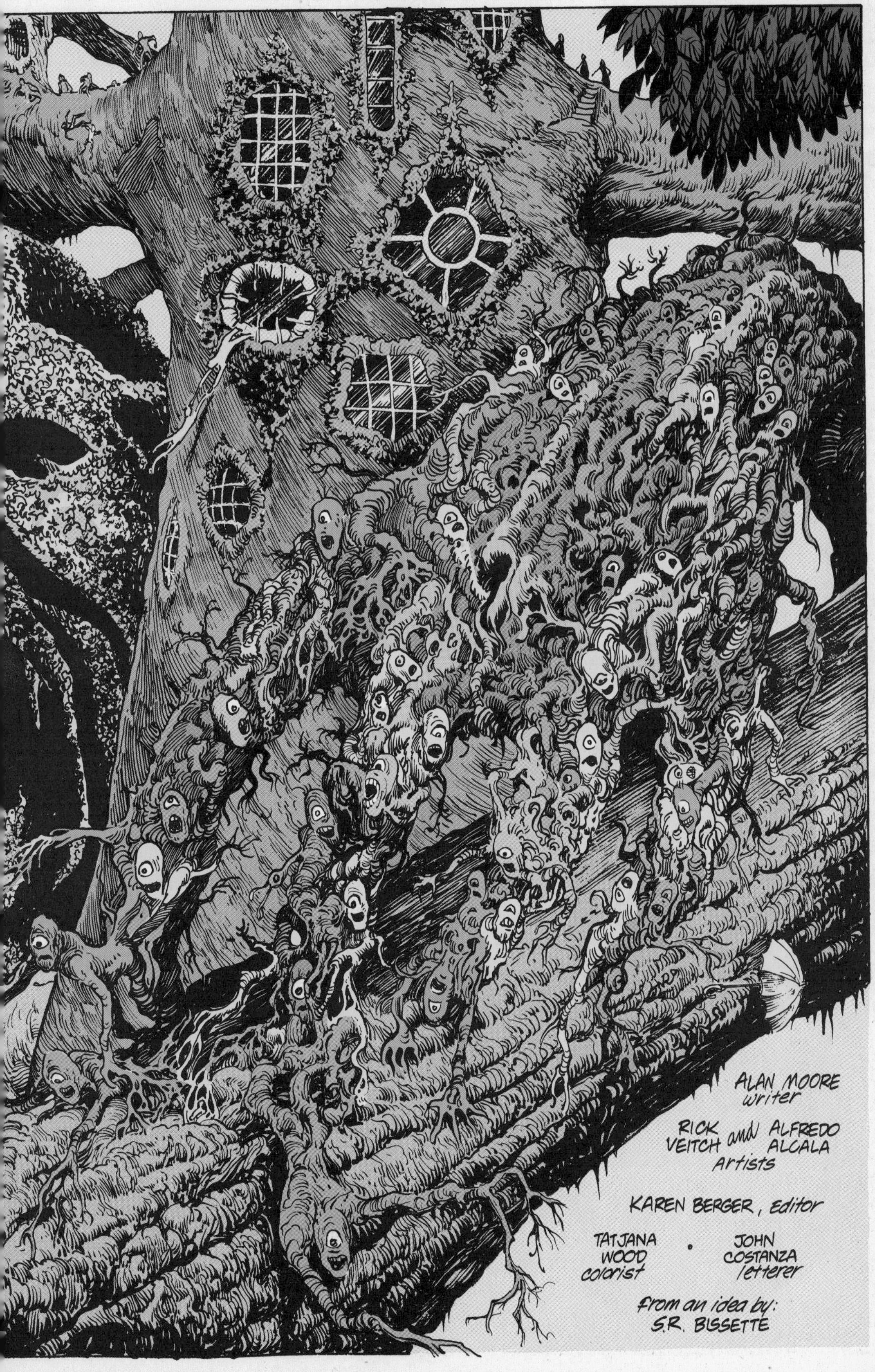
ALAN MOORE
writer
RICK VEITCH and ALFREDO ALCALA
Artists
KAREN BERGER, Editor
TATJANA WOOD
colorist
JOHN COSTANZA
letterer
from an idea by:
S.R. BISSETTE

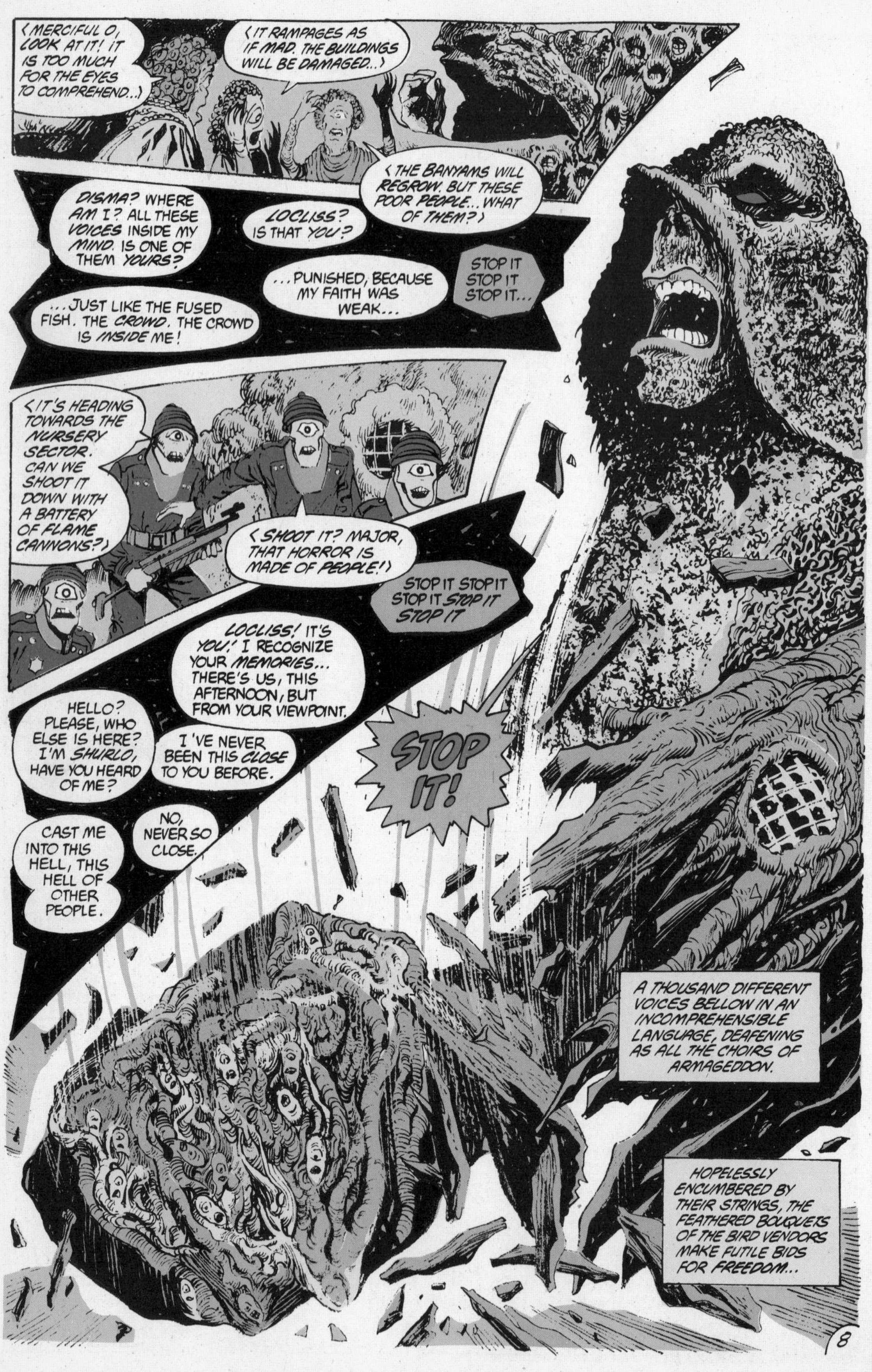

⟨MERCIFUL O, LOOK AT IT! IT IS TOO MUCH FOR THE EYES TO COMPREHEND...⟩
⟨IT RAMPAGES AS IF MAD. THE BUILDINGS WILL BE DAMAGED...⟩
⟨THE BANYAMS WILL REGROW. BUT THESE POOR PEOPLE... WHAT OF THEM?⟩
DISMA? WHERE AM I? ALL THESE VOICES INSIDE MY MIND. IS ONE OF THEM YOURS?
LOCLISS? IS THAT YOU?
...PUNISHED, BECAUSE MY FAITH WAS WEAK...
STOP IT STOP IT STOP IT...
...JUST LIKE THE FUSED FISH. THE CROWD. THE CROWD IS INSIDE ME!
⟨IT'S HEADING TOWARDS THE NURSERY SECTOR. CAN WE SHOOT IT DOWN WITH A BATTERY OF FLAME CANNONS?⟩
⟨SHOOT IT? MAJOR, THAT HORROR IS MADE OF PEOPLE!⟩
STOP IT STOP IT STOP IT STOP IT STOP IT
LOCLISS! IT'S YOU! I RECOGNIZE YOUR MEMORIES... THERE'S US, THIS AFTERNOON, BUT FROM YOUR VIEWPOINT.
HELLO? PLEASE, WHO ELSE IS HERE? I'M SHURLO, HAVE YOU HEARD OF ME?
I'VE NEVER BEEN THIS CLOSE TO YOU BEFORE.
STOP IT!
CAST ME INTO THIS HELL, THIS HELL OF OTHER PEOPLE.
NO, NEVER SO CLOSE.
A THOUSAND DIFFERENT VOICES BELLOW IN AN INCOMPREHENSIBLE LANGUAGE, DEAFENING AS ALL THE CHOIRS OF ARMAGEDDON.
HOPELESSLY ENCUMBERED BY THEIR STRINGS, THE FEATHERED BOUQUETS OF THE BIRD VENDORS MAKE FUTILE BIDS FOR FREEDOM...
8

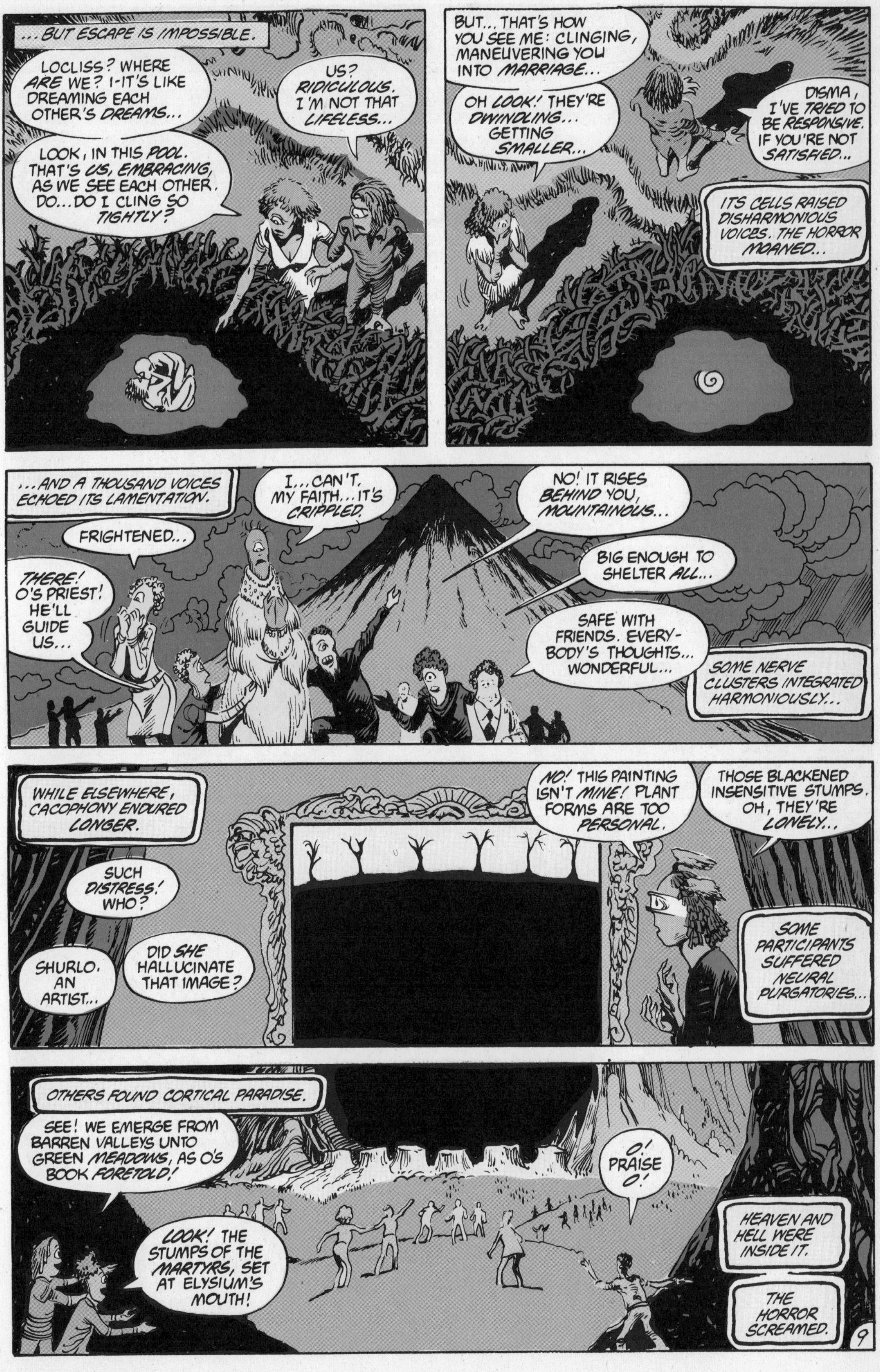
...BUT ESCAPE IS IMPOSSIBLE.
LOCLISS? WHERE ARE WE? I-IT'S LIKE DREAMING EACH OTHER'S DREAMS...
US? RIDICULOUS. I'M NOT THAT LIFELESS...
LOOK, IN THIS POOL. THAT'S US, EMBRACING, AS WE SEE EACH OTHER. DO...DO I CLING SO TIGHTLY?
BUT... THAT'S HOW YOU SEE ME: CLINGING, MANEUVERING YOU INTO MARRIAGE...
OH LOOK! THEY'RE DWINDLING... GETTING SMALLER...
DISMA, I'VE TRIED TO BE RESPONSIVE. IF YOU'RE NOT SATISFIED...
ITS CELLS RAISED DISHARMONIOUS VOICES. THE HORROR MOANED...
...AND A THOUSAND VOICES ECHOED ITS LAMENTATION.
I...CAN'T. MY FAITH...IT'S CRIPPLED.
NO! IT RISES BEHIND YOU, MOUNTAINOUS...
FRIGHTENED...
BIG ENOUGH TO SHELTER ALL...
THERE! O'S PRIEST! HE'LL GUIDE US...
SAFE WITH FRIENDS. EVERY-BODY'S THOUGHTS... WONDERFUL...
SOME NERVE CLUSTERS INTEGRATED HARMONIOUSLY...
WHILE ELSEWHERE, CACOPHONY ENDURED LONGER.
NO! THIS PAINTING ISN'T MINE! PLANT FORMS ARE TOO PERSONAL.
THOSE BLACKENED INSENSITIVE STUMPS. OH, THEY'RE LONELY...
SUCH DISTRESS! WHO?
SHURLO. AN ARTIST...
DID SHE HALLUCINATE THAT IMAGE?
SOME PARTICIPANTS SUFFERED NEURAL PURGATORIES...
OTHERS FOUND CORTICAL PARADISE.
SEE! WE EMERGE FROM BARREN VALLEYS UNTO GREEN MEADOWS, AS O'S BOOK FORETOLD!
O! PRAISE O!
LOOK! THE STUMPS OF THE MARTYRS, SET AT ELYSIUM'S MOUTH!
HEAVEN AND HELL WERE INSIDE IT.
THE HORROR SCREAMED.
9

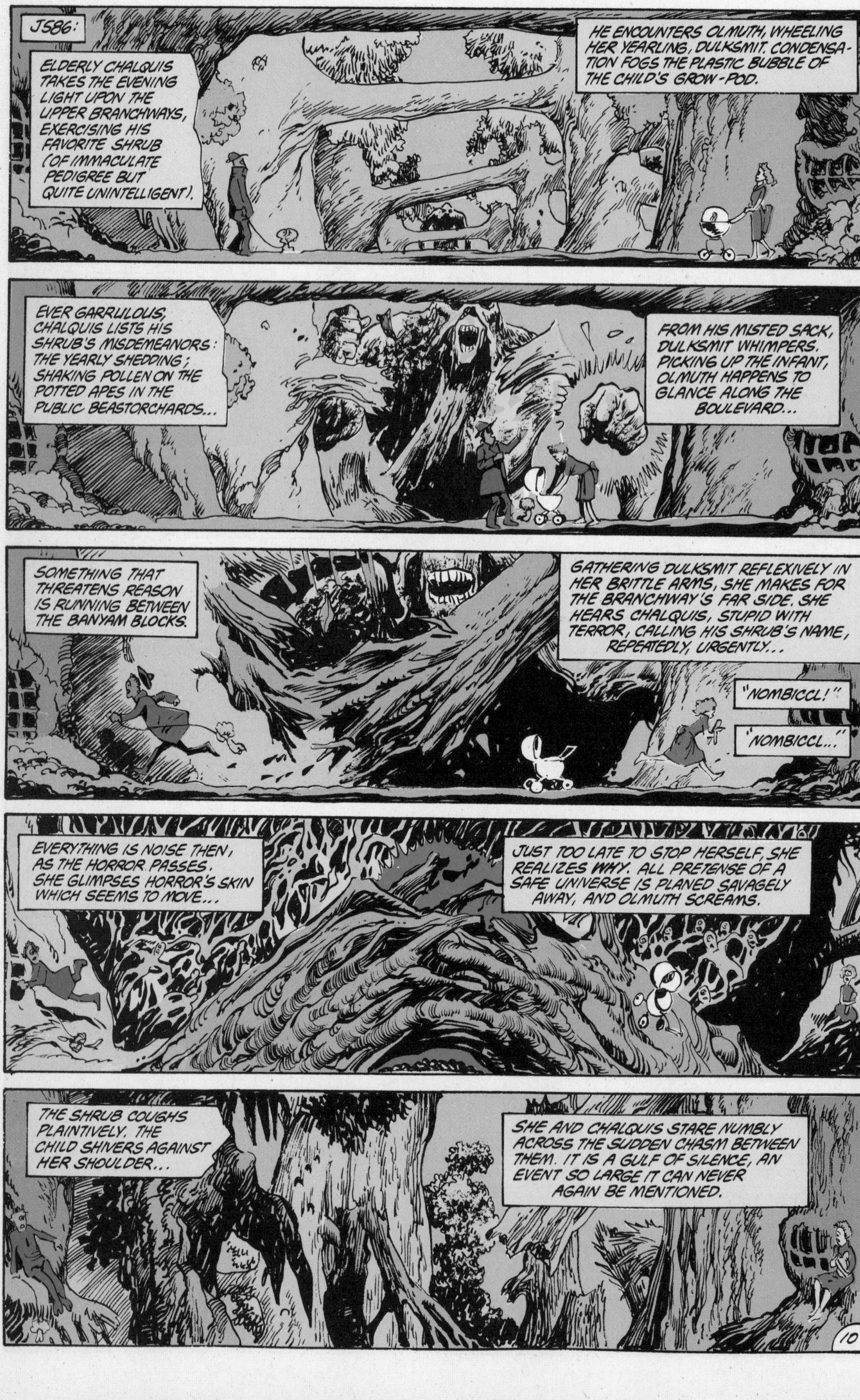
JS86:
ELDERLY CHALQUIS TAKES THE EVENING LIGHT UPON THE UPPER BRANCHWAYS, EXERCISING HIS FAVORITE SHRUB (OF IMMACULATE PEDIGREE BUT QUITE UNINTELLIGENT).
HE ENCOUNTERS OLMUTH, WHEELING HER YEARLING, DULKSMIT. CONDENSATION FOGS THE PLASTIC BUBBLE OF THE CHILD'S GROW-POD.
EVER GARRULOUS, CHALQUIS LISTS HIS SHRUB'S MISDEMEANORS: THE YEARLY SHEDDING; SHAKING POLLEN ON THE POTTED APES IN THE PUBLIC BEASTORCHARDS...
FROM HIS MISTED SACK, DULKSMIT WHIMPERS. PICKING UP THE INFANT, OLMUTH HAPPENS TO GLANCE ALONG THE BOULEVARD...
SOMETHING THAT THREATENS REASON IS RUNNING BETWEEN THE BANYAM BLOCKS.
GATHERING DULKSMIT REFLEXIVELY IN HER BRITTLE ARMS, SHE MAKES FOR THE BRANCHWAY'S FAR SIDE. SHE HEARS CHALQUIS, STUPID WITH TERROR, CALLING HIS SHRUB'S NAME, REPEATEDLY, URGENTLY...
"NOMBICCL!"
"NOMBICCL..."
EVERYTHING IS NOISE THEN, AS THE HORROR PASSES. SHE GLIMPSES HORROR'S SKIN WHICH SEEMS TO MOVE...
JUST TOO LATE TO STOP HERSELF, SHE REALIZES WHY. ALL PRETENSE OF A SAFE UNIVERSE IS PLANED SAVAGELY AWAY, AND OLMUTH SCREAMS.
THE SHRUB COUGHS PLAINTIVELY. THE CHILD SHIVERS AGAINST HER SHOULDER...
SHE AND CHALQUIS STARE NUMBLY ACROSS THE SUDDEN CHASM BETWEEN THEM. IT IS A GULF OF SILENCE, AN EVENT SO LARGE IT CAN NEVER AGAIN BE MENTIONED.
10

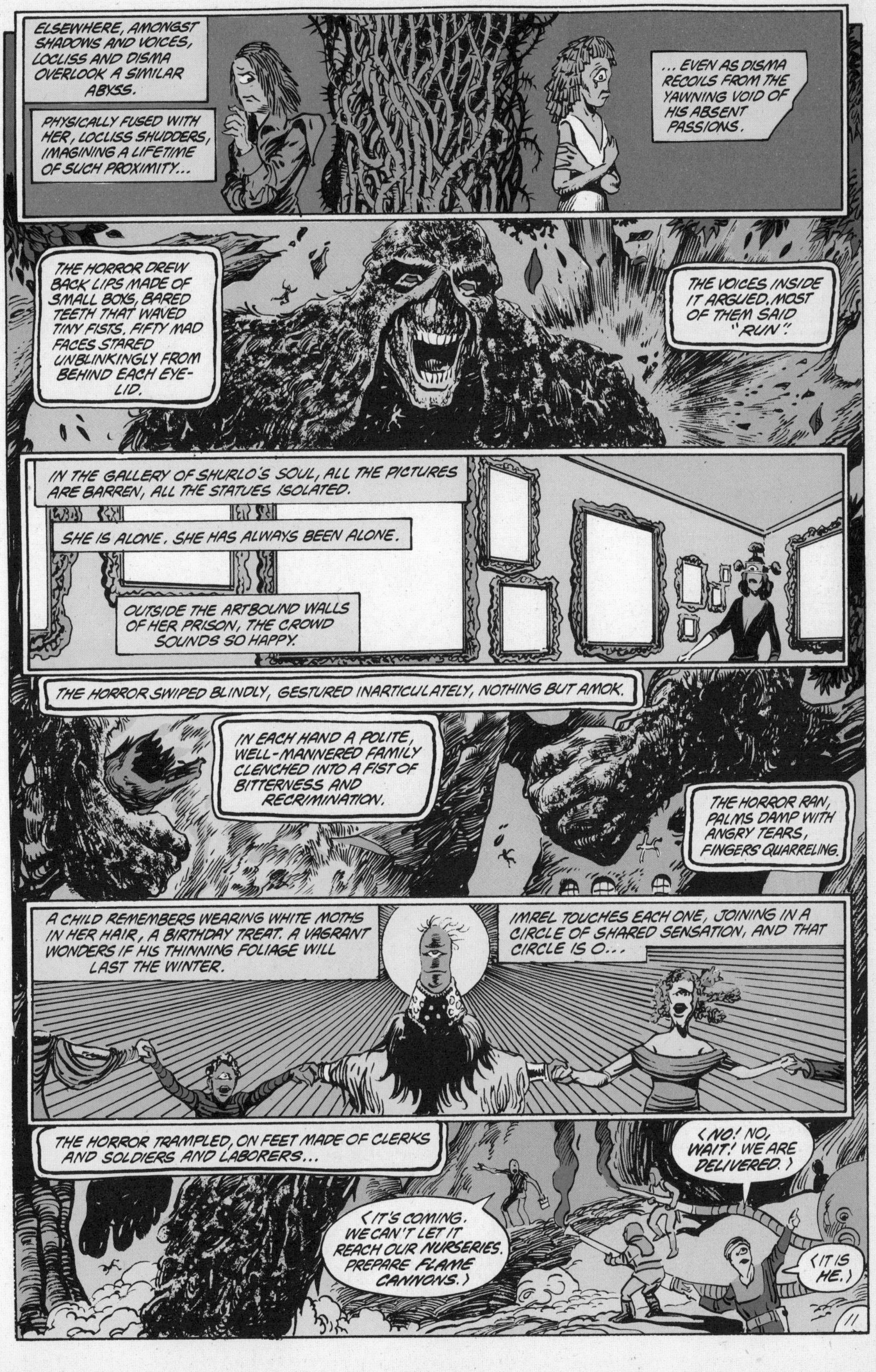
ELSEWHERE, AMONGST SHADOWS AND VOICES, LOCLISS AND DISMA OVERLOOK A SIMILAR ABYSS.
PHYSICALLY FUSED WITH HER, LOCLISS SHUDDERS, IMAGINING A LIFETIME OF SUCH PROXIMITY...
...EVEN AS DISMA RECOILS FROM THE YAWNING VOID OF HIS ABSENT PASSIONS.
THE HORROR DREW BACK LIPS MADE OF SMALL BOYS, BARED TEETH THAT WAVED TINY FISTS. FIFTY MAD FACES STARED UNBLINKINGLY FROM BEHIND EACH EYE-LID.
THE VOICES INSIDE IT ARGUED. MOST OF THEM SAID "RUN".
IN THE GALLERY OF SHURLO'S SOUL, ALL THE PICTURES ARE BARREN, ALL THE STATUES ISOLATED.
SHE IS ALONE. SHE HAS ALWAYS BEEN ALONE.
OUTSIDE THE ARTBOUND WALLS OF HER PRISON, THE CROWD SOUNDS SO HAPPY.
THE HORROR SWIPED BLINDLY, GESTURED INARTICULATELY, NOTHING BUT AMOK.
IN EACH HAND A POLITE, WELL-MANNERED FAMILY CLENCHED INTO A FIST OF BITTERNESS AND RECRIMINATION.
THE HORROR RAN, PALMS DAMP WITH ANGRY TEARS, FINGERS QUARRELING.
A CHILD REMEMBERS WEARING WHITE MOTHS IN HER HAIR, A BIRTHDAY TREAT. A VAGRANT WONDERS IF HIS THINNING FOLIAGE WILL LAST THE WINTER.
IMREL TOUCHES EACH ONE, JOINING IN A CIRCLE OF SHARED SENSATION, AND THAT CIRCLE IS O...
THE HORROR TRAMPLED, ON FEET MADE OF CLERKS AND SOLDIERS AND LABORERS...
<NO! NO, WAIT! WE ARE DELIVERED.>
<IT'S COMING. WE CAN'T LET IT REACH OUR NURSERIES. PREPARE FLAME CANNONS.>
<IT IS HE.>
11

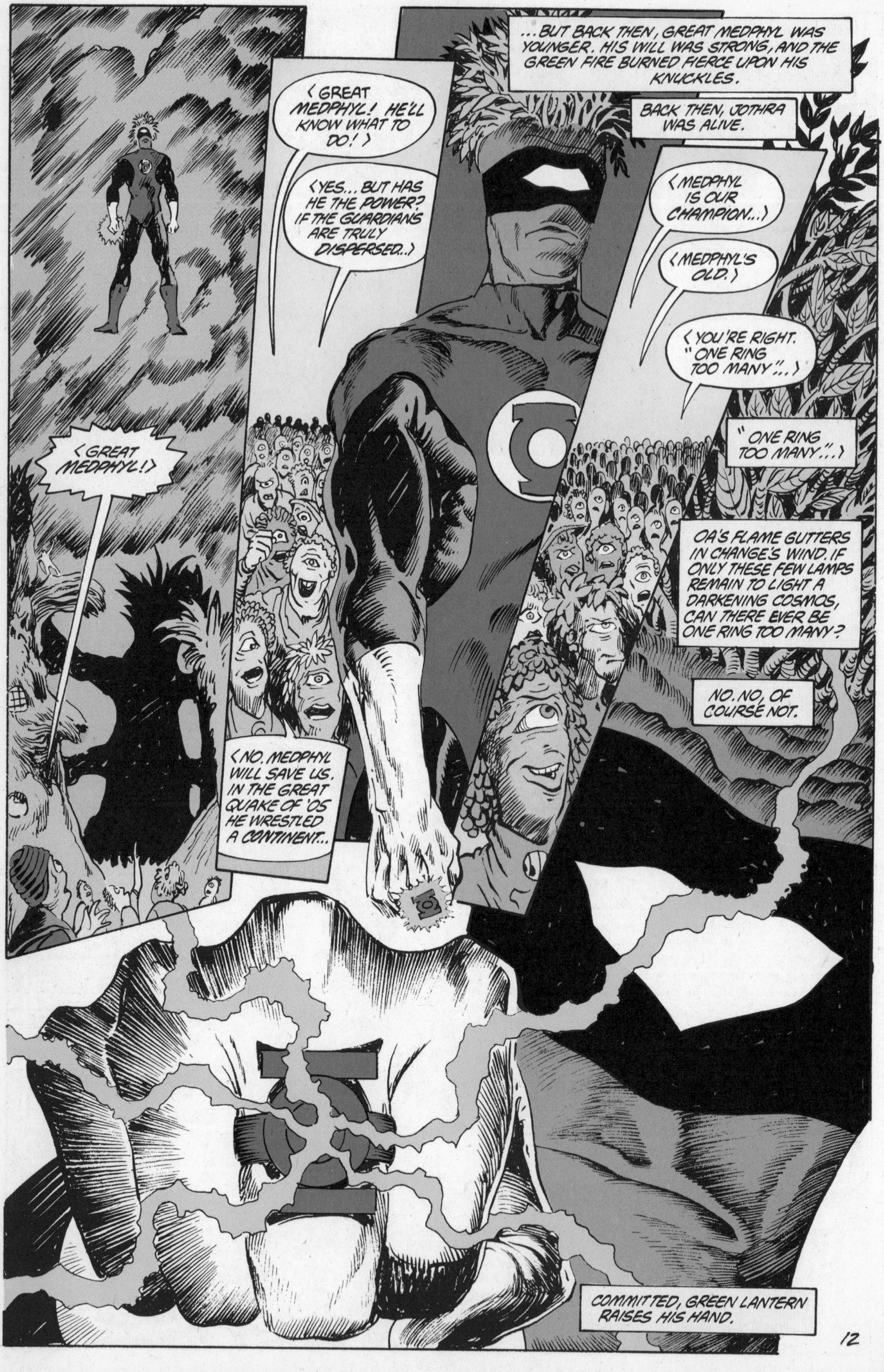
...BUT BACK THEN, GREAT MEDPHYL WAS YOUNGER. HIS WILL WAS STRONG, AND THE GREEN FIRE BURNED FIERCE UPON HIS KNUCKLES.
BACK THEN, JOTHRA WAS ALIVE.
< GREAT MEDPHYL! >
< GREAT MEDPHYL! HE'LL KNOW WHAT TO DO! >
< YES... BUT HAS HE THE POWER? IF THE GUARDIANS ARE TRULY DISPERSED...>
< NO. MEDPHYL WILL SAVE US. IN THE GREAT QUAKE OF 'OS HE WRESTLED A CONTINENT...
< MEDPHYL IS OUR CHAMPION...>
< MEDPHYL'S OLD. >
< YOU'RE RIGHT. "ONE RING TOO MANY"...>
"ONE RING TOO MANY"...>
OA'S FLAME GUTTERS IN CHANGE'S WIND. IF ONLY THESE FEW LAMPS REMAIN TO LIGHT A DARKENING COSMOS, CAN THERE EVER BE ONE RING TOO MANY?
NO. NO, OF COURSE NOT.
COMMITTED, GREEN LANTERN RAISES HIS HAND.
12

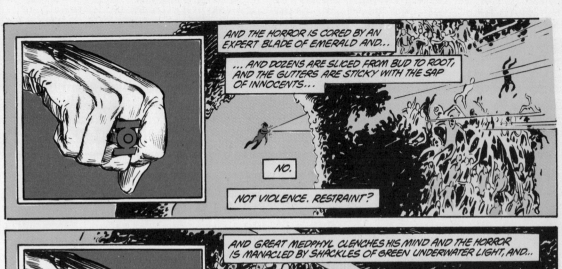

AND THE HORROR IS CORED BY AN EXPERT BLADE OF EMERALD AND...

...AND DOZENS ARE SLICED FROM BUD TO ROOT, AND THE GUTTERS ARE STICKY WITH THE SAP OF INNOCENTS...

NO.

NOT VIOLENCE. RESTRAINT?

AND GREAT MEDPHYL CLENCHES HIS MIND AND THE HORROR IS MANACLED BY SHACKLES OF GREEN UNDERWATER LIGHT, AND...

...AND CHILDREN ARE CRUSHED AGAINST AN UNYIELDING PHOSPHORESCENT, SPLINTERING AS THE MONSTER STRUGGLES AGAINST HIS CHAINS...

NO. SOMETHING ELSE. STUNNING IT, PERHAPS...

...AND THE HORROR STAGGERS, THEN TOPPLES, AN AVALANCHE OF SCREAMING TIMBER, A LOGSLIDE OF PEOPLE, AND THEIR UNIDENTIFIABLE FRAGMENTS ARE SCATTERED OVER SEVERAL BLOCKS...

NO, NO, NO, NO!

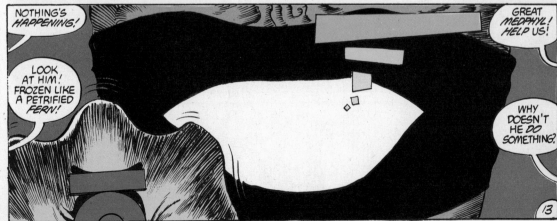

NOTHING'S HAPPENING!

LOOK AT HIM! FROZEN LIKE A PETRIFIED FERN!

GREAT MEDPHYL! HELP US!

WHY DOESN'T HE DO SOMETHING.

13

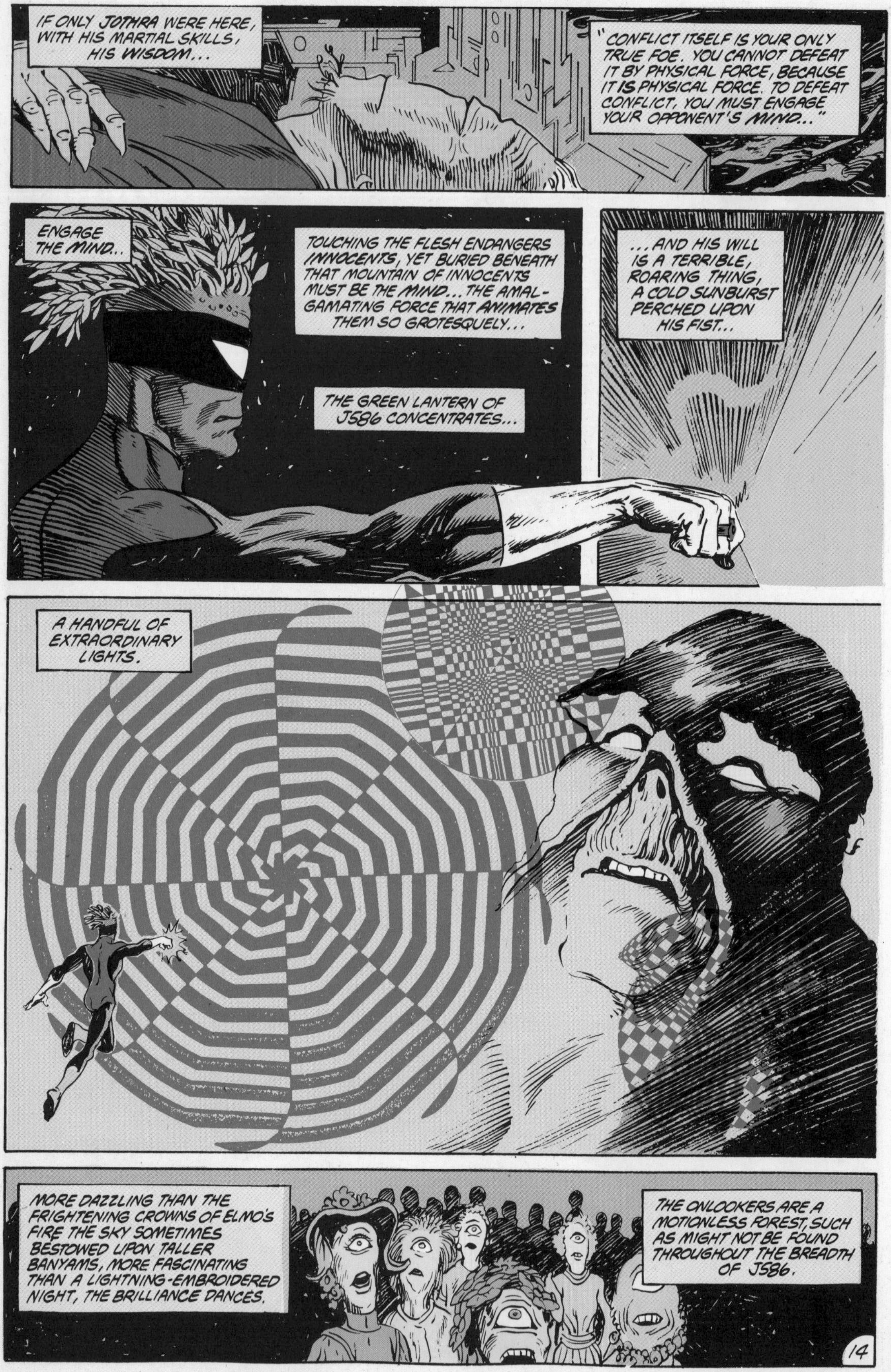
IF ONLY JOTHRA WERE HERE, WITH HIS MARTIAL SKILLS, HIS WISDOM...
"CONFLICT ITSELF IS YOUR ONLY TRUE FOE. YOU CANNOT DEFEAT IT BY PHYSICAL FORCE, BECAUSE IT IS PHYSICAL FORCE. TO DEFEAT CONFLICT, YOU MUST ENGAGE YOUR OPPONENT'S MIND..."
ENGAGE THE MIND...
TOUCHING THE FLESH ENDANGERS INNOCENTS, YET BURIED BENEATH THAT MOUNTAIN OF INNOCENTS MUST BE THE MIND... THE AMAL-GAMATING FORCE THAT ANIMATES THEM SO GROTESQUELY...
THE GREEN LANTERN OF J586 CONCENTRATES...
...AND HIS WILL IS A TERRIBLE, ROARING THING, A COLD SUNBURST PERCHED UPON HIS FIST...
A HANDFUL OF EXTRAORDINARY LIGHTS.
MORE DAZZLING THAN THE FRIGHTENING CROWNS OF ELMO'S FIRE THE SKY SOMETIMES BESTOWED UPON TALLER BANYAMS, MORE FASCINATING THAN A LIGHTNING-EMBROIDERED NIGHT, THE BRILLIANCE DANCES.
THE ONLOOKERS ARE A MOTIONLESS FOREST, SUCH AS MIGHT NOT BE FOUND THROUGHOUT THE BREADTH OF J586.
14

THE HORROR PAUSES, CAPTIVATED BY A MOIRÉ OF FLUORESCENT LIME. TO EITHER SIDE PULSE STROBES OF ELECTRIC JADE. CAREFULLY, MEDPHYL INCREASES THEIR FREQUENCY.

AT NINETEEN CYCLES PER SECOND THE HORROR BECOMES RIGID, TRANSFIXED...

THE MIND OF ANY CORPORATE ENTITY MUST HARBOR SOME DEGREE OF CONFUSION. A CONFUSED MIND IS NOT DIFFICULT TO DISTRACT, OFFERING LITTLE RESISTANCE.

THUS DISTRACTED, THE HORROR MAY PERHAPS BE DISMANTLED.

THIS, AT LEAST, IS MEDPHYL'S PLAN.

THROUGH THE SHIMMERING GLAMOUR, THE GREEN LANTERN EXTRUDES RAY TENTACLES, POWERFUL AND SENSITIVE, ALL THE WHILE MAINTAINING THE STROBING OPTIC DISPLAY.

WITH SOME SATISFACTION HE NOTES THAT HE'D NOT HAVE DARED ATTEMPT THIS AS A YOUNGER BEING.

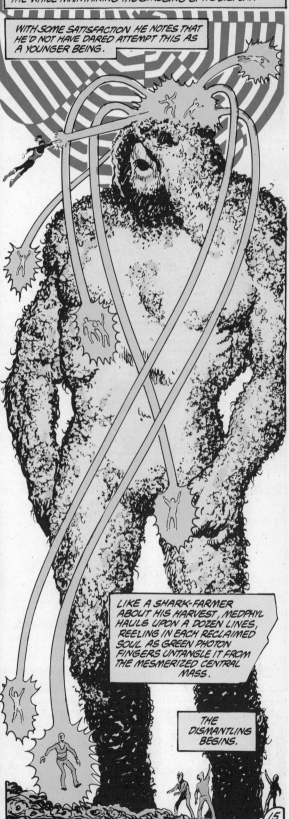

LIKE A SHARK-FARMER ABOUT HIS HARVEST, MEDPHYL HAULS UPON A DOZEN LINES, REELING IN EACH RECLAIMED SOUL AS GREEN PHOTON FINGERS UNTANGLE IT FROM THE MESMERIZED CENTRAL MASS.

THE DISMANTLING BEGINS.

15

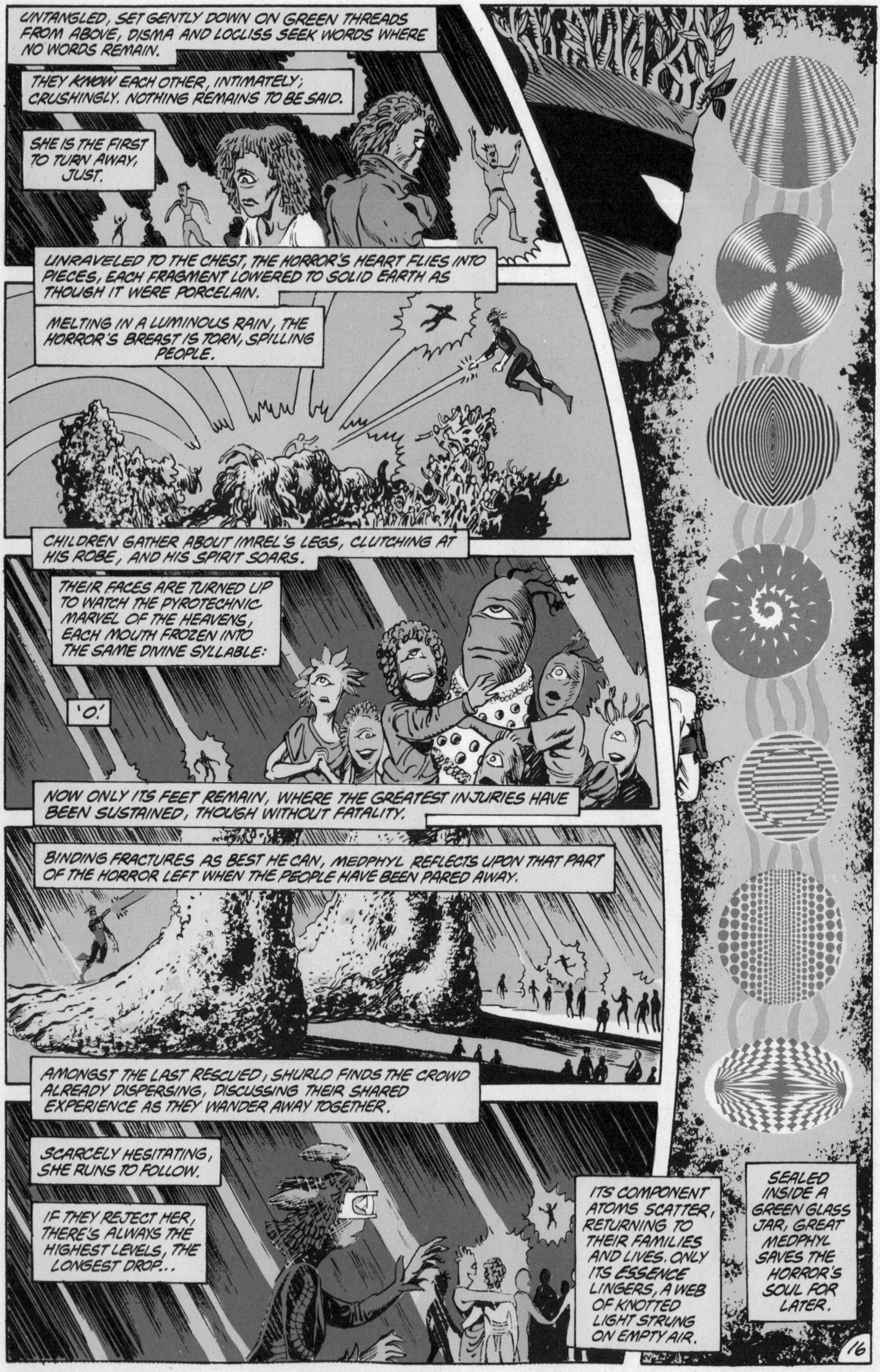
UNTANGLED, SET GENTLY DOWN ON GREEN THREADS FROM ABOVE, DISMA AND LOCLISS SEEK WORDS WHERE NO WORDS REMAIN.
THEY KNOW EACH OTHER, INTIMATELY; CRUSHINGLY. NOTHING REMAINS TO BE SAID.
SHE IS THE FIRST TO TURN AWAY, JUST.
UNRAVELED TO THE CHEST, THE HORROR'S HEART FLIES INTO PIECES, EACH FRAGMENT LOWERED TO SOLID EARTH AS THOUGH IT WERE PORCELAIN.
MELTING IN A LUMINOUS RAIN, THE HORROR'S BREAST IS TORN, SPILLING PEOPLE.
CHILDREN GATHER ABOUT IMREL'S LEGS, CLUTCHING AT HIS ROBE, AND HIS SPIRIT SOARS.
THEIR FACES ARE TURNED UP TO WATCH THE PYROTECHNIC MARVEL OF THE HEAVENS, EACH MOUTH FROZEN INTO THE SAME DIVINE SYLLABLE:
'O.'
NOW ONLY ITS FEET REMAIN, WHERE THE GREATEST INJURIES HAVE BEEN SUSTAINED, THOUGH WITHOUT FATALITY.
BINDING FRACTURES AS BEST HE CAN, MEDPHYL REFLECTS UPON THAT PART OF THE HORROR LEFT WHEN THE PEOPLE HAVE BEEN PARED AWAY.
AMONGST THE LAST RESCUED, SHURLO FINDS THE CROWD ALREADY DISPERSING, DISCUSSING THEIR SHARED EXPERIENCE AS THEY WANDER AWAY TOGETHER.
SCARCELY HESITATING, SHE RUNS TO FOLLOW.
IF THEY REJECT HER, THERE'S ALWAYS THE HIGHEST LEVELS, THE LONGEST DROP...
ITS COMPONENT ATOMS SCATTER, RETURNING TO THEIR FAMILIES AND LIVES. ONLY ITS ESSENCE LINGERS, A WEB OF KNOTTED LIGHT STRUNG ON EMPTY AIR.
SEALED INSIDE A GREEN GLASS JAR, GREAT MEDPHYL SAVES THE HORROR'S SOUL FOR LATER.
16

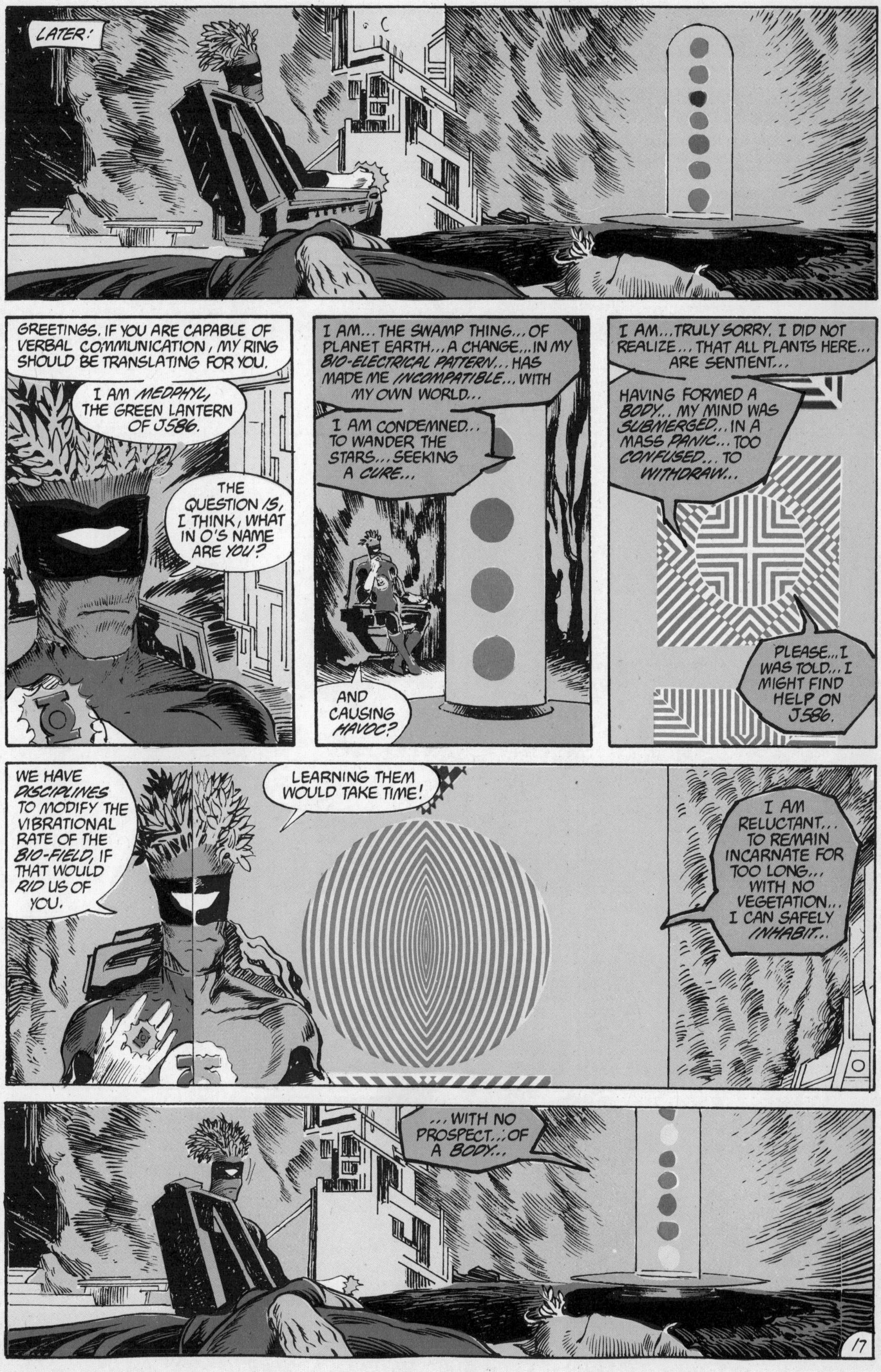
LATER:
GREETINGS. IF YOU ARE CAPABLE OF VERBAL COMMUNICATION, MY RING SHOULD BE TRANSLATING FOR YOU.
I AM MEDPHYL, THE GREEN LANTERN OF J586.
THE QUESTION IS, I THINK, WHAT IN O'S NAME ARE YOU?
I AM... THE SWAMP THING... OF PLANET EARTH... A CHANGE... IN MY BIO-ELECTRICAL PATTERN... HAS MADE ME INCOMPATIBLE... WITH MY OWN WORLD...
I AM CONDEMNED... TO WANDER THE STARS... SEEKING A CURE...
AND CAUSING HAVOC?
I AM... TRULY SORRY. I DID NOT REALIZE... THAT ALL PLANTS HERE... ARE SENTIENT...
HAVING FORMED A BODY... MY MIND WAS SUBMERGED... IN A MASS PANIC... TOO CONFUSED... TO WITHDRAW...
PLEASE... I WAS TOLD... I MIGHT FIND HELP ON J586.
WE HAVE DISCIPLINES TO MODIFY THE VIBRATIONAL RATE OF THE BIO-FIELD, IF THAT WOULD RID US OF YOU.
LEARNING THEM WOULD TAKE TIME!
I AM RELUCTANT... TO REMAIN INCARNATE FOR TOO LONG... WITH NO VEGETATION... I CAN SAFELY INHABIT...
...WITH NO PROSPECT... OF A BODY...
17

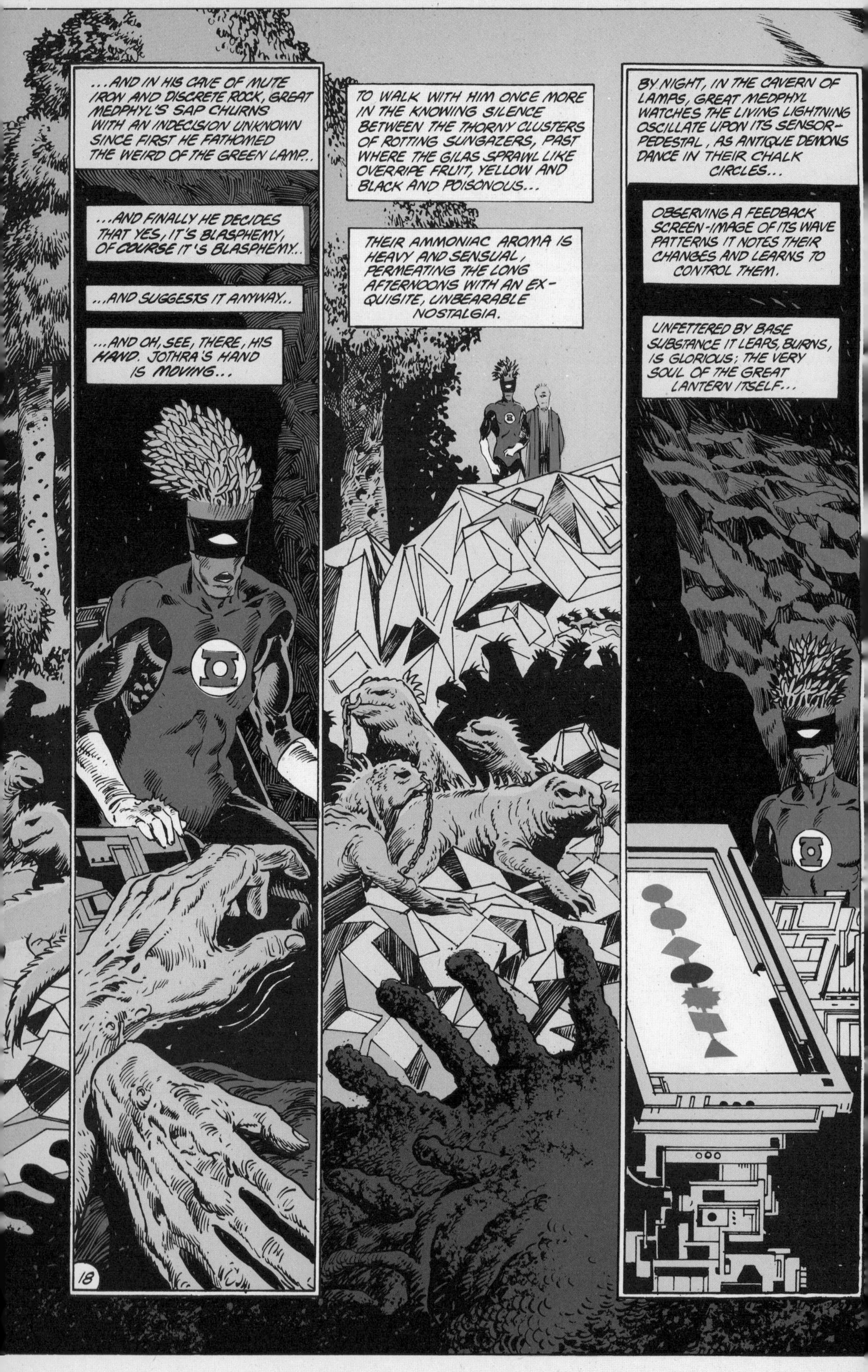
...AND IN HIS CAVE OF MUTE IRON AND DISCRETE ROCK, GREAT MEDPHYL'S SAP CHURNS WITH AN INDECISION UNKNOWN SINCE FIRST HE FATHOMED THE WEIRD OF THE GREEN LAMP...
...AND FINALLY HE DECIDES THAT YES, IT'S BLASPHEMY, OF COURSE IT'S BLASPHEMY...
...AND SUGGESTS IT ANYWAY...
...AND OH, SEE, THERE, HIS HAND. JOTHRA'S HAND IS MOVING...
TO WALK WITH HIM ONCE MORE IN THE KNOWING SILENCE BETWEEN THE THORNY CLUSTERS OF ROTTING SUNGAZERS, PAST WHERE THE GILAS SPRAWL LIKE OVERRIPE FRUIT, YELLOW AND BLACK AND POISONOUS...
THEIR AMMONIAC AROMA IS HEAVY AND SENSUAL, PERMEATING THE LONG AFTERNOONS WITH AN EXQUISITE, UNBEARABLE NOSTALGIA.
BY NIGHT, IN THE CAVERN OF LAMPS, GREAT MEDPHYL WATCHES THE LIVING LIGHTNING OSCILLATE UPON ITS SENSOR-PEDESTAL, AS ANTIQUE DEMONS DANCE IN THEIR CHALK CIRCLES...
OBSERVING A FEEDBACK SCREEN-IMAGE OF ITS WAVE PATTERNS IT NOTES THEIR CHANGES AND LEARNS TO CONTROL THEM.
UNFETTERED BY BASE SUBSTANCE IT LEAPS, BURNS, IS GLORIOUS: THE VERY SOUL OF THE GREAT LANTERN ITSELF...
18

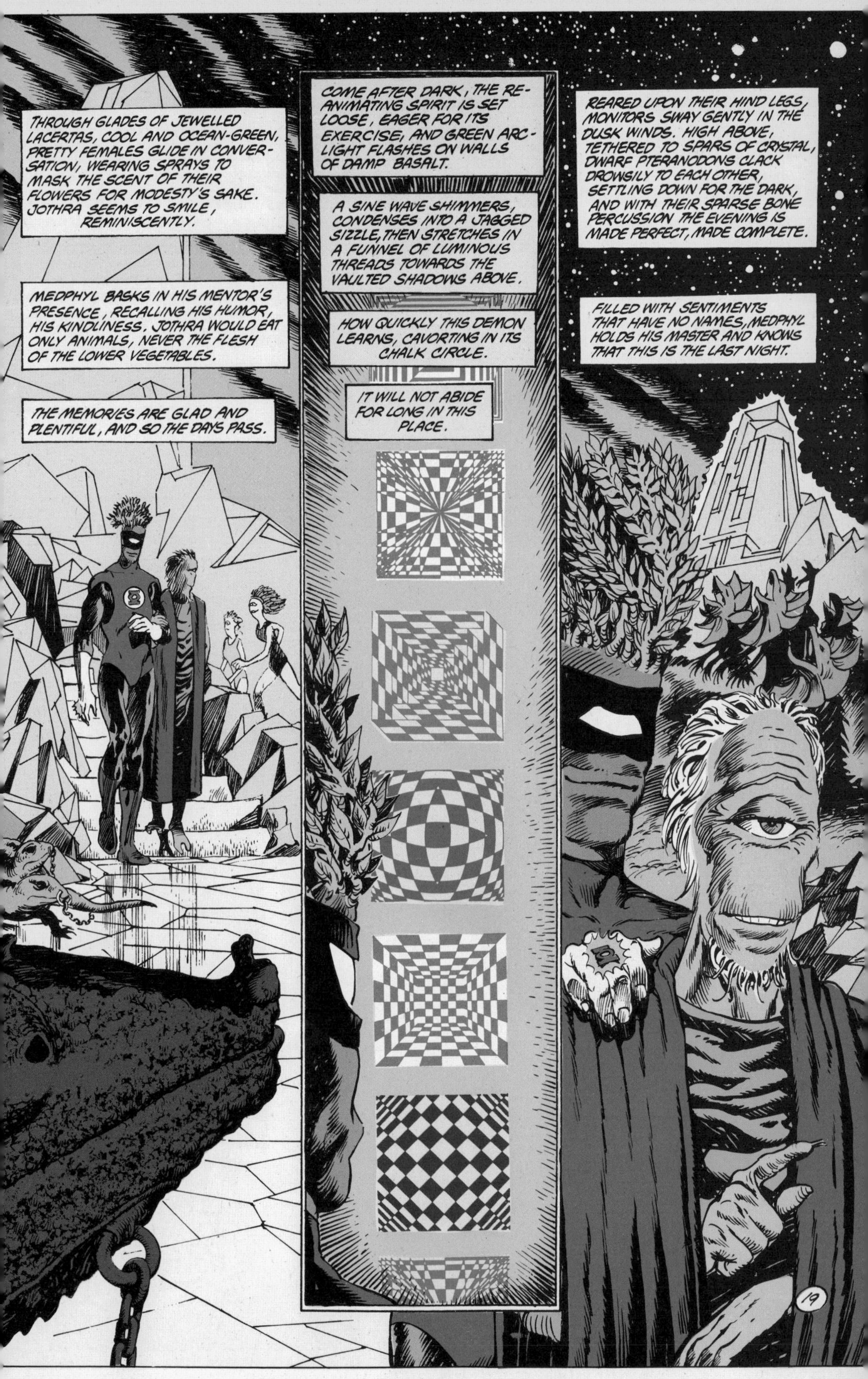
THROUGH GLADES OF JEWELLED LACERTAS, COOL AND OCEAN-GREEN, PRETTY FEMALES GLIDE IN CONVERSATION, WEARING SPRAYS TO MASK THE SCENT OF THEIR FLOWERS FOR MODESTY'S SAKE. JOTHRA SEEMS TO SMILE, REMINISCENTLY.
MEDPHYL BASKS IN HIS MENTOR'S PRESENCE, RECALLING HIS HUMOR, HIS KINDLINESS. JOTHRA WOULD EAT ONLY ANIMALS, NEVER THE FLESH OF THE LOWER VEGETABLES.
THE MEMORIES ARE GLAD AND PLENTIFUL, AND SO THE DAYS PASS.
COME AFTER DARK, THE RE-ANIMATING SPIRIT IS SET LOOSE, EAGER FOR ITS EXERCISE; AND GREEN ARC-LIGHT FLASHES ON WALLS OF DAMP BASALT.
A SINE WAVE SHIMMERS, CONDENSES INTO A JAGGED SIZZLE, THEN STRETCHES IN A FUNNEL OF LUMINOUS THREADS TOWARDS THE VAULTED SHADOWS ABOVE.
HOW QUICKLY THIS DEMON LEARNS, CAVORTING IN ITS CHALK CIRCLE.
IT WILL NOT ABIDE FOR LONG IN THIS PLACE.
REARED UPON THEIR HIND LEGS, MONITORS SWAY GENTLY IN THE DUSK WINDS. HIGH ABOVE, TETHERED TO SPARS OF CRYSTAL, DWARF PTERANODONS CLACK DROWSILY TO EACH OTHER, SETTLING DOWN FOR THE DARK, AND WITH THEIR SPARSE BONE PERCUSSION THE EVENING IS MADE PERFECT, MADE COMPLETE.
FILLED WITH SENTIMENTS THAT HAVE NO NAMES, MEDPHYL HOLDS HIS MASTER AND KNOWS THAT THIS IS THE LAST NIGHT.
19

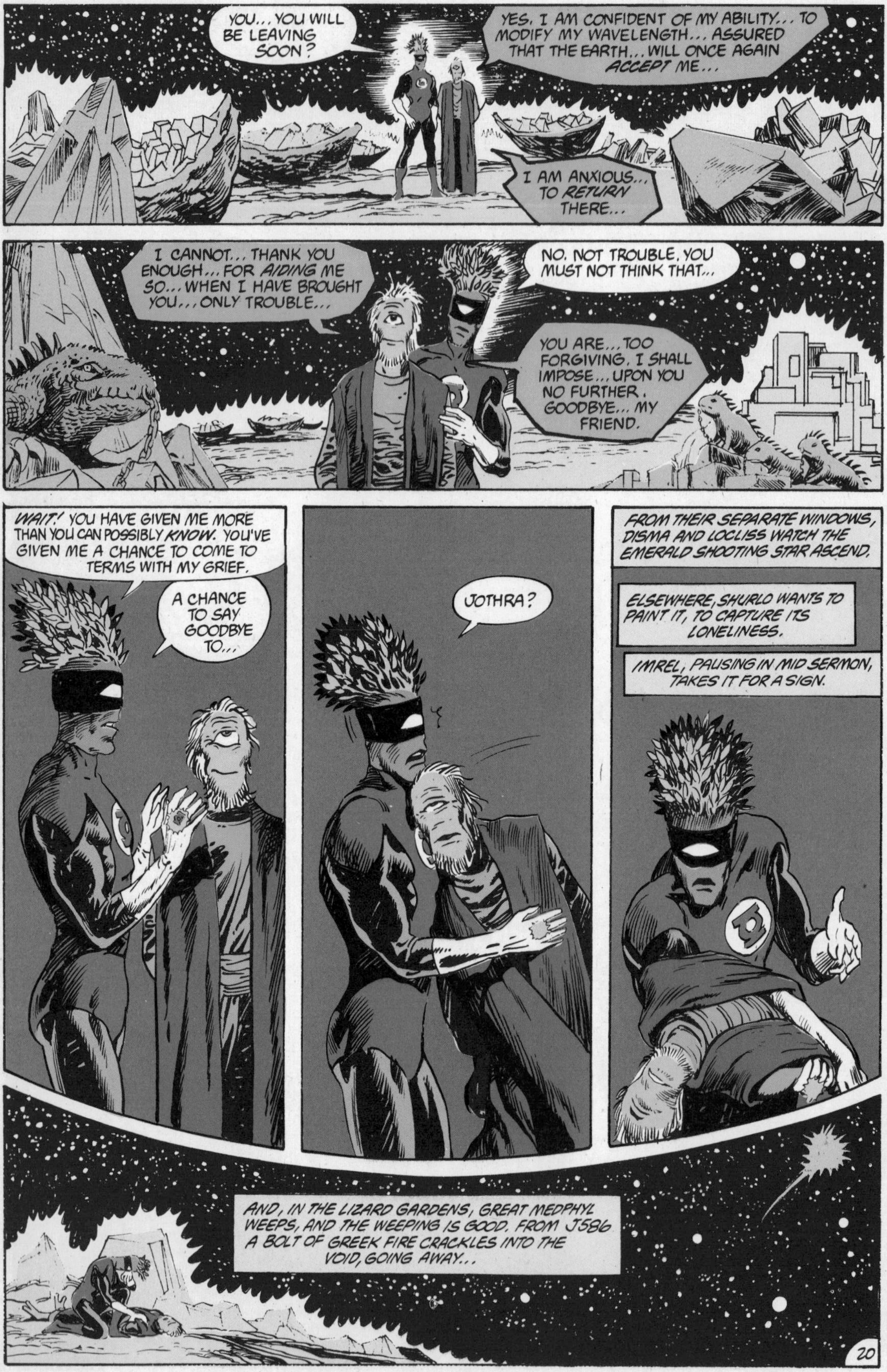
YOU... YOU WILL BE LEAVING SOON?
YES. I AM CONFIDENT OF MY ABILITY... TO MODIFY MY WAVELENGTH... ASSURED THAT THE EARTH... WILL ONCE AGAIN ACCEPT ME...
I AM ANXIOUS... TO RETURN THERE...
I CANNOT... THANK YOU ENOUGH... FOR AIDING ME SO... WHEN I HAVE BROUGHT YOU... ONLY TROUBLE...
NO. NOT TROUBLE. YOU MUST NOT THINK THAT...
YOU ARE... TOO FORGIVING. I SHALL IMPOSE... UPON YOU NO FURTHER. GOODBYE... MY FRIEND.
WAIT! YOU HAVE GIVEN ME MORE THAN YOU CAN POSSIBLY KNOW. YOU'VE GIVEN ME A CHANCE TO COME TO TERMS WITH MY GRIEF.
A CHANCE TO SAY GOODBYE TO...
JOTHRA?
FROM THEIR SEPARATE WINDOWS, DISMA AND LOCLISS WATCH THE EMERALD SHOOTING STAR ASCEND.
ELSEWHERE, SHURLO WANTS TO PAINT IT, TO CAPTURE ITS LONELINESS.
IMREL, PAUSING IN MID SERMON, TAKES IT FOR A SIGN.
AND, IN THE LIZARD GARDENS, GREAT MEDPHYL WEEPS, AND THE WEEPING IS GOOD. FROM J586 A BOLT OF GREEK FIRE CRACKLES INTO THE VOID, GOING AWAY...
20

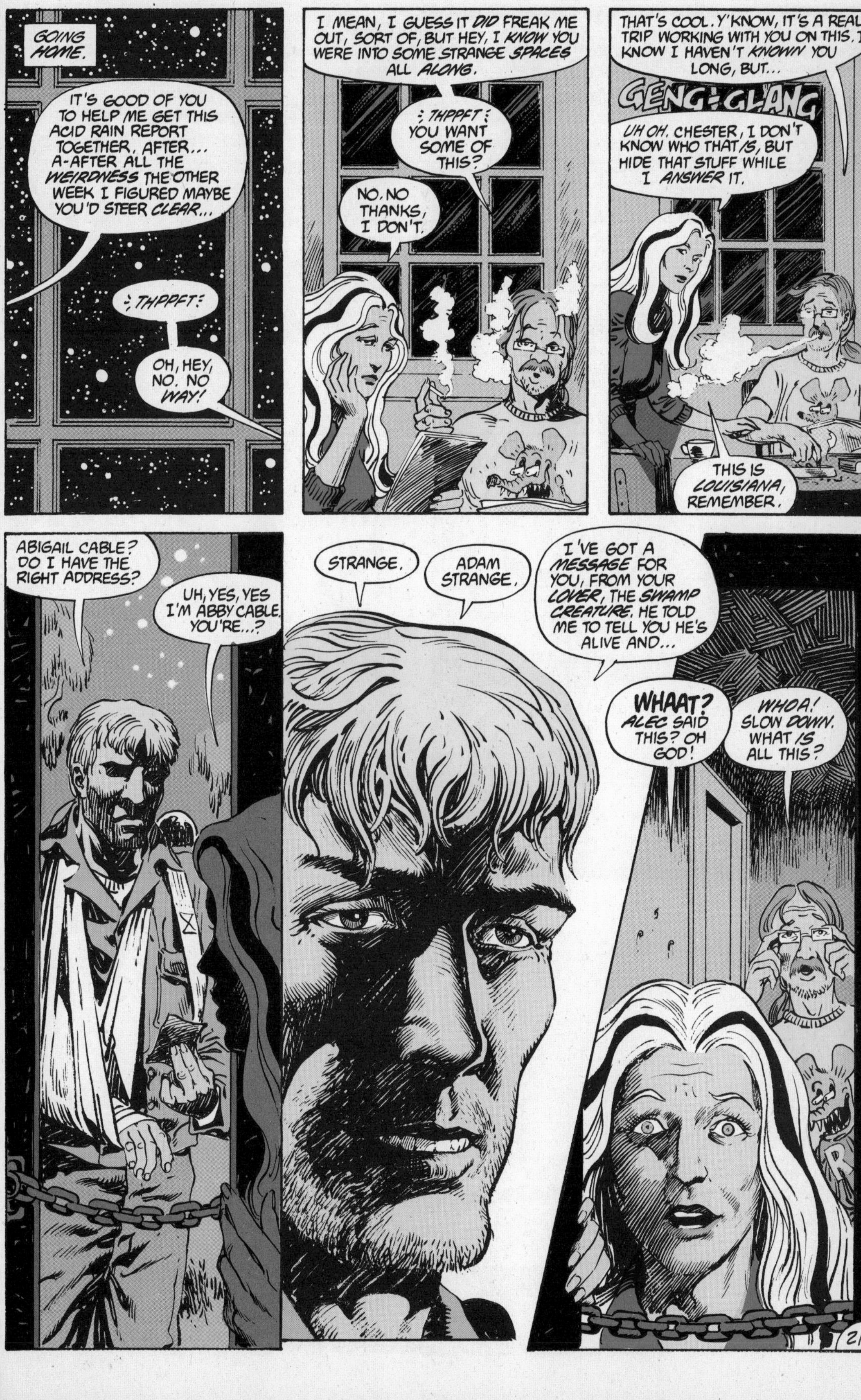
GOING HOME.
IT'S GOOD OF YOU TO HELP ME GET THIS ACID RAIN REPORT TOGETHER. AFTER... A-AFTER ALL THE WEIRDNESS THE OTHER WEEK I FIGURED MAYBE YOU'D STEER CLEAR...
THPPFT
OH, HEY, NO. NO WAY!
I MEAN, I GUESS IT DID FREAK ME OUT, SORT OF, BUT HEY, I KNOW YOU WERE INTO SOME STRANGE SPACES ALL ALONG.
THPPFT YOU WANT SOME OF THIS?
NO. NO THANKS, I DON'T.
THAT'S COOL. Y'KNOW, IT'S A REAL TRIP WORKING WITH YOU ON THIS. I KNOW I HAVEN'T KNOWN YOU LONG, BUT...
GENG GLANG
UH OH. CHESTER, I DON'T KNOW WHO THAT IS, BUT HIDE THAT STUFF WHILE I ANSWER IT.
THIS IS LOUISIANA, REMEMBER.
ABIGAIL CABLE? DO I HAVE THE RIGHT ADDRESS?
UH, YES, YES I'M ABBY CABLE. YOU'RE...?
STRANGE.
ADAM STRANGE.
I'VE GOT A MESSAGE FOR YOU, FROM YOUR LOVER, THE SWAMP CREATURE. HE TOLD ME TO TELL YOU HE'S ALIVE AND...
WHAAT? ALEC SAID THIS? OH GOD!
WHOA! SLOW DOWN. WHAT IS ALL THIS?
21

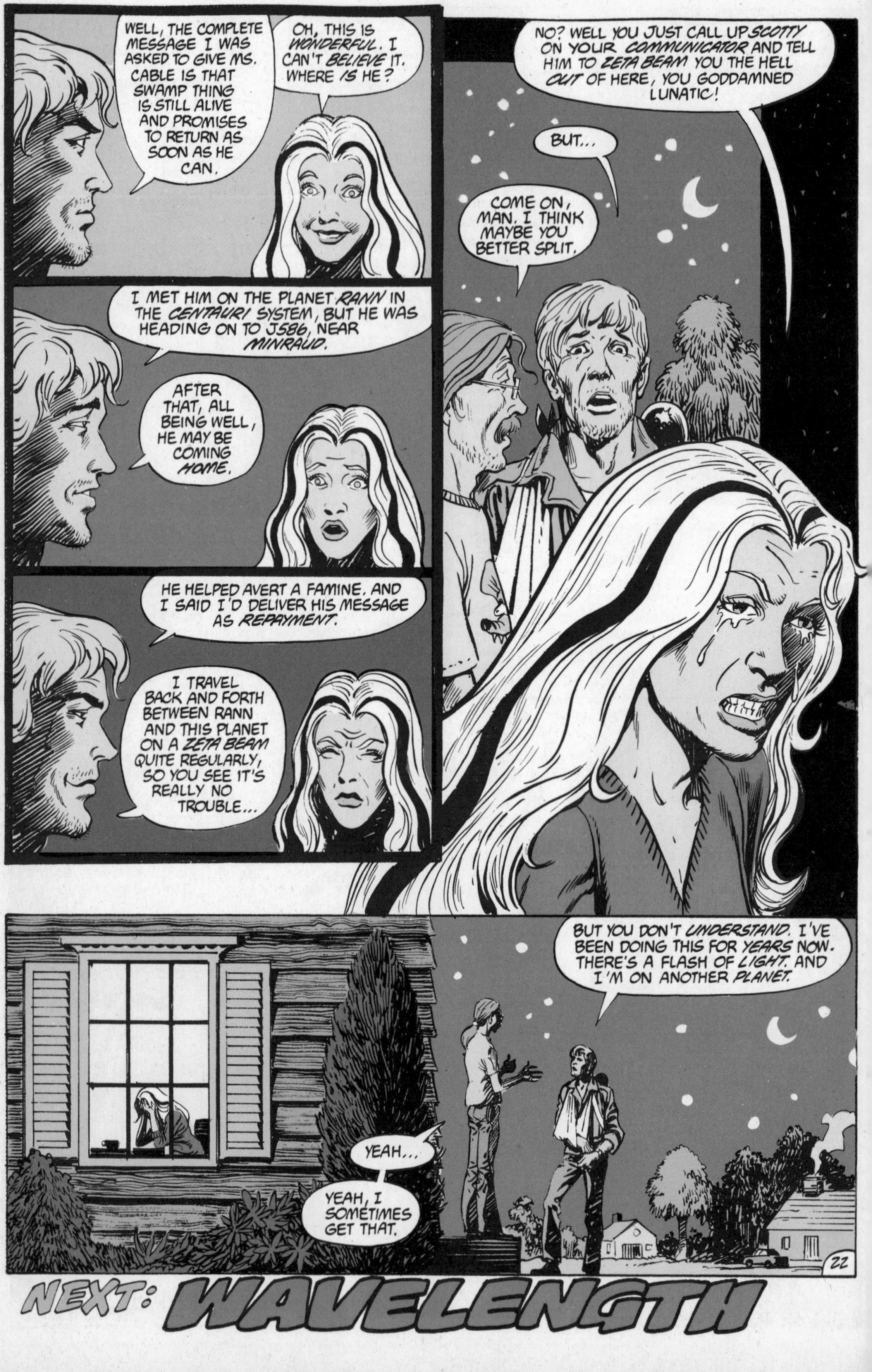
WELL, THE COMPLETE MESSAGE I WAS ASKED TO GIVE MS. CABLE IS THAT SWAMP THING IS STILL ALIVE AND PROMISES TO RETURN AS SOON AS HE CAN.
OH, THIS IS WONDERFUL. I CAN'T BELIEVE IT. WHERE IS HE?
I MET HIM ON THE PLANET RANN IN THE CENTAURI SYSTEM, BUT HE WAS HEADING ON TO J586, NEAR MINRAUD.
AFTER THAT, ALL BEING WELL, HE MAY BE COMING HOME.
HE HELPED AVERT A FAMINE, AND I SAID I'D DELIVER HIS MESSAGE AS REPAYMENT.
I TRAVEL BACK AND FORTH BETWEEN RANN AND THIS PLANET ON A ZETA BEAM QUITE REGULARLY, SO YOU SEE IT'S REALLY NO TROUBLE...
NO? WELL YOU JUST CALL UP SCOTTY ON YOUR COMMUNICATOR AND TELL HIM TO ZETA BEAM YOU THE HELL OUT OF HERE, YOU GODDAMNED LUNATIC!
BUT...
COME ON, MAN. I THINK MAYBE YOU BETTER SPLIT.
BUT YOU DON'T UNDERSTAND. I'VE BEEN DOING THIS FOR YEARS NOW. THERE'S A FLASH OF LIGHT. AND I'M ON ANOTHER PLANET.
YEAH...
YEAH, I SOMETIMES GET THAT.
22
NEXT: WAVELENGTH

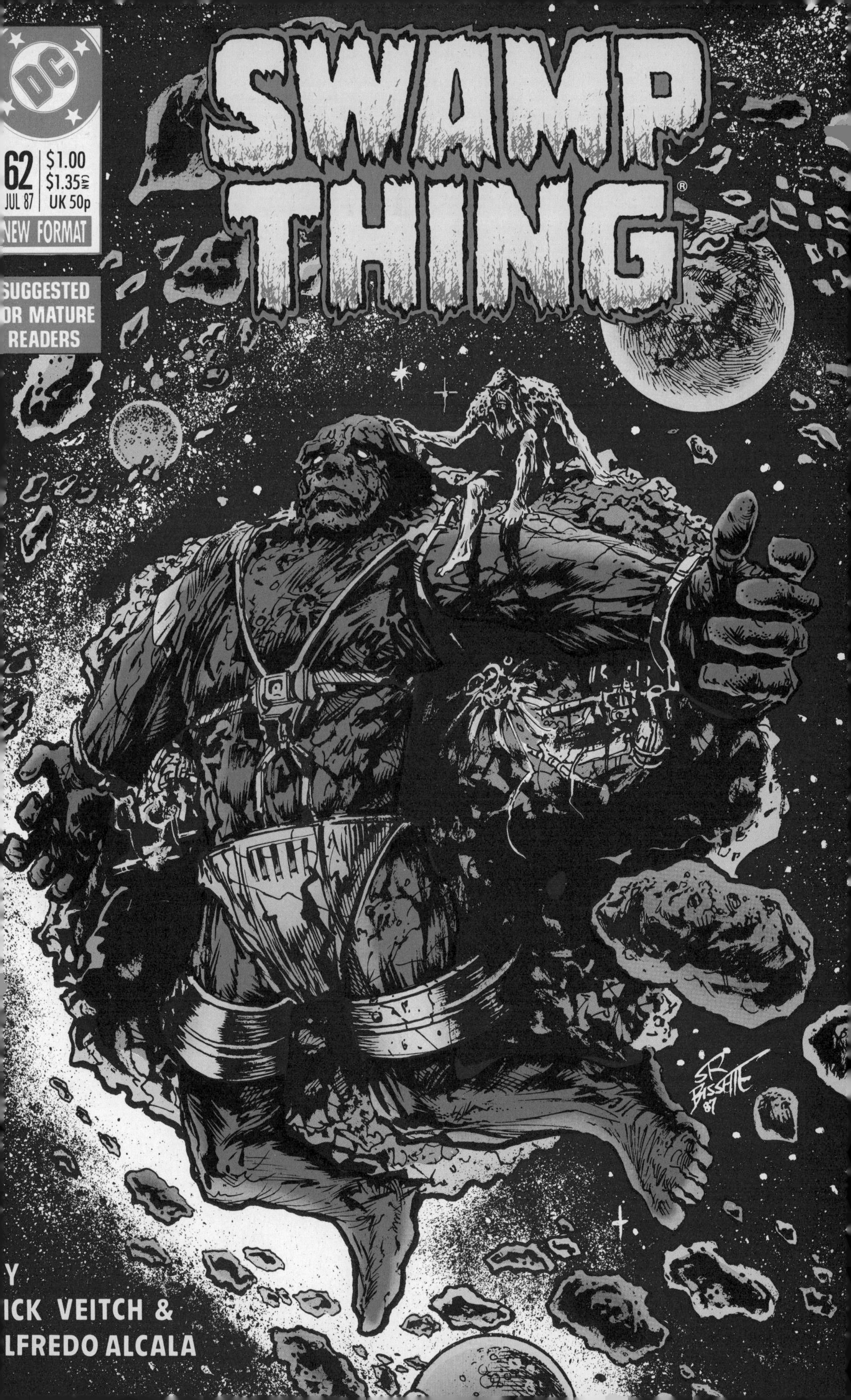

DC
62
$1.00
$1.35
JUL 87
UK 50p
NEW FORMAT
SWAMP THING
UGGESTED
OR MATURE
READERS
SR BISSETTE '87
Y
ICK VEITCH &
LFREDO ALCALA

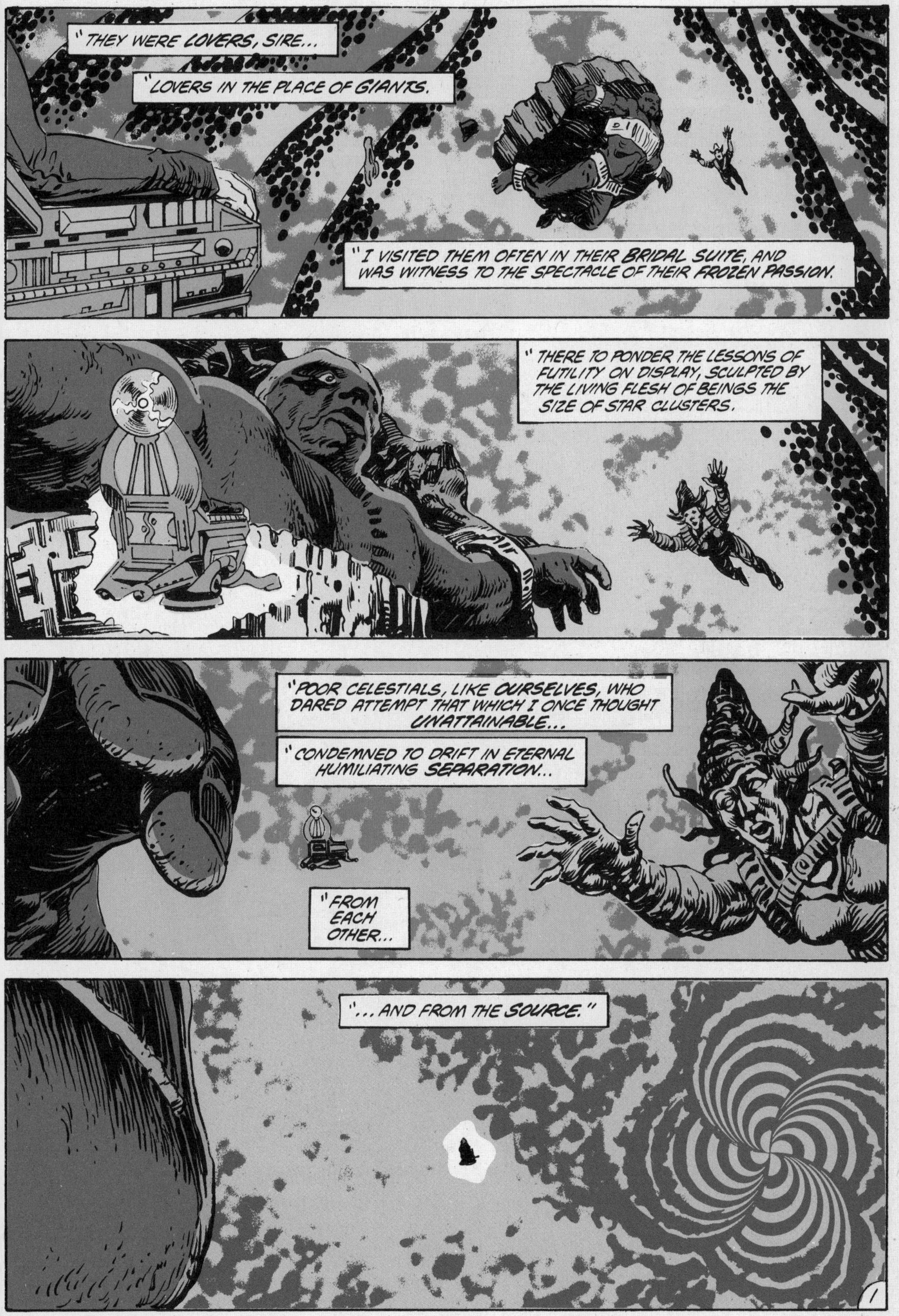
"THEY WERE LOVERS, SIRE...
"LOVERS IN THE PLACE OF GIANTS.
"I VISITED THEM OFTEN IN THEIR BRIDAL SUITE, AND WAS WITNESS TO THE SPECTACLE OF THEIR FROZEN PASSION.
"THERE TO PONDER THE LESSONS OF FUTILITY ON DISPLAY, SCULPTED BY THE LIVING FLESH OF BEINGS THE SIZE OF STAR CLUSTERS.
"POOR CELESTIALS, LIKE OURSELVES, WHO DARED ATTEMPT THAT WHICH I ONCE THOUGHT UNATTAINABLE...
"CONDEMNED TO DRIFT IN ETERNAL HUMILIATING SEPARATION...
"FROM EACH OTHER...
"...AND FROM THE SOURCE."
1

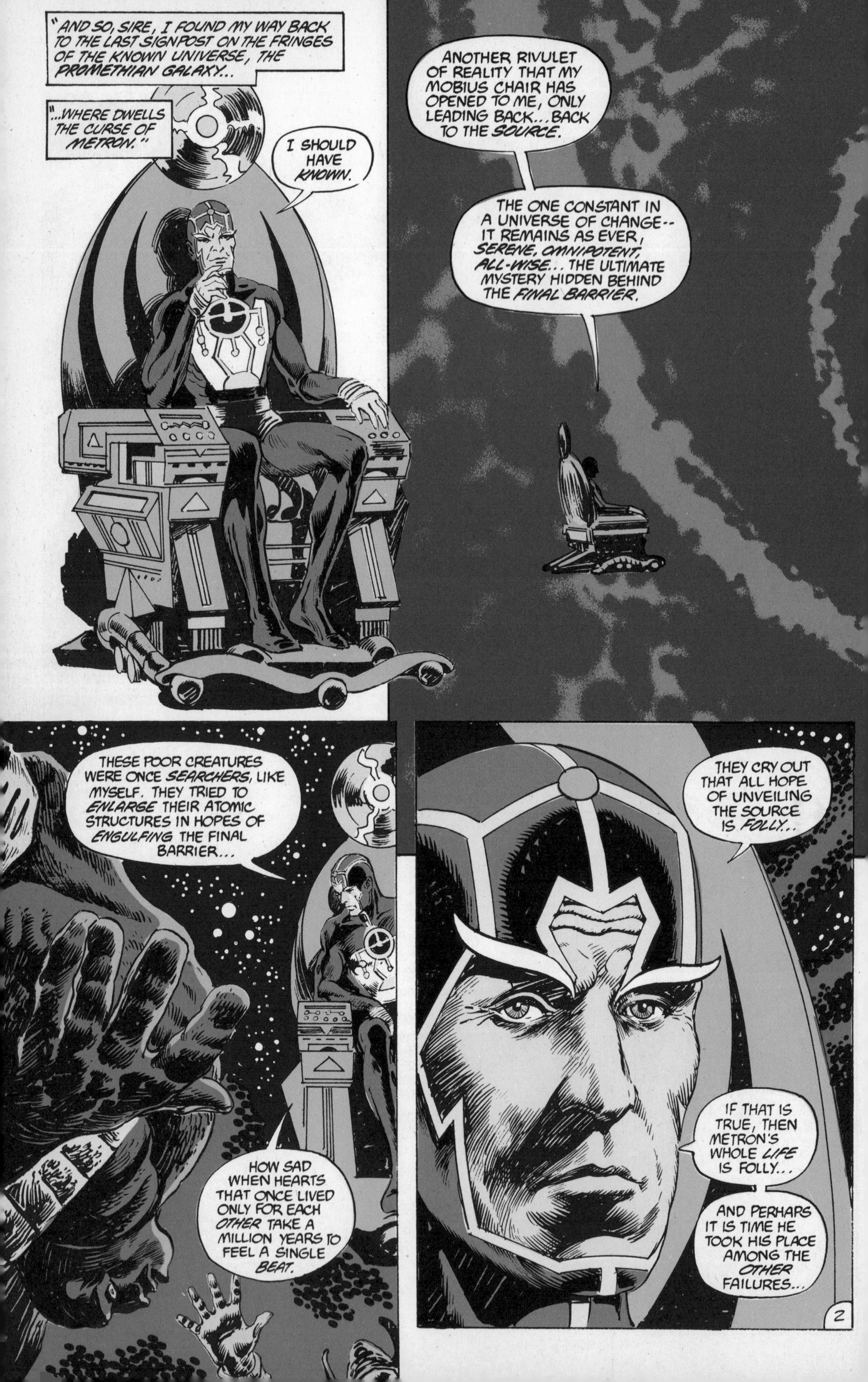
"AND SO, SIRE, I FOUND MY WAY BACK TO THE LAST SIGNPOST ON THE FRINGES OF THE KNOWN UNIVERSE, THE PROMETHIAN GALAXY...
"...WHERE DWELLS THE CURSE OF METRON."
I SHOULD HAVE KNOWN.
ANOTHER RIVULET OF REALITY THAT MY MOBIUS CHAIR HAS OPENED TO ME, ONLY LEADING BACK... BACK TO THE SOURCE.
THE ONE CONSTANT IN A UNIVERSE OF CHANGE-- IT REMAINS AS EVER, SERENE, OMNIPOTENT, ALL-WISE... THE ULTIMATE MYSTERY HIDDEN BEHIND THE FINAL BARRIER.
THESE POOR CREATURES WERE ONCE SEARCHERS, LIKE MYSELF. THEY TRIED TO ENLARGE THEIR ATOMIC STRUCTURES IN HOPES OF ENGULFING THE FINAL BARRIER...
HOW SAD WHEN HEARTS THAT ONCE LIVED ONLY FOR EACH OTHER TAKE A MILLION YEARS TO FEEL A SINGLE BEAT.
THEY CRY OUT THAT ALL HOPE OF UNVEILING THE SOURCE IS FOLLY...
IF THAT IS TRUE, THEN METRON'S WHOLE LIFE IS FOLLY...
AND PERHAPS IT IS TIME HE TOOK HIS PLACE AMONG THE OTHER FAILURES...
2

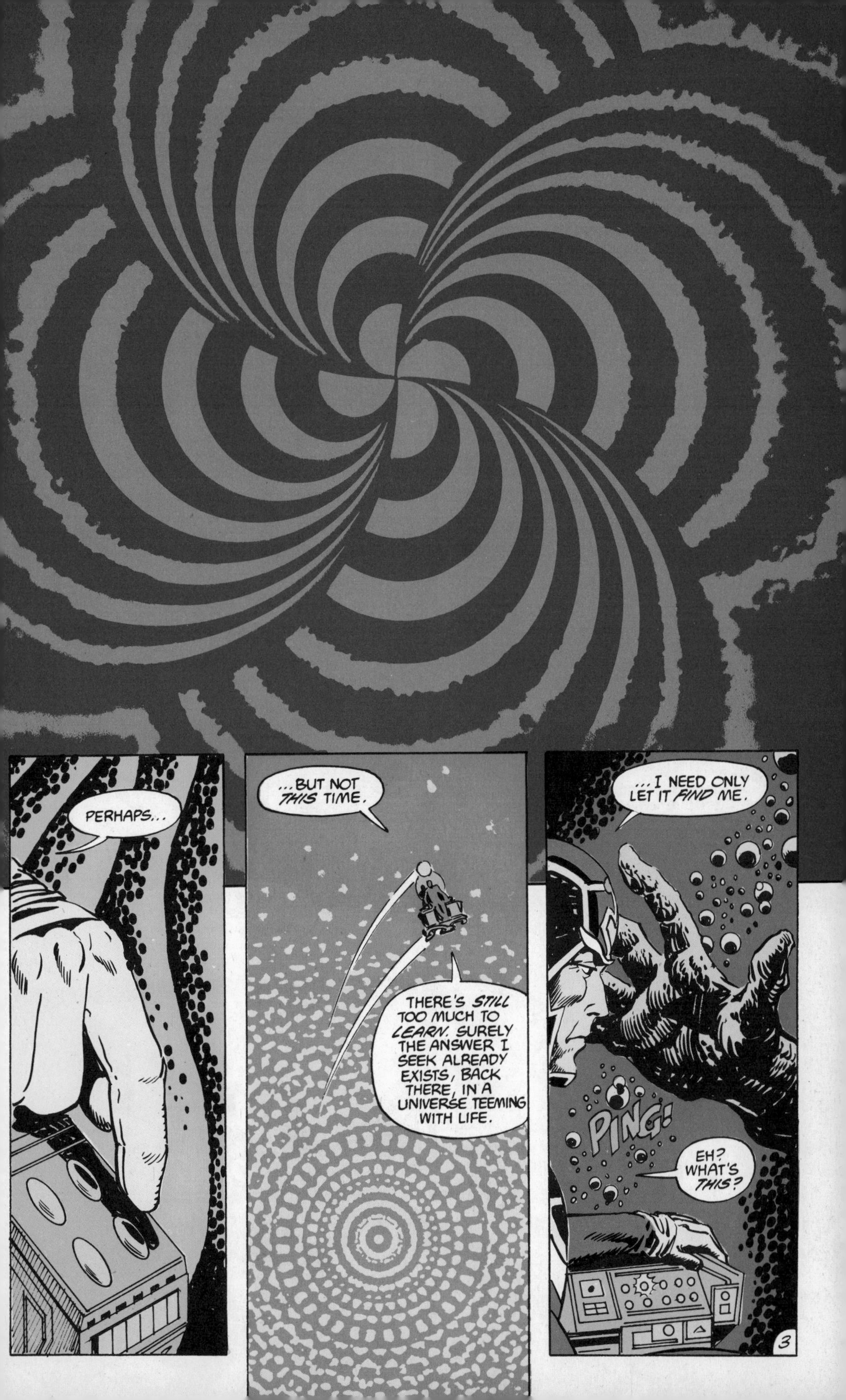
PERHAPS...
...BUT NOT THIS TIME.
THERE'S STILL TOO MUCH TO LEARN. SURELY THE ANSWER I SEEK ALREADY EXISTS, BACK THERE, IN A UNIVERSE TEEMING WITH LIFE.
...I NEED ONLY LET IT FIND ME.
PING!
EH? WHAT'S THIS?
3

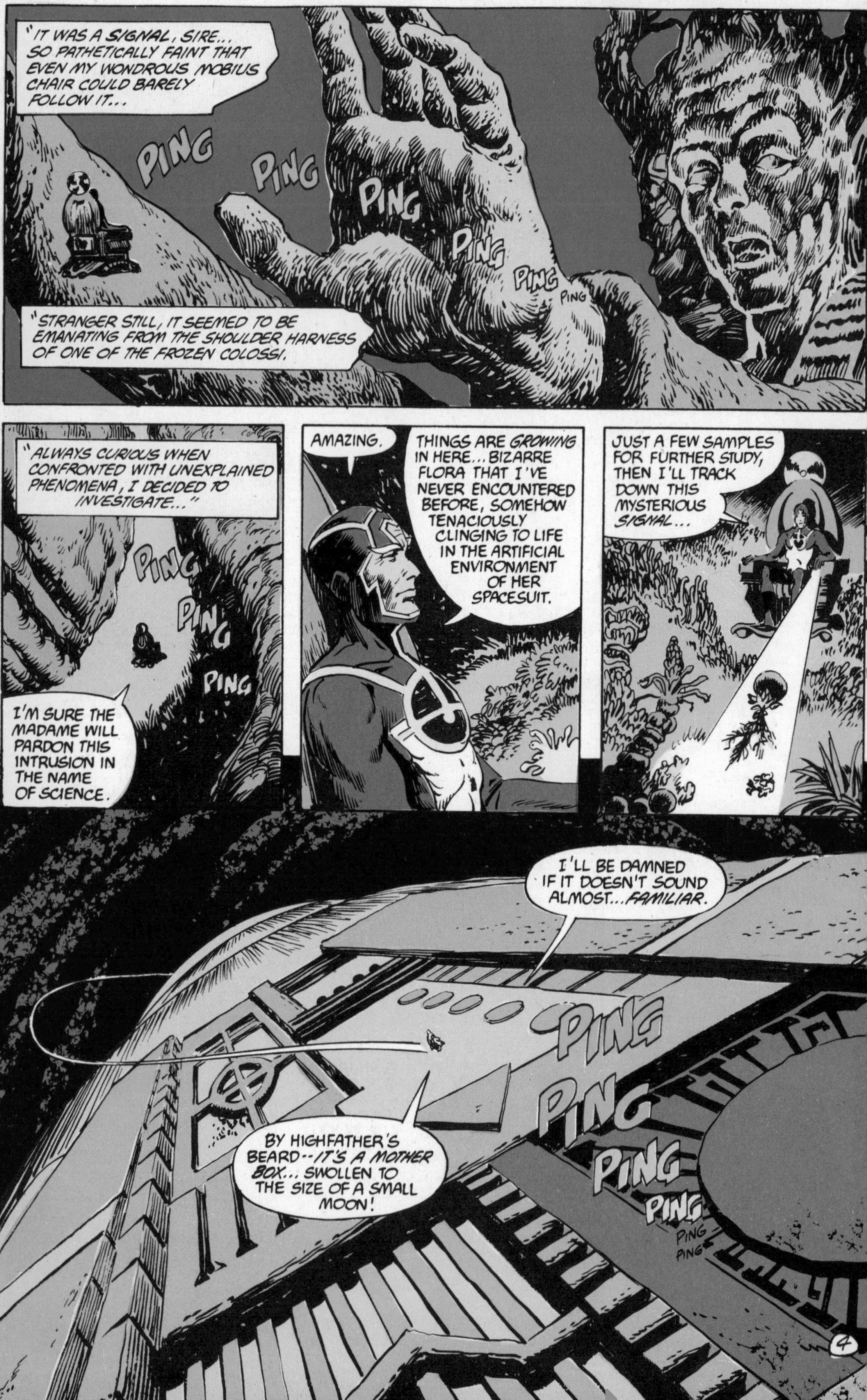
"IT WAS A SIGNAL, SIRE... SO PATHETICALLY FAINT THAT EVEN MY WONDROUS MOBIUS CHAIR COULD BARELY FOLLOW IT...
PING PING PING PING PING PING
"STRANGER STILL, IT SEEMED TO BE EMANATING FROM THE SHOULDER HARNESS OF ONE OF THE FROZEN COLOSSI.
"ALWAYS CURIOUS WHEN CONFRONTED WITH UNEXPLAINED PHENOMENA, I DECIDED TO INVESTIGATE..."
PING PING PING
I'M SURE THE MADAME WILL PARDON THIS INTRUSION IN THE NAME OF SCIENCE.
AMAZING.
THINGS ARE GROWING IN HERE... BIZARRE FLORA THAT I'VE NEVER ENCOUNTERED BEFORE, SOMEHOW TENACIOUSLY CLINGING TO LIFE IN THE ARTIFICIAL ENVIRONMENT OF HER SPACESUIT.
JUST A FEW SAMPLES FOR FURTHER STUDY, THEN I'LL TRACK DOWN THIS MYSTERIOUS SIGNAL...
I'LL BE DAMNED IF IT DOESN'T SOUND ALMOST... FAMILIAR.
BY HIGHFATHER'S BEARD--IT'S A MOTHER BOX... SWOLLEN TO THE SIZE OF A SMALL MOON!
PING PING PING PING PING PING
4

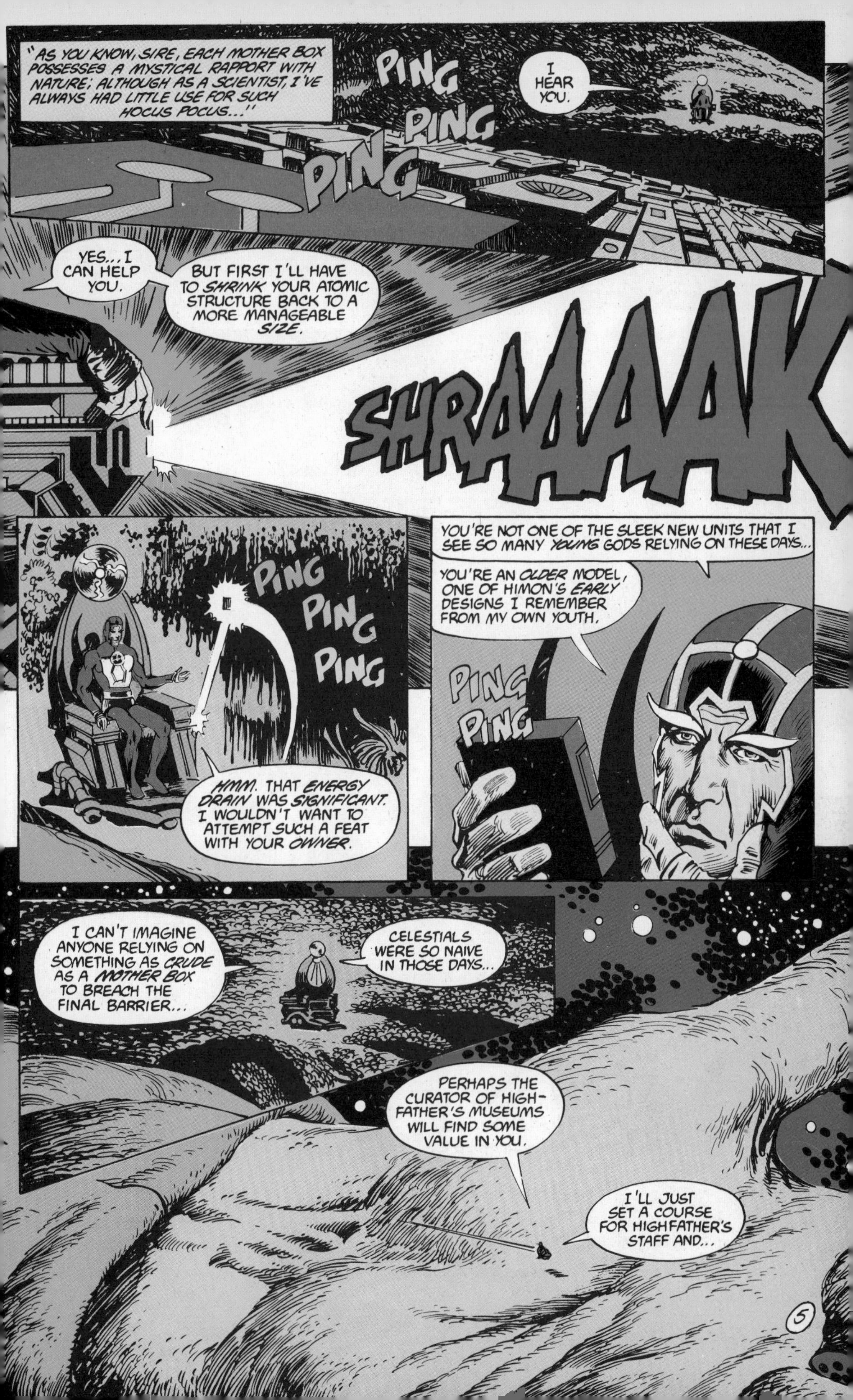
"AS YOU KNOW, SIRE, EACH MOTHER BOX POSSESSES A MYSTICAL RAPPORT WITH NATURE; ALTHOUGH AS A SCIENTIST, I'VE ALWAYS HAD LITTLE USE FOR SUCH HOCUS POCUS..."
PING PING PING
I HEAR YOU.
YES... I CAN HELP YOU.
BUT FIRST I'LL HAVE TO SHRINK YOUR ATOMIC STRUCTURE BACK TO A MORE MANAGEABLE SIZE.
SHRAAAAK
PING PING PING
HMM. THAT ENERGY DRAIN WAS SIGNIFICANT. I WOULDN'T WANT TO ATTEMPT SUCH A FEAT WITH YOUR OWNER.
YOU'RE NOT ONE OF THE SLEEK NEW UNITS THAT I SEE SO MANY YOUNG GODS RELYING ON THESE DAYS...
YOU'RE AN OLDER MODEL, ONE OF HIMON'S EARLY DESIGNS I REMEMBER FROM MY OWN YOUTH.
PING PING
I CAN'T IMAGINE ANYONE RELYING ON SOMETHING AS CRUDE AS A MOTHER BOX TO BREACH THE FINAL BARRIER...
CELESTIALS WERE SO NAIVE IN THOSE DAYS...
PERHAPS THE CURATOR OF HIGH-FATHER'S MUSEUMS WILL FIND SOME VALUE IN YOU.
I'LL JUST SET A COURSE FOR HIGHFATHER'S STAFF AND...
5

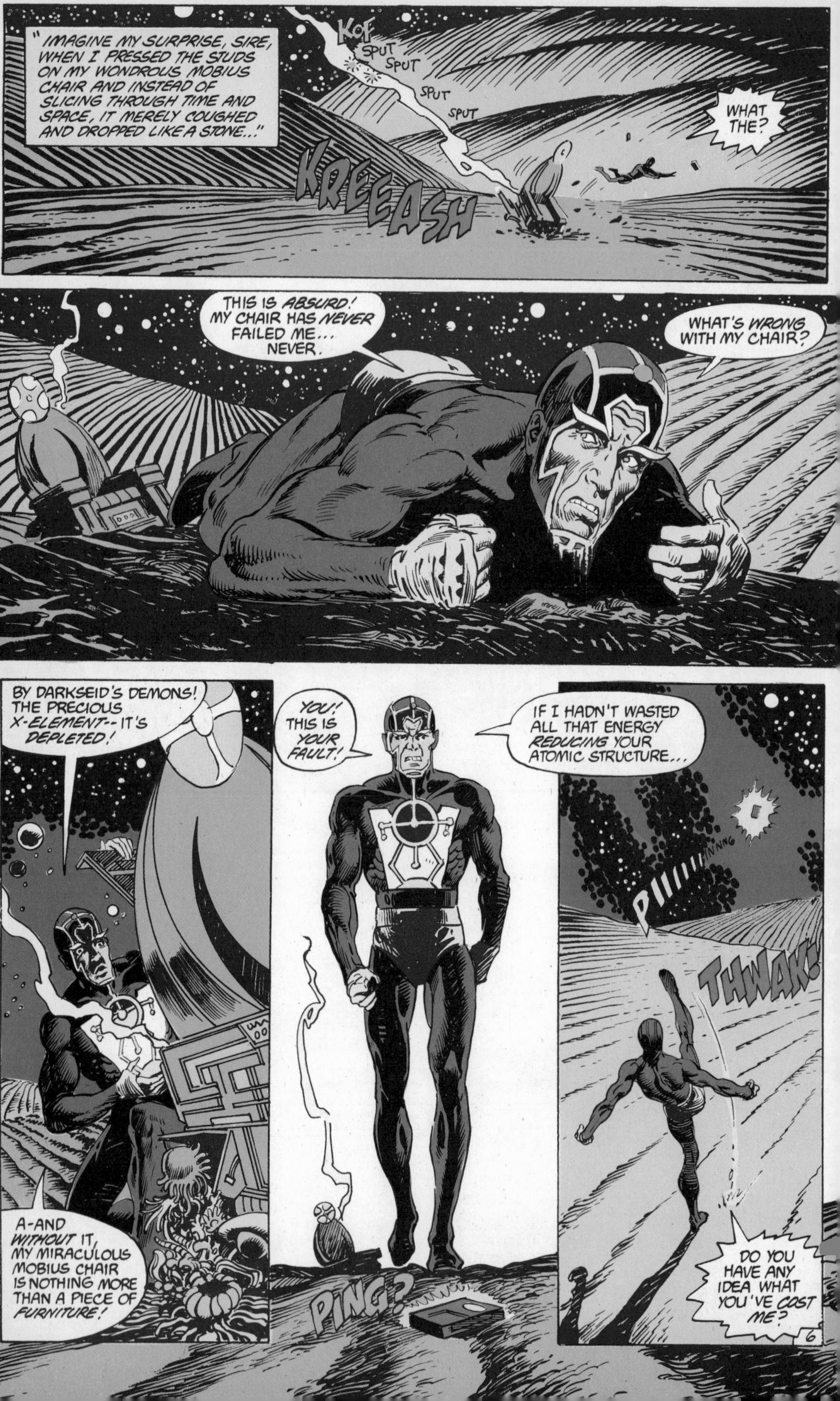
"IMAGINE MY SURPRISE, SIRE, WHEN I PRESSED THE STUDS ON MY WONDROUS MOBIUS CHAIR AND INSTEAD OF SLICING THROUGH TIME AND SPACE, IT MERELY COUGHED AND DROPPED LIKE A STONE..."
KOF
SPUT SPUT
SPUT
SPUT
WHAT THE?
KREEASH
THIS IS ABSURD! MY CHAIR HAS NEVER FAILED ME... NEVER.
WHAT'S WRONG WITH MY CHAIR?
BY DARKSEID'S DEMONS! THE PRECIOUS X-ELEMENT-- IT'S DEPLETED!
A-AND WITHOUT IT, MY MIRACULOUS MOBIUS CHAIR IS NOTHING MORE THAN A PIECE OF FURNITURE!
YOU! THIS IS YOUR FAULT!
PING?
IF I HADN'T WASTED ALL THAT ENERGY REDUCING YOUR ATOMIC STRUCTURE...
PIIIIIINNNG
THWAK!
DO YOU HAVE ANY IDEA WHAT YOU'VE COST ME?
6

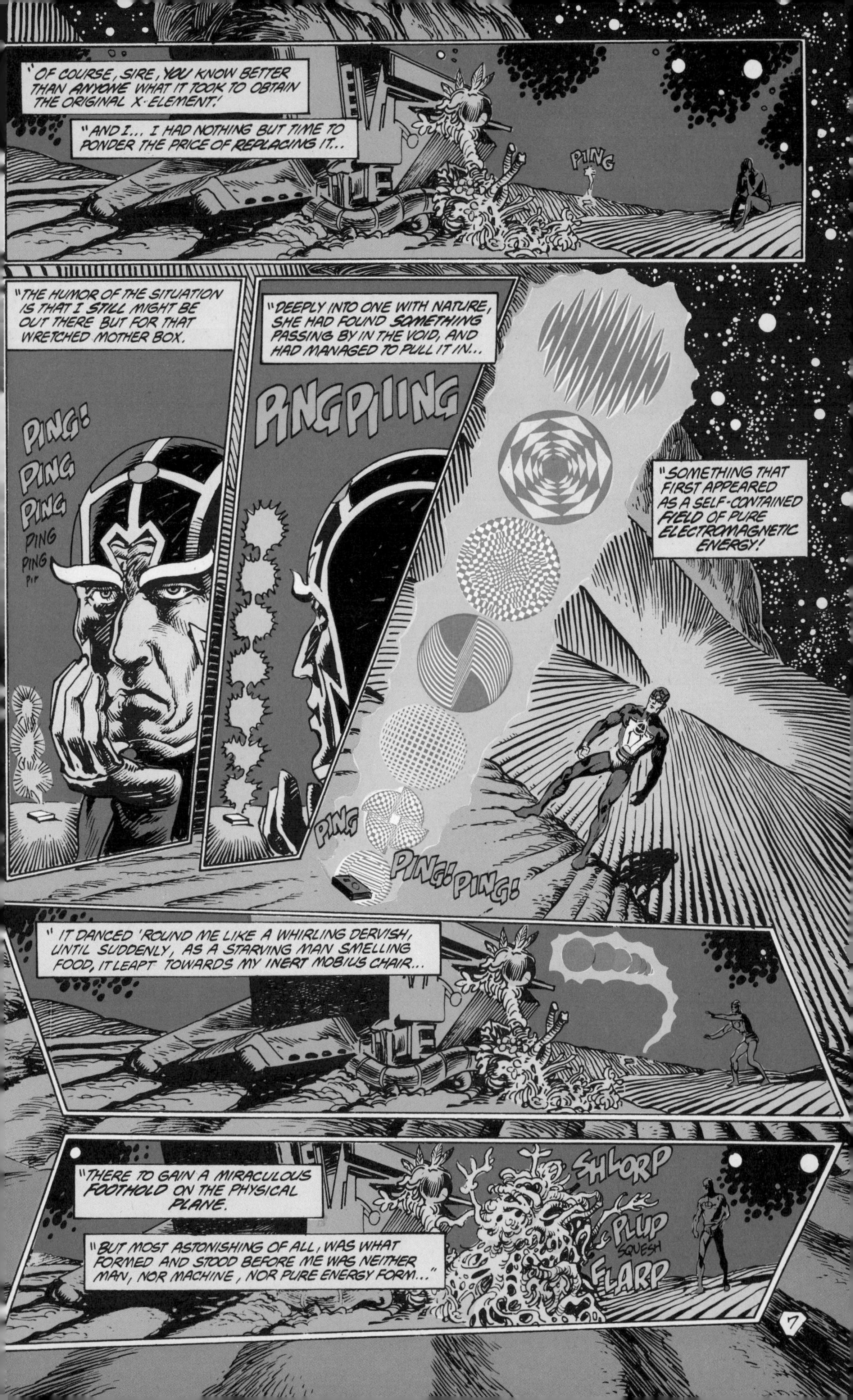
"OF COURSE, SIRE, YOU KNOW BETTER THAN ANYONE WHAT IT TOOK TO OBTAIN THE ORIGINAL X-ELEMENT!
"AND I... I HAD NOTHING BUT TIME TO PONDER THE PRICE OF REPLACING IT...
PING
"THE HUMOR OF THE SITUATION IS THAT I STILL MIGHT BE OUT THERE BUT FOR THAT WRETCHED MOTHER BOX.
PING! PING PING PING PING PI
"DEEPLY INTO ONE WITH NATURE, SHE HAD FOUND SOMETHING PASSING BY IN THE VOID, AND HAD MANAGED TO PULL IT IN...
PINGPIIING
"SOMETHING THAT FIRST APPEARED AS A SELF-CONTAINED FIELD OF PURE ELECTROMAGNETIC ENERGY!
PING PING! PING!
" IT DANCED 'ROUND ME LIKE A WHIRLING DERVISH, UNTIL SUDDENLY, AS A STARVING MAN SMELLING FOOD, IT LEAPT TOWARDS MY INERT MOBIUS CHAIR...
"THERE TO GAIN A MIRACULOUS FOOTHOLD ON THE PHYSICAL PLANE.
"BUT MOST ASTONISHING OF ALL, WAS WHAT FORMED AND STOOD BEFORE ME WAS NEITHER MAN, NOR MACHINE, NOR PURE ENERGY FORM..."
SHLORP
PLUP
SQUESH
FLARP
7

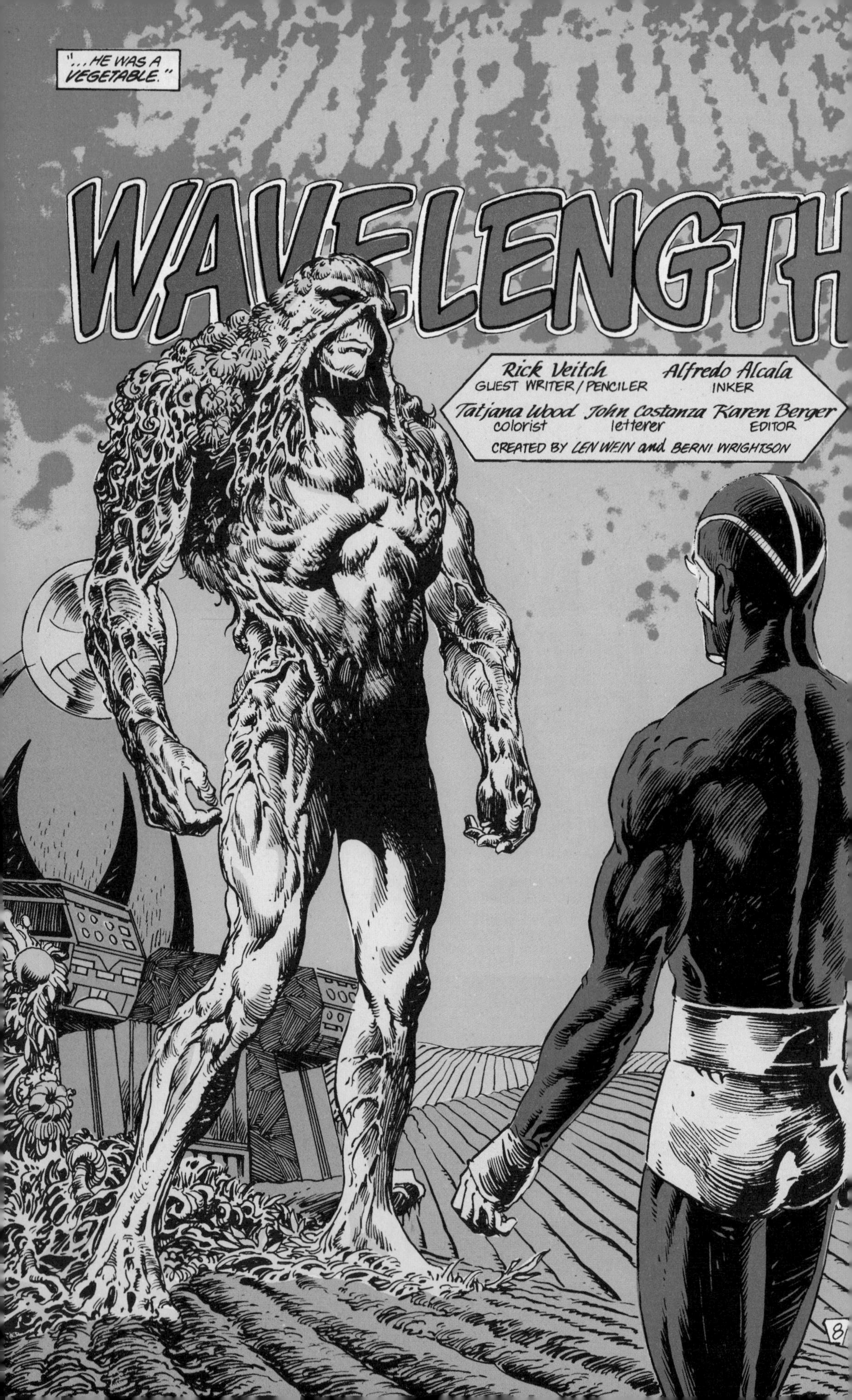

"...HE WAS A VEGETABLE."
WAVELENGTH
Rick Veitch GUEST WRITER/PENCILER
Alfredo Alcala INKER
Tatjana Wood colorist
John Costanza letterer
Karen Berger EDITOR
CREATED BY LEN WEIN and BERNI WRIGHTSON
8

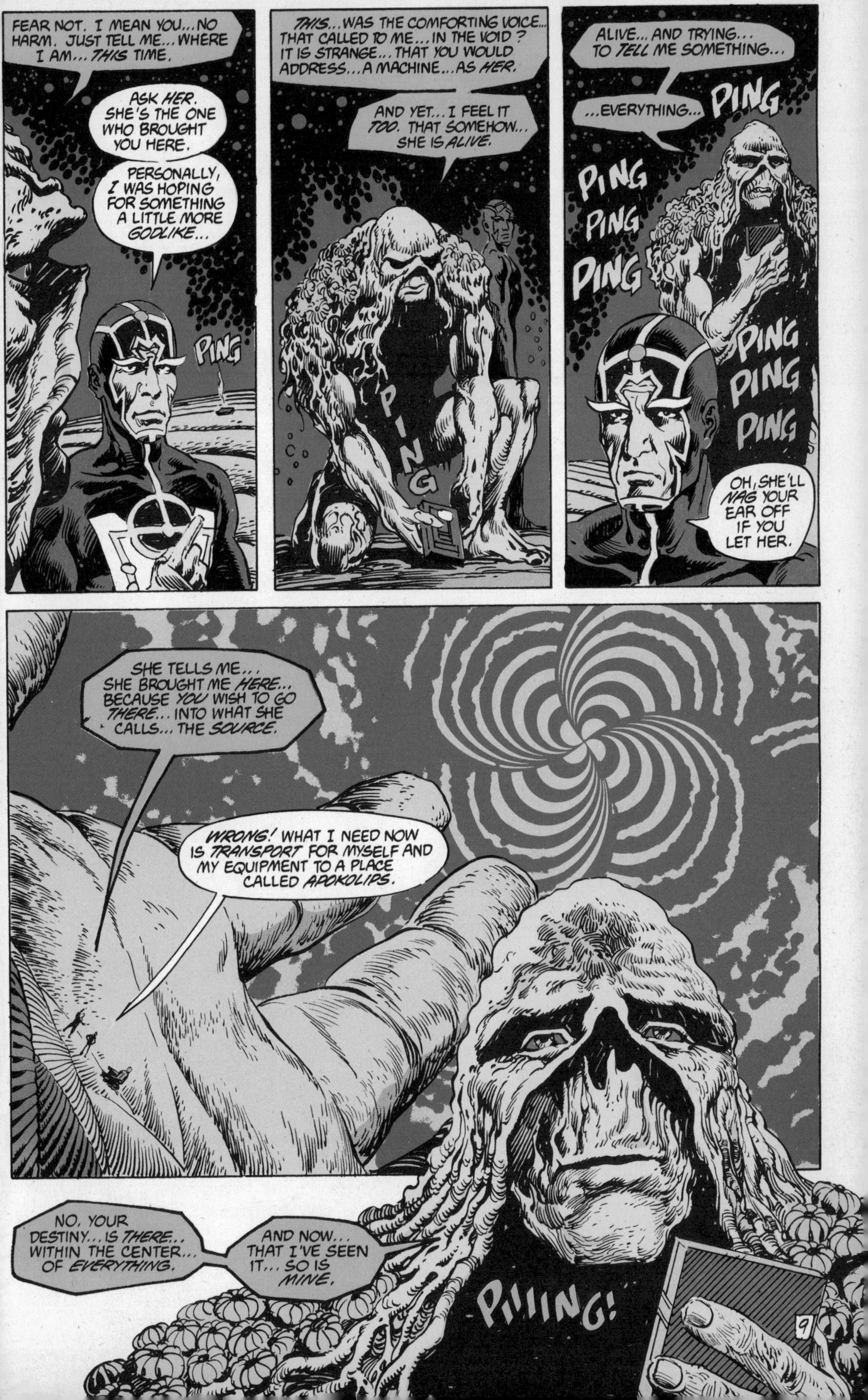
FEAR NOT. I MEAN YOU... NO HARM. JUST TELL ME... WHERE I AM... THIS TIME.
ASK HER. SHE'S THE ONE WHO BROUGHT YOU HERE.
PERSONALLY, I WAS HOPING FOR SOMETHING A LITTLE MORE GODLIKE...
PING
THIS... WAS THE COMFORTING VOICE... THAT CALLED TO ME... IN THE VOID? IT IS STRANGE... THAT YOU WOULD ADDRESS... A MACHINE... AS HER.
AND YET... I FEEL IT TOO. THAT SOMEHOW... SHE IS ALIVE.
PING
ALIVE... AND TRYING... TO TELL ME SOMETHING...
...EVERYTHING...
PING
PING
PING
PING
PING
PING
PING
OH, SHE'LL NAG YOUR EAR OFF IF YOU LET HER.
SHE TELLS ME... SHE BROUGHT ME HERE... BECAUSE YOU WISH TO GO THERE... INTO WHAT SHE CALLS... THE SOURCE.
WRONG! WHAT I NEED NOW IS TRANSPORT FOR MYSELF AND MY EQUIPMENT TO A PLACE CALLED APOKOLIPS.
NO, YOUR DESTINY... IS THERE... WITHIN THE CENTER... OF EVERYTHING.
AND NOW... THAT I'VE SEEN IT... SO IS MINE.
PIIIING!
9

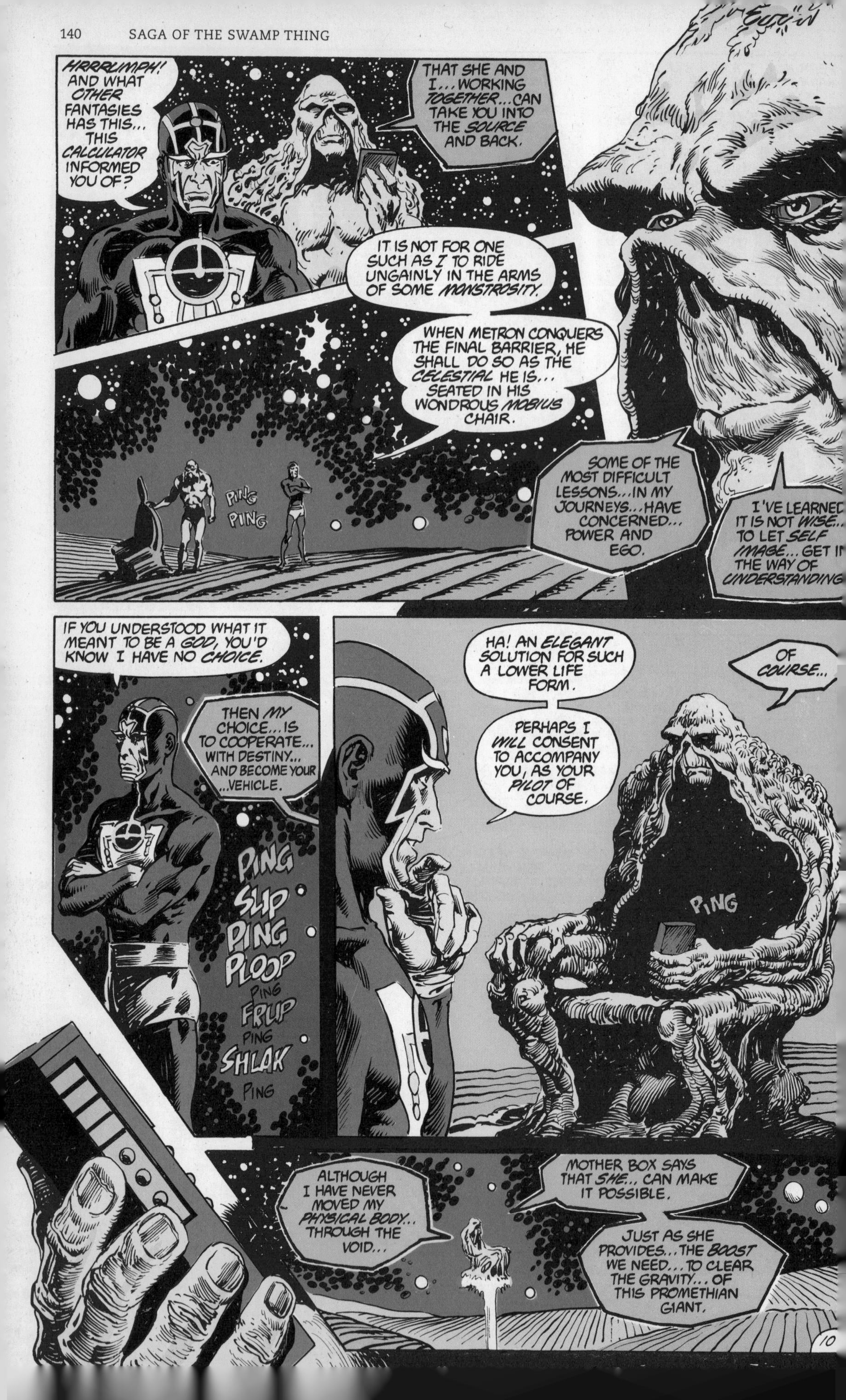
HRRRUMPH! AND WHAT OTHER FANTASIES HAS THIS... THIS CALCULATOR INFORMED YOU OF?
THAT SHE AND I... WORKING TOGETHER... CAN TAKE YOU INTO THE SOURCE AND BACK.
IT IS NOT FOR ONE SUCH AS I TO RIDE UNGAINLY IN THE ARMS OF SOME MONSTROSITY.
WHEN METRON CONQUERS THE FINAL BARRIER, HE SHALL DO SO AS THE CELESTIAL HE IS... SEATED IN HIS WONDROUS MOBIUS CHAIR.
PING
PING
SOME OF THE MOST DIFFICULT LESSONS... IN MY JOURNEYS... HAVE CONCERNED... POWER AND EGO.
I'VE LEARNED IT IS NOT WISE... TO LET SELF IMAGE... GET IN THE WAY OF UNDERSTANDING.
IF YOU UNDERSTOOD WHAT IT MEANT TO BE A GOD, YOU'D KNOW I HAVE NO CHOICE.
THEN MY CHOICE... IS TO COOPERATE... WITH DESTINY... AND BECOME YOUR ...VEHICLE.
PING
SLIP
PING
PLOOP
PING
FRUP
PING
SHLAK
PING
HA! AN ELEGANT SOLUTION FOR SUCH A LOWER LIFE FORM.
PERHAPS I WILL CONSENT TO ACCOMPANY YOU, AS YOUR PILOT OF COURSE.
OF COURSE...
PING
ALTHOUGH I HAVE NEVER MOVED MY PHYSICAL BODY... THROUGH THE VOID...
MOTHER BOX SAYS THAT SHE... CAN MAKE IT POSSIBLE.
JUST AS SHE PROVIDES... THE BOOST WE NEED... TO CLEAR THE GRAVITY... OF THIS PROMETHIAN GIANT.
10

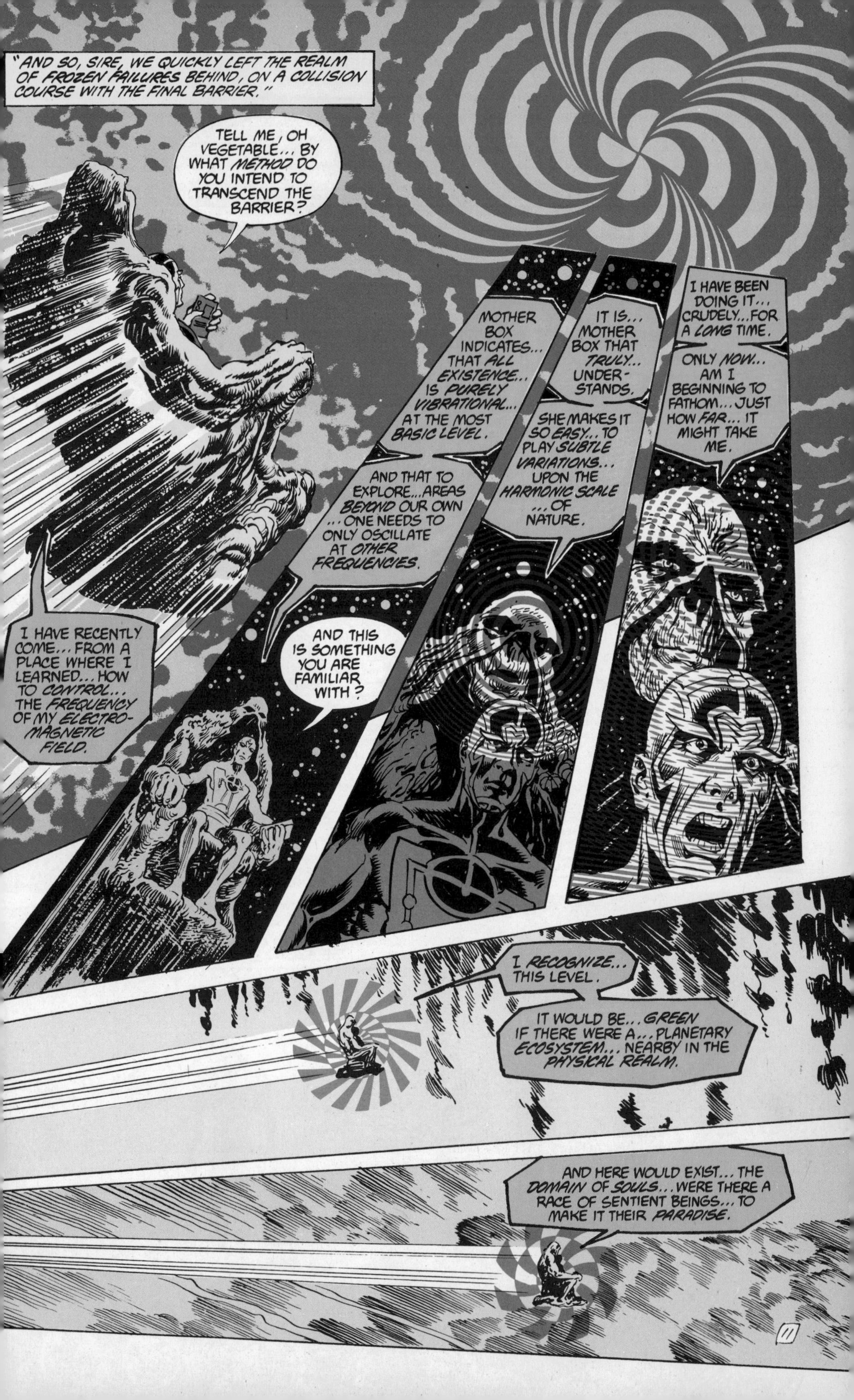
"AND SO, SIRE, WE QUICKLY LEFT THE REALM OF FROZEN FAILURES BEHIND, ON A COLLISION COURSE WITH THE FINAL BARRIER."
TELL ME, OH VEGETABLE... BY WHAT METHOD DO YOU INTEND TO TRANSCEND THE BARRIER?
I HAVE RECENTLY COME... FROM A PLACE WHERE I LEARNED... HOW TO CONTROL... THE FREQUENCY OF MY ELECTRO-MAGNETIC FIELD.
AND THIS IS SOMETHING YOU ARE FAMILIAR WITH?
MOTHER BOX INDICATES... THAT ALL EXISTENCE... IS PURELY VIBRATIONAL... AT THE MOST BASIC LEVEL.
AND THAT TO EXPLORE...AREAS BEYOND OUR OWN ...ONE NEEDS TO ONLY OSCILLATE AT OTHER FREQUENCIES.
IT IS... MOTHER BOX THAT TRULY... UNDER-STANDS.
SHE MAKES IT SO EASY... TO PLAY SUBTLE VARIATIONS... UPON THE HARMONIC SCALE ...OF NATURE.
I HAVE BEEN DOING IT... CRUDELY...FOR A LONG TIME.
ONLY NOW... AM I BEGINNING TO FATHOM... JUST HOW FAR... IT MIGHT TAKE ME.
I RECOGNIZE... THIS LEVEL.
IT WOULD BE... GREEN IF THERE WERE A... PLANETARY ECOSYSTEM... NEARBY IN THE PHYSICAL REALM.
AND HERE WOULD EXIST... THE DOMAIN OF SOULS... WERE THERE A RACE OF SENTIENT BEINGS... TO MAKE IT THEIR PARADISE.

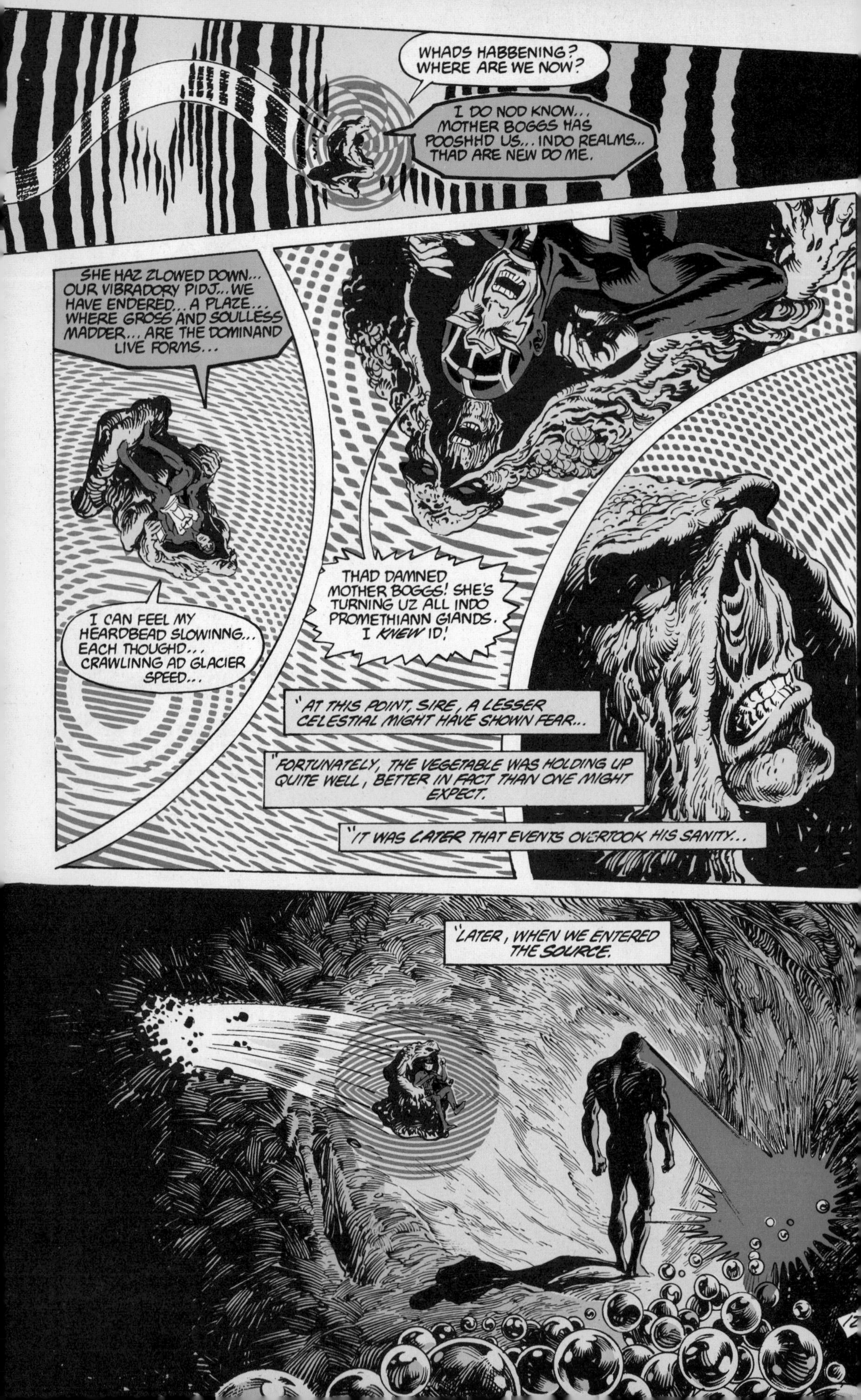
WHADS HABBENING? WHERE ARE WE NOW?
I DO NOD KNOW... MOTHER BOGGS HAS POOSHHD US... INDO REALMS... THAD ARE NEW DO ME.
SHE HAZ ZLOWED DOWN... OUR VIBRADORY PIDJ...WE HAVE ENDERED... A PLAZE... WHERE GROSS AND SOULLESS MADDER... ARE THE DOMINAND LIVE FORMS...
I CAN FEEL MY HEARDBEAD SLOWINNG... EACH THOUGHD... CRAWLINNG AD GLACIER SPEED...
THAD DAMNED MOTHER BOGGS! SHE'S TURNING UZ ALL INDO PROMETHIANN GIANDS. I KNEW ID!
"AT THIS POINT, SIRE, A LESSER CELESTIAL MIGHT HAVE SHOWN FEAR...
"FORTUNATELY, THE VEGETABLE WAS HOLDING UP QUITE WELL, BETTER IN FACT THAN ONE MIGHT EXPECT.
"IT WAS LATER THAT EVENTS OVERTOOK HIS SANITY...
"LATER, WHEN WE ENTERED THE SOURCE.

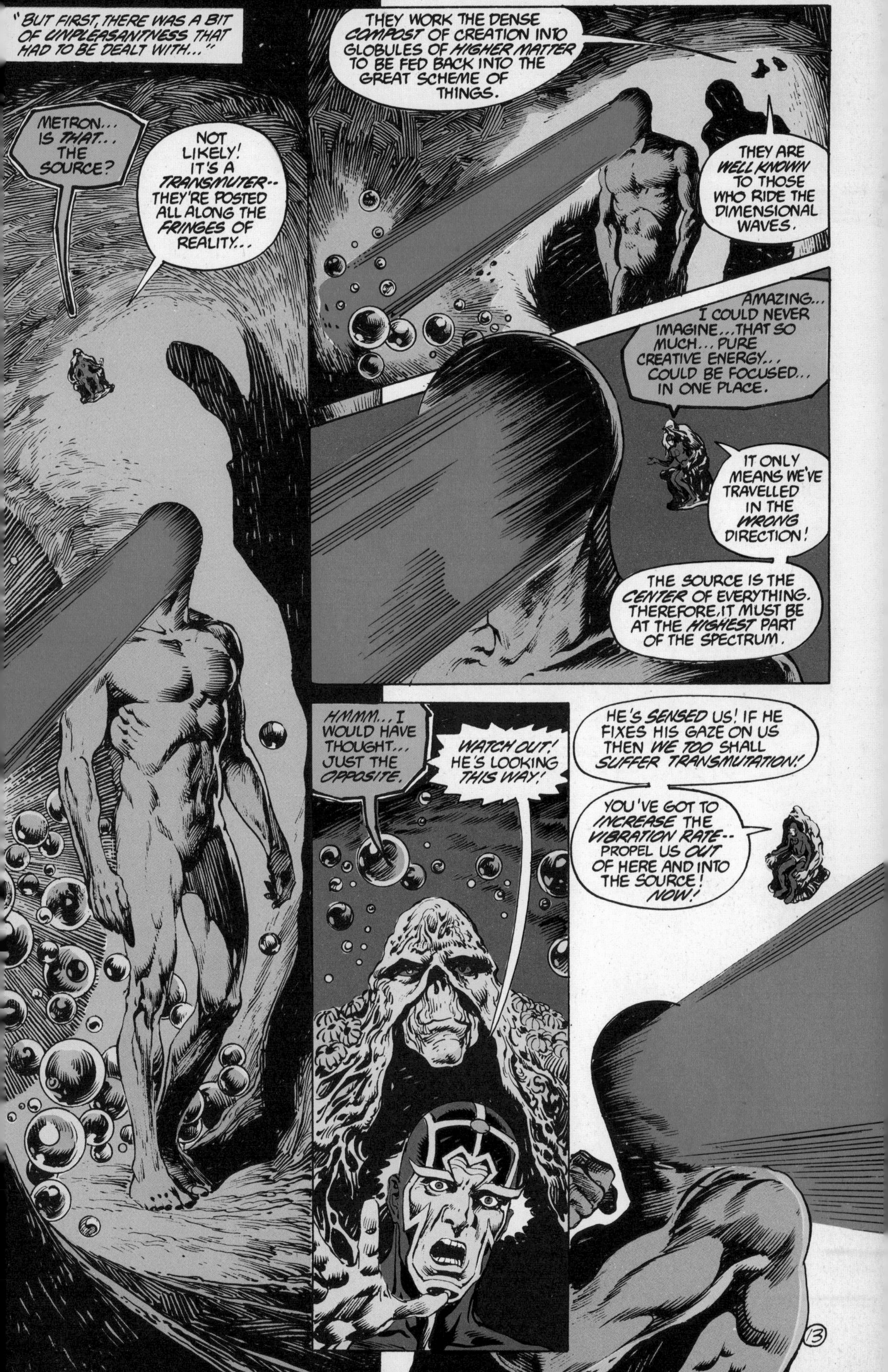

"BUT FIRST, THERE WAS A BIT OF UNPLEASANTNESS THAT HAD TO BE DEALT WITH..."
METRON... IS THAT... THE SOURCE?
NOT LIKELY! IT'S A TRANSMUTER-- THEY'RE POSTED ALL ALONG THE FRINGES OF REALITY...
THEY WORK THE DENSE COMPOST OF CREATION INTO GLOBULES OF HIGHER MATTER TO BE FED BACK INTO THE GREAT SCHEME OF THINGS.
THEY ARE WELL KNOWN TO THOSE WHO RIDE THE DIMENSIONAL WAVES.
AMAZING... I COULD NEVER IMAGINE... THAT SO MUCH... PURE CREATIVE ENERGY... COULD BE FOCUSED... IN ONE PLACE.
IT ONLY MEANS WE'VE TRAVELLED IN THE WRONG DIRECTION!
THE SOURCE IS THE CENTER OF EVERYTHING. THEREFORE, IT MUST BE AT THE HIGHEST PART OF THE SPECTRUM.
HMMM... I WOULD HAVE THOUGHT... JUST THE OPPOSITE.
WATCH OUT! HE'S LOOKING THIS WAY!
HE'S SENSED US! IF HE FIXES HIS GAZE ON US THEN WE TOO SHALL SUFFER TRANSMUTATION!
YOU'VE GOT TO INCREASE THE VIBRATION RATE-- PROPEL US OUT OF HERE AND INTO THE SOURCE! NOW!
13

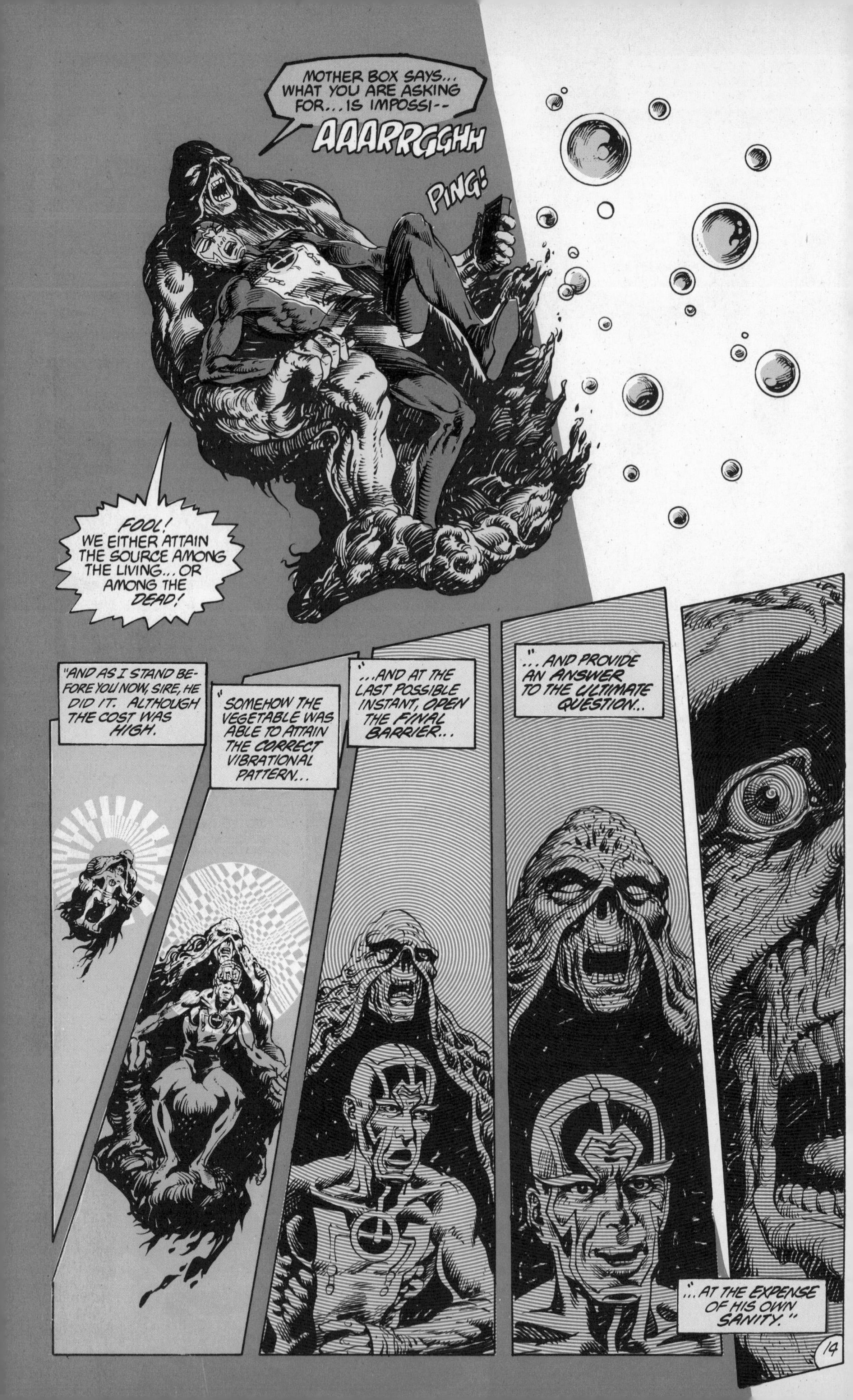

MOTHER BOX SAYS... WHAT YOU ARE ASKING FOR... IS IMPOSSI--
AAARRGGHH
PING!
FOOL! WE EITHER ATTAIN THE SOURCE AMONG THE LIVING... OR AMONG THE DEAD!
"AND AS I STAND BEFORE YOU NOW, SIRE, HE DID IT. ALTHOUGH THE COST WAS HIGH.
"SOMEHOW THE VEGETABLE WAS ABLE TO ATTAIN THE CORRECT VIBRATIONAL PATTERN...
"...AND AT THE LAST POSSIBLE INSTANT, OPEN THE FINAL BARRIER...
"... AND PROVIDE AN ANSWER TO THE ULTIMATE QUESTION...
"...AT THE EXPENSE OF HIS OWN SANITY."

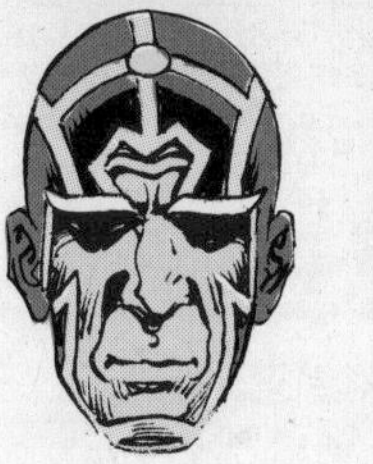

"AS I COME NOW TO THE INEFFABLE CLIMAX OF MY STORY, MY DESPAIR AS A NARRATOR BEGINS. TO DESCRIBE THE SOURCE... HOW DOES ONE CONVEY THE ACT OF SEEING ALL OF INFINITY WITHIN ONE GIGANTIC INSTANT? TO DRINK IN BILLIONS OF ACTIONS, THE TOTALITY OF EVERYTHING, OBSERVED FROM EVERY POINT IN THE UNIVERSE, ALL IN LESS TIME THAN IT TAKES TO DRAW A SINGLE BREATH. EVEN MY GREAT INTELLECT WAS OVERWHELMED BY IT, SIRE. WHAT MY EYES SAW WAS SIMULTANEOUS AND OCCUPYING THE SAME POINT, SO I CAN ONLY ACCOUNT FOR WHAT WONDERS I WAS ABLE TO FOCUS ON AND REMEMBER IN THAT TIDAL WAVE OF INFORMATION...

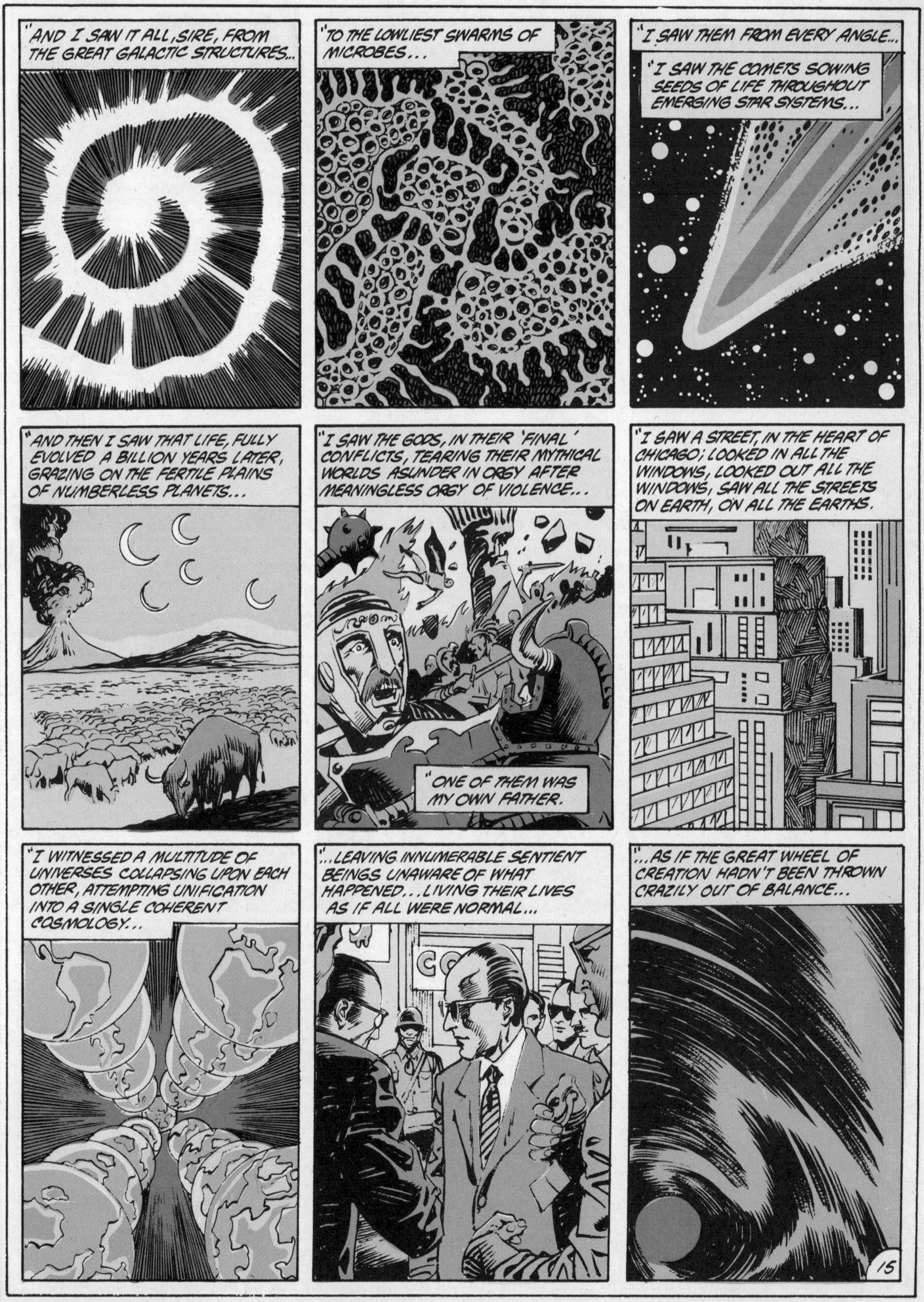
"AND I SAW IT ALL, SIRE, FROM THE GREAT GALACTIC STRUCTURES...
"TO THE LOWLIEST SWARMS OF MICROBES...
"I SAW THEM FROM EVERY ANGLE...
"I SAW THE COMETS SOWING SEEDS OF LIFE THROUGHOUT EMERGING STAR SYSTEMS...
"AND THEN I SAW THAT LIFE, FULLY EVOLVED A BILLION YEARS LATER, GRAZING ON THE FERTILE PLAINS OF NUMBERLESS PLANETS...
"I SAW THE GODS, IN THEIR 'FINAL' CONFLICTS, TEARING THEIR MYTHICAL WORLDS ASUNDER IN ORGY AFTER MEANINGLESS ORGY OF VIOLENCE...
"ONE OF THEM WAS MY OWN FATHER.
"I SAW A STREET, IN THE HEART OF CHICAGO; LOOKED IN ALL THE WINDOWS, LOOKED OUT ALL THE WINDOWS, SAW ALL THE STREETS ON EARTH, ON ALL THE EARTHS.
"I WITNESSED A MULTITUDE OF UNIVERSES COLLAPSING UPON EACH OTHER, ATTEMPTING UNIFICATION INTO A SINGLE COHERENT COSMOLOGY...
"...LEAVING INNUMERABLE SENTIENT BEINGS UNAWARE OF WHAT HAPPENED... LIVING THEIR LIVES AS IF ALL WERE NORMAL...
"...AS IF THE GREAT WHEEL OF CREATION HADN'T BEEN THROWN CRAZILY OUT OF BALANCE...
15

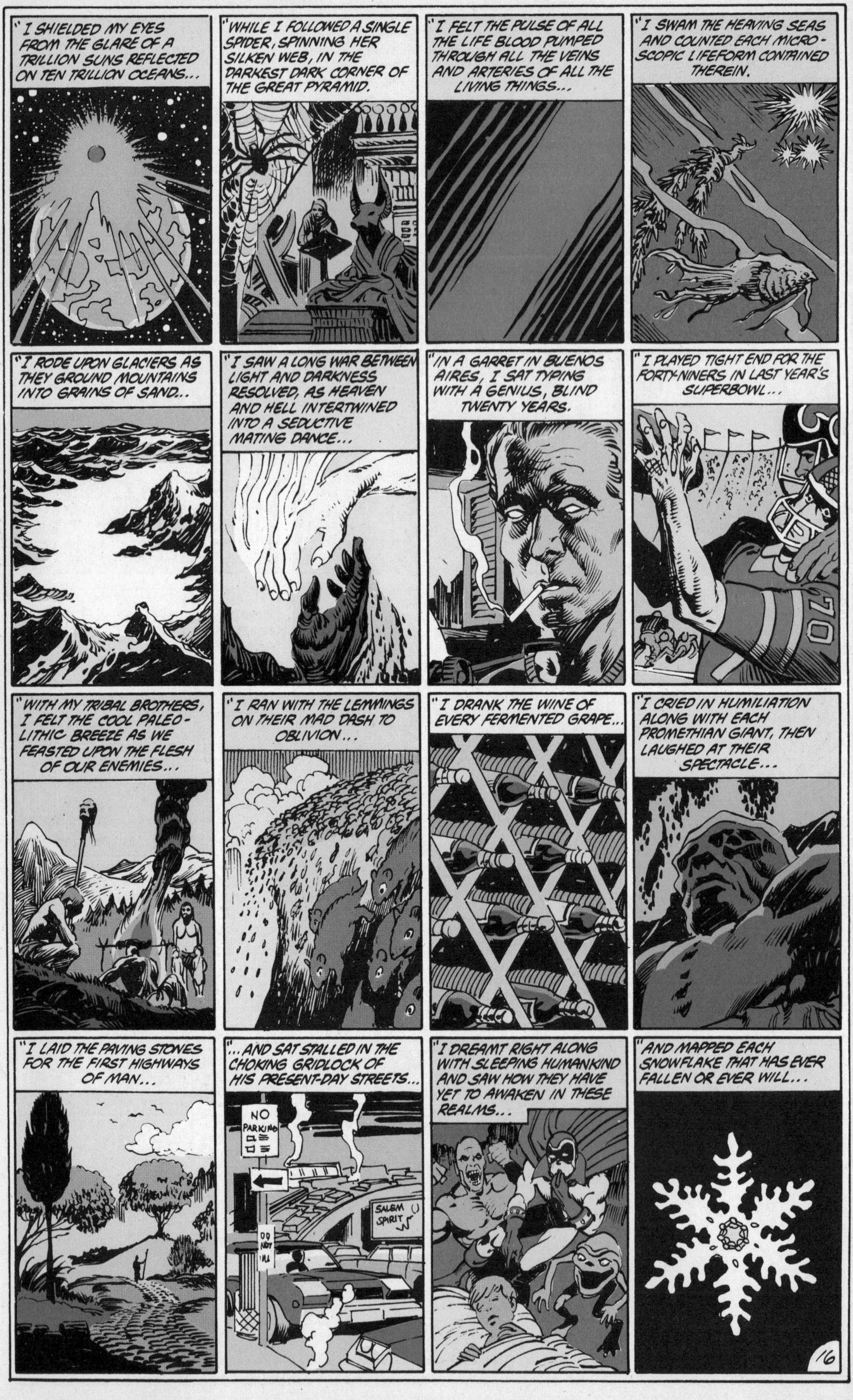
"I SHIELDED MY EYES FROM THE GLARE OF A TRILLION SUNS REFLECTED ON TEN TRILLION OCEANS...
"WHILE I FOLLOWED A SINGLE SPIDER, SPINNING HER SILKEN WEB, IN THE DARKEST DARK CORNER OF THE GREAT PYRAMID.
"I FELT THE PULSE OF ALL THE LIFE BLOOD PUMPED THROUGH ALL THE VEINS AND ARTERIES OF ALL THE LIVING THINGS...
"I SWAM THE HEAVING SEAS AND COUNTED EACH MICRO-SCOPIC LIFEFORM CONTAINED THEREIN.
"I RODE UPON GLACIERS AS THEY GROUND MOUNTAINS INTO GRAINS OF SAND...
"I SAW A LONG WAR BETWEEN LIGHT AND DARKNESS RESOLVED, AS HEAVEN AND HELL INTERTWINED INTO A SEDUCTIVE MATING DANCE...
"IN A GARRET IN BUENOS AIRES, I SAT TYPING WITH A GENIUS, BLIND TWENTY YEARS.
"I PLAYED TIGHT END FOR THE FORTY-NINERS IN LAST YEAR'S SUPERBOWL...
70
"WITH MY TRIBAL BROTHERS, I FELT THE COOL PALEO-LITHIC BREEZE AS WE FEASTED UPON THE FLESH OF OUR ENEMIES...
"I RAN WITH THE LEMMINGS ON THEIR MAD DASH TO OBLIVION...
"I DRANK THE WINE OF EVERY FERMENTED GRAPE...
"I CRIED IN HUMILIATION ALONG WITH EACH PROMETHIAN GIANT, THEN LAUGHED AT THEIR SPECTACLE...
"I LAID THE PAVING STONES FOR THE FIRST HIGHWAYS OF MAN...
"...AND SAT STALLED IN THE CHOKING GRIDLOCK OF HIS PRESENT-DAY STREETS...
NO PARKING
SALEM SPIRIT
"I DREAMT RIGHT ALONG WITH SLEEPING HUMANKIND AND SAW HOW THEY HAVE YET TO AWAKEN IN THESE REALMS...
"AND MAPPED EACH SNOWFLAKE THAT HAS EVER FALLEN OR EVER WILL...
16

"I SMELT RANCID GREASE DRIPPING ON A STOVETOP COUNTER..."

"...AND WONDERED AT THE BEAUTY OF THE TAJ MAHAL..."

"I FLEW WITH PTERO-DACTYLS, WINGS BEATING FURIOUSLY IN AN ATTEMPT TO OUTRACE EXTINCTION..."

"I SAW THE SEASONS OF THE YEAR UNFOLDING, ALL THE SEASONS OF ALL THE YEARS..."

"A BABY KITTEN, SUFFERING DISTEMPER..."

"ALL THE PAWNS MOVED IN ALL THE GAMES EVER PLAYED..."

"A PEACOCK, SPREADING HIS FEATHERS, REVEALING THE GAZE OF A HUNDRED JEWELED EYES..."

"I SAW THE HEEL OF A SHOE, CRUSHING A DELICATE FLOWER..."

"...THE MANIA AND DELUSIONS THAT ACCOMPANY ALL CIVILIZATIONS.

"I WATCHED THE ELEMENTS BEING FORMED WITHIN THE CRUCIBLES OF THE STARS..."

"...THE GASES THAT BREW IN THE CLOSED SYSTEMS OF THE PLANETS...

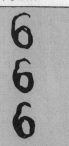

"THE OMENS THAT AUGUR ALL FUTURE ACTS...

"...A GAMBLER'S DISCARDS.

"I SAW TIME, NOT AS A LINEAR PROGRESSION OF EVENTS, BUT AS A SINGLE HARMONIC EXPLOSION...

"I SAW A PEBBLE, TOSSED INTO A POND, RIPPLING OUT IN PERFECT CONCENTRIC PATTERNS...

"I FOLLOWED THE SPOOR OF THE YETI...

"I LIFTED THE COLUMNS OF THE ACROPOLIS IN FEAR AND HONOR OF THE GODS...

"I KNEW THE HUBRIS OF OUR ANCESTORS AS THEY LOOKED DOWN ON THESE OFFERINGS...

"I SAW A GREAT SHIP, ITS RUDDER GONE, SIDES SPLIT ASUNDER BY A TREACHEROUS REEF...

"I WAS THE REEF, A COMPLETE ECOSYSTEM WELCOMING THE SHIP'S CREW TO MY WATERY BOSOM...

"I FELT THE MOTHER BOX, AND UNDERSTOOD HER COMMUNION WITH NATURE...

PING!

PING!

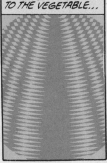

"...HER CONNECTION TO THE VEGETABLE...

"AND HIS CONNECTION TO EARTH.

"I SAW HIS FACE SCREAMING AS THE MADNESS OVERCAME HIM...

"I SAW MY FACE..."

17

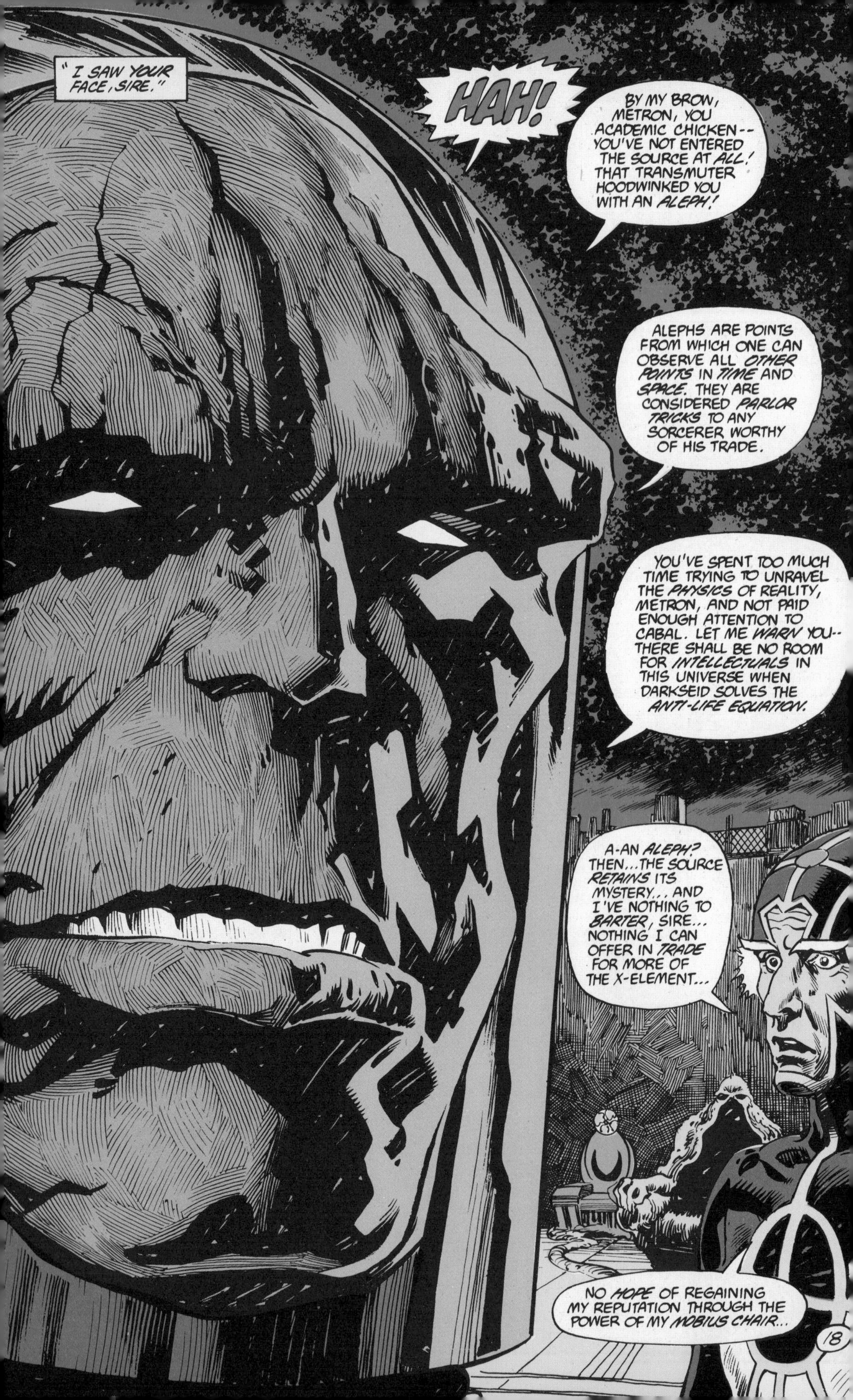
"I SAW YOUR FACE, SIRE."
HAH!
BY MY BROW, METRON, YOU ACADEMIC CHICKEN-- YOU'VE NOT ENTERED THE SOURCE AT ALL! THAT TRANSMUTER HOODWINKED YOU WITH AN ALEPH!
ALEPHS ARE POINTS FROM WHICH ONE CAN OBSERVE ALL OTHER POINTS IN TIME AND SPACE. THEY ARE CONSIDERED PARLOR TRICKS TO ANY SORCERER WORTHY OF HIS TRADE.
YOU'VE SPENT TOO MUCH TIME TRYING TO UNRAVEL THE PHYSICS OF REALITY, METRON, AND NOT PAID ENOUGH ATTENTION TO CABAL. LET ME WARN YOU-- THERE SHALL BE NO ROOM FOR INTELLECTUALS IN THIS UNIVERSE WHEN DARKSEID SOLVES THE ANTI-LIFE EQUATION.
A-AN ALEPH? THEN... THE SOURCE RETAINS ITS MYSTERY... AND I'VE NOTHING TO BARTER, SIRE... NOTHING I CAN OFFER IN TRADE FOR MORE OF THE X-ELEMENT...
NO HOPE OF REGAINING MY REPUTATION THROUGH THE POWER OF MY MOBIUS CHAIR...
18

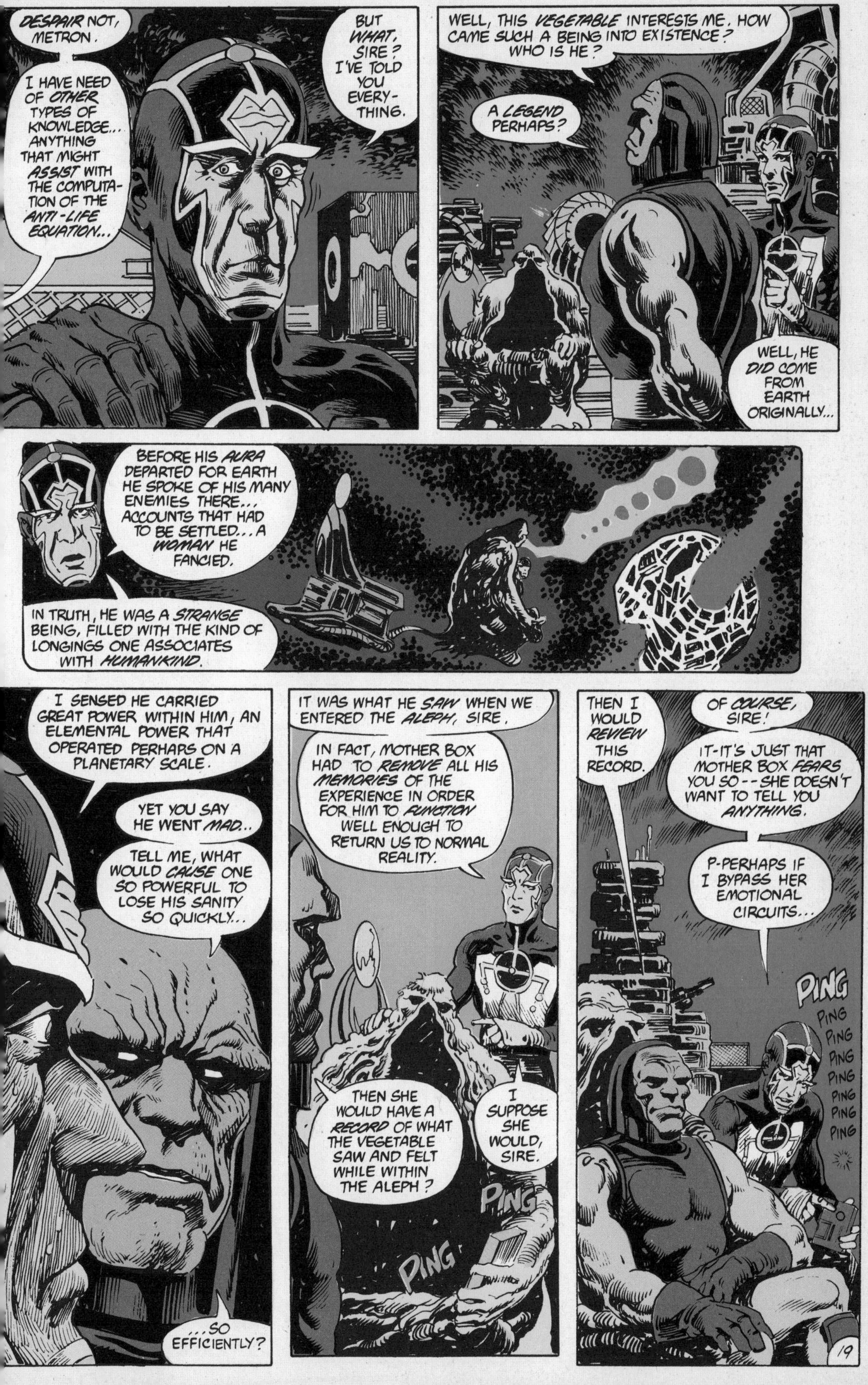
DESPAIR NOT, METRON.
I HAVE NEED OF OTHER TYPES OF KNOWLEDGE... ANYTHING THAT MIGHT ASSIST WITH THE COMPUTATION OF THE ANTI-LIFE EQUATION...
BUT WHAT, SIRE? I'VE TOLD YOU EVERYTHING.
WELL, THIS VEGETABLE INTERESTS ME. HOW CAME SUCH A BEING INTO EXISTENCE? WHO IS HE?
A LEGEND PERHAPS?
WELL, HE DID COME FROM EARTH ORIGINALLY...
BEFORE HIS AURA DEPARTED FOR EARTH HE SPOKE OF HIS MANY ENEMIES THERE... ACCOUNTS THAT HAD TO BE SETTLED... A WOMAN HE FANCIED.
IN TRUTH, HE WAS A STRANGE BEING, FILLED WITH THE KIND OF LONGINGS ONE ASSOCIATES WITH HUMANKIND.
I SENSED HE CARRIED GREAT POWER WITHIN HIM, AN ELEMENTAL POWER THAT OPERATED PERHAPS ON A PLANETARY SCALE.
YET YOU SAY HE WENT MAD...
TELL ME, WHAT WOULD CAUSE ONE SO POWERFUL TO LOSE HIS SANITY SO QUICKLY...
...SO EFFICIENTLY?
IT WAS WHAT HE SAW WHEN WE ENTERED THE ALEPH, SIRE.
IN FACT, MOTHER BOX HAD TO REMOVE ALL HIS MEMORIES OF THE EXPERIENCE IN ORDER FOR HIM TO FUNCTION WELL ENOUGH TO RETURN US TO NORMAL REALITY.
THEN SHE WOULD HAVE A RECORD OF WHAT THE VEGETABLE SAW AND FELT WHILE WITHIN THE ALEPH?
I SUPPOSE SHE WOULD, SIRE.
PING
PING
THEN I WOULD REVIEW THIS RECORD.
OF COURSE, SIRE!
IT-IT'S JUST THAT MOTHER BOX FEARS YOU SO--SHE DOESN'T WANT TO TELL YOU ANYTHING.
P-PERHAPS IF I BYPASS HER EMOTIONAL CIRCUITS...
PING
PING
PING
PING
PING
PING
PING
PING
19

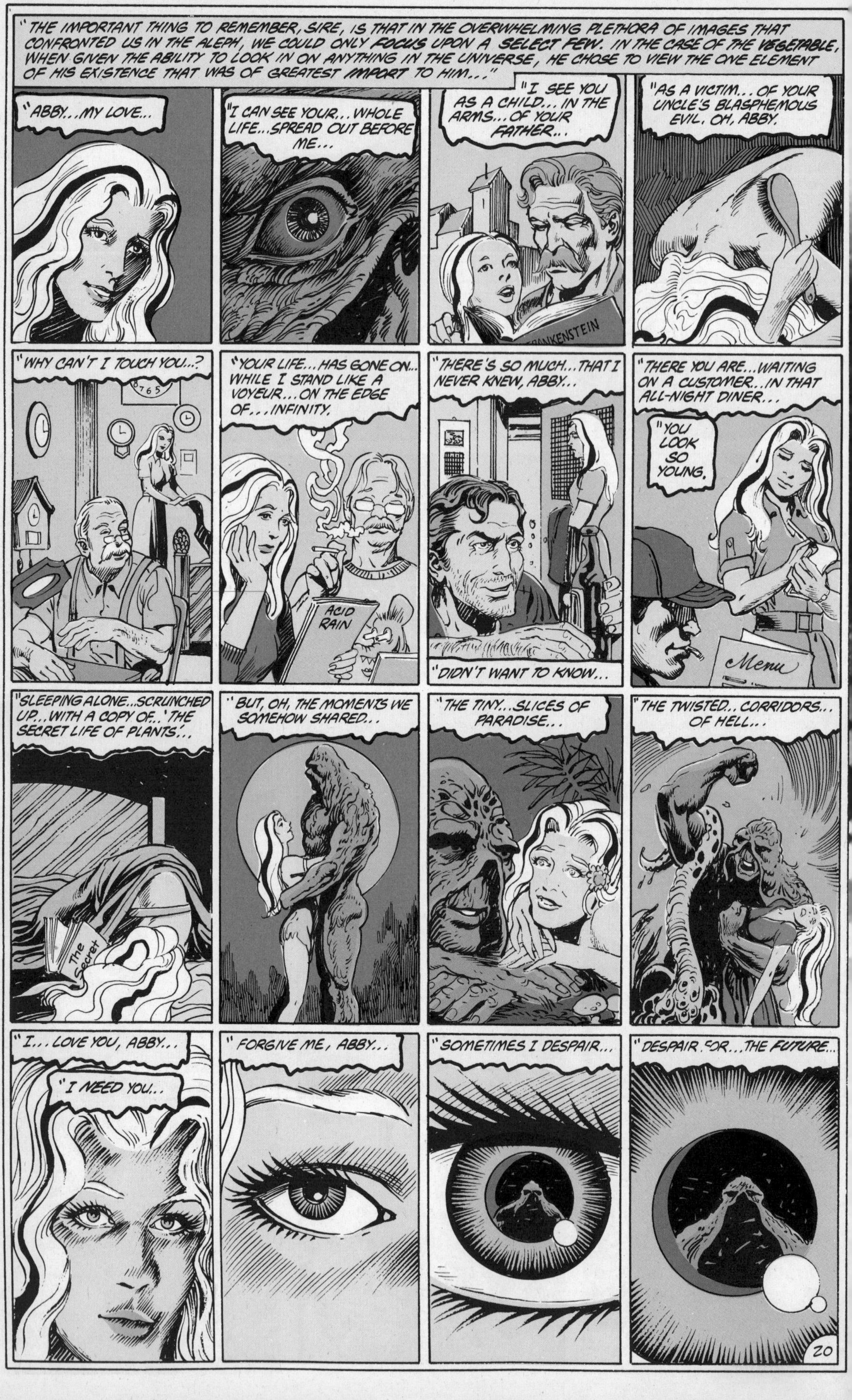
"THE IMPORTANT THING TO REMEMBER, SIRE, IS THAT IN THE OVERWHELMING PLETHORA OF IMAGES THAT CONFRONTED US IN THE ALEPH, WE COULD ONLY FOCUS UPON A SELECT FEW. IN THE CASE OF THE VEGETABLE, WHEN GIVEN THE ABILITY TO LOOK IN ON ANYTHING IN THE UNIVERSE, HE CHOSE TO VIEW THE ONE ELEMENT OF HIS EXISTENCE THAT WAS OF GREATEST IMPORT TO HIM..."
"ABBY...MY LOVE...
"I CAN SEE YOUR...WHOLE LIFE...SPREAD OUT BEFORE ME...
"I SEE YOU AS A CHILD...IN THE ARMS...OF YOUR FATHER...
FRANKENSTEIN
"AS A VICTIM...OF YOUR UNCLE'S BLASPHEMOUS EVIL. OH, ABBY.
"WHY CAN'T I TOUCH YOU...?
"YOUR LIFE...HAS GONE ON...WHILE I STAND LIKE A VOYEUR...ON THE EDGE OF...INFINITY.
ACID RAIN
"THERE'S SO MUCH...THAT I NEVER KNEW, ABBY...
"DIDN'T WANT TO KNOW...
"THERE YOU ARE...WAITING ON A CUSTOMER...IN THAT ALL-NIGHT DINER...
"YOU LOOK SO YOUNG.
Menu
"SLEEPING ALONE...SCRUNCHED UP...WITH A COPY OF...'THE SECRET LIFE OF PLANTS'...
The Secret
"BUT, OH, THE MOMENTS WE SOMEHOW SHARED...
"THE TINY...SLICES OF PARADISE...
"THE TWISTED...CORRIDORS...OF HELL...
"I...LOVE YOU, ABBY...
"I NEED YOU...
"FORGIVE ME, ABBY...
"SOMETIMES I DESPAIR...
"DESPAIR FOR...THE FUTURE...
20

"THE FUTURE...OUR FUTURE...TOGETHER?

"OH, PLEASE...

"EMBRACING YOU? YOUR FULL LIPS BRUSHING MY OWN...?

"IN THE SWAMP...FREE FROM ALL PRYING...?

"IS IT POSSIBLE?

"A WHITE HAND... SLOWLY TURNING GREEN...

"I'M DIVING...FOR PEARLS IN AN OCEAN OF EMERALD...LIGHT.

"I SEE YOU LOST...BUT HAPPY...LAUGHING... THERE IS NO DANGER...

"NOTHING TO FEAR...

"THE WHITE HAND...NOW EMERALD...GRASPING THE YOUNG SHOOT...

"CONSTANTINE...?

"A CARNIVOROUS PLANT...THE SIZE OF... A FOOTBALL STADIUM...

"...ABBY, WHAT ARE YOU AND CONSTANTINE...?

"THE PARLIAMENT OF TREES...DEMANDING...

"ABBY...?

"BUT I LOVE...

"A MAN...BURNING... RUNNING FOR THE SWAMPS.

"BURNING...

"A PARCHED...AND CHALKY HAND... NOW GREEN... PULLING THE SHOOT... OUT BY THE ROOTS...

"ANOTHER MAN BURNS...

"ABBY...

"THE GREEN DIMEN- SION...WITHERING... ROTTING...DROPPING AWAY PIECEMEAL.

"ABBY, YOUR LOVE...

"A WITCH DOCTOR...DEEP IN THE NEW GUINEA RAIN FOREST...GRINDING POWDERS IN A CEREMONIAL BOWL...

"YOUR LOVE...

"MORE BURNING...A WOMAN, SCREAMING...

"YOUR LOVE WAS ALL...

"MY NAME IS ALEC OLSEN...NO! HOLLAND...

"YOUR LOVE WAS ALL THAT KEPT ME...

"THE BURNING...NO-- PLEASE DON'T LET ME...

"ALL THAT KEPT ME...

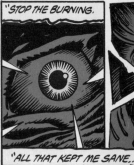

"STOP THE BURNING.

"ALL THAT KEPT ME SANE..."

PING! PING! PING! PING! PING! PING! PING! PING! PING!

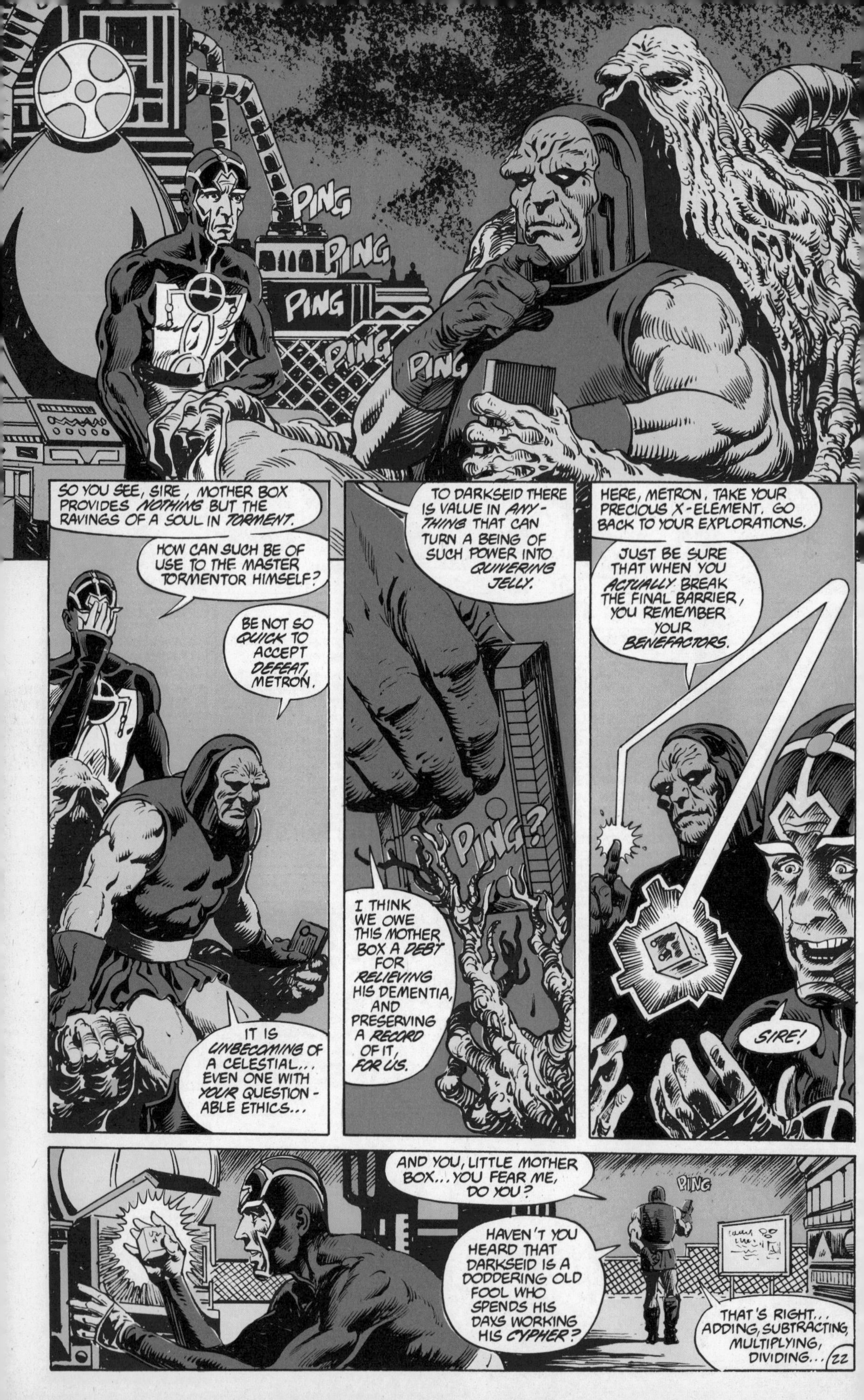
PING
PING
PING
PING
PING
SO YOU SEE, SIRE, MOTHER BOX PROVIDES NOTHING BUT THE RAVINGS OF A SOUL IN TORMENT.
HOW CAN SUCH BE OF USE TO THE MASTER TORMENTOR HIMSELF?
BE NOT SO QUICK TO ACCEPT DEFEAT, METRON.
IT IS UNBECOMING OF A CELESTIAL... EVEN ONE WITH YOUR QUESTION-ABLE ETHICS...
TO DARKSEID THERE IS VALUE IN ANY-THING THAT CAN TURN A BEING OF SUCH POWER INTO QUIVERING JELLY.
PING?
I THINK WE OWE THIS MOTHER BOX A DEBT FOR RELIEVING HIS DEMENTIA, AND PRESERVING A RECORD OF IT, FOR US.
HERE, METRON, TAKE YOUR PRECIOUS X-ELEMENT. GO BACK TO YOUR EXPLORATIONS.
JUST BE SURE THAT WHEN YOU ACTUALLY BREAK THE FINAL BARRIER, YOU REMEMBER YOUR BENEFACTORS.
SIRE!
AND YOU, LITTLE MOTHER BOX... YOU FEAR ME, DO YOU?
PING
HAVEN'T YOU HEARD THAT DARKSEID IS A DODDERING OLD FOOL WHO SPENDS HIS DAYS WORKING HIS CYPHER?
THAT'S RIGHT... ADDING, SUBTRACTING, MULTIPLYING, DIVIDING...
22

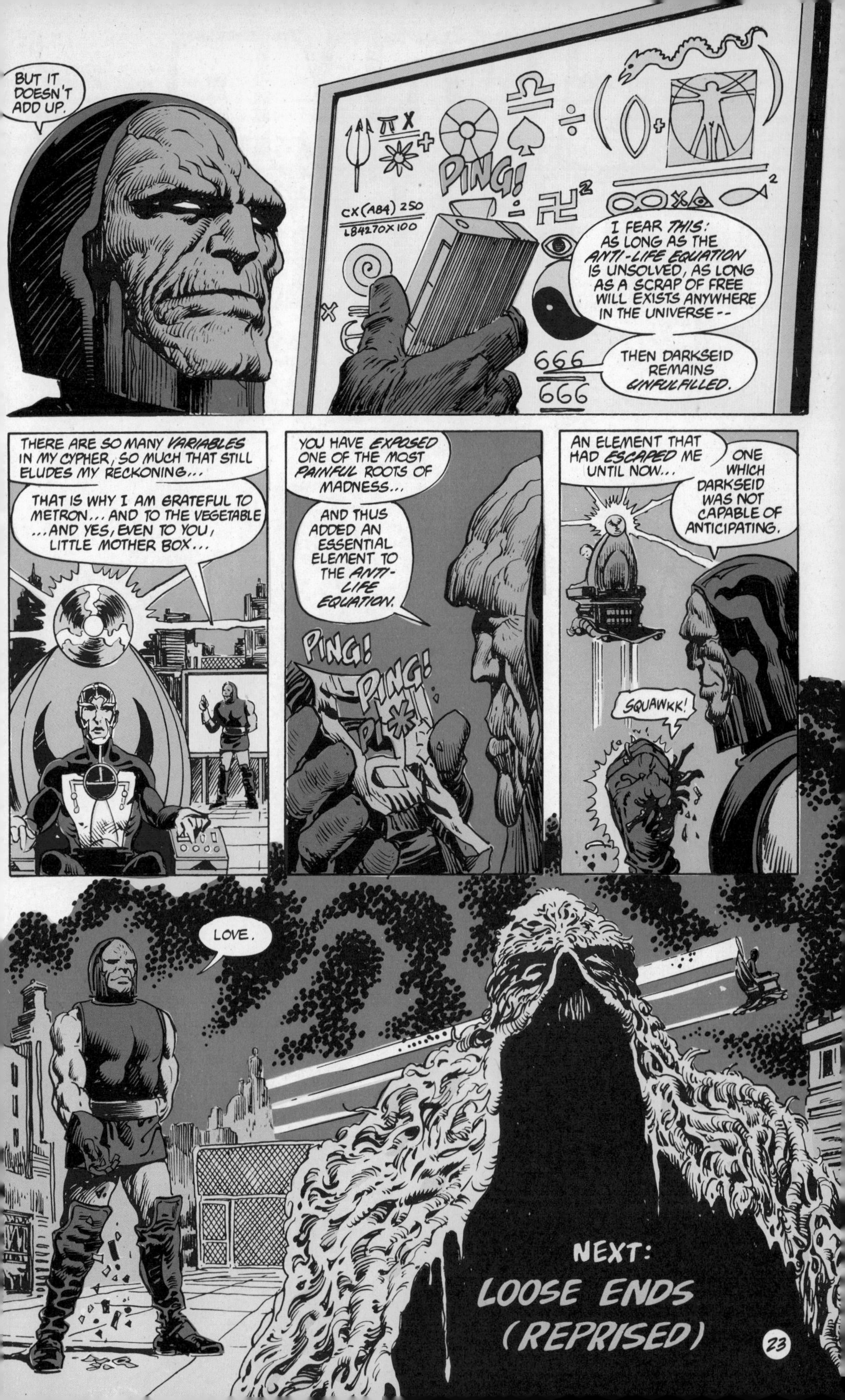

BUT IT DOESN'T ADD UP.
PING!
CX(AB4) 250
LB4270X100
666
666
I FEAR THIS: AS LONG AS THE ANTI-LIFE EQUATION IS UNSOLVED, AS LONG AS A SCRAP OF FREE WILL EXISTS ANYWHERE IN THE UNIVERSE--
THEN DARKSEID REMAINS UNFULFILLED.
THERE ARE SO MANY VARIABLES IN MY CYPHER, SO MUCH THAT STILL ELUDES MY RECKONING...
THAT IS WHY I AM GRATEFUL TO METRON... AND TO THE VEGETABLE ...AND YES, EVEN TO YOU, LITTLE MOTHER BOX...
YOU HAVE EXPOSED ONE OF THE MOST PAINFUL ROOTS OF MADNESS...
AND THUS ADDED AN ESSENTIAL ELEMENT TO THE ANTI-LIFE EQUATION.
PING!
PING!
AN ELEMENT THAT HAD ESCAPED ME UNTIL NOW...
ONE WHICH DARKSEID WAS NOT CAPABLE OF ANTICIPATING.
SQUAWKK!
LOVE.
NEXT:
LOOSE ENDS (REPRISED)

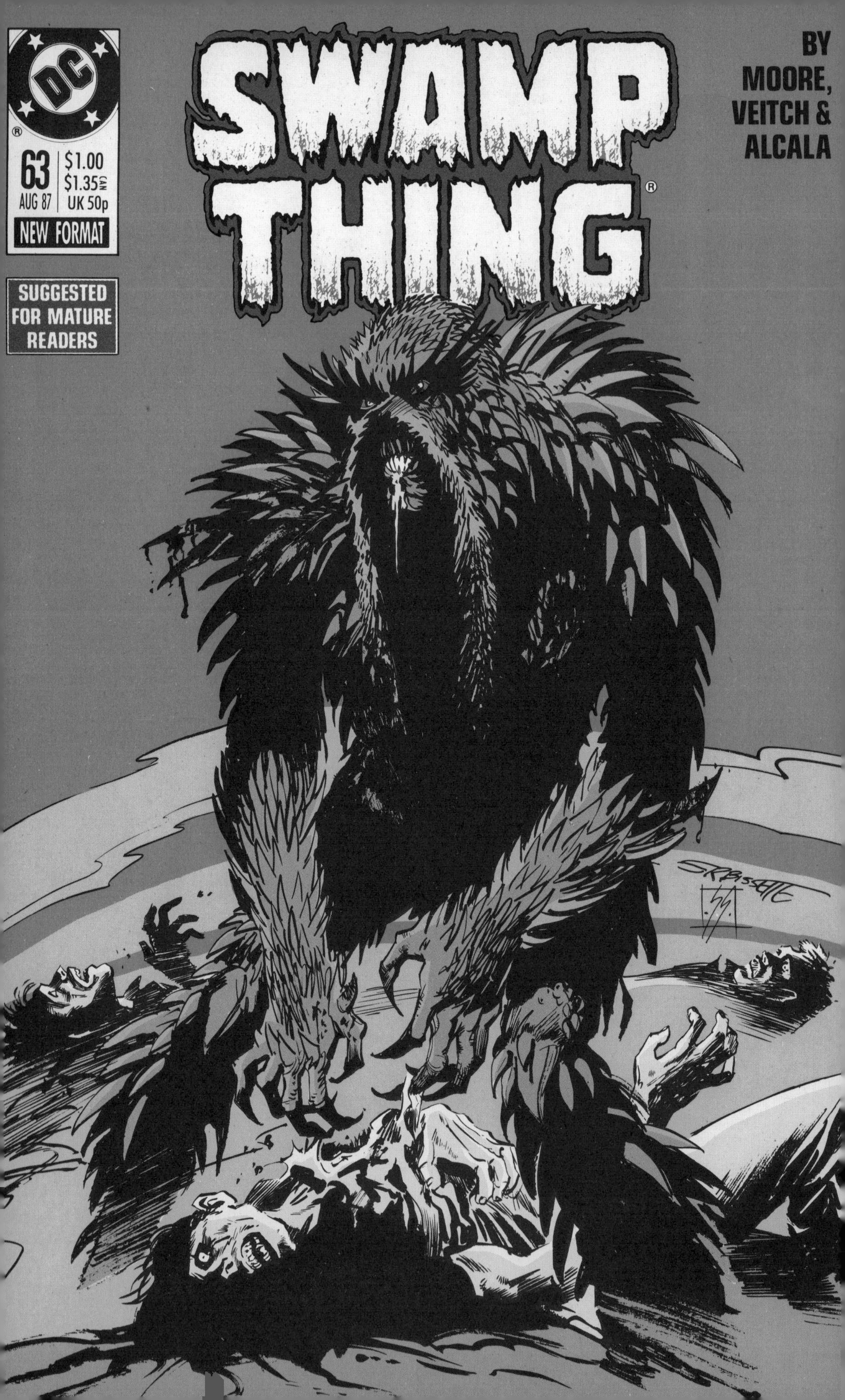
SWAMP THING
BY MOORE, VEITCH & ALCALA
63
$1.00
$1.35 CAN
AUG 87
UK 50p
NEW FORMAT
SUGGESTED FOR MATURE READERS

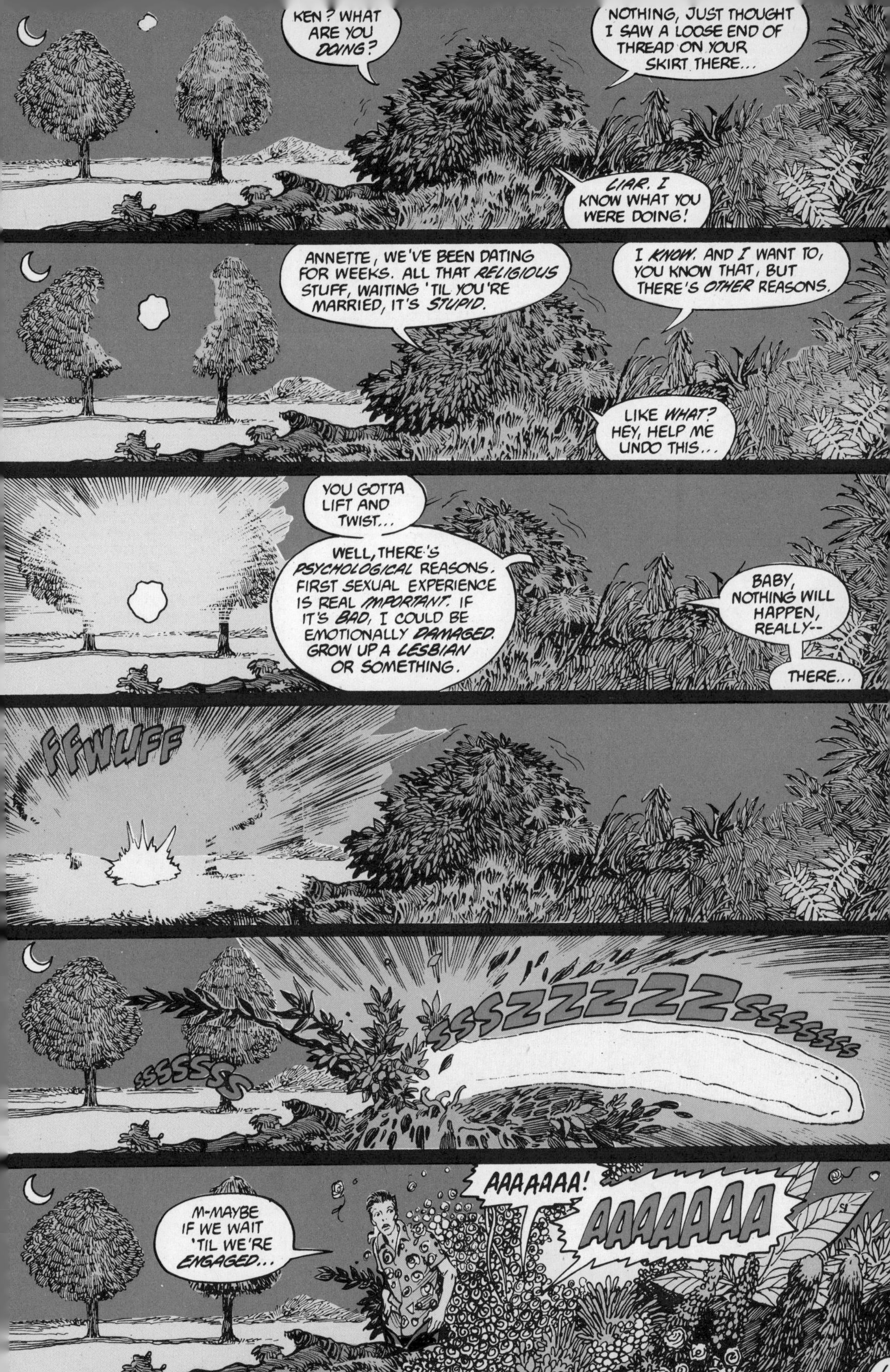
KEN? WHAT ARE YOU DOING?
NOTHING, JUST THOUGHT I SAW A LOOSE END OF THREAD ON YOUR SKIRT THERE...
LIAR. I KNOW WHAT YOU WERE DOING!
ANNETTE, WE'VE BEEN DATING FOR WEEKS. ALL THAT RELIGIOUS STUFF, WAITING 'TIL YOU'RE MARRIED, IT'S STUPID.
I KNOW. AND I WANT TO, YOU KNOW THAT, BUT THERE'S OTHER REASONS.
LIKE WHAT? HEY, HELP ME UNDO THIS...
YOU GOTTA LIFT AND TWIST...
WELL, THERE'S PSYCHOLOGICAL REASONS. FIRST SEXUAL EXPERIENCE IS REAL IMPORTANT. IF IT'S BAD, I COULD BE EMOTIONALLY DAMAGED. GROW UP A LESBIAN OR SOMETHING.
BABY, NOTHING WILL HAPPEN, REALLY--
THERE...
FFWUFF
SSSZZZZZSSSSSSSS
SSSSSSS
M-MAYBE IF WE WAIT 'TIL WE'RE ENGAGED...
AAAAAAA!
AAAAAAA
1

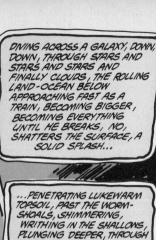

DIVING ACROSS A GALAXY, DOWN, DOWN, THROUGH STARS AND STARS AND STARS AND FINALLY CLOUDS, THE ROLLING LAND-OCEAN BELOW APPROACHING FAST AS A TRAIN, BECOMING BIGGER, BECOMING EVERYTHING UNTIL HE BREAKS, NO, SHATTERS THE SURFACE, A SOLID SPLASH...

...PENETRATING LUKEWARM TOPSOIL, PAST THE WORM-SHOALS, SHIMMERING, WRITHING IN THE SHALLOWS, PLUNGING DEEPER, THROUGH THE THRILLING COLD STREAMS OF THE CLAYBEDS AND OH, OH THE FEELING AND HE IS HOME...

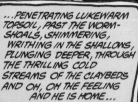

FINALLY, HOME.

ABOVE GREAT GEOLOGIC WAVES OF EARTH AND ROCK RACE IMPERCEPTIBLY CROSS-CONTINENT TO BREAK, PERHAPS, A MILLION YEARS FROM NOW, AGAINST THE SEA.

ABOVE, THE TREESTUMPS RADIATE PALE TENDRILS, ROTTEN STARS BENEATH WHICH SKELETONS OF CATS AND HORSES HANG SUSPENDED IN THE STEAD OF CLOUDS. THE COAL SEAM IS A REEF OF JET, ITS PLATES PRECARIOUSLY STACKED, LIKE DIRTY DISHES, AND, BELOW THAT, MONSTERS, MONSTERS AND THEIR FOOTPRINTS BEFORE MILES OF STONE AND ULTIMATELY FIRE.

THE BURIED RIVERBED'S A PEBBLE RIBBON WHERE THE FISHBONES HOVER, DREAMING OF THEIR FORMER LIVES, AND THERE, AMONGST THE KEELS OF ROCKS, HE THINKS OF HER, THE IMPRINT OF THEIR LAST EMBRACE A CHERISHED BRUISE UPON HIS SPIRIT, PURPLE STILL AND TENDER, DESPITE ALL THE LONG AND HOLLOW MONTHS ALONE.

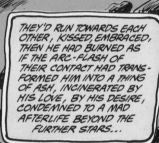

THEY'D RUN TOWARDS EACH OTHER, KISSED, EMBRACED, THEN HE HAD BURNED AS IF THE ARC-FLASH OF THEIR CONTACT HAD TRANSFORMED HIM INTO A THING OF ASH, INCINERATED BY HIS LOVE, BY HIS DESIRE, CONDEMNED TO A MAD AFTERLIFE BEYOND THE FURTHER STARS...

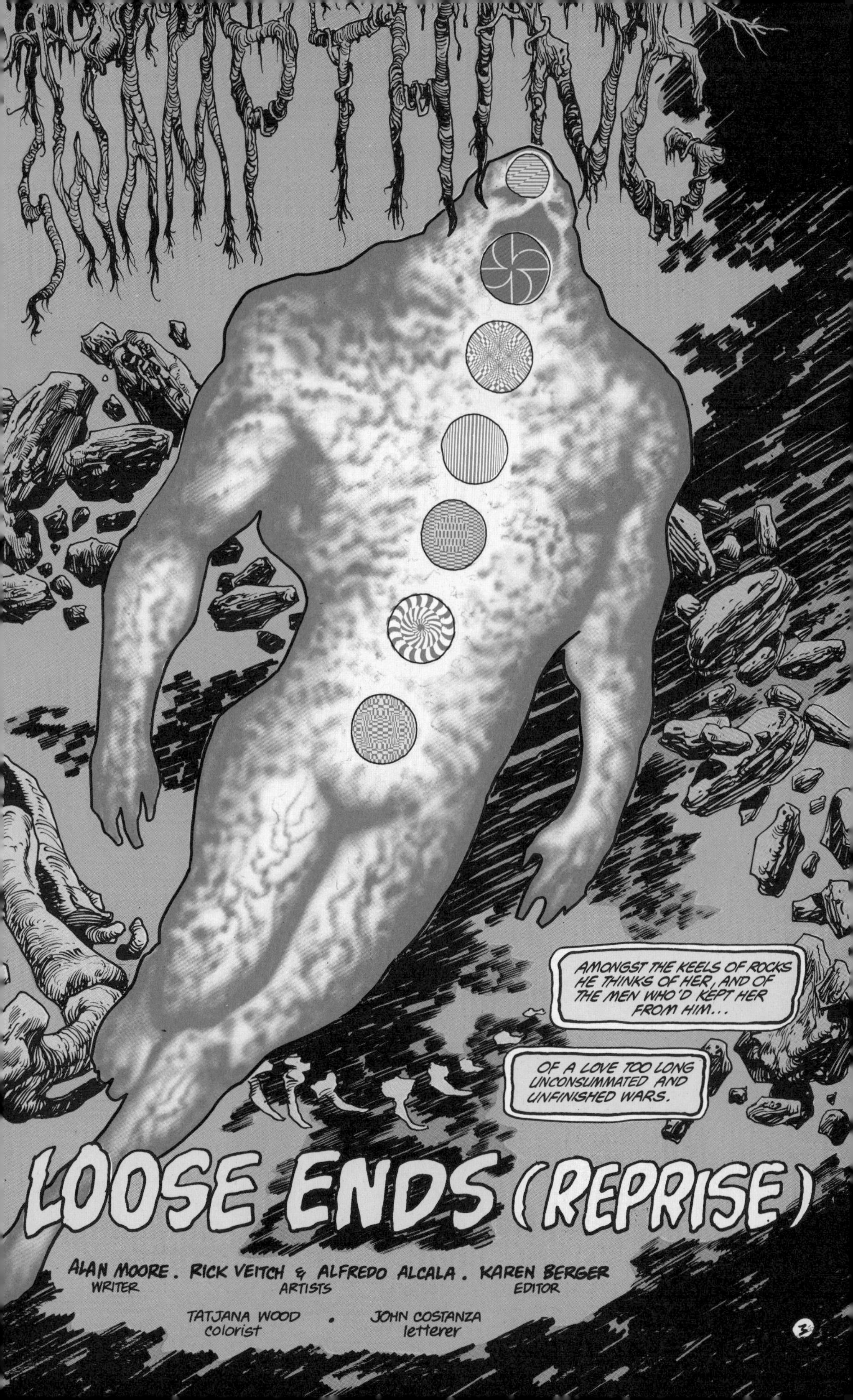
SWAMP THING
AMONGST THE KEELS OF ROCKS HE THINKS OF HER, AND OF THE MEN WHO'D KEPT HER FROM HIM...
OF A LOVE TOO LONG UNCONSUMMATED AND UNFINISHED WARS.
LOOSE ENDS (REPRISE)
ALAN MOORE . RICK VEITCH & ALFREDO ALCALA . KAREN BERGER
WRITER ARTISTS EDITOR
TATJANA WOOD . JOHN COSTANZA
colorist letterer
3

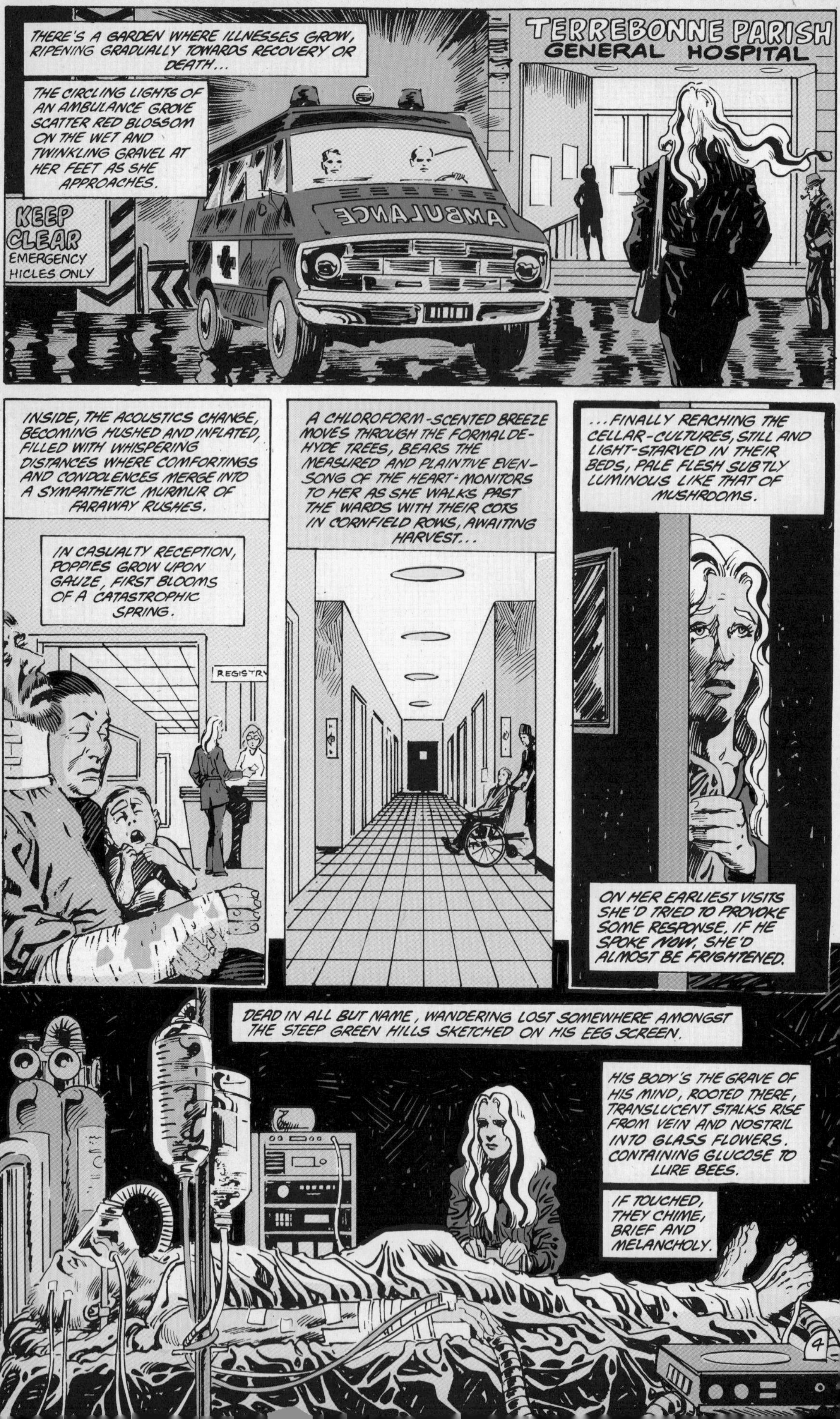
THERE'S A GARDEN WHERE ILLNESSES GROW, RIPENING GRADUALLY TOWARDS RECOVERY OR DEATH...
TERREBONNE PARISH GENERAL HOSPITAL
THE CIRCLING LIGHTS OF AN AMBULANCE GROVE SCATTER RED BLOSSOM ON THE WET AND TWINKLING GRAVEL AT HER FEET AS SHE APPROACHES.
KEEP CLEAR EMERGENCY HICLES ONLY
AMBULANCE
INSIDE, THE ACOUSTICS CHANGE, BECOMING HUSHED AND INFLATED, FILLED WITH WHISPERING DISTANCES WHERE COMFORTINGS AND CONDOLENCES MERGE INTO A SYMPATHETIC MURMUR OF FARAWAY RUSHES.
IN CASUALTY RECEPTION, POPPIES GROW UPON GAUZE, FIRST BLOOMS OF A CATASTROPHIC SPRING.
REGISTRY
A CHLOROFORM-SCENTED BREEZE MOVES THROUGH THE FORMALDEHYDE TREES, BEARS THE MEASURED AND PLAINTIVE EVEN-SONG OF THE HEART-MONITORS TO HER AS SHE WALKS PAST THE WARDS WITH THEIR COTS IN CORNFIELD ROWS, AWAITING HARVEST...
...FINALLY REACHING THE CELLAR-CULTURES, STILL AND LIGHT-STARVED IN THEIR BEDS, PALE FLESH SUBTLY LUMINOUS LIKE THAT OF MUSHROOMS.
ON HER EARLIEST VISITS SHE'D TRIED TO PROVOKE SOME RESPONSE. IF HE SPOKE NOW, SHE'D ALMOST BE FRIGHTENED.
DEAD IN ALL BUT NAME, WANDERING LOST SOMEWHERE AMONGST THE STEEP GREEN HILLS SKETCHED ON HIS EEG SCREEN.
HIS BODY'S THE GRAVE OF HIS MIND, ROOTED THERE, TRANSLUCENT STALKS RISE FROM VEIN AND NOSTRIL INTO GLASS FLOWERS. CONTAINING GLUCOSE TO LURE BEES.
IF TOUCHED, THEY CHIME, BRIEF AND MELANCHOLY.
4

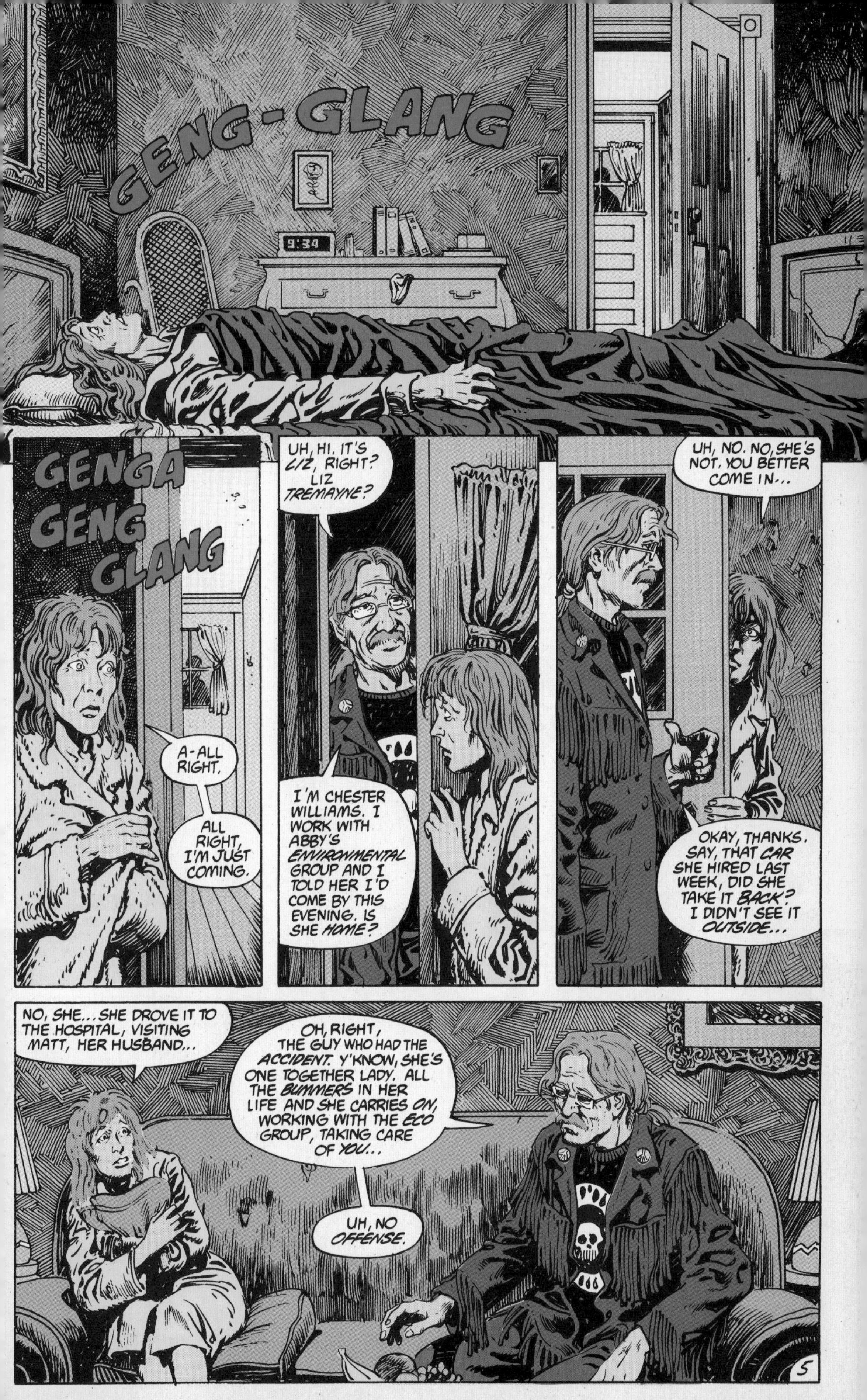
GENG-GLANG
9:34
GENGA GENG GLANG
A-ALL RIGHT.
ALL RIGHT, I'M JUST COMING.
UH, HI. IT'S LIZ, RIGHT? LIZ TREMAYNE?
I'M CHESTER WILLIAMS. I WORK WITH ABBY'S ENVIRONMENTAL GROUP AND I TOLD HER I'D COME BY THIS EVENING. IS SHE HOME?
UH, NO. NO, SHE'S NOT. YOU BETTER COME IN...
OKAY, THANKS. SAY, THAT CAR SHE HIRED LAST WEEK, DID SHE TAKE IT BACK? I DIDN'T SEE IT OUTSIDE...
NO, SHE... SHE DROVE IT TO THE HOSPITAL, VISITING MATT, HER HUSBAND...
OH, RIGHT, THE GUY WHO HAD THE ACCIDENT. Y'KNOW, SHE'S ONE TOGETHER LADY. ALL THE BUMMERS IN HER LIFE AND SHE CARRIES ON, WORKING WITH THE ECO GROUP, TAKING CARE OF YOU...
UH, NO OFFENSE.

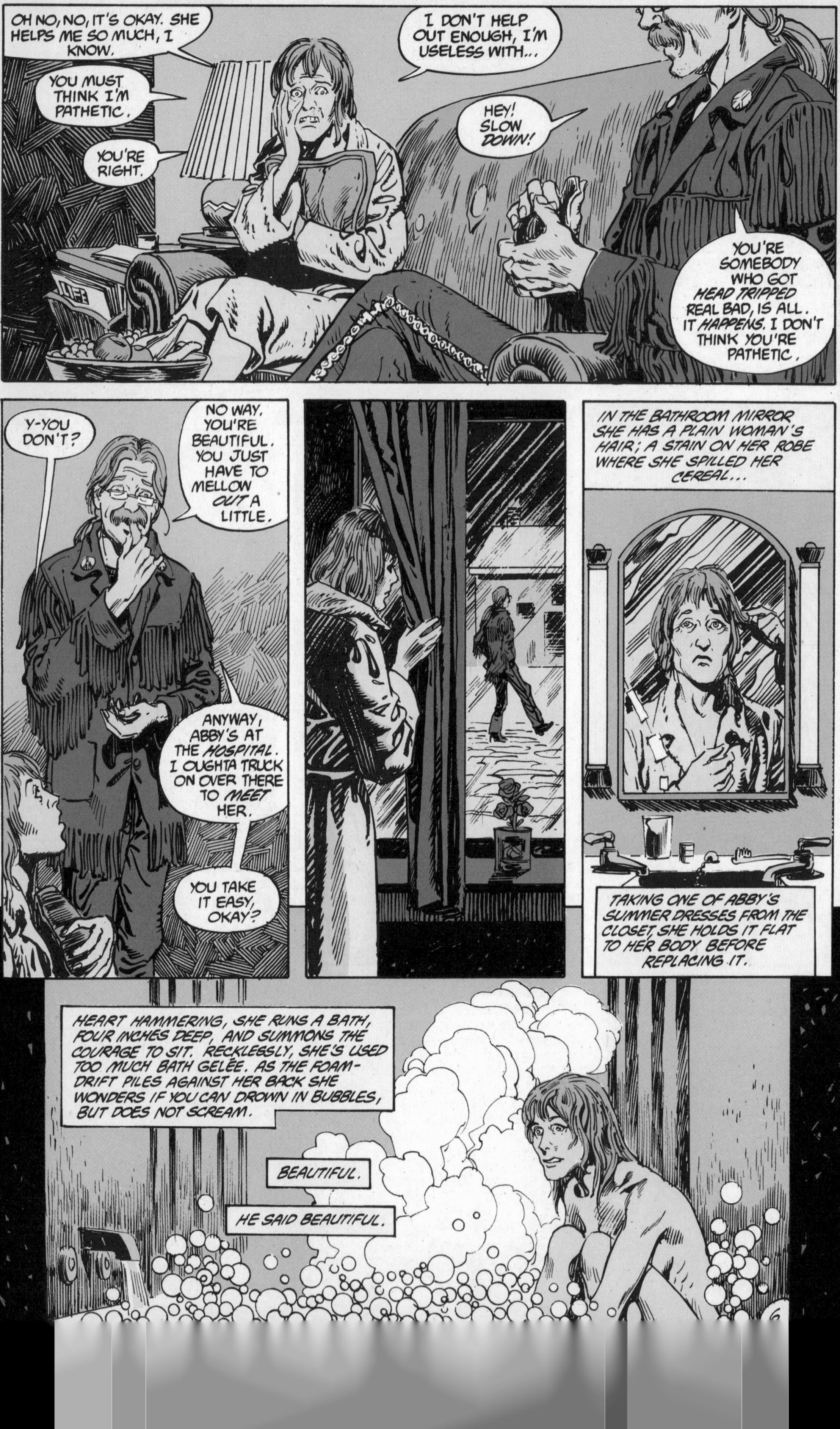
OH NO, NO, IT'S OKAY. SHE HELPS ME SO MUCH, I KNOW.
YOU MUST THINK I'M PATHETIC.
YOU'RE RIGHT.
I DON'T HELP OUT ENOUGH, I'M USELESS WITH...
HEY! SLOW DOWN!
YOU'RE SOMEBODY WHO GOT HEAD TRIPPED REAL BAD, IS ALL. IT HAPPENS. I DON'T THINK YOU'RE PATHETIC.
Y-YOU DON'T?
NO WAY. YOU'RE BEAUTIFUL. YOU JUST HAVE TO MELLOW OUT A LITTLE.
ANYWAY, ABBY'S AT THE HOSPITAL. I OUGHTA TRUCK ON OVER THERE TO MEET HER.
YOU TAKE IT EASY, OKAY?
IN THE BATHROOM MIRROR SHE HAS A PLAIN WOMAN'S HAIR; A STAIN ON HER ROBE WHERE SHE SPILLED HER CEREAL...
TAKING ONE OF ABBY'S SUMMER DRESSES FROM THE CLOSET, SHE HOLDS IT FLAT TO HER BODY BEFORE REPLACING IT.
HEART HAMMERING, SHE RUNS A BATH, FOUR INCHES DEEP, AND SUMMONS THE COURAGE TO SIT. RECKLESSLY, SHE'S USED TOO MUCH BATH GELÉE. AS THE FOAM-DRIFT PILES AGAINST HER BACK SHE WONDERS IF YOU CAN DROWN IN BUBBLES, BUT DOES NOT SCREAM.
BEAUTIFUL.
HE SAID BEAUTIFUL.
6

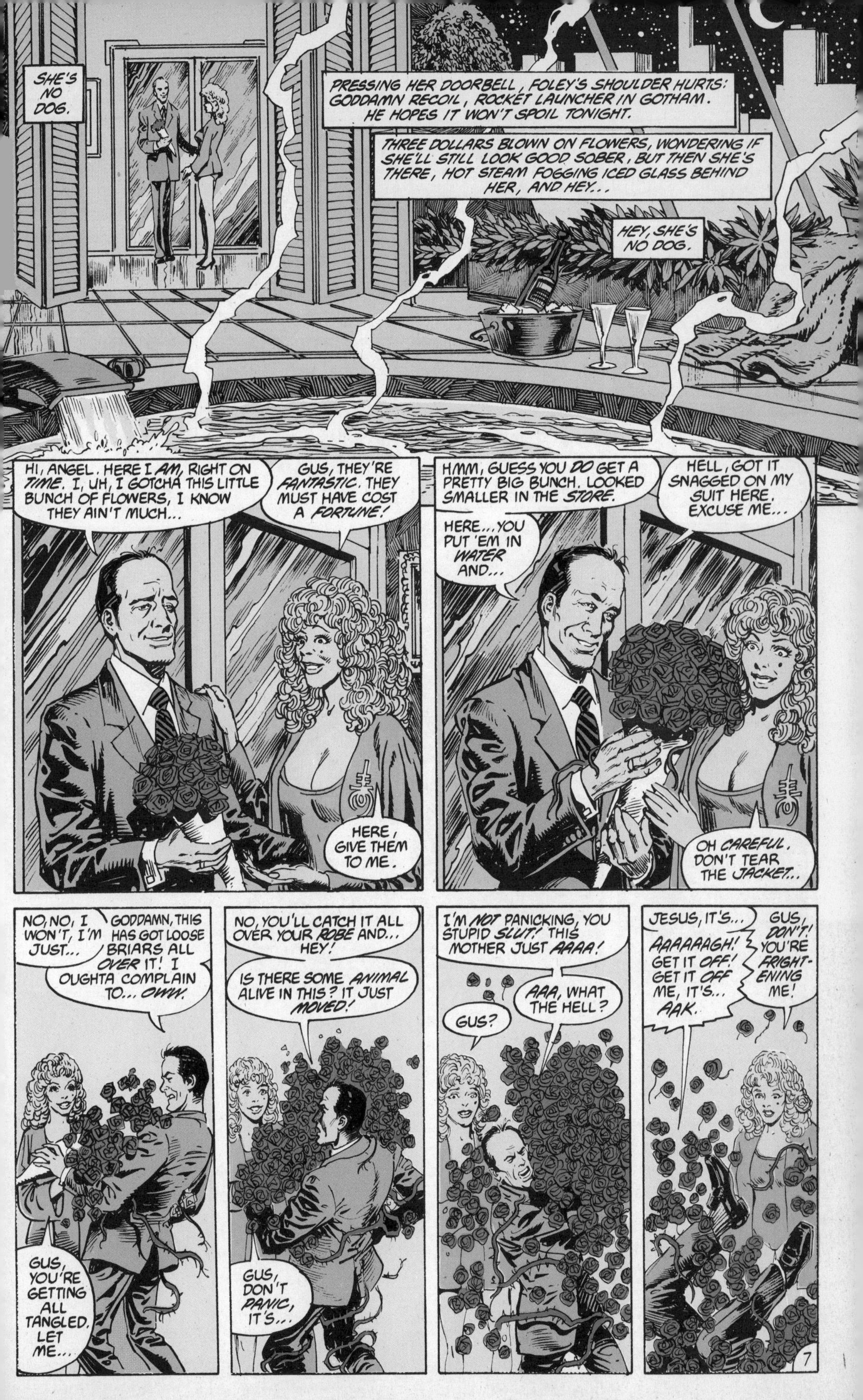
SHE'S NO DOG.
PRESSING HER DOORBELL, FOLEY'S SHOULDER HURTS: GODDAMN RECOIL, ROCKET LAUNCHER IN GOTHAM. HE HOPES IT WON'T SPOIL TONIGHT.
THREE DOLLARS BLOWN ON FLOWERS, WONDERING IF SHE'LL STILL LOOK GOOD SOBER, BUT THEN SHE'S THERE, HOT STEAM FOGGING ICED GLASS BEHIND HER, AND HEY...
HEY, SHE'S NO DOG.
HI, ANGEL. HERE I AM, RIGHT ON TIME. I, UH, I GOTCHA THIS LITTLE BUNCH OF FLOWERS, I KNOW THEY AIN'T MUCH...
GUS, THEY'RE FANTASTIC. THEY MUST HAVE COST A FORTUNE!
HERE, GIVE THEM TO ME.
H'MM, GUESS YOU DO GET A PRETTY BIG BUNCH. LOOKED SMALLER IN THE STORE.
HERE... YOU PUT 'EM IN WATER AND...
HELL, GOT IT SNAGGED ON MY SUIT HERE. EXCUSE ME...
OH CAREFUL. DON'T TEAR THE JACKET...
NO, NO, I WON'T, I'M JUST...
GODDAMN, THIS HAS GOT LOOSE BRIARS ALL OVER IT! I OUGHTA COMPLAIN TO... OWW.
GUS, YOU'RE GETTING ALL TANGLED. LET ME...
NO, YOU'LL CATCH IT ALL OVER YOUR ROBE AND... HEY!
IS THERE SOME ANIMAL ALIVE IN THIS? IT JUST MOVED!
GUS, DON'T PANIC, IT'S...
I'M NOT PANICKING, YOU STUPID SLUT! THIS MOTHER JUST AAAA!
GUS?
AAA, WHAT THE HELL?
JESUS, IT'S...
AAAAAAGH! GET IT OFF! GET IT OFF ME, IT'S... AAK.
GUS, DON'T! YOU'RE FRIGHT-ENING ME!
7

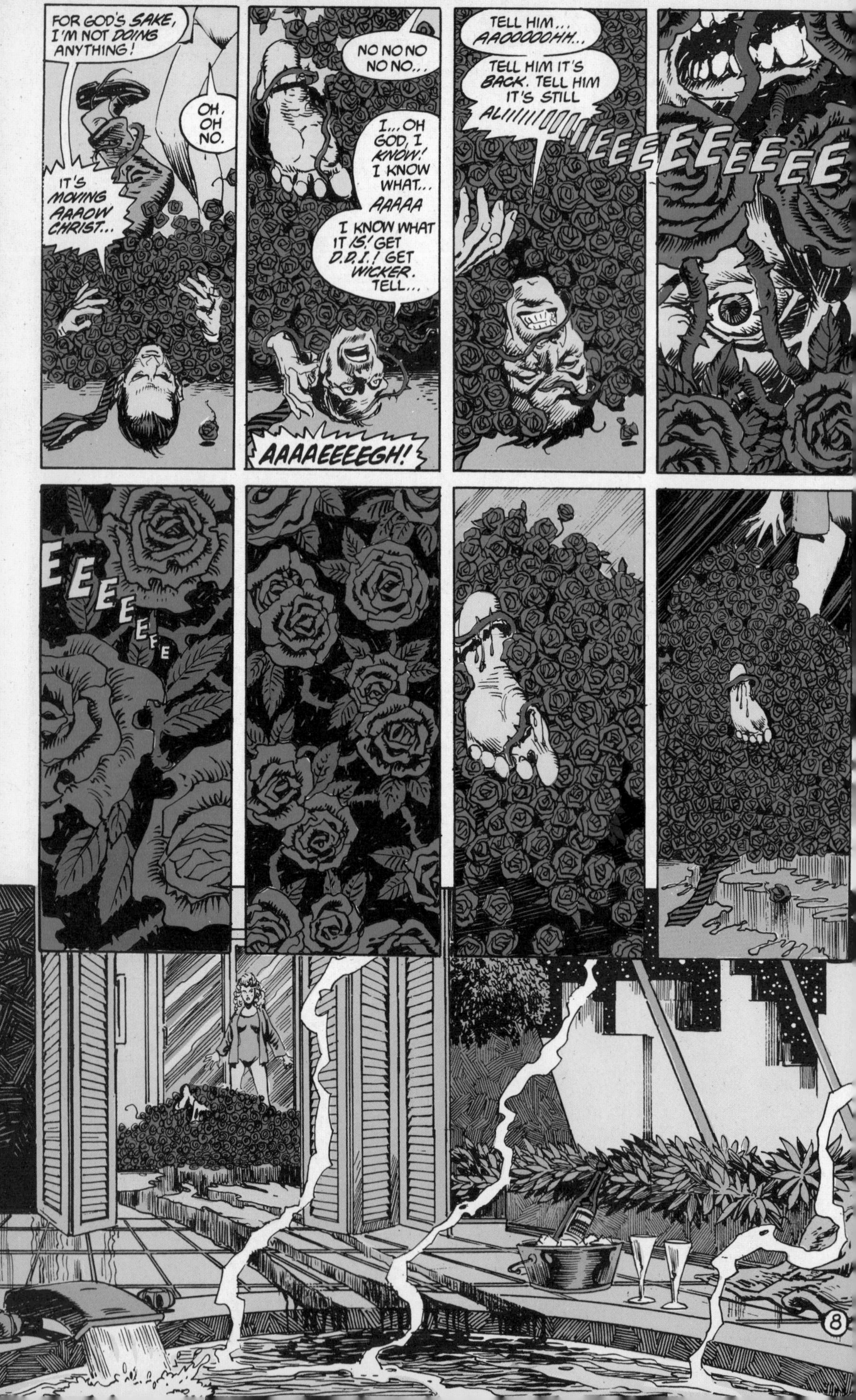
FOR GOD'S SAKE, I'M NOT DOING ANYTHING!
OH, OH NO.
IT'S MOVING AAAOW CHRIST...
NO NO NO NO NO...
I...OH GOD, I KNOW! I KNOW WHAT... AAAAA
I KNOW WHAT IT IS! GET D.D.I.! GET WICKER. TELL...
AAAAEEEEGH!
TELL HIM... AAOOOOOHH...
TELL HIM IT'S BACK. TELL HIM IT'S STILL ALIIIIIIIIIIIEEEEEEEEEEE
EEEEEEE
8

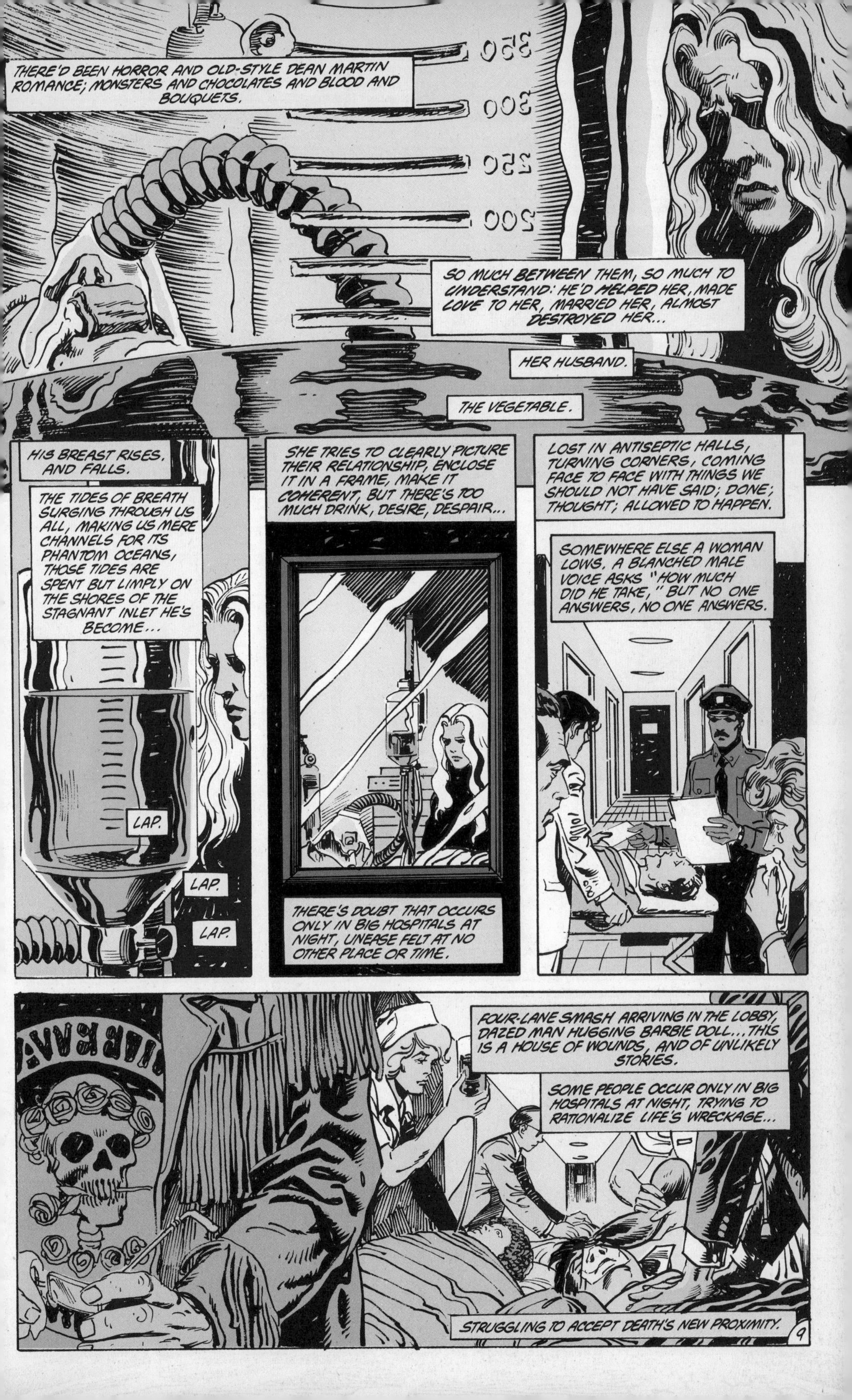
THERE'D BEEN HORROR AND OLD-STYLE DEAN MARTIN ROMANCE; MONSTERS AND CHOCOLATES AND BLOOD AND BOUQUETS.
SO MUCH BETWEEN THEM, SO MUCH TO UNDERSTAND: HE'D HELPED HER, MADE LOVE TO HER, MARRIED HER, ALMOST DESTROYED HER...
HER HUSBAND.
THE VEGETABLE.
HIS BREAST RISES. AND FALLS.
THE TIDES OF BREATH SURGING THROUGH US ALL, MAKING US MERE CHANNELS FOR ITS PHANTOM OCEANS, THOSE TIDES ARE SPENT BUT LIMPLY ON THE SHORES OF THE STAGNANT INLET HE'S BECOME...
LAP.
LAP.
LAP.
SHE TRIES TO CLEARLY PICTURE THEIR RELATIONSHIP, ENCLOSE IT IN A FRAME, MAKE IT COHERENT, BUT THERE'S TOO MUCH DRINK, DESIRE, DESPAIR...
THERE'S DOUBT THAT OCCURS ONLY IN BIG HOSPITALS AT NIGHT, UNEASE FELT AT NO OTHER PLACE OR TIME.
LOST IN ANTISEPTIC HALLS, TURNING CORNERS, COMING FACE TO FACE WITH THINGS WE SHOULD NOT HAVE SAID; DONE; THOUGHT; ALLOWED TO HAPPEN.
SOMEWHERE ELSE A WOMAN LOWS. A BLANCHED MALE VOICE ASKS "HOW MUCH DID HE TAKE," BUT NO ONE ANSWERS, NO ONE ANSWERS.
FOUR-LANE SMASH ARRIVING IN THE LOBBY, DAZED MAN HUGGING BARBIE DOLL... THIS IS A HOUSE OF WOUNDS, AND OF UNLIKELY STORIES.
SOME PEOPLE OCCUR ONLY IN BIG HOSPITALS AT NIGHT, TRYING TO RATIONALIZE LIFE'S WRECKAGE...
STRUGGLING TO ACCEPT DEATH'S NEW PROXIMITY.
9

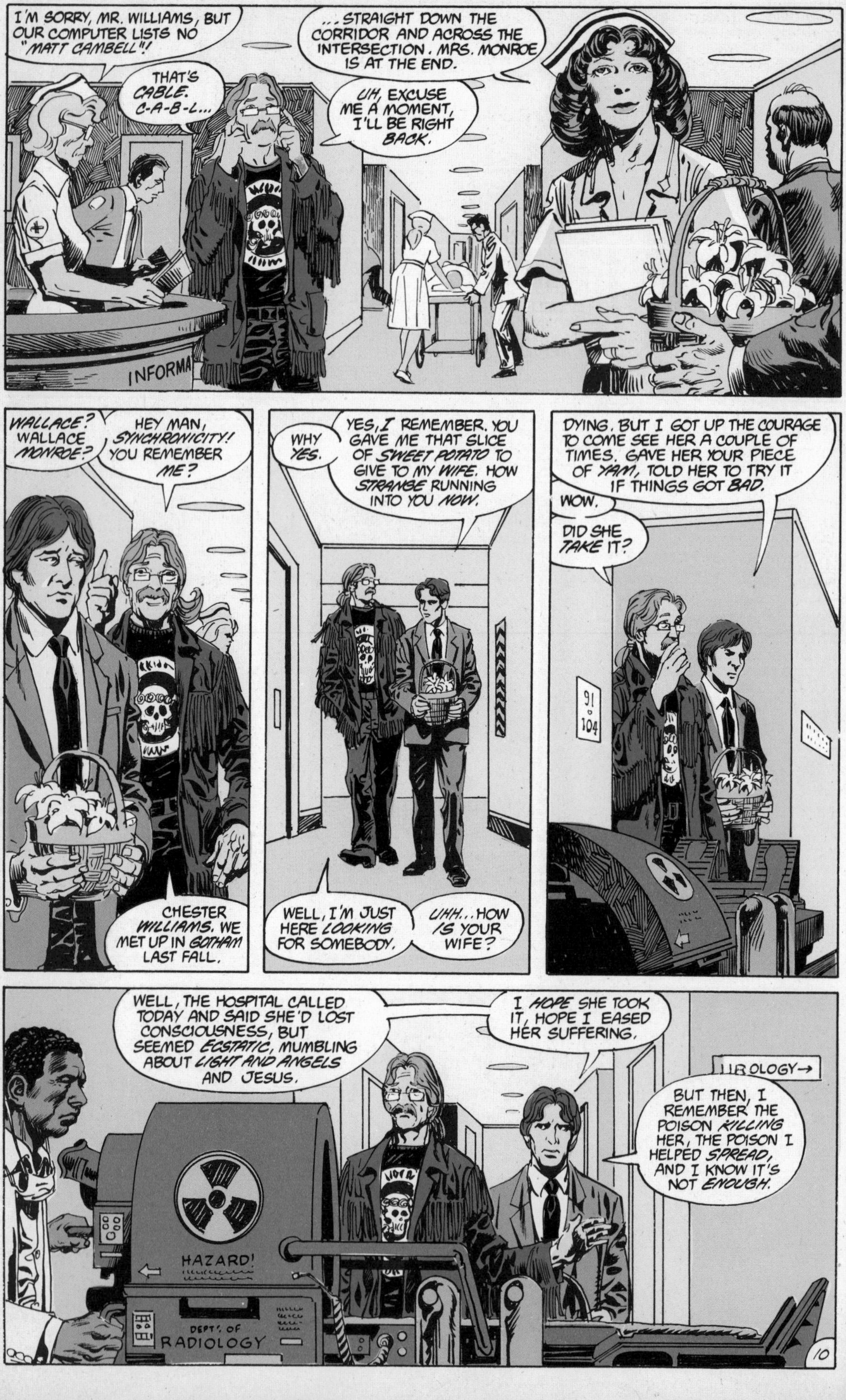
I'M SORRY, MR. WILLIAMS, BUT OUR COMPUTER LISTS NO "MATT CAMBELL"!
THAT'S CABLE. C-A-B-L...
...STRAIGHT DOWN THE CORRIDOR AND ACROSS THE INTERSECTION. MRS. MONROE IS AT THE END.
UH, EXCUSE ME A MOMENT, I'LL BE RIGHT BACK.
INFORMA
WALLACE? WALLACE MONROE?
HEY MAN, SYNCHRONICITY! YOU REMEMBER ME?
CHESTER WILLIAMS. WE MET UP IN GOTHAM LAST FALL.
WHY YES.
YES, I REMEMBER. YOU GAVE ME THAT SLICE OF SWEET POTATO TO GIVE TO MY WIFE. HOW STRANGE RUNNING INTO YOU NOW.
WELL, I'M JUST HERE LOOKING FOR SOMEBODY.
UHH... HOW IS YOUR WIFE?
DYING. BUT I GOT UP THE COURAGE TO COME SEE HER A COUPLE OF TIMES. GAVE HER YOUR PIECE OF YAM, TOLD HER TO TRY IT IF THINGS GOT BAD.
WOW.
DID SHE TAKE IT?
91
104
WELL, THE HOSPITAL CALLED TODAY AND SAID SHE'D LOST CONSCIOUSNESS, BUT SEEMED ECSTATIC, MUMBLING ABOUT LIGHT AND ANGELS AND JESUS.
I HOPE SHE TOOK IT, HOPE I EASED HER SUFFERING.
UROLOGY→
BUT THEN, I REMEMBER THE POISON KILLING HER, THE POISON I HELPED SPREAD, AND I KNOW IT'S NOT ENOUGH.
HAZARD!
DEPT. OF RADIOLOGY
10

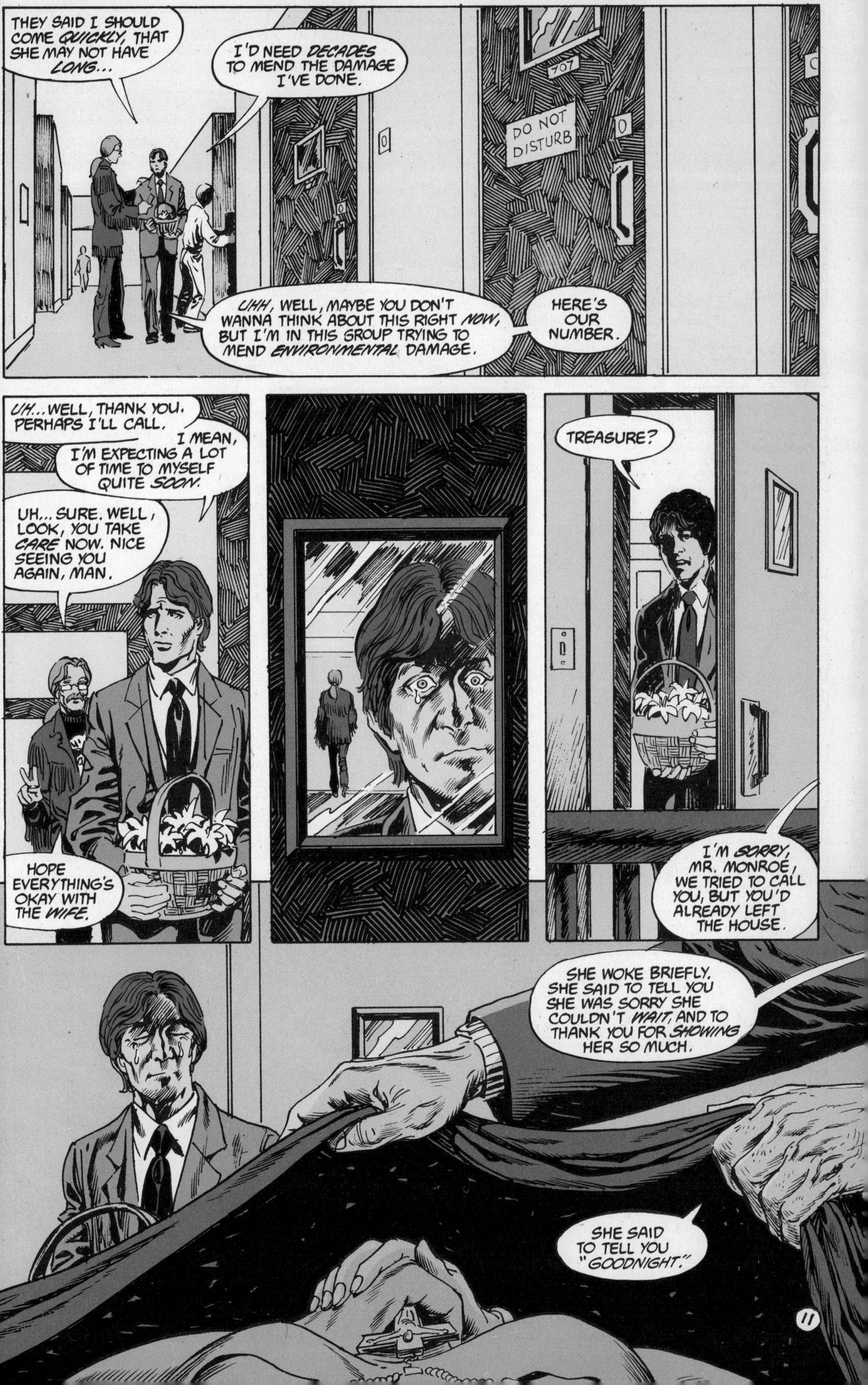
THEY SAID I SHOULD COME *QUICKLY*, THAT SHE MAY NOT HAVE *LONG*...
I'D NEED *DECADES* TO MEND THE DAMAGE I'VE DONE.
707
DO NOT DISTURB
UHH, WELL, *MAYBE* YOU DON'T WANNA THINK ABOUT THIS RIGHT *NOW*, BUT I'M IN THIS GROUP TRYING TO MEND *ENVIRONMENTAL* DAMAGE.
HERE'S OUR NUMBER.
UH... WELL, THANK YOU. PERHAPS I'LL CALL.
I MEAN, I'M EXPECTING A LOT OF TIME TO MYSELF QUITE *SOON*.
UH... SURE. WELL, LOOK, YOU TAKE *CARE* NOW. NICE SEEING YOU AGAIN, MAN.
HOPE EVERYTHING'S OKAY WITH THE *WIFE*.
TREASURE?
I'M *SORRY*, MR. MONROE, WE TRIED TO CALL YOU, BUT YOU'D ALREADY LEFT THE HOUSE.
SHE WOKE BRIEFLY. SHE SAID TO TELL YOU SHE WAS SORRY SHE COULDN'T *WAIT*, AND TO THANK YOU FOR *SHOWING* HER SO MUCH.
SHE SAID TO TELL YOU "*GOODNIGHT*."
11

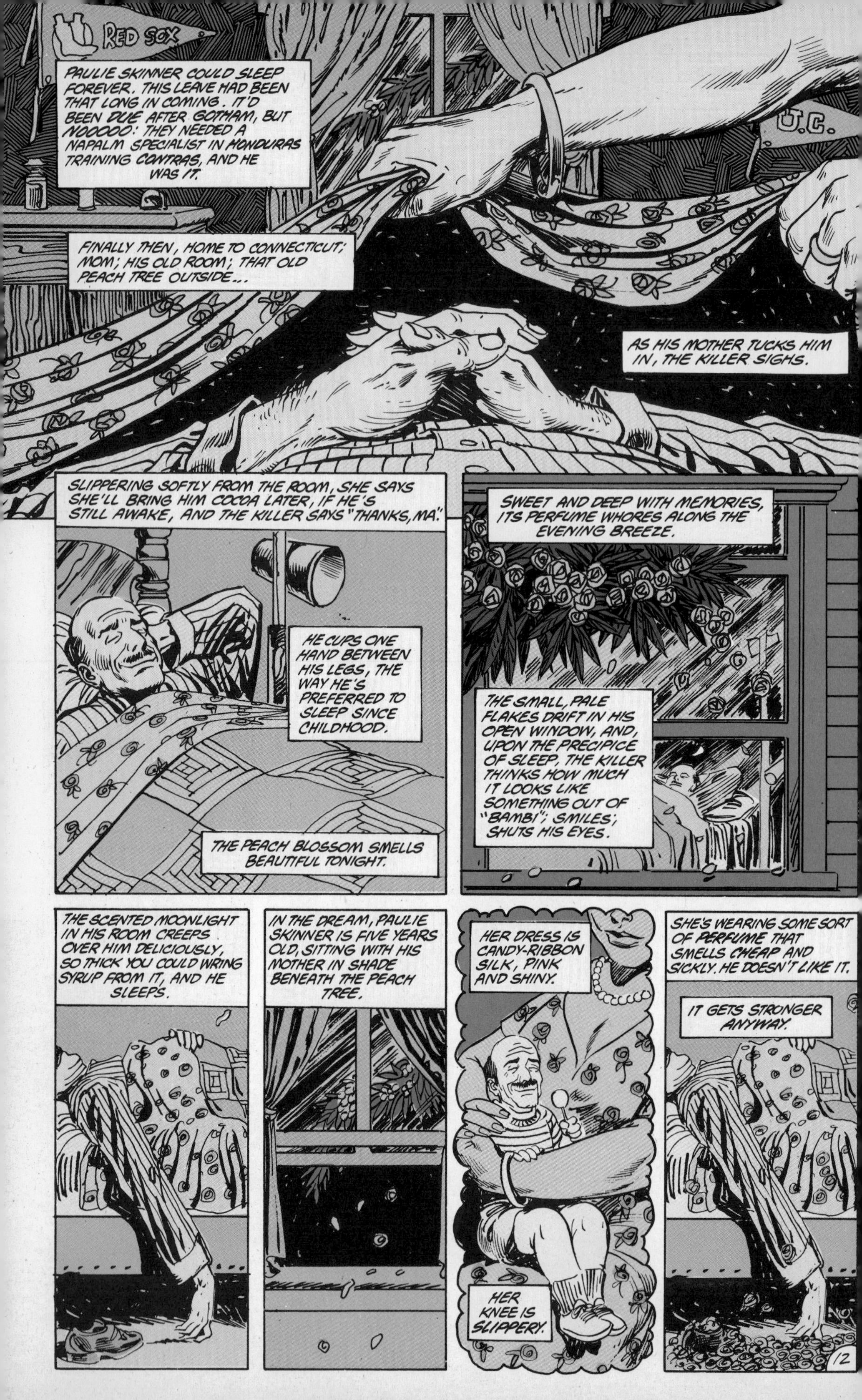
RED SOX
PAULIE SKINNER COULD SLEEP FOREVER. THIS LEAVE HAD BEEN THAT LONG IN COMING. IT'D BEEN DUE AFTER GOTHAM, BUT NOOOOO: THEY NEEDED A NAPALM SPECIALIST IN HONDURAS TRAINING CONTRAS, AND HE WAS IT.
U.C.
FINALLY THEN, HOME TO CONNECTICUT; MOM; HIS OLD ROOM; THAT OLD PEACH TREE OUTSIDE...
AS HIS MOTHER TUCKS HIM IN, THE KILLER SIGHS.
SLIPPERING SOFTLY FROM THE ROOM, SHE SAYS SHE'LL BRING HIM COCOA LATER, IF HE'S STILL AWAKE, AND THE KILLER SAYS "THANKS, MA."
HE CUPS ONE HAND BETWEEN HIS LEGS, THE WAY HE'S PREFERRED TO SLEEP SINCE CHILDHOOD.
THE PEACH BLOSSOM SMELLS BEAUTIFUL TONIGHT.
SWEET AND DEEP WITH MEMORIES, ITS PERFUME WHORES ALONG THE EVENING BREEZE.
THE SMALL, PALE FLAKES DRIFT IN HIS OPEN WINDOW, AND, UPON THE PRECIPICE OF SLEEP, THE KILLER THINKS HOW MUCH IT LOOKS LIKE SOMETHING OUT OF "BAMBI"; SMILES; SHUTS HIS EYES.
THE SCENTED MOONLIGHT IN HIS ROOM CREEPS OVER HIM DELICIOUSLY, SO THICK YOU COULD WRING SYRUP FROM IT, AND HE SLEEPS.
IN THE DREAM, PAULIE SKINNER IS FIVE YEARS OLD, SITTING WITH HIS MOTHER IN SHADE BENEATH THE PEACH TREE.
HER DRESS IS CANDY-RIBBON SILK, PINK AND SHINY.
HER KNEE IS SLIPPERY.
SHE'S WEARING SOME SORT OF PERFUME THAT SMELLS CHEAP AND SICKLY. HE DOESN'T LIKE IT.
IT GETS STRONGER ANYWAY.

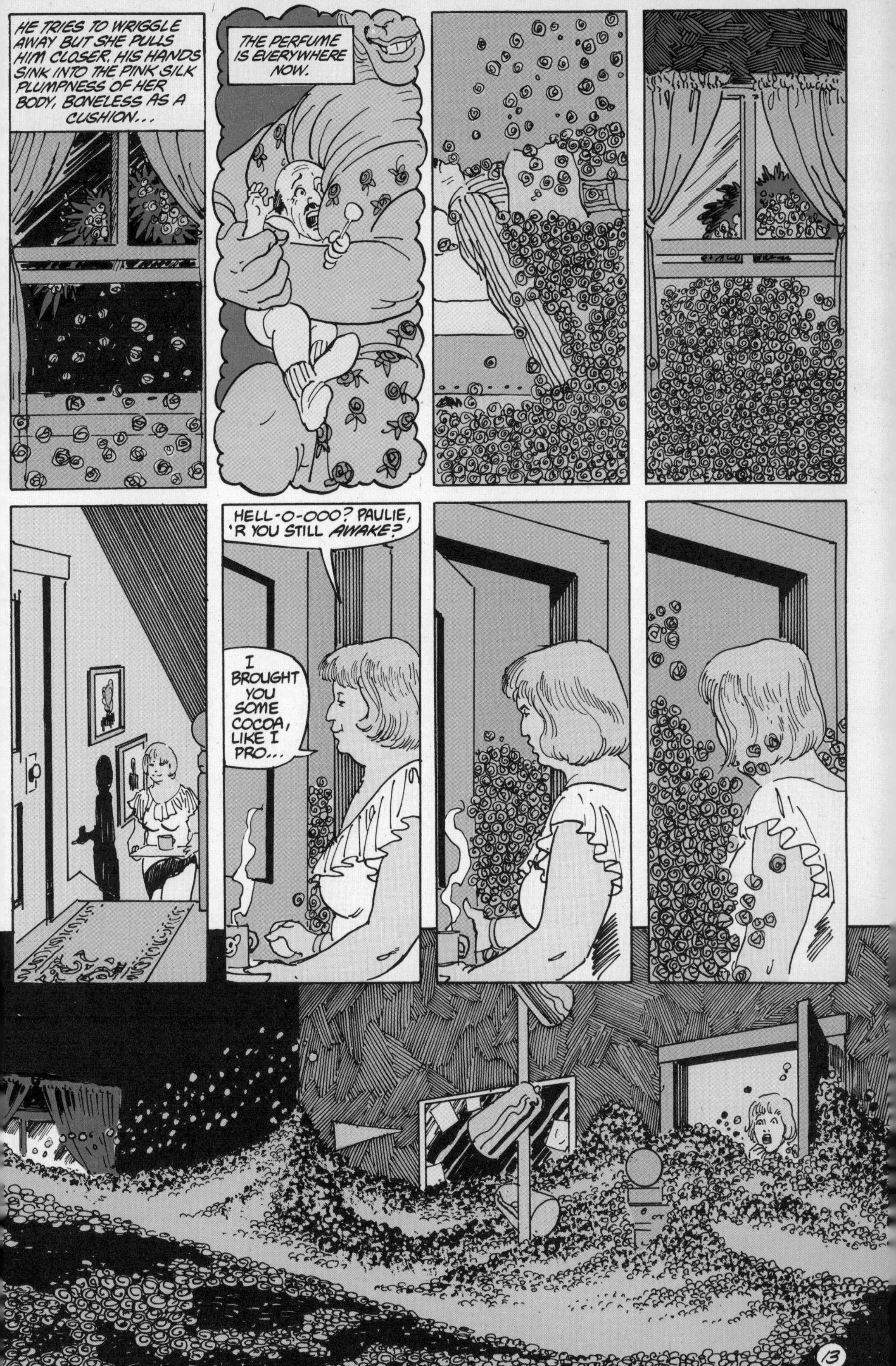
HE TRIES TO WRIGGLE AWAY BUT SHE PULLS HIM CLOSER. HIS HANDS SINK INTO THE PINK SILK PLUMPNESS OF HER BODY, BONELESS AS A CUSHION...
THE PERFUME IS EVERYWHERE NOW.
HELL-O-OOO? PAULIE, 'R YOU STILL AWAKE?
I BROUGHT YOU SOME COCOA, LIKE I PRO...

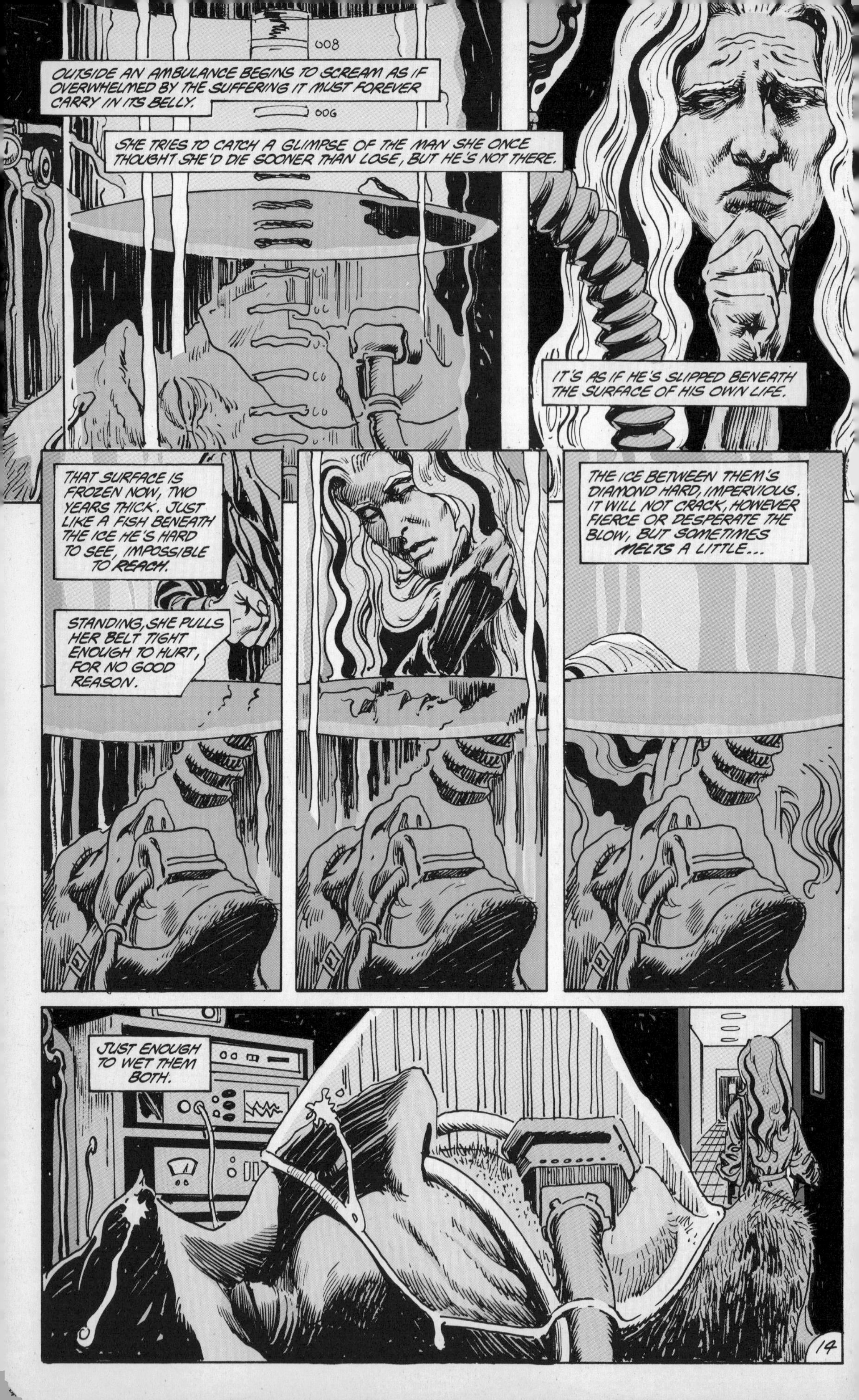
OUTSIDE AN AMBULANCE BEGINS TO SCREAM AS IF OVERWHELMED BY THE SUFFERING IT MUST FOREVER CARRY IN ITS BELLY.
SHE TRIES TO CATCH A GLIMPSE OF THE MAN SHE ONCE THOUGHT SHE'D DIE SOONER THAN LOSE, BUT HE'S NOT THERE.
IT'S AS IF HE'S SLIPPED BENEATH THE SURFACE OF HIS OWN LIFE.
THAT SURFACE IS FROZEN NOW, TWO YEARS THICK. JUST LIKE A FISH BENEATH THE ICE HE'S HARD TO SEE, IMPOSSIBLE TO REACH.
STANDING, SHE PULLS HER BELT TIGHT ENOUGH TO HURT, FOR NO GOOD REASON.
THE ICE BETWEEN THEM'S DIAMOND HARD, IMPERVIOUS. IT WILL NOT CRACK, HOWEVER FIERCE OR DESPERATE THE BLOW, BUT SOMETIMES MELTS A LITTLE...
JUST ENOUGH TO WET THEM BOTH.

HEY! ABBY! I FINALLY *CONNECTED* WITH YOU!

LIZ TOLD ME YOU WERE HERE. I FIGURED I'D COME *OVER.*

ALL VISIT MUS REGI AT DES

HOW'S THINGS WITH YOUR, UH, YOUR *EX-HUSBAND?*

OH, WELL, HE TOLD ME ABOUT THE *MOVIES* HE'D SEEN, AND WE DISCUSSED *POLITICS* AND HE SAID HE LIKED MY *OUTFIT...*

REALLY?

NO.

LOOK, I'M *SORRY.* SINCE *ALEC* DIED, COMING HERE TO SEE *MATT,* I JUST FEEL *EMPTY,* LIKE I DON'T HAVE ENOUGH STUFF TO MOURN BOTH OF THEM.

DO YOU MIND IF WE SKIP THE ECO-BUSINESS TONIGHT? I WANT TO DRIVE OUT TO THE SWAMPS.

YOU WANT TO BE ALONE?

ALONE?

CHESTER, LATELY I'VE BEEN WORKING WITH *OLD* PEOPLE, WHOSE KIDS HAVE STUCK THEM IN A HOME WITH A LOT OF PEOPLE THEY DON'T *KNOW* AND I JUST THINK *"CHRIST,"* YOU KNOW?

NO...

NO, I DON'T WANT TO BE ALONE.

TERREBONNE GENERAL HOSPITAL AMBULANCE

TERRE

AM

15

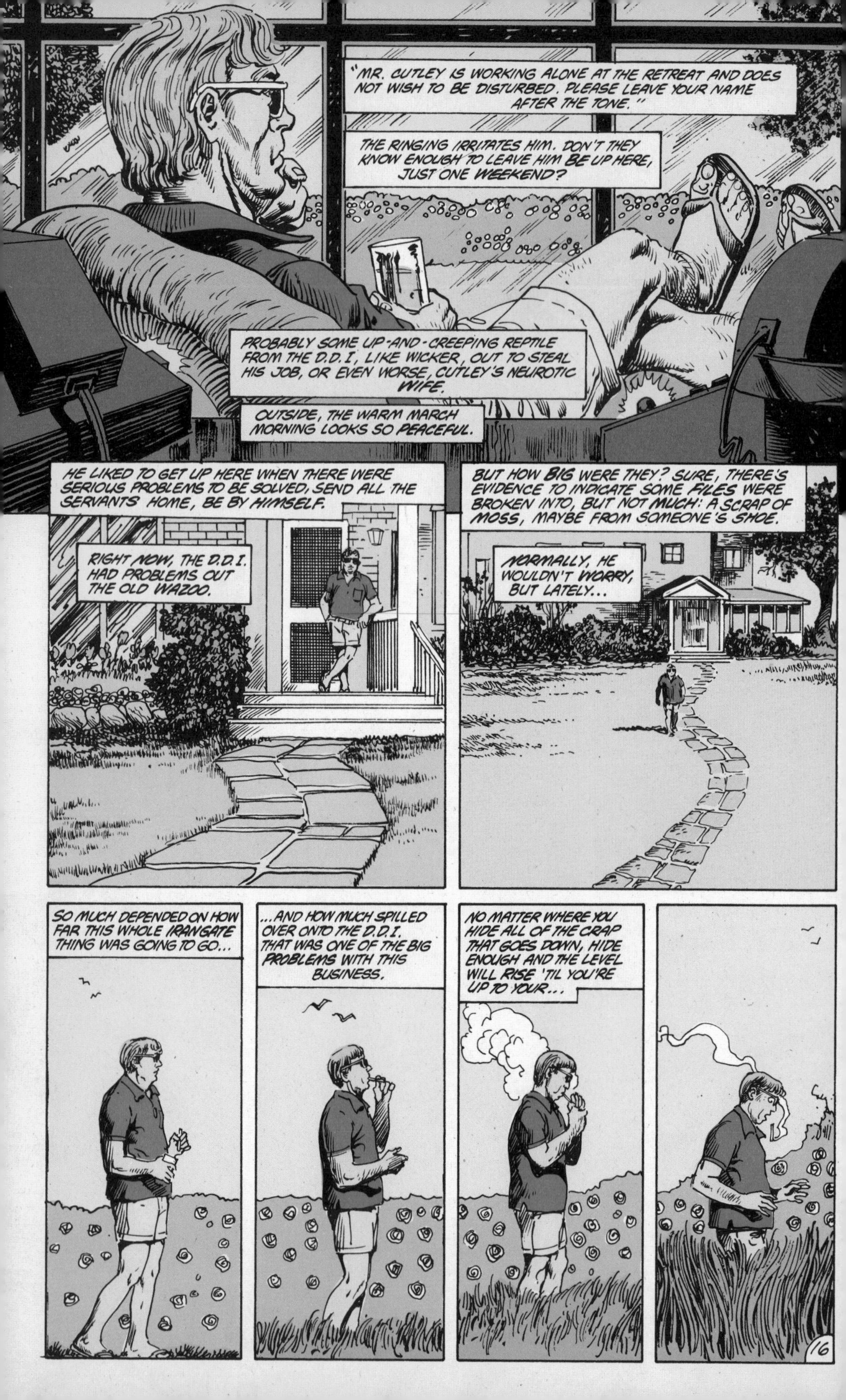
"MR. CUTLEY IS WORKING ALONE AT THE RETREAT AND DOES NOT WISH TO BE DISTURBED. PLEASE LEAVE YOUR NAME AFTER THE TONE."
THE RINGING IRRITATES HIM. DON'T THEY KNOW ENOUGH TO LEAVE HIM BE UP HERE, JUST ONE WEEKEND?
PROBABLY SOME UP-AND-CREEPING REPTILE FROM THE D.D.I., LIKE WICKER, OUT TO STEAL HIS JOB, OR EVEN WORSE, CUTLEY'S NEUROTIC WIFE.
OUTSIDE, THE WARM MARCH MORNING LOOKS SO PEACEFUL.
HE LIKED TO GET UP HERE WHEN THERE WERE SERIOUS PROBLEMS TO BE SOLVED, SEND ALL THE SERVANTS HOME, BE BY HIMSELF.
RIGHT NOW, THE D.D.I. HAD PROBLEMS OUT THE OLD WAZOO.
BUT HOW BIG WERE THEY? SURE, THERE'S EVIDENCE TO INDICATE SOME FILES WERE BROKEN INTO, BUT NOT MUCH: A SCRAP OF MOSS, MAYBE FROM SOMEONE'S SHOE.
NORMALLY, HE WOULDN'T WORRY, BUT LATELY...
SO MUCH DEPENDED ON HOW FAR THIS WHOLE IRANGATE THING WAS GOING TO GO...
...AND HOW MUCH SPILLED OVER ONTO THE D.D.I. THAT WAS ONE OF THE BIG PROBLEMS WITH THIS BUSINESS.
NO MATTER WHERE YOU HIDE ALL OF THE CRAP THAT GOES DOWN, HIDE ENOUGH AND THE LEVEL WILL RISE 'TIL YOU'RE UP TO YOUR...

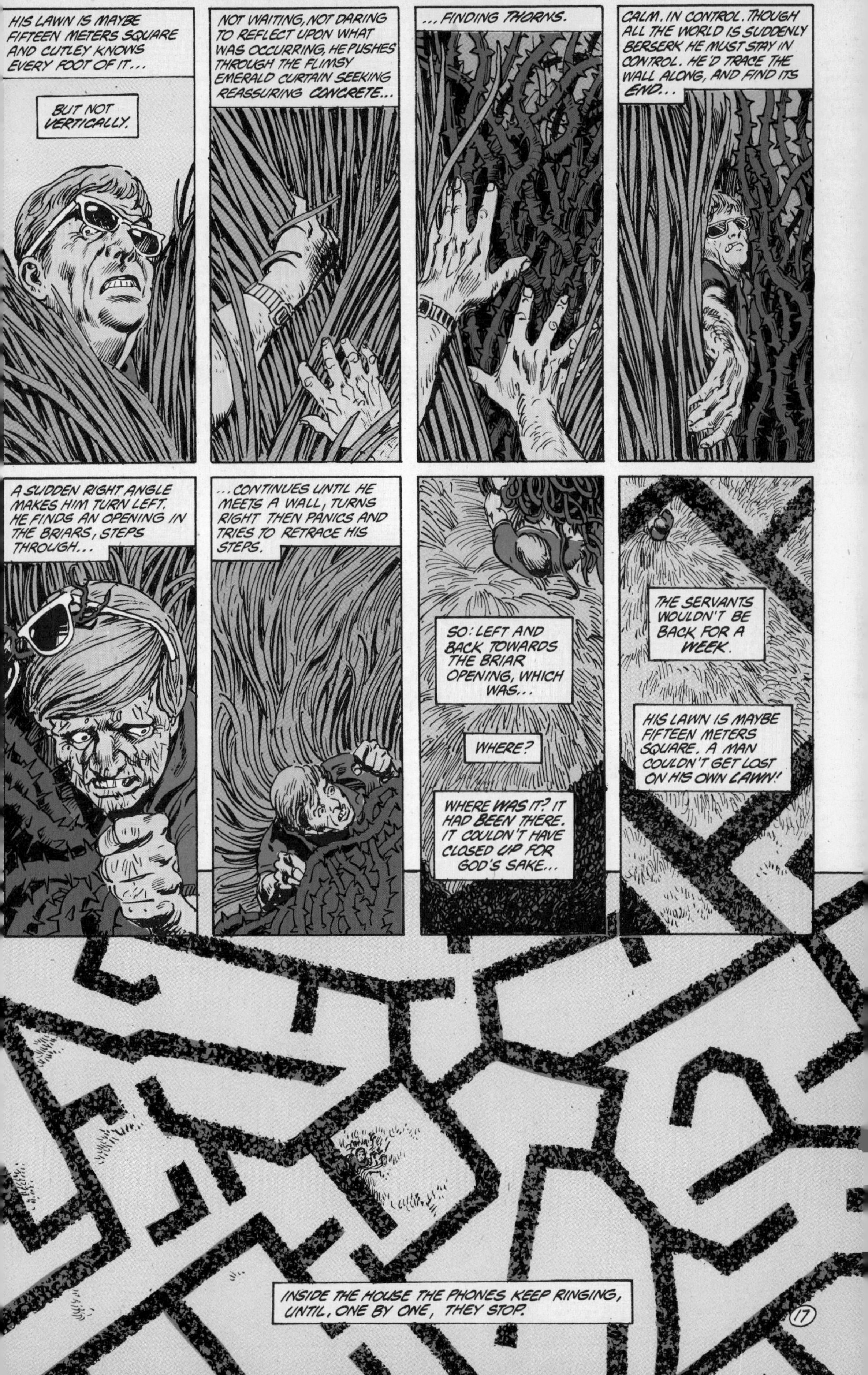
HIS LAWN IS MAYBE FIFTEEN METERS SQUARE AND CUTLEY KNOWS EVERY FOOT OF IT...
BUT NOT VERTICALLY.
NOT WAITING, NOT DARING TO REFLECT UPON WHAT WAS OCCURRING, HE PUSHES THROUGH THE FLIMSY EMERALD CURTAIN SEEKING REASSURING CONCRETE...
...FINDING THORNS.
CALM. IN CONTROL. THOUGH ALL THE WORLD IS SUDDENLY BERSERK HE MUST STAY IN CONTROL. HE'D TRACE THE WALL ALONG, AND FIND ITS END...
A SUDDEN RIGHT ANGLE MAKES HIM TURN LEFT. HE FINDS AN OPENING IN THE BRIARS, STEPS THROUGH...
...CONTINUES UNTIL HE MEETS A WALL, TURNS RIGHT THEN PANICS AND TRIES TO RETRACE HIS STEPS.
SO: LEFT AND BACK TOWARDS THE BRIAR OPENING, WHICH WAS...
WHERE?
WHERE WAS IT? IT HAD BEEN THERE. IT COULDN'T HAVE CLOSED UP FOR GOD'S SAKE...
THE SERVANTS WOULDN'T BE BACK FOR A WEEK.
HIS LAWN IS MAYBE FIFTEEN METERS SQUARE. A MAN COULDN'T GET LOST ON HIS OWN LAWN!
INSIDE THE HOUSE THE PHONES KEEP RINGING, UNTIL, ONE BY ONE, THEY STOP.

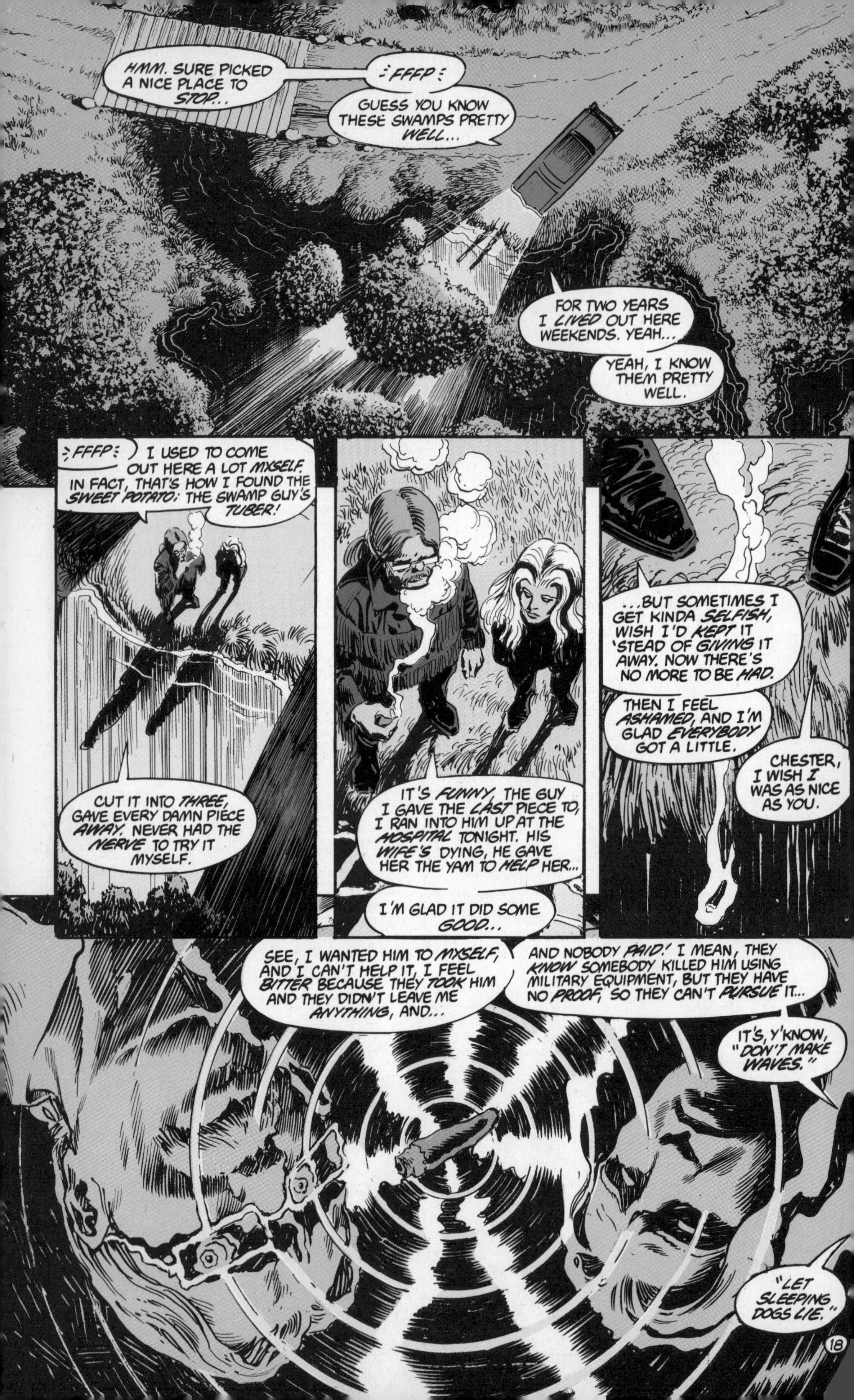
HMM. SURE PICKED A NICE PLACE TO STOP...
:FFFP:
GUESS YOU KNOW THESE SWAMPS PRETTY WELL...
FOR TWO YEARS I LIVED OUT HERE WEEKENDS. YEAH...
YEAH, I KNOW THEM PRETTY WELL.
:FFFP:
I USED TO COME OUT HERE A LOT MYSELF. IN FACT, THAT'S HOW I FOUND THE SWEET POTATO; THE SWAMP GUY'S TUBER!
CUT IT INTO THREE, GAVE EVERY DAMN PIECE AWAY. NEVER HAD THE NERVE TO TRY IT MYSELF.
IT'S FUNNY. THE GUY I GAVE THE LAST PIECE TO, I RAN INTO HIM UP AT THE HOSPITAL TONIGHT. HIS WIFE'S DYING, HE GAVE HER THE YAM TO HELP HER...
I'M GLAD IT DID SOME GOOD...
...BUT SOMETIMES I GET KINDA SELFISH, WISH I'D KEPT IT 'STEAD OF GIVING IT AWAY. NOW THERE'S NO MORE TO BE HAD.
THEN I FEEL ASHAMED, AND I'M GLAD EVERYBODY GOT A LITTLE.
CHESTER, I WISH I WAS AS NICE AS YOU.
SEE, I WANTED HIM TO MYSELF, AND I CAN'T HELP IT, I FEEL BITTER BECAUSE THEY TOOK HIM AND THEY DIDN'T LEAVE ME ANYTHING, AND...
AND NOBODY PAID! I MEAN, THEY KNOW SOMEBODY KILLED HIM USING MILITARY EQUIPMENT, BUT THEY HAVE NO PROOF, SO THEY CAN'T PURSUE IT...
IT'S, Y'KNOW, "DON'T MAKE WAVES."
"LET SLEEPING DOGS LIE."

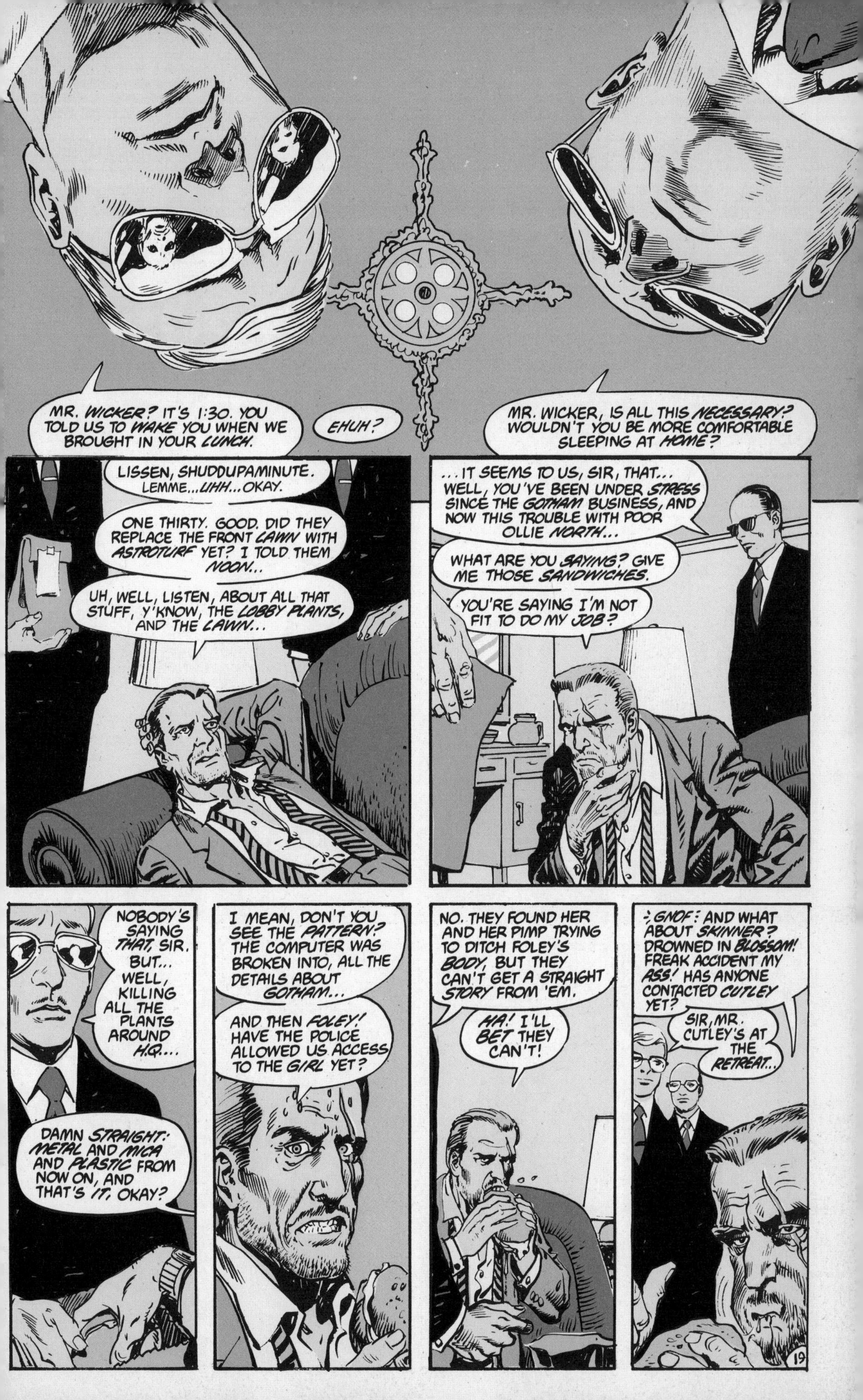
MR. WICKER? IT'S 1:30. YOU TOLD US TO WAKE YOU WHEN WE BROUGHT IN YOUR LUNCH.
EHUH?
MR. WICKER, IS ALL THIS NECESSARY? WOULDN'T YOU BE MORE COMFORTABLE SLEEPING AT HOME?
LISSEN, SHUDDUPAMINUTE. LEMME...UHH...OKAY.
ONE THIRTY. GOOD. DID THEY REPLACE THE FRONT LAWN WITH ASTROTURF YET? I TOLD THEM NOON...
UH, WELL, LISTEN, ABOUT ALL THAT STUFF, Y'KNOW, THE LOBBY PLANTS, AND THE LAWN...
...IT SEEMS TO US, SIR, THAT... WELL, YOU'VE BEEN UNDER STRESS SINCE THE GOTHAM BUSINESS, AND NOW THIS TROUBLE WITH POOR OLLIE NORTH...
WHAT ARE YOU SAYING? GIVE ME THOSE SANDWICHES.
YOU'RE SAYING I'M NOT FIT TO DO MY JOB?
NOBODY'S SAYING THAT, SIR. BUT... WELL, KILLING ALL THE PLANTS AROUND H.Q....
DAMN STRAIGHT: METAL AND MICA AND PLASTIC FROM NOW ON, AND THAT'S IT, OKAY?
I MEAN, DON'T YOU SEE THE PATTERN? THE COMPUTER WAS BROKEN INTO, ALL THE DETAILS ABOUT GOTHAM...
AND THEN FOLEY! HAVE THE POLICE ALLOWED US ACCESS TO THE GIRL YET?
NO. THEY FOUND HER AND HER PIMP TRYING TO DITCH FOLEY'S BODY, BUT THEY CAN'T GET A STRAIGHT STORY FROM 'EM.
HA! I'LL BET THEY CAN'T!
:GNOF: AND WHAT ABOUT SKINNER? DROWNED IN BLOSSOM! FREAK ACCIDENT MY ASS! HAS ANYONE CONTACTED CUTLEY YET?
SIR, MR. CUTLEY'S AT THE RETREAT...

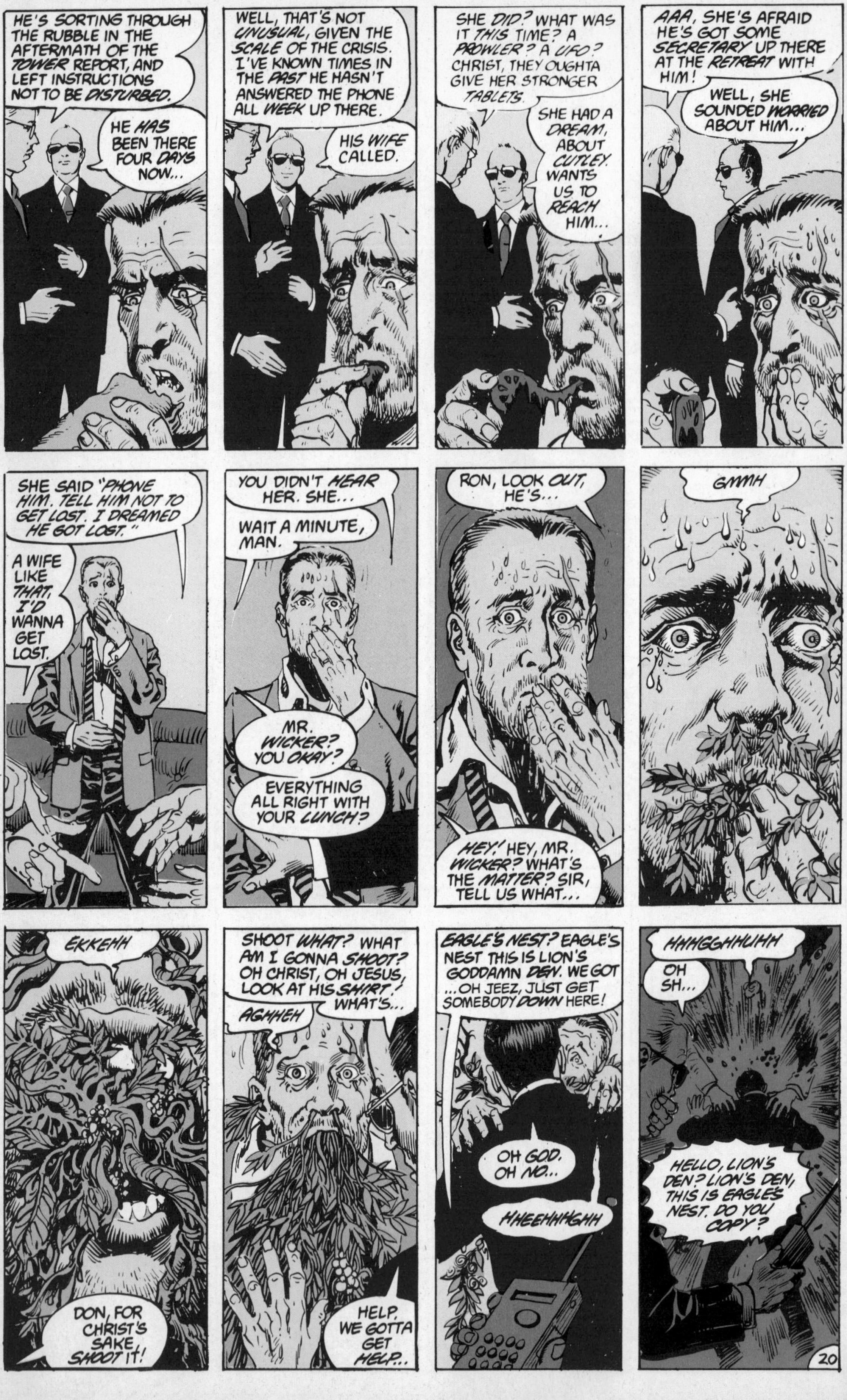
HE'S SORTING THROUGH THE RUBBLE IN THE AFTERMATH OF THE TOWER REPORT, AND LEFT INSTRUCTIONS NOT TO BE DISTURBED.
HE HAS BEEN THERE FOUR DAYS NOW...
WELL, THAT'S NOT UNUSUAL, GIVEN THE SCALE OF THE CRISIS. I'VE KNOWN TIMES IN THE PAST HE HASN'T ANSWERED THE PHONE ALL WEEK UP THERE.
HIS WIFE CALLED.
SHE DID? WHAT WAS IT THIS TIME? A PROWLER? A UFO? CHRIST, THEY OUGHTA GIVE HER STRONGER TABLETS.
SHE HAD A DREAM, ABOUT CUTLEY. WANTS US TO REACH HIM...
AAA, SHE'S AFRAID HE'S GOT SOME SECRETARY UP THERE AT THE RETREAT WITH HIM!
WELL, SHE SOUNDED WORRIED ABOUT HIM...
SHE SAID "PHONE HIM. TELL HIM NOT TO GET LOST. I DREAMED HE GOT LOST."
A WIFE LIKE THAT, I'D WANNA GET LOST.
YOU DIDN'T HEAR HER. SHE...
WAIT A MINUTE, MAN.
MR. WICKER? YOU OKAY?
EVERYTHING ALL RIGHT WITH YOUR LUNCH?
RON, LOOK OUT, HE'S...
HEY! HEY, MR. WICKER? WHAT'S THE MATTER? SIR, TELL US WHAT...
GMMH
EKKEHH
DON, FOR CHRIST'S SAKE SHOOT IT!
SHOOT WHAT? WHAT AM I GONNA SHOOT? OH CHRIST, OH JESUS, LOOK AT HIS SHIRT! WHAT'S...
AGHHEH
HELP, WE GOTTA GET HELP...
EAGLE'S NEST? EAGLE'S NEST THIS IS LION'S GODDAMN DEN. WE GOT ...OH JEEZ, JUST GET SOMEBODY DOWN HERE!
OH GOD. OH NO...
HHEEHHHGHH
HHHGGHHUHH
OH SH...
HELLO, LION'S DEN? LION'S DEN, THIS IS EAGLE'S NEST. DO YOU COPY?
20

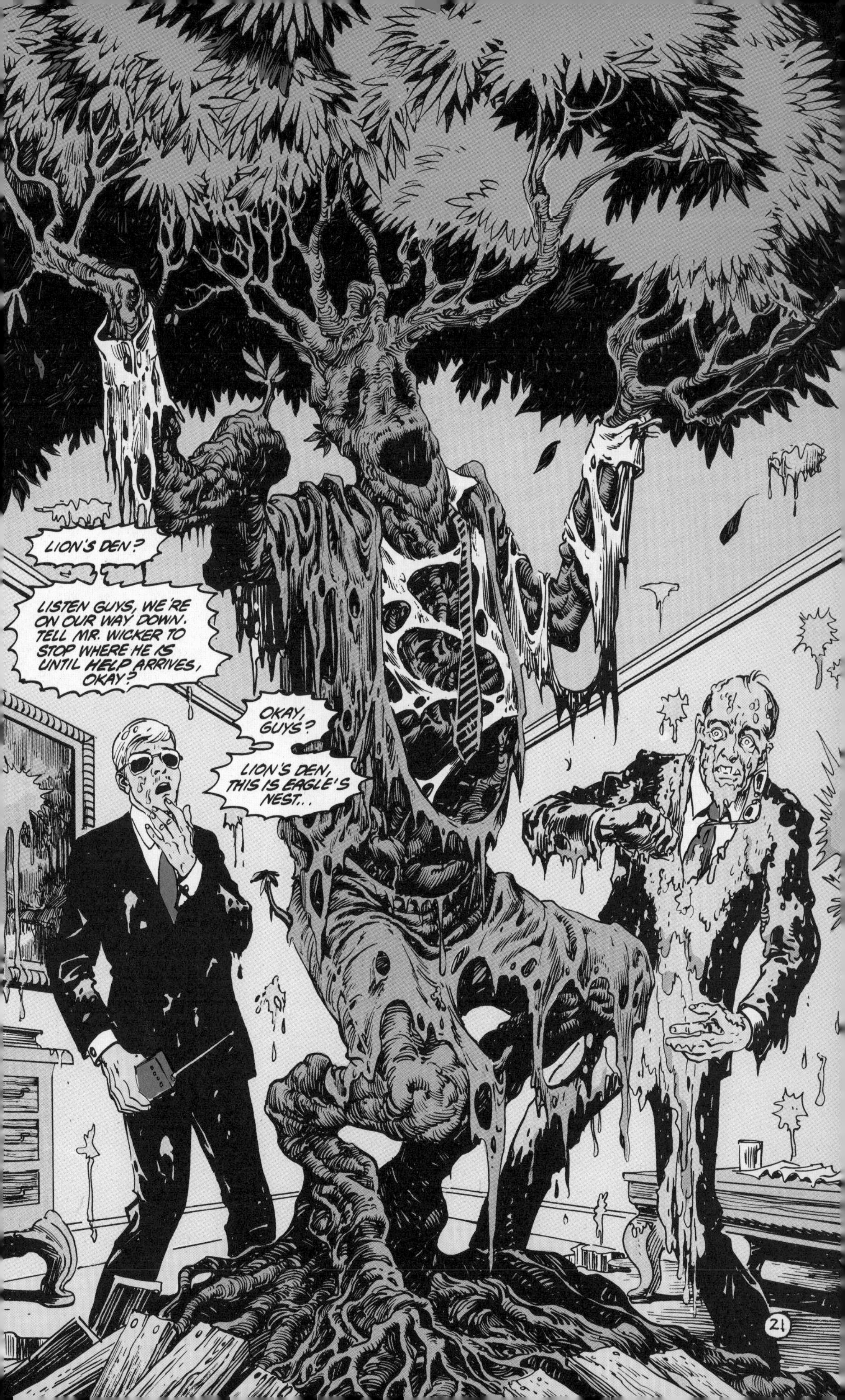
LION'S DEN?
LISTEN GUYS, WE'RE ON OUR WAY DOWN. TELL MR. WICKER TO STOP WHERE HE IS UNTIL HELP ARRIVES, OKAY?
OKAY, GUYS?
LION'S DEN, THIS IS EAGLE'S NEST...
21

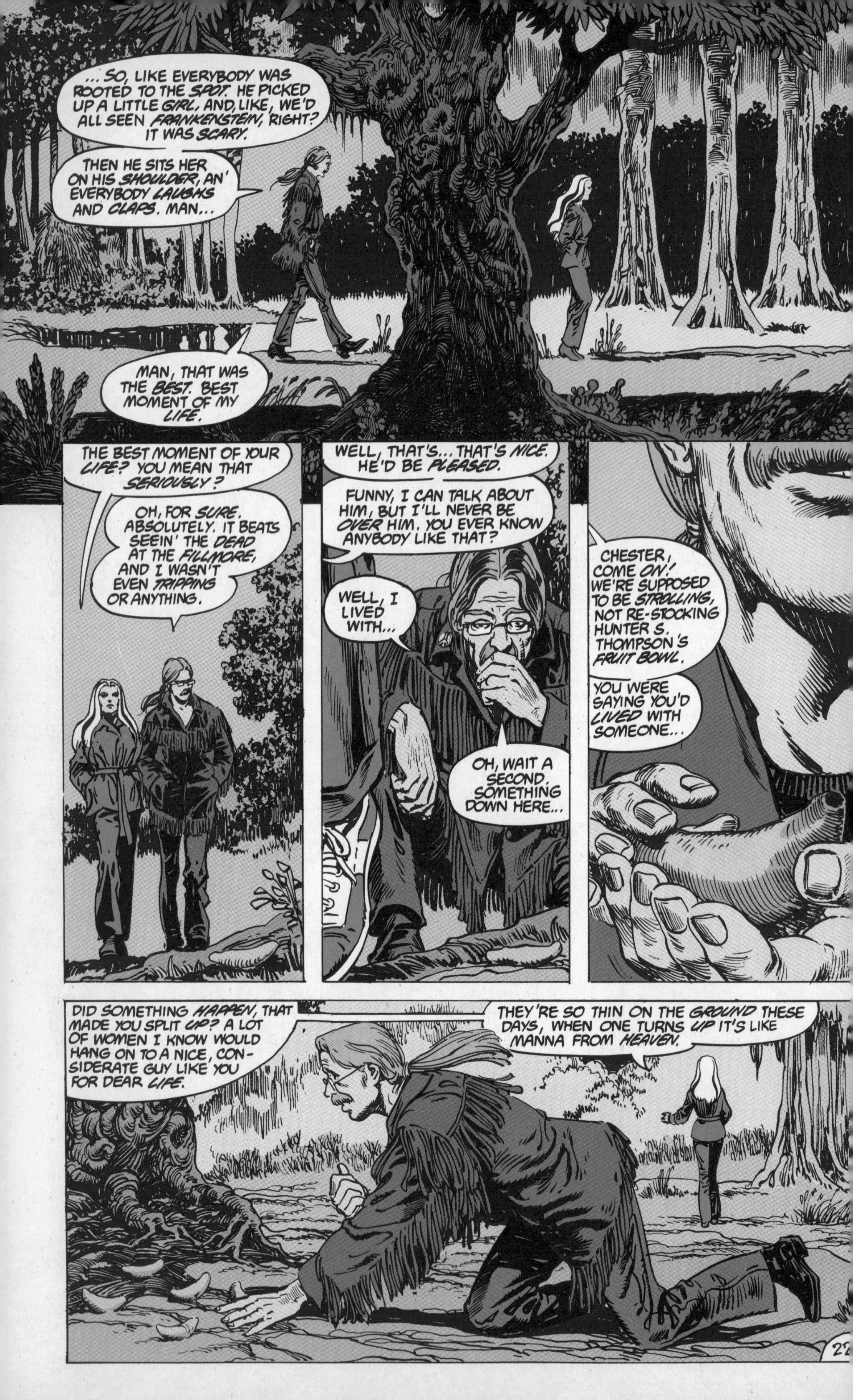
...SO, LIKE EVERYBODY WAS ROOTED TO THE SPOT. HE PICKED UP A LITTLE GIRL, AND, LIKE, WE'D ALL SEEN FRANKENSTEIN, RIGHT? IT WAS SCARY.
THEN HE SITS HER ON HIS SHOULDER, AN' EVERYBODY LAUGHS AND CLAPS. MAN...
MAN, THAT WAS THE BEST. BEST MOMENT OF MY LIFE.
THE BEST MOMENT OF YOUR LIFE? YOU MEAN THAT SERIOUSLY?
OH, FOR SURE. ABSOLUTELY. IT BEATS SEEIN' THE DEAD AT THE FILLMORE, AND I WASN'T EVEN TRIPPING OR ANYTHING.
WELL, THAT'S... THAT'S NICE. HE'D BE PLEASED.
FUNNY, I CAN TALK ABOUT HIM, BUT I'LL NEVER BE OVER HIM. YOU EVER KNOW ANYBODY LIKE THAT?
WELL, I LIVED WITH...
OH, WAIT A SECOND. SOMETHING DOWN HERE...
CHESTER, COME ON! WE'RE SUPPOSED TO BE STROLLING, NOT RE-STOCKING HUNTER S. THOMPSON'S FRUIT BOWL.
YOU WERE SAYING YOU'D LIVED WITH SOMEONE...
DID SOMETHING HAPPEN, THAT MADE YOU SPLIT UP? A LOT OF WOMEN I KNOW WOULD HANG ON TO A NICE, CONSIDERATE GUY LIKE YOU FOR DEAR LIFE.
THEY'RE SO THIN ON THE GROUND THESE DAYS, WHEN ONE TURNS UP IT'S LIKE MANNA FROM HEAVEN.
22

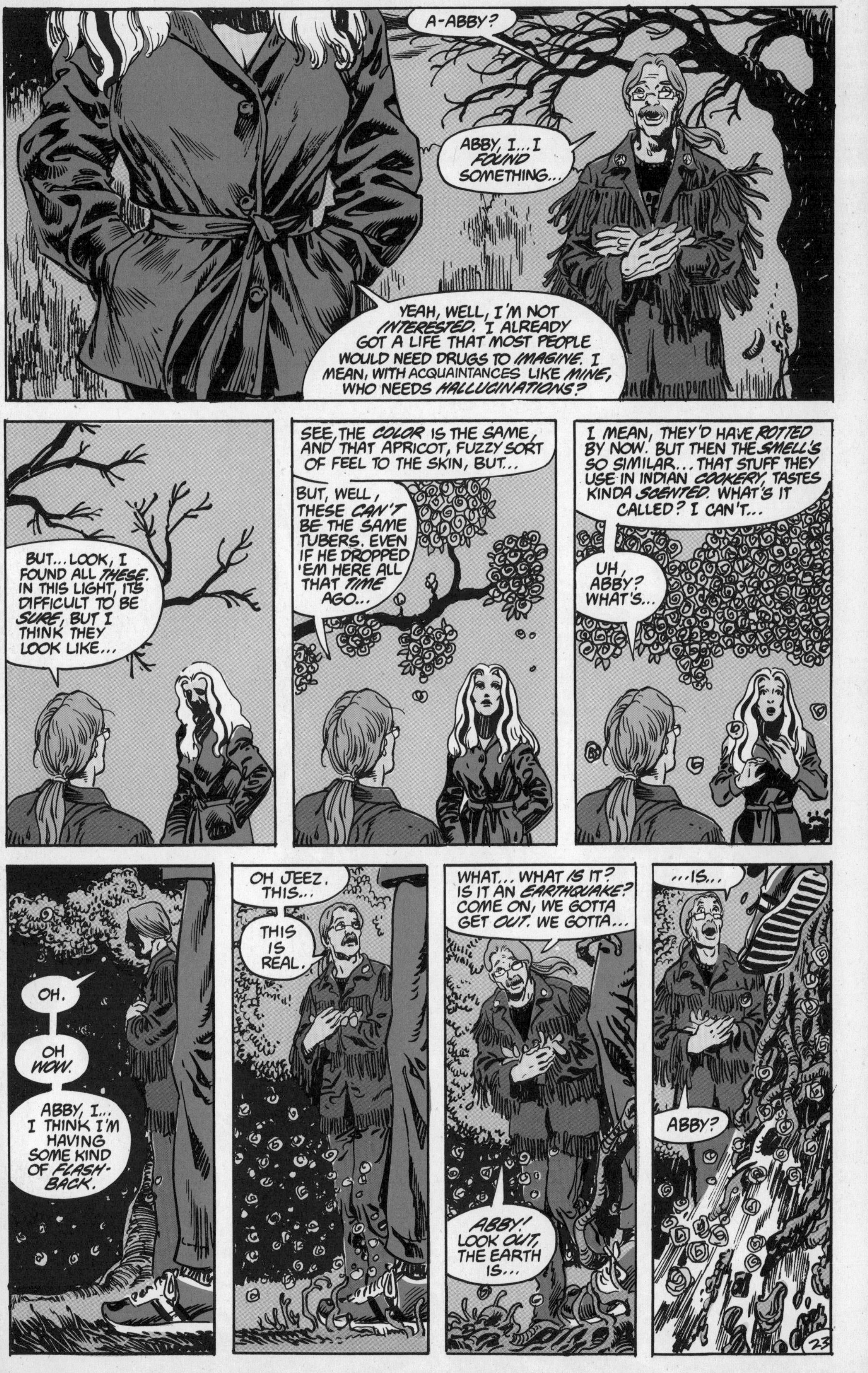
A-ABBY?
ABBY, I... I FOUND SOMETHING...
YEAH, WELL, I'M NOT INTERESTED. I ALREADY GOT A LIFE THAT MOST PEOPLE WOULD NEED DRUGS TO IMAGINE. I MEAN, WITH ACQUAINTANCES LIKE MINE, WHO NEEDS HALLUCINATIONS?
BUT... LOOK, I FOUND ALL THESE. IN THIS LIGHT, ITS DIFFICULT TO BE SURE, BUT I THINK THEY LOOK LIKE...
SEE, THE COLOR IS THE SAME, AND THAT APRICOT, FUZZY SORT OF FEEL TO THE SKIN, BUT...
BUT, WELL, THESE CAN'T BE THE SAME TUBERS. EVEN IF HE DROPPED 'EM HERE ALL THAT TIME AGO...
I MEAN, THEY'D HAVE ROTTED BY NOW. BUT THEN THE SMELL'S SO SIMILAR... THAT STUFF THEY USE IN INDIAN COOKERY, TASTES KINDA SCENTED. WHAT'S IT CALLED? I CAN'T...
UH, ABBY? WHAT'S...
OH.
OH WOW.
ABBY, I... I THINK I'M HAVING SOME KIND OF FLASH-BACK.
OH JEEZ. THIS...
THIS IS REAL.
WHAT... WHAT IS IT? IS IT AN EARTHQUAKE? COME ON, WE GOTTA GET OUT. WE GOTTA...
ABBY! LOOK OUT, THE EARTH IS...
...IS...
ABBY?
23

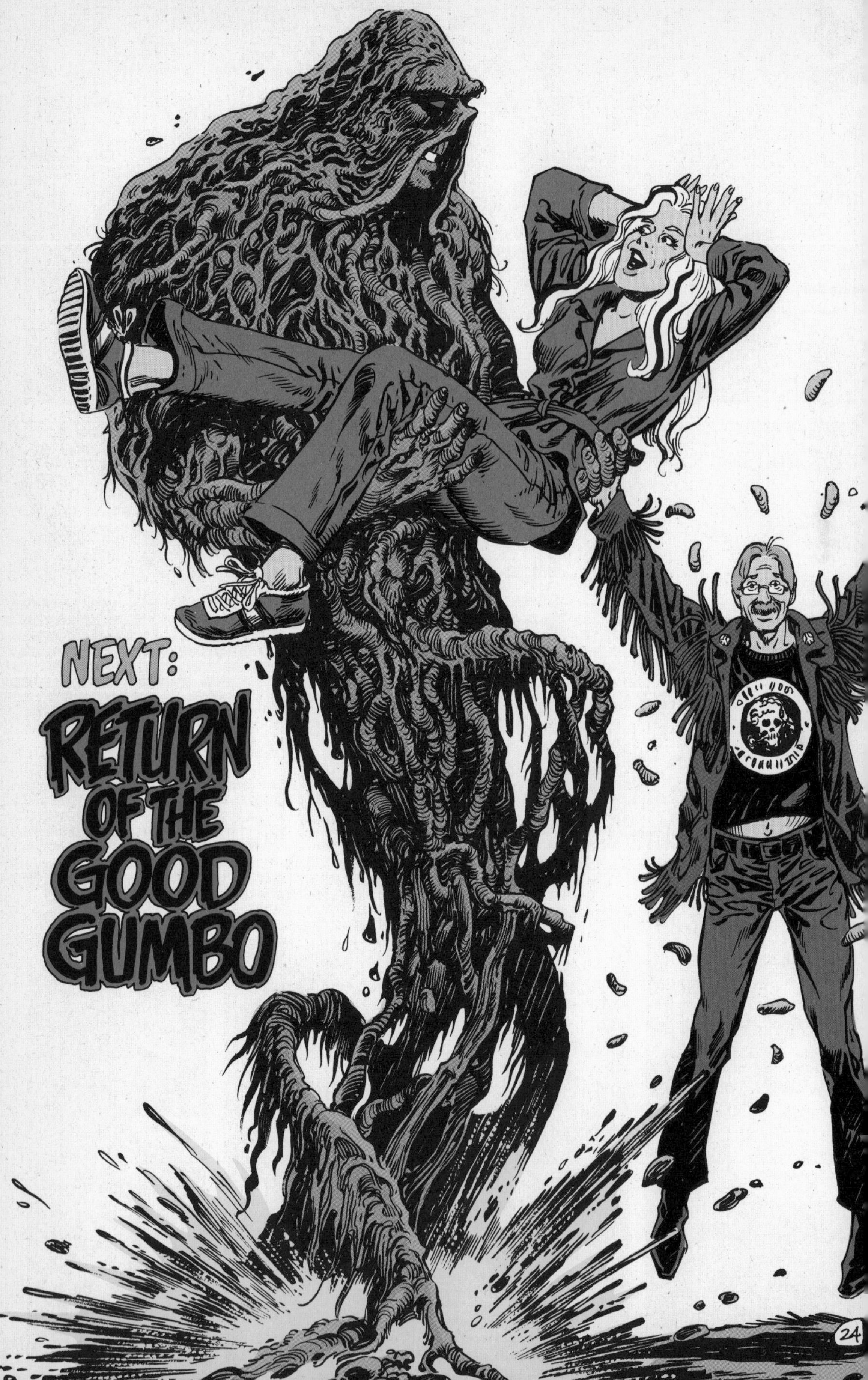
NEXT:
RETURN OF THE GOOD GUMBO
24

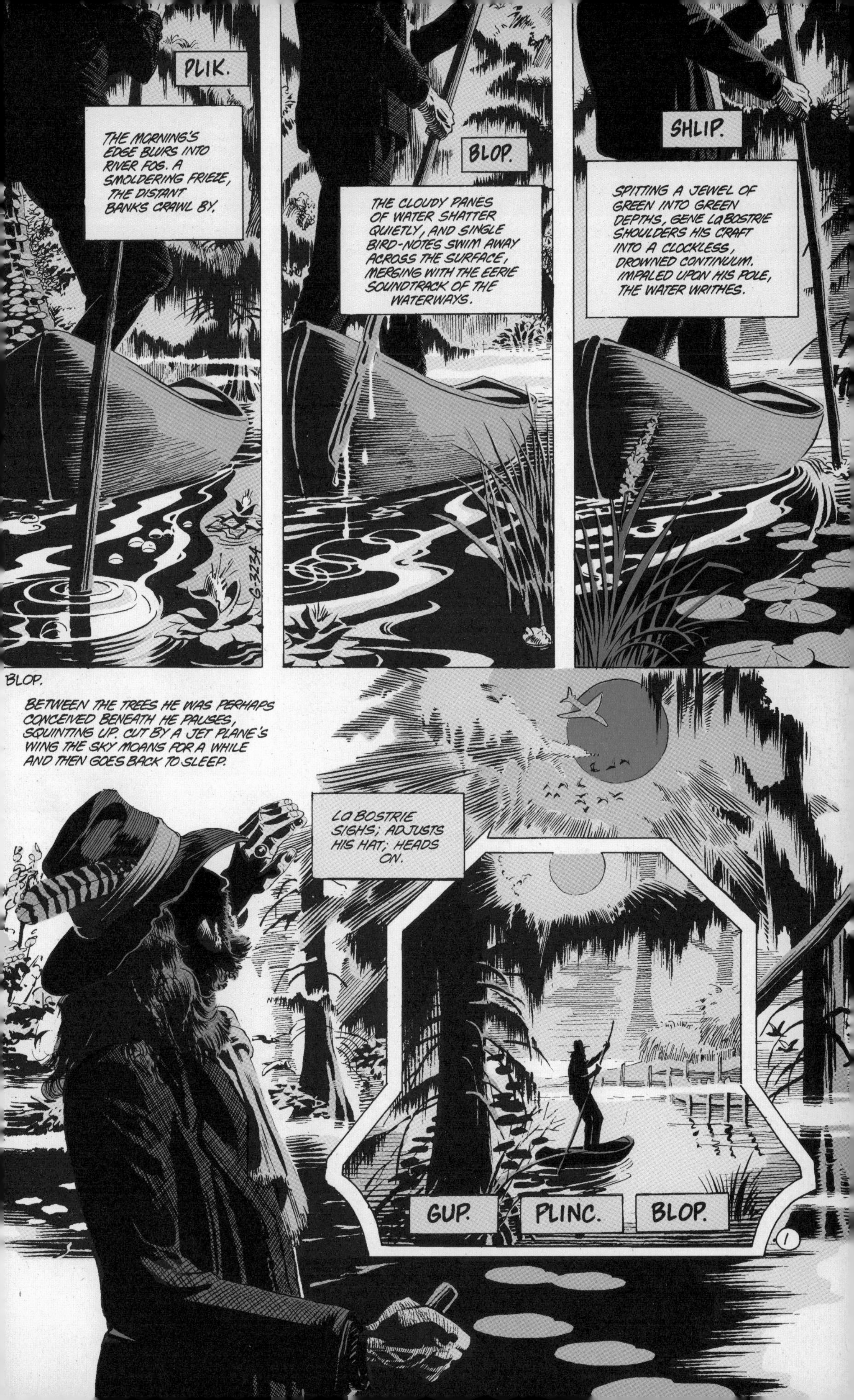
PLIK.
THE MORNING'S EDGE BLURS INTO RIVER FOG. A SMOLDERING FRIEZE, THE DISTANT BANKS CRAWL BY.
BLOP.
THE CLOUDY PANES OF WATER SHATTER QUIETLY, AND SINGLE BIRD-NOTES SWIM AWAY ACROSS THE SURFACE, MERGING WITH THE EERIE SOUNDTRACK OF THE WATERWAYS.
SHLIP.
SPITTING A JEWEL OF GREEN INTO GREEN DEPTHS, GENE LaBOSTRIE SHOULDERS HIS CRAFT INTO A CLOCKLESS, DROWNED CONTINUUM. IMPALED UPON HIS POLE, THE WATER WRITHES.
BLOP.
BETWEEN THE TREES HE WAS PERHAPS CONCEIVED BENEATH HE PAUSES, SQUINTING UP. CUT BY A JET PLANE'S WING THE SKY MOANS FOR A WHILE AND THEN GOES BACK TO SLEEP.
LaBOSTRIE SIGHS; ADJUSTS HIS HAT; HEADS ON.
GUP.
PLINC.
BLOP.
1

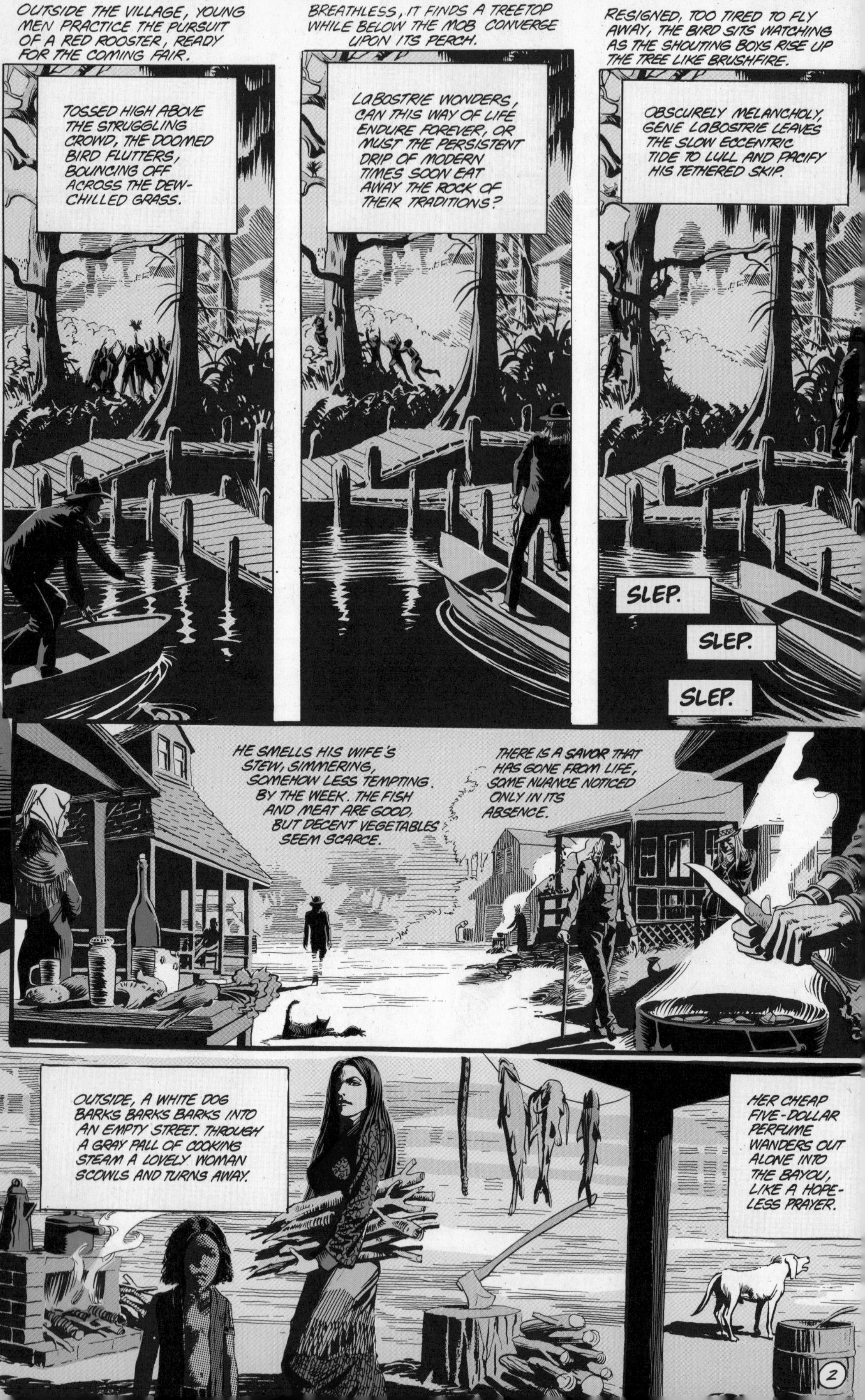
OUTSIDE THE VILLAGE, YOUNG MEN PRACTICE THE PURSUIT OF A RED ROOSTER, READY FOR THE COMING FAIR.
TOSSED HIGH ABOVE THE STRUGGLING CROWD, THE DOOMED BIRD FLUTTERS, BOUNCING OFF ACROSS THE DEW-CHILLED GRASS.
BREATHLESS, IT FINDS A TREETOP WHILE BELOW THE MOB CONVERGE UPON ITS PERCH.
LaBOSTRIE WONDERS, CAN THIS WAY OF LIFE ENDURE FOREVER, OR MUST THE PERSISTENT DRIP OF MODERN TIMES SOON EAT AWAY THE ROCK OF THEIR TRADITIONS?
RESIGNED, TOO TIRED TO FLY AWAY, THE BIRD SITS WATCHING AS THE SHOUTING BOYS RISE UP THE TREE LIKE BRUSHFIRE.
OBSCURELY MELANCHOLY, GENE LaBOSTRIE LEAVES THE SLOW ECCENTRIC TIDE TO LULL AND PACIFY HIS TETHERED SKIP.
SLEP.
SLEP.
SLEP.
HE SMELLS HIS WIFE'S STEW, SIMMERING, SOMEHOW LESS TEMPTING BY THE WEEK. THE FISH AND MEAT ARE GOOD, BUT DECENT VEGETABLES SEEM SCARCE.
THERE IS A SAVOR THAT HAS GONE FROM LIFE, SOME NUANCE NOTICED ONLY IN ITS ABSENCE.
OUTSIDE, A WHITE DOG BARKS BARKS BARKS INTO AN EMPTY STREET. THROUGH A GRAY PALL OF COOKING STEAM A LOVELY WOMAN SCOWLS AND TURNS AWAY.
HER CHEAP FIVE-DOLLAR PERFUME WANDERS OUT ALONE INTO THE BAYOU, LIKE A HOPE-LESS PRAYER.
2

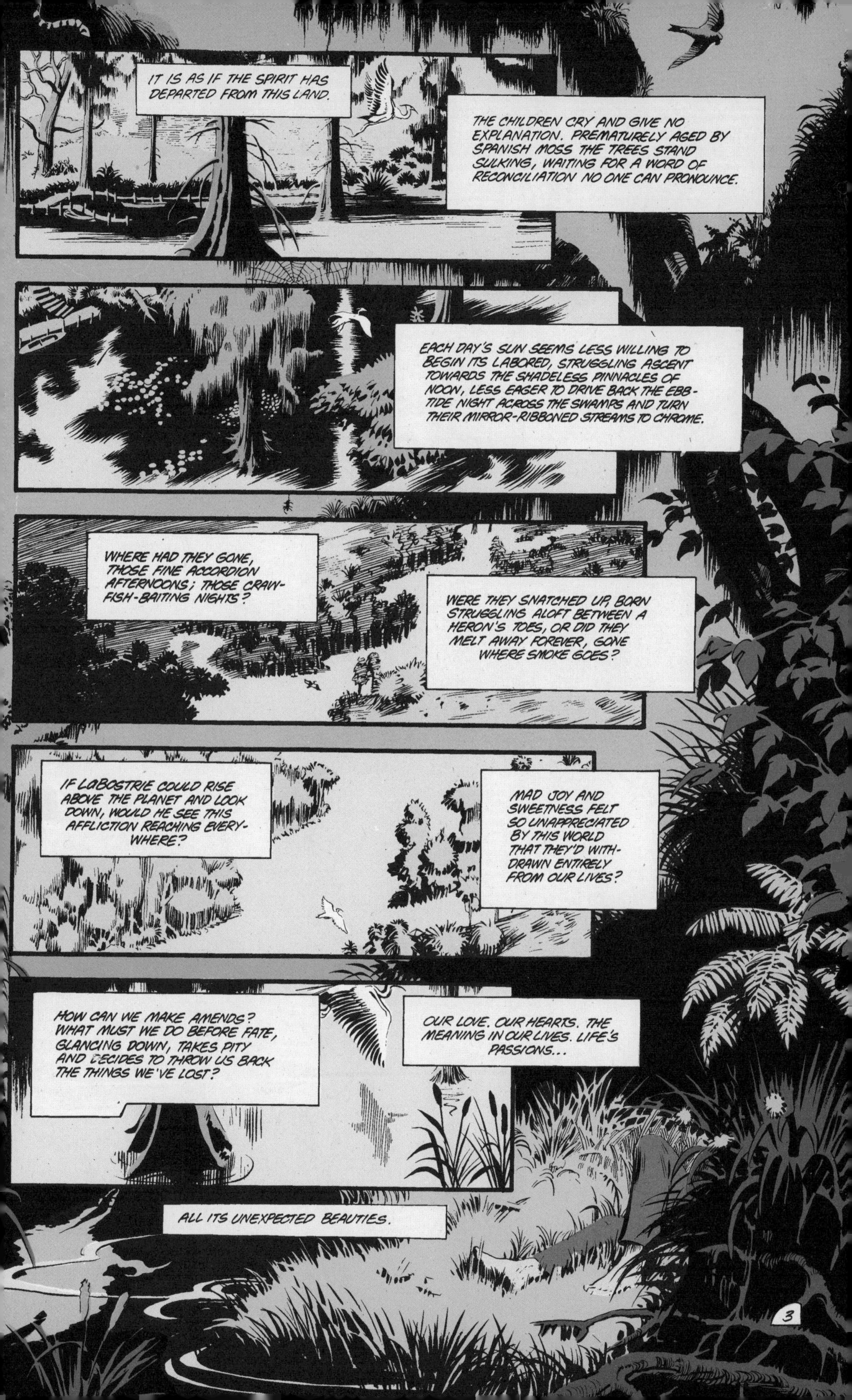
IT IS AS IF THE SPIRIT HAS DEPARTED FROM THIS LAND.
THE CHILDREN CRY AND GIVE NO EXPLANATION. PREMATURELY AGED BY SPANISH MOSS THE TREES STAND SULKING, WAITING FOR A WORD OF RECONCILIATION NO ONE CAN PRONOUNCE.
EACH DAY'S SUN SEEMS LESS WILLING TO BEGIN ITS LABORED, STRUGGLING ASCENT TOWARDS THE SHADELESS PINNACLES OF NOON, LESS EAGER TO DRIVE BACK THE EBB-TIDE NIGHT ACROSS THE SWAMPS AND TURN THEIR MIRROR-RIBBONED STREAMS TO CHROME.
WHERE HAD THEY GONE, THOSE FINE ACCORDION AFTERNOONS; THOSE CRAW-FISH-BAITING NIGHTS?
WERE THEY SNATCHED UP, BORN STRUGGLING ALOFT BETWEEN A HERON'S TOES, OR DID THEY MELT AWAY FOREVER, GONE WHERE SMOKE GOES?
IF LABOSTRIE COULD RISE ABOVE THE PLANET AND LOOK DOWN, WOULD HE SEE THIS AFFLICTION REACHING EVERY-WHERE?
MAD JOY AND SWEETNESS FELT SO UNAPPRECIATED BY THIS WORLD THAT THEY'D WITH-DRAWN ENTIRELY FROM OUR LIVES?
HOW CAN WE MAKE AMENDS? WHAT MUST WE DO BEFORE FATE, GLANCING DOWN, TAKES PITY AND DECIDES TO THROW US BACK THE THINGS WE'VE LOST?
OUR LOVE. OUR HEARTS. THE MEANING IN OUR LIVES. LIFE'S PASSIONS...
ALL ITS UNEXPECTED BEAUTIES.

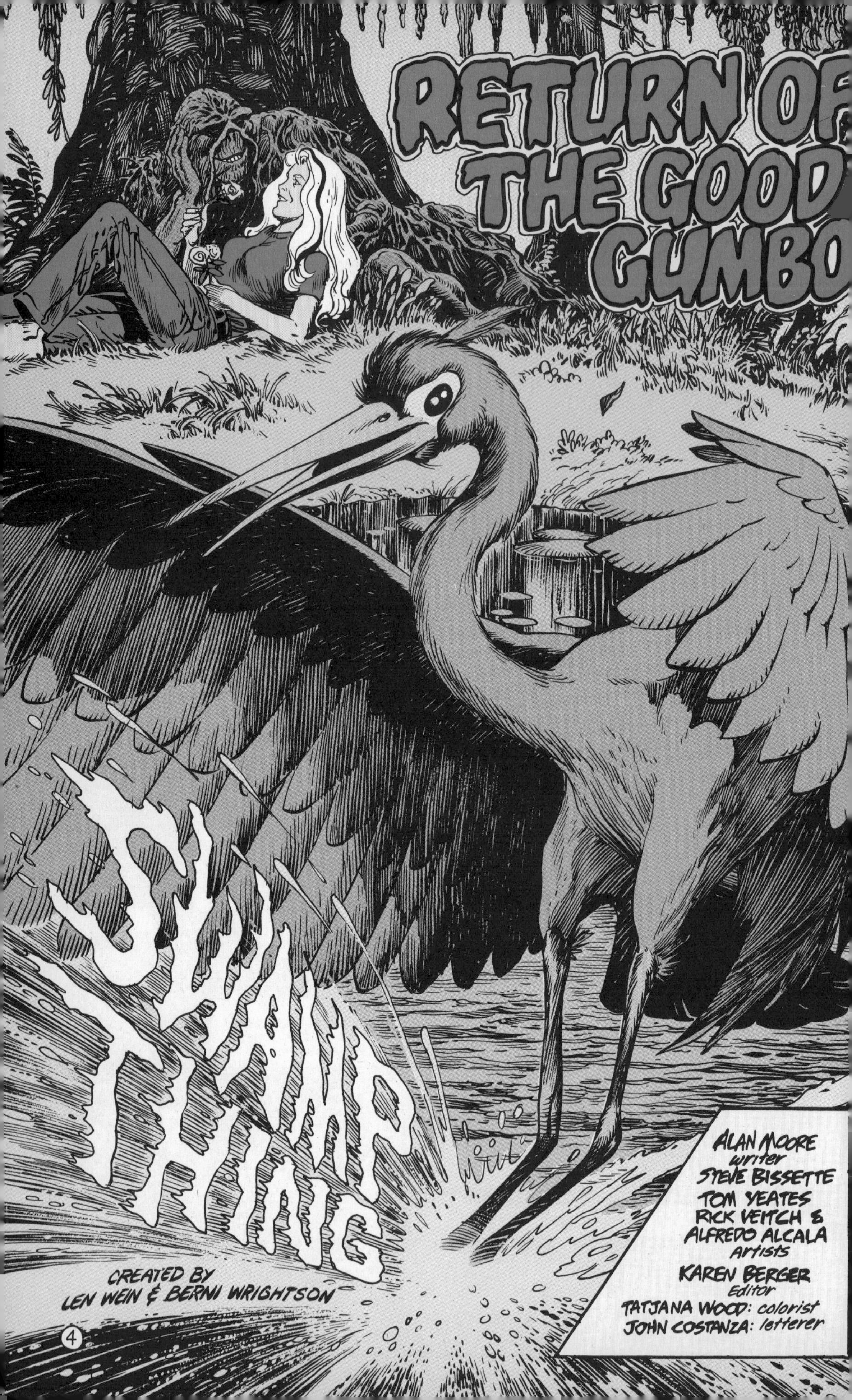
RETURN OF THE GOOD GUMBO
SWAMP THING
CREATED BY LEN WEIN & BERNI WRIGHTSON
ALAN MOORE writer
STEVE BISSETTE
TOM YEATES
RICK VEITCH &
ALFREDO ALCALA
Artists
KAREN BERGER
Editor
TATJANA WOOD: colorist
JOHN COSTANZA: letterer
4

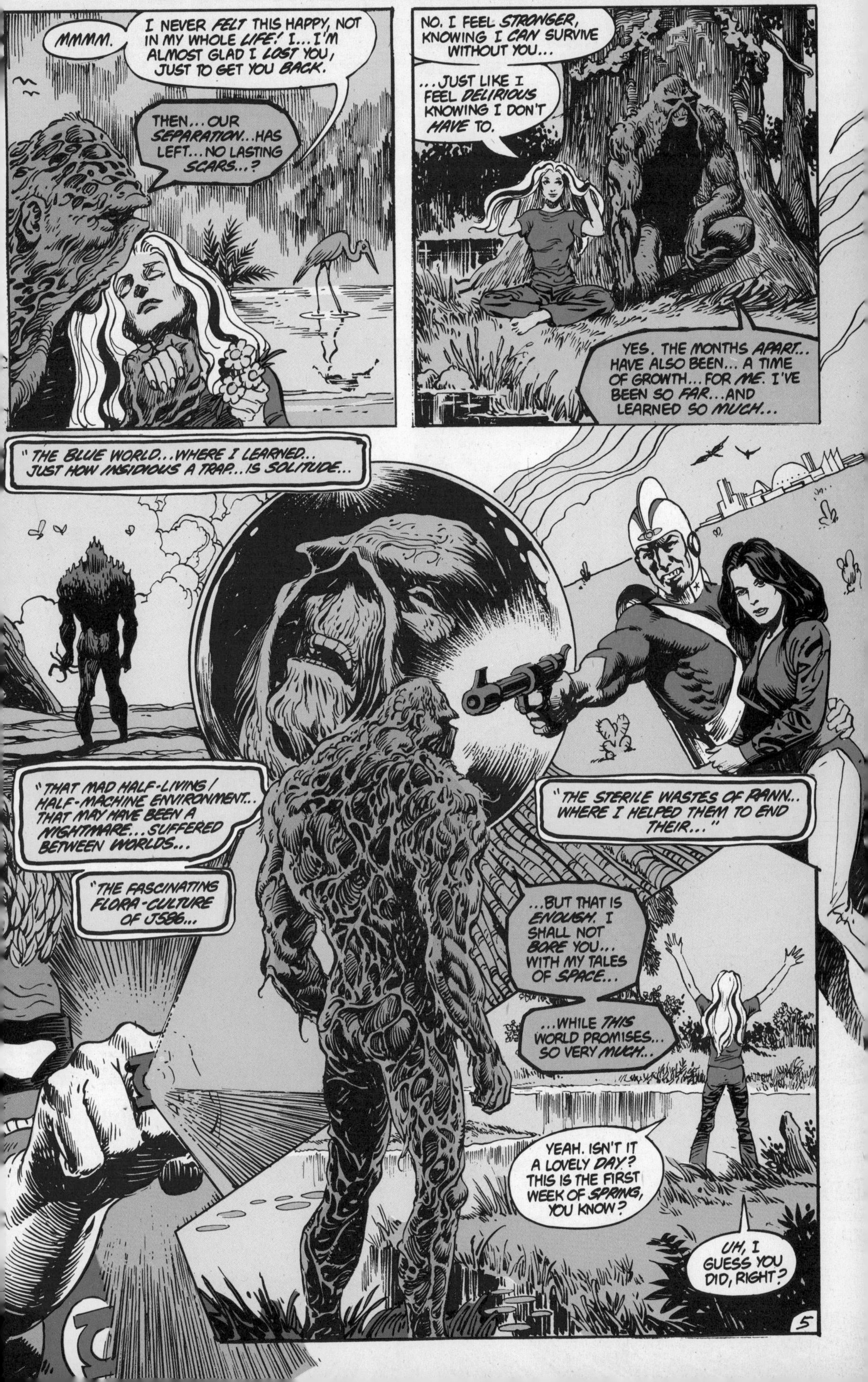
MMMM.
I NEVER FELT THIS HAPPY, NOT IN MY WHOLE LIFE! I...I'M ALMOST GLAD I LOST YOU, JUST TO GET YOU BACK.
THEN...OUR SEPARATION...HAS LEFT...NO LASTING SCARS...?
NO. I FEEL STRONGER, KNOWING I CAN SURVIVE WITHOUT YOU...
...JUST LIKE I FEEL DELIRIOUS KNOWING I DON'T HAVE TO.
YES. THE MONTHS APART... HAVE ALSO BEEN... A TIME OF GROWTH... FOR ME. I'VE BEEN SO FAR...AND LEARNED SO MUCH...
"THE BLUE WORLD...WHERE I LEARNED... JUST HOW INSIDIOUS A TRAP...IS SOLITUDE...
"THAT MAD HALF-LIVING/ HALF-MACHINE ENVIRONMENT... THAT MAY HAVE BEEN A NIGHTMARE...SUFFERED BETWEEN WORLDS...
"THE FASCINATING FLORA-CULTURE OF J586...
"THE STERILE WASTES OF RANN... WHERE I HELPED THEM TO END THEIR..."
...BUT THAT IS ENOUGH. I SHALL NOT BORE YOU... WITH MY TALES OF SPACE...
...WHILE THIS WORLD PROMISES... SO VERY MUCH...
YEAH. ISN'T IT A LOVELY DAY? THIS IS THE FIRST WEEK OF SPRING, YOU KNOW?
UH, I GUESS YOU DID, RIGHT?
5

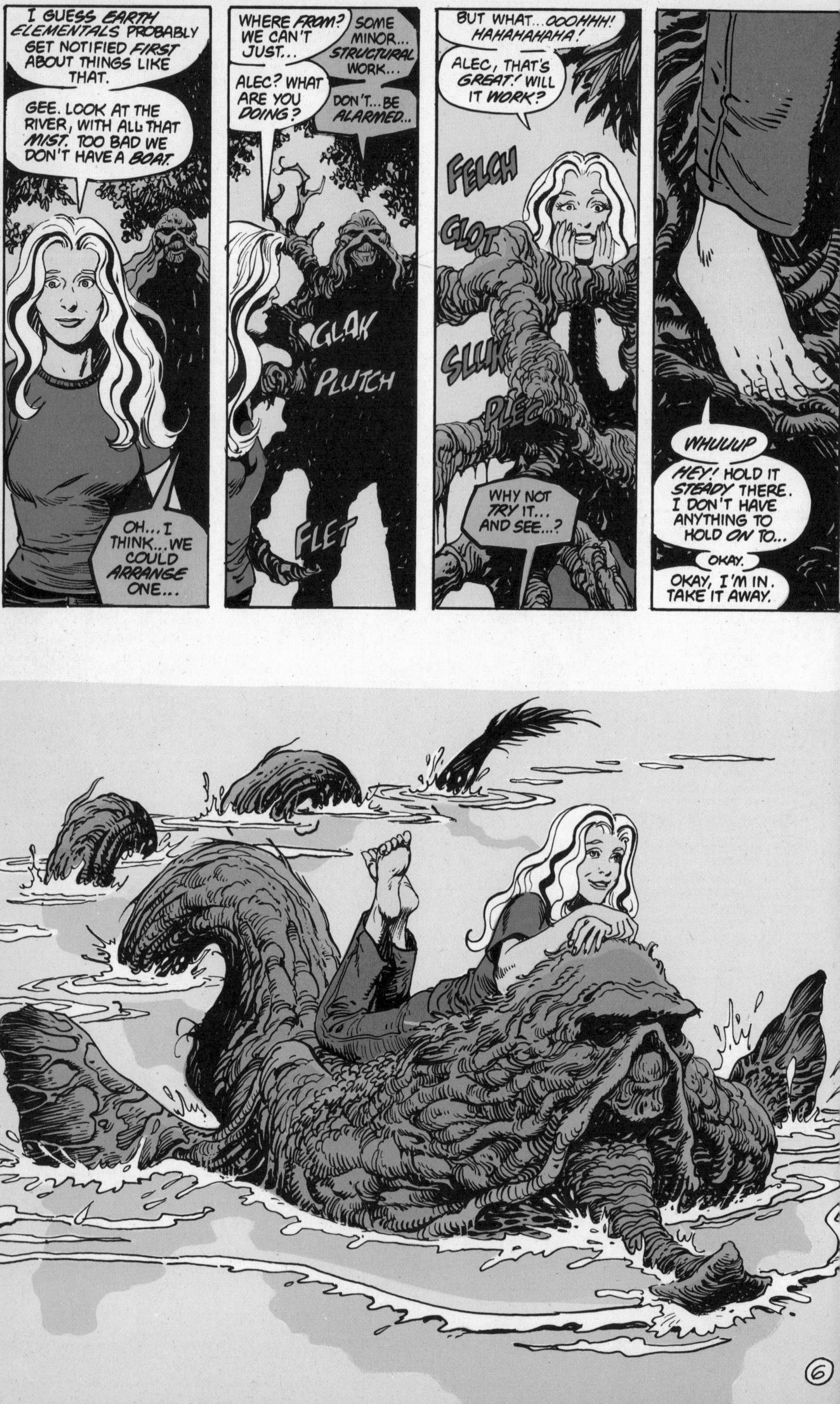
I GUESS EARTH ELEMENTALS PROBABLY GET NOTIFIED FIRST ABOUT THINGS LIKE THAT.
GEE. LOOK AT THE RIVER, WITH ALL THAT MIST. TOO BAD WE DON'T HAVE A BOAT.
OH... I THINK... WE COULD ARRANGE ONE...
WHERE FROM? WE CAN'T JUST...
SOME MINOR... STRUCTURAL WORK...
ALEC? WHAT ARE YOU DOING?
DON'T... BE ALARMED...
GLAK
PLUTCH
FLET
BUT WHAT... OOOHHH! HAHAHAHAHA!
ALEC, THAT'S GREAT! WILL IT WORK?
FELCH
GLOT
SLUK
PLEC
WHY NOT TRY IT... AND SEE...?
WHUUUP
HEY! HOLD IT STEADY THERE. I DON'T HAVE ANYTHING TO HOLD ON TO...
OKAY.
OKAY, I'M IN. TAKE IT AWAY.
6

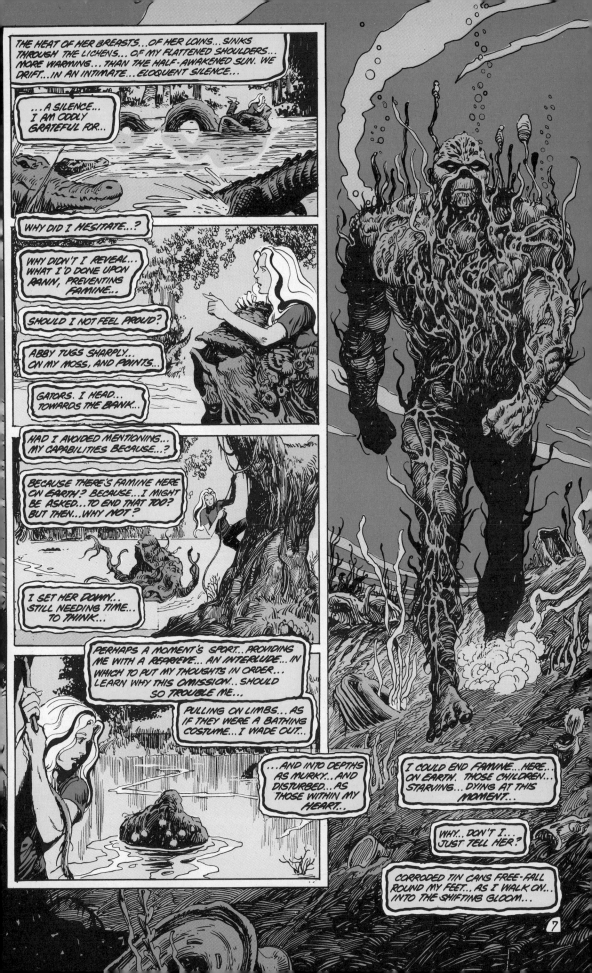

THE HEAT OF HER BREASTS...OF HER LOINS...SINKS THROUGH THE LICHENS... OF MY FLATTENED SHOULDERS... MORE WARMING...THAN THE HALF-AWAKENED SUN. WE DRIFT...IN AN INTIMATE...ELOQUENT SILENCE...

...A SILENCE... I AM ODDLY GRATEFUL FOR...

WHY DID I HESITATE...?

WHY DIDN'T I REVEAL... WHAT I'D DONE UPON RANN, PREVENTING FAMINE...

SHOULD I NOT FEEL PROUD?

ABBY TUGS SHARPLY... ON MY MOSS, AND POINTS...

GATORS. I HEAD... TOWARDS THE BANK...

HAD I AVOIDED MENTIONING... MY CAPABILITIES BECAUSE...?

BECAUSE THERE'S FAMINE HERE ON EARTH? BECAUSE...I MIGHT BE ASKED...TO END THAT TOO? BUT THEN...WHY NOT?

I SET HER DOWN... STILL NEEDING TIME... TO THINK...

PERHAPS A MOMENT'S SPORT...PROVIDING ME WITH A REPRIEVE... AN INTERLUDE...IN WHICH TO PUT MY THOUGHTS IN ORDER... LEARN WHY THIS OMISSION...SHOULD SO TROUBLE ME...

PULLING ON LIMBS... AS IF THEY WERE A BATHING COSTUME... I WADE OUT...

...AND INTO DEPTHS AS MURKY...AND DISTURBED...AS THOSE WITHIN MY HEART...

I COULD END FAMINE...HERE... ON EARTH. THOSE CHILDREN... STARVING...DYING AT THIS MOMENT...

WHY...DON'T I... JUST TELL HER?

CORRODED TIN CANS FREE-FALL ROUND MY FEET...AS I WALK ON... INTO THE SHIFTING GLOOM...

7

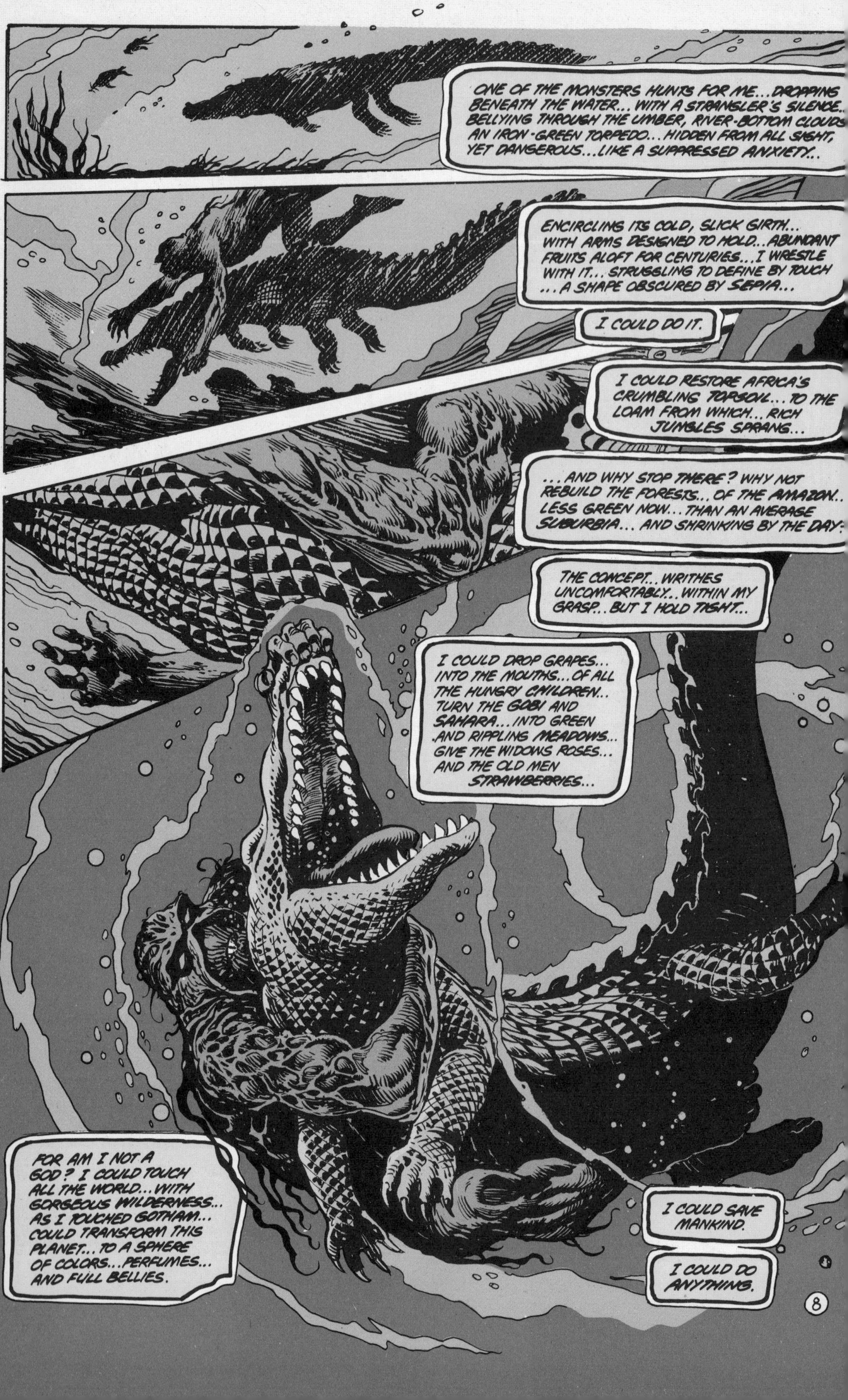
ONE OF THE MONSTERS HUNTS FOR ME... DROPPING BENEATH THE WATER... WITH A STRANGLER'S SILENCE... BELLYING THROUGH THE UMBER, RIVER-BOTTOM CLOUDS, AN IRON-GREEN TORPEDO... HIDDEN FROM ALL SIGHT, YET DANGEROUS... LIKE A SUPPRESSED ANXIETY...
ENCIRCLING ITS COLD, SLICK GIRTH... WITH ARMS DESIGNED TO HOLD... ABUNDANT FRUITS ALOFT FOR CENTURIES... I WRESTLE WITH IT... STRUGGLING TO DEFINE BY TOUCH ... A SHAPE OBSCURED BY SEPIA...
I COULD DO IT.
I COULD RESTORE AFRICA'S CRUMBLING TOPSOIL... TO THE LOAM FROM WHICH... RICH JUNGLES SPRANG...
...AND WHY STOP THERE? WHY NOT REBUILD THE FORESTS... OF THE AMAZON... LESS GREEN NOW... THAN AN AVERAGE SUBURBIA... AND SHRINKING BY THE DAY.
THE CONCEPT... WRITHES UNCOMFORTABLY... WITHIN MY GRASP... BUT I HOLD TIGHT...
I COULD DROP GRAPES... INTO THE MOUTHS... OF ALL THE HUNGRY CHILDREN... TURN THE GOBI AND SAHARA... INTO GREEN AND RIPPLING MEADOWS... GIVE THE WIDOWS ROSES... AND THE OLD MEN STRAWBERRIES...
FOR AM I NOT A GOD? I COULD TOUCH ALL THE WORLD... WITH GORGEOUS WILDERNESS... AS I TOUCHED GOTHAM... COULD TRANSFORM THIS PLANET... TO A SPHERE OF COLORS... PERFUMES... AND FULL BELLIES.
I COULD SAVE MANKIND.
I COULD DO ANYTHING.
8

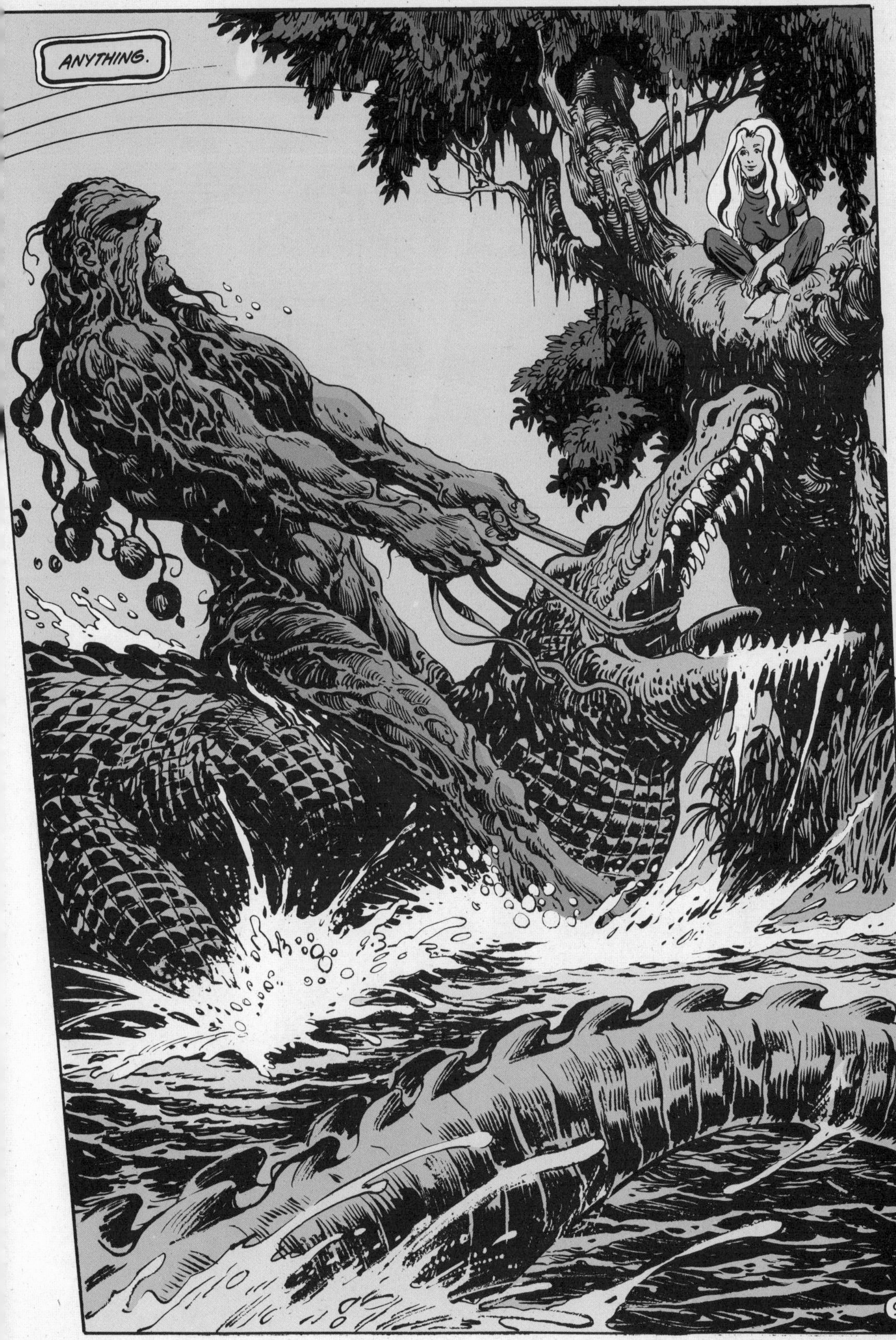
ANYTHING.
9

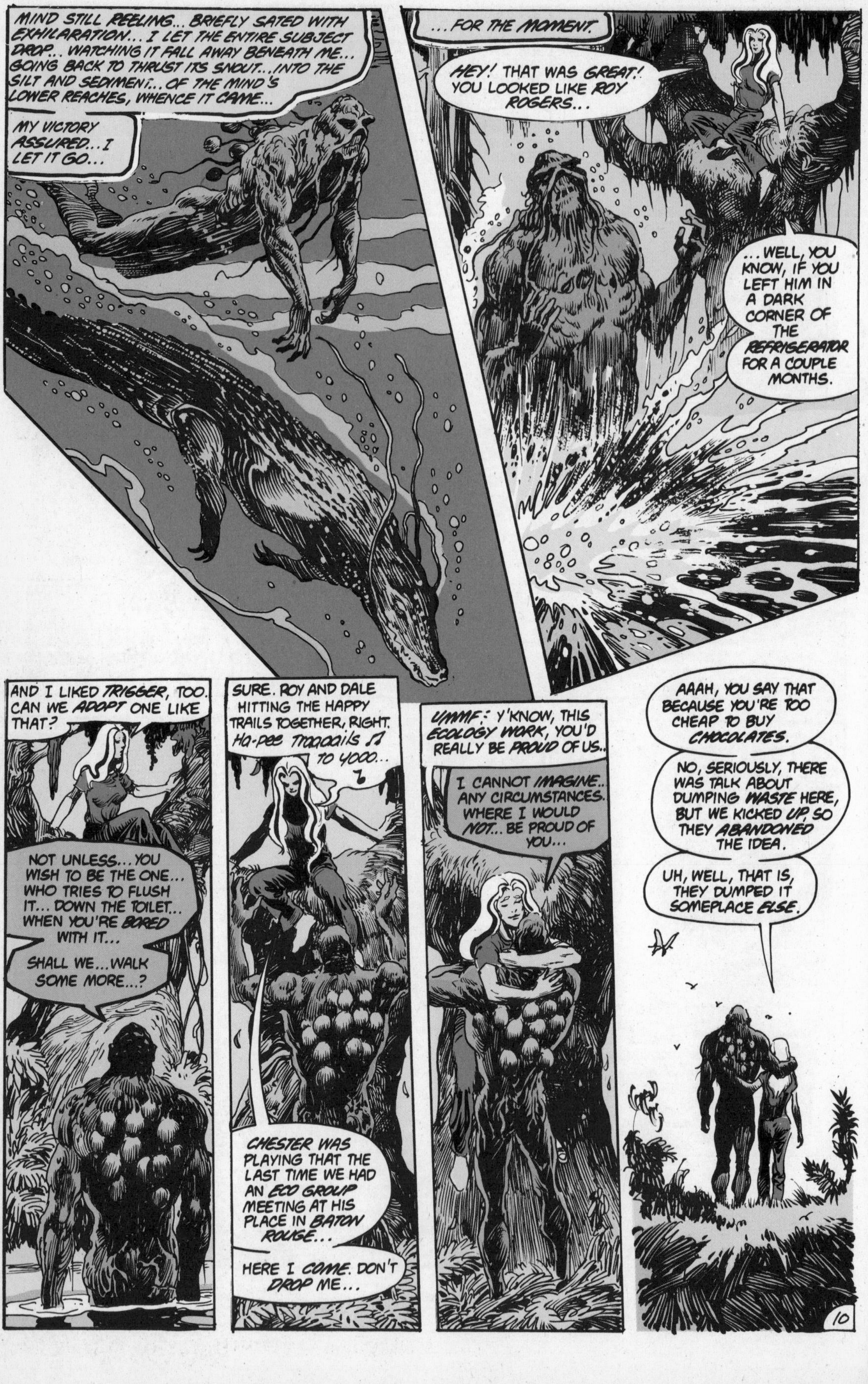
MIND STILL REELING... BRIEFLY SATED WITH EXHILARATION... I LET THE ENTIRE SUBJECT DROP... WATCHING IT FALL AWAY BENEATH ME... GOING BACK TO THRUST ITS SNOUT... INTO THE SILT AND SEDIMENT... OF THE MIND'S LOWER REACHES, WHENCE IT CAME...
MY VICTORY ASSURED... I LET IT GO...
...FOR THE MOMENT.
HEY! THAT WAS GREAT! YOU LOOKED LIKE ROY ROGERS...
...WELL, YOU KNOW, IF YOU LEFT HIM IN A DARK CORNER OF THE REFRIGERATOR FOR A COUPLE MONTHS.
AND I LIKED TRIGGER, TOO. CAN WE ADOPT ONE LIKE THAT?
NOT UNLESS... YOU WISH TO BE THE ONE... WHO TRIES TO FLUSH IT... DOWN THE TOILET... WHEN YOU'RE BORED WITH IT...
SHALL WE... WALK SOME MORE...?
SURE. ROY AND DALE HITTING THE HAPPY TRAILS TOGETHER, RIGHT. Ha-pee Traaaails ♫ to yooo...
CHESTER WAS PLAYING THAT THE LAST TIME WE HAD AN ECO GROUP MEETING AT HIS PLACE IN BATON ROUGE...
HERE I COME. DON'T DROP ME...
UMMF: Y'KNOW, THIS ECOLOGY WORK, YOU'D REALLY BE PROUD OF US...
I CANNOT IMAGINE... ANY CIRCUMSTANCES... WHERE I WOULD NOT... BE PROUD OF YOU...
AAAH, YOU SAY THAT BECAUSE YOU'RE TOO CHEAP TO BUY CHOCOLATES.
NO, SERIOUSLY, THERE WAS TALK ABOUT DUMPING WASTE HERE, BUT WE KICKED UP, SO THEY ABANDONED THE IDEA.
UH, WELL, THAT IS, THEY DUMPED IT SOMEPLACE ELSE.
10

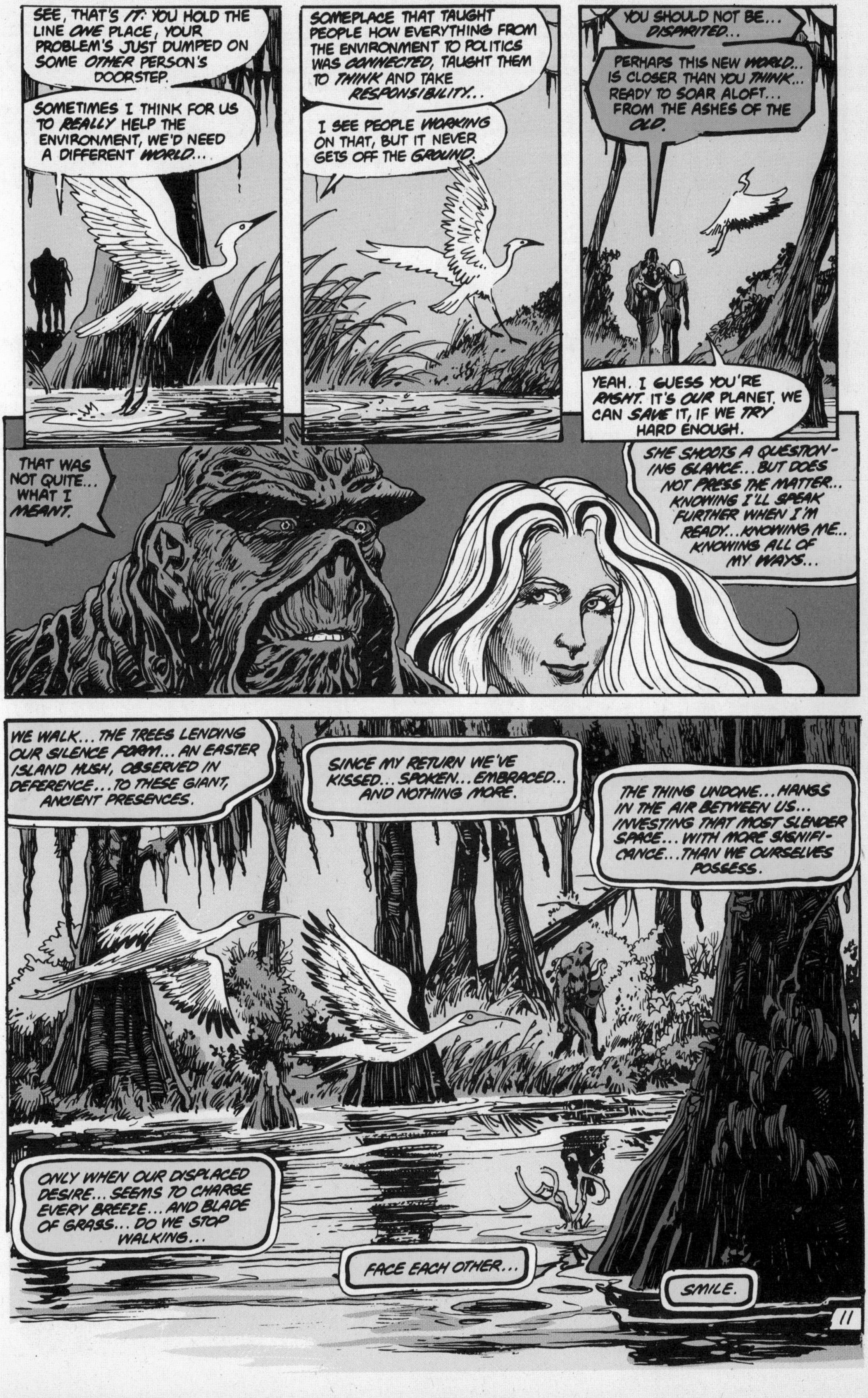
SEE, THAT'S IT: YOU HOLD THE LINE ONE PLACE, YOUR PROBLEM'S JUST DUMPED ON SOME OTHER PERSON'S DOORSTEP.
SOMETIMES I THINK FOR US TO REALLY HELP THE ENVIRONMENT, WE'D NEED A DIFFERENT WORLD...
SOMEPLACE THAT TAUGHT PEOPLE HOW EVERYTHING FROM THE ENVIRONMENT TO POLITICS WAS CONNECTED, TAUGHT THEM TO THINK AND TAKE RESPONSIBILITY...
I SEE PEOPLE WORKING ON THAT, BUT IT NEVER GETS OFF THE GROUND.
YOU SHOULD NOT BE... DISPIRITED...
PERHAPS THIS NEW WORLD... IS CLOSER THAN YOU THINK... READY TO SOAR ALOFT... FROM THE ASHES OF THE OLD.
YEAH. I GUESS YOU'RE RIGHT. IT'S OUR PLANET. WE CAN SAVE IT, IF WE TRY HARD ENOUGH.
THAT WAS NOT QUITE... WHAT I MEANT.
SHE SHOOTS A QUESTIONING GLANCE... BUT DOES NOT PRESS THE MATTER... KNOWING I'LL SPEAK FURTHER WHEN I'M READY... KNOWING ME... KNOWING ALL OF MY WAYS...
WE WALK... THE TREES LENDING OUR SILENCE FORM... AN EASTER ISLAND HUSH, OBSERVED IN DEFERENCE... TO THESE GIANT, ANCIENT PRESENCES.
SINCE MY RETURN WE'VE KISSED... SPOKEN... EMBRACED... AND NOTHING MORE.
THE THING UNDONE... HANGS IN THE AIR BETWEEN US... INVESTING THAT MOST SLENDER SPACE... WITH MORE SIGNIFICANCE... THAN WE OURSELVES POSSESS.
ONLY WHEN OUR DISPLACED DESIRE... SEEMS TO CHARGE EVERY BREEZE... AND BLADE OF GRASS... DO WE STOP WALKING...
FACE EACH OTHER...
SMILE.
11

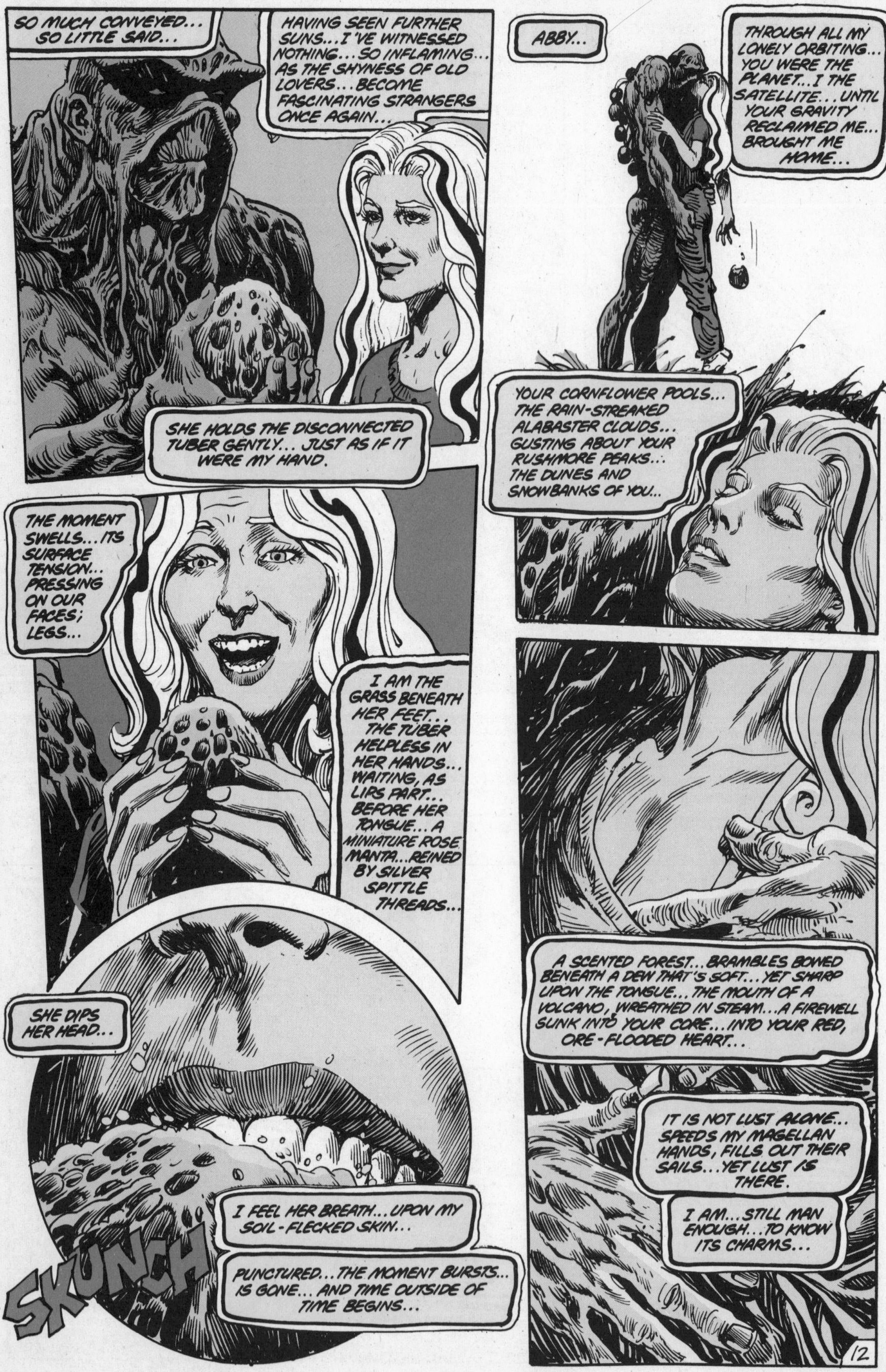
SO MUCH CONVEYED... SO LITTLE SAID...
HAVING SEEN FURTHER SUNS...I'VE WITNESSED NOTHING...SO INFLAMING... AS THE SHYNESS OF OLD LOVERS...BECOME FASCINATING STRANGERS ONCE AGAIN...
SHE HOLDS THE DISCONNECTED TUBER GENTLY... JUST AS IF IT WERE MY HAND.
ABBY...
THROUGH ALL MY LONELY ORBITING... YOU WERE THE PLANET...I THE SATELLITE...UNTIL YOUR GRAVITY RECLAIMED ME... BROUGHT ME HOME...
YOUR CORNFLOWER POOLS... THE RAIN-STREAKED ALABASTER CLOUDS... GUSTING ABOUT YOUR RUSHMORE PEAKS... THE DUNES AND SNOWBANKS OF YOU...
THE MOMENT SWELLS... ITS SURFACE TENSION... PRESSING ON OUR FACES; LEGS...
I AM THE GRASS BENEATH HER FEET... THE TUBER HELPLESS IN HER HANDS... WAITING, AS LIPS PART... BEFORE HER TONGUE... A MINIATURE ROSE MANTA...REINED BY SILVER SPITTLE THREADS...
SHE DIPS HER HEAD...
I FEEL HER BREATH...UPON MY SOIL-FLECKED SKIN...
SKUNCH
PUNCTURED...THE MOMENT BURSTS... IS GONE... AND TIME OUTSIDE OF TIME BEGINS...
A SCENTED FOREST...BRAMBLES BOWED BENEATH A DEW THAT'S SOFT...YET SHARP UPON THE TONGUE...THE MOUTH OF A VOLCANO, WREATHED IN STEAM...A FIREWELL SUNK INTO YOUR CORE...INTO YOUR RED, ORE-FLOODED HEART...
IT IS NOT LUST ALONE... SPEEDS MY MAGELLAN HANDS, FILLS OUT THEIR SAILS...YET LUST IS THERE.
I AM...STILL MAN ENOUGH...TO KNOW ITS CHARMS...
12

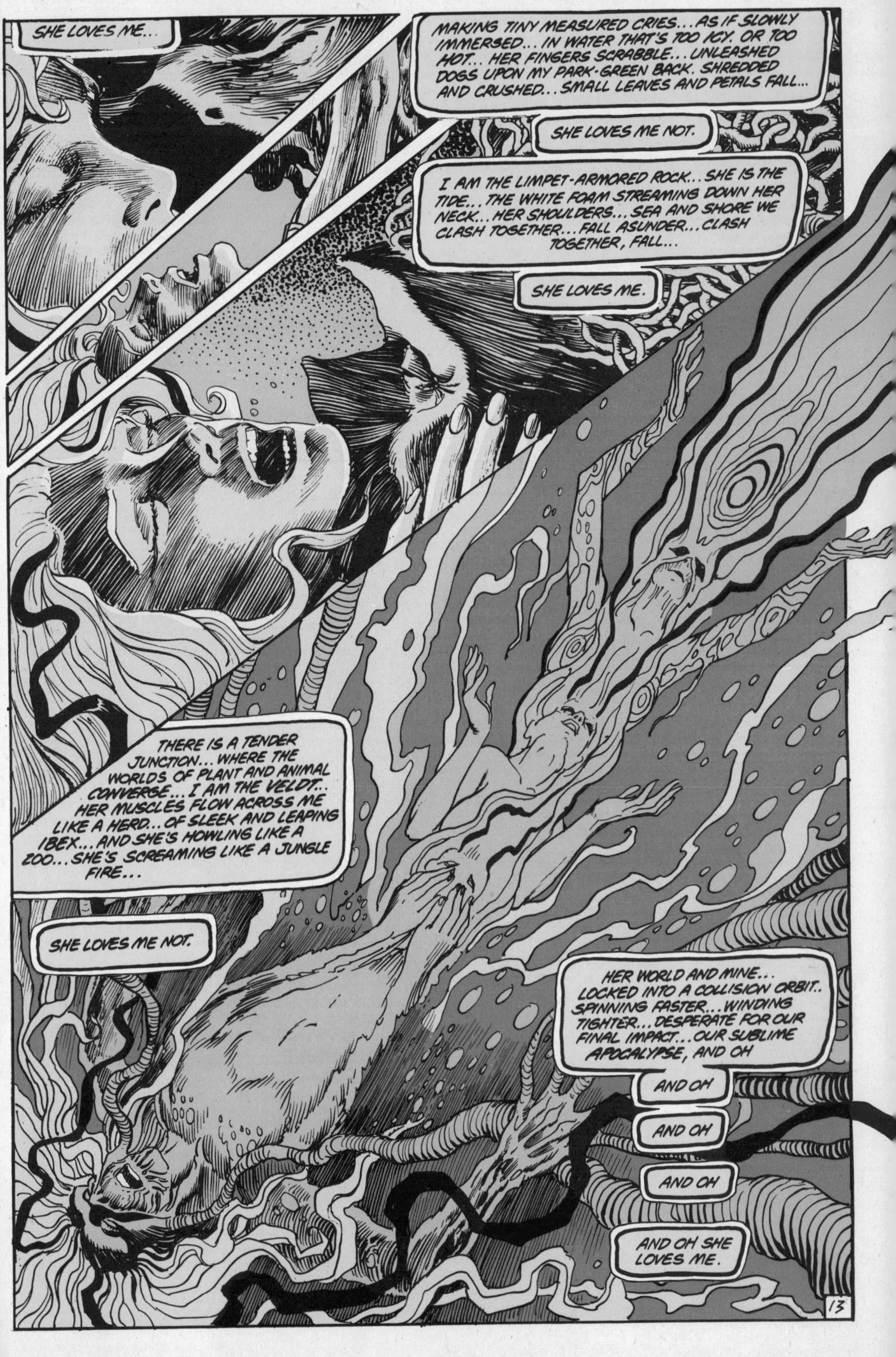
SHE LOVES ME...
MAKING TINY MEASURED CRIES... AS IF SLOWLY IMMERSED... IN WATER THAT'S TOO ICY. OR TOO HOT... HER FINGERS SCRABBLE... UNLEASHED DOGS UPON MY PARK-GREEN BACK. SHREDDED AND CRUSHED... SMALL LEAVES AND PETALS FALL...
SHE LOVES ME NOT.
I AM THE LIMPET-ARMORED ROCK... SHE IS THE TIDE... THE WHITE FOAM STREAMING DOWN HER NECK... HER SHOULDERS... SEA AND SHORE WE CLASH TOGETHER... FALL ASUNDER... CLASH TOGETHER, FALL...
SHE LOVES ME.
THERE IS A TENDER JUNCTION... WHERE THE WORLDS OF PLANT AND ANIMAL CONVERSE... I AM THE VELDT... HER MUSCLES FLOW ACROSS ME LIKE A HERD... OF SLEEK AND LEAPING IBEX... AND SHE'S HOWLING LIKE A ZOO... SHE'S SCREAMING LIKE A JUNGLE FIRE...
SHE LOVES ME NOT.
HER WORLD AND MINE... LOCKED INTO A COLLISION ORBIT.. SPINNING FASTER... WINDING TIGHTER... DESPERATE FOR OUR FINAL IMPACT... OUR SUBLIME APOCALYPSE, AND OH
AND OH
AND OH
AND OH
AND OH SHE LOVES ME.
13

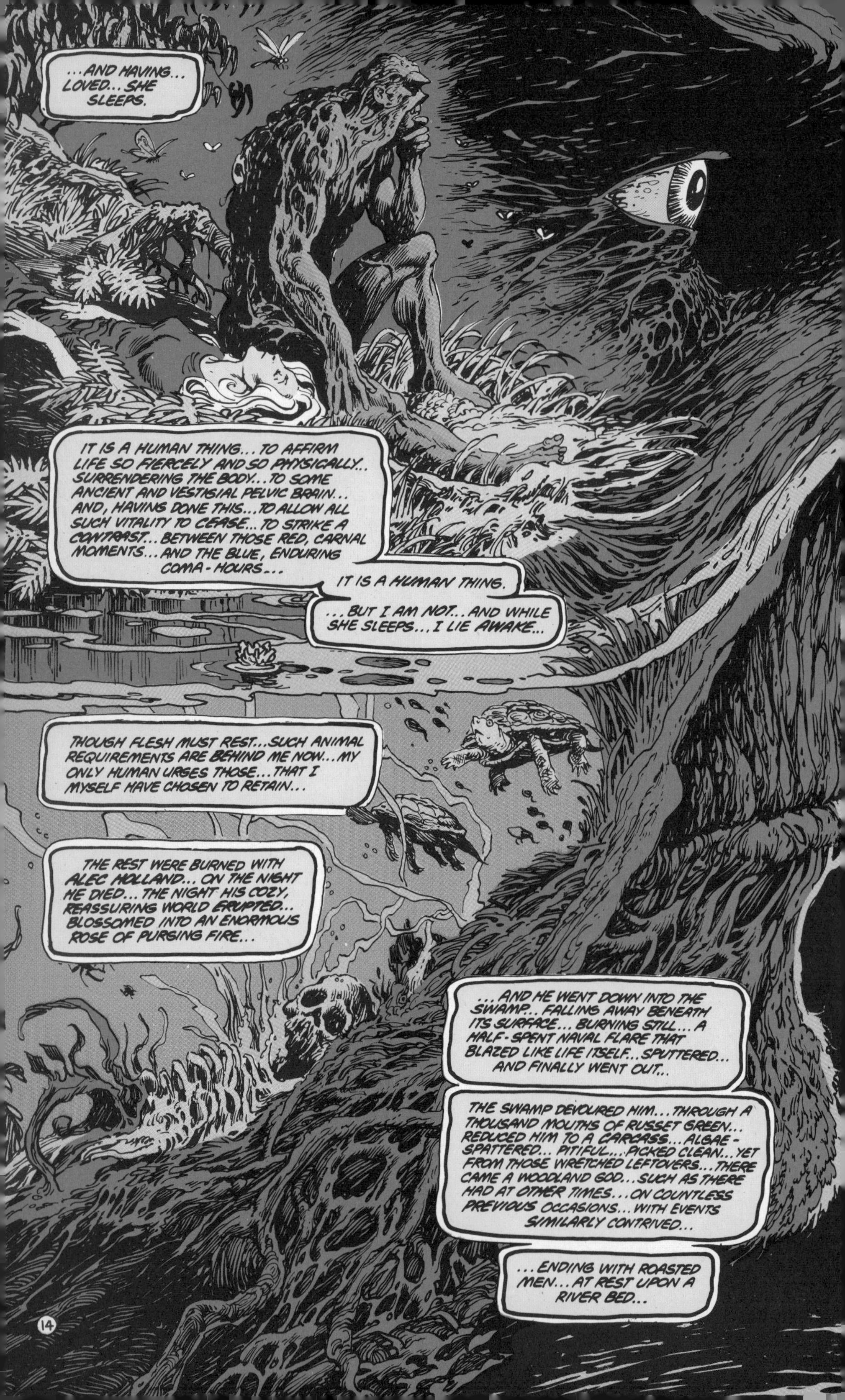
...AND HAVING... LOVED... SHE SLEEPS.
IT IS A HUMAN THING... TO AFFIRM LIFE SO FIERCELY AND SO PHYSICALLY... SURRENDERING THE BODY... TO SOME ANCIENT AND VESTIGIAL PELVIC BRAIN... AND, HAVING DONE THIS... TO ALLOW ALL SUCH VITALITY TO CEASE... TO STRIKE A CONTRAST... BETWEEN THOSE RED, CARNAL MOMENTS... AND THE BLUE, ENDURING COMA-HOURS...
IT IS A HUMAN THING.
...BUT I AM NOT... AND WHILE SHE SLEEPS... I LIE AWAKE...
THOUGH FLESH MUST REST... SUCH ANIMAL REQUIREMENTS ARE BEHIND ME NOW... MY ONLY HUMAN URGES THOSE... THAT I MYSELF HAVE CHOSEN TO RETAIN...
THE REST WERE BURNED WITH ALEC HOLLAND... ON THE NIGHT HE DIED... THE NIGHT HIS COZY, REASSURING WORLD ERUPTED... BLOSSOMED INTO AN ENORMOUS ROSE OF PURGING FIRE...
...AND HE WENT DOWN INTO THE SWAMP... FALLING AWAY BENEATH ITS SURFACE... BURNING STILL... A HALF-SPENT NAVAL FLARE THAT BLAZED LIKE LIFE ITSELF... SPUTTERED... AND FINALLY WENT OUT...
THE SWAMP DEVOURED HIM... THROUGH A THOUSAND MOUTHS OF RUSSET GREEN... REDUCED HIM TO A CARCASS... ALGAE-SPATTERED... PITIFUL... PICKED CLEAN... YET FROM THOSE WRETCHED LEFTOVERS... THERE CAME A WOODLAND GOD... SUCH AS THERE HAD AT OTHER TIMES... ON COUNTLESS PREVIOUS OCCASIONS... WITH EVENTS SIMILARLY CONTRIVED...
...ENDING WITH ROASTED MEN... AT REST UPON A RIVER BED...
14

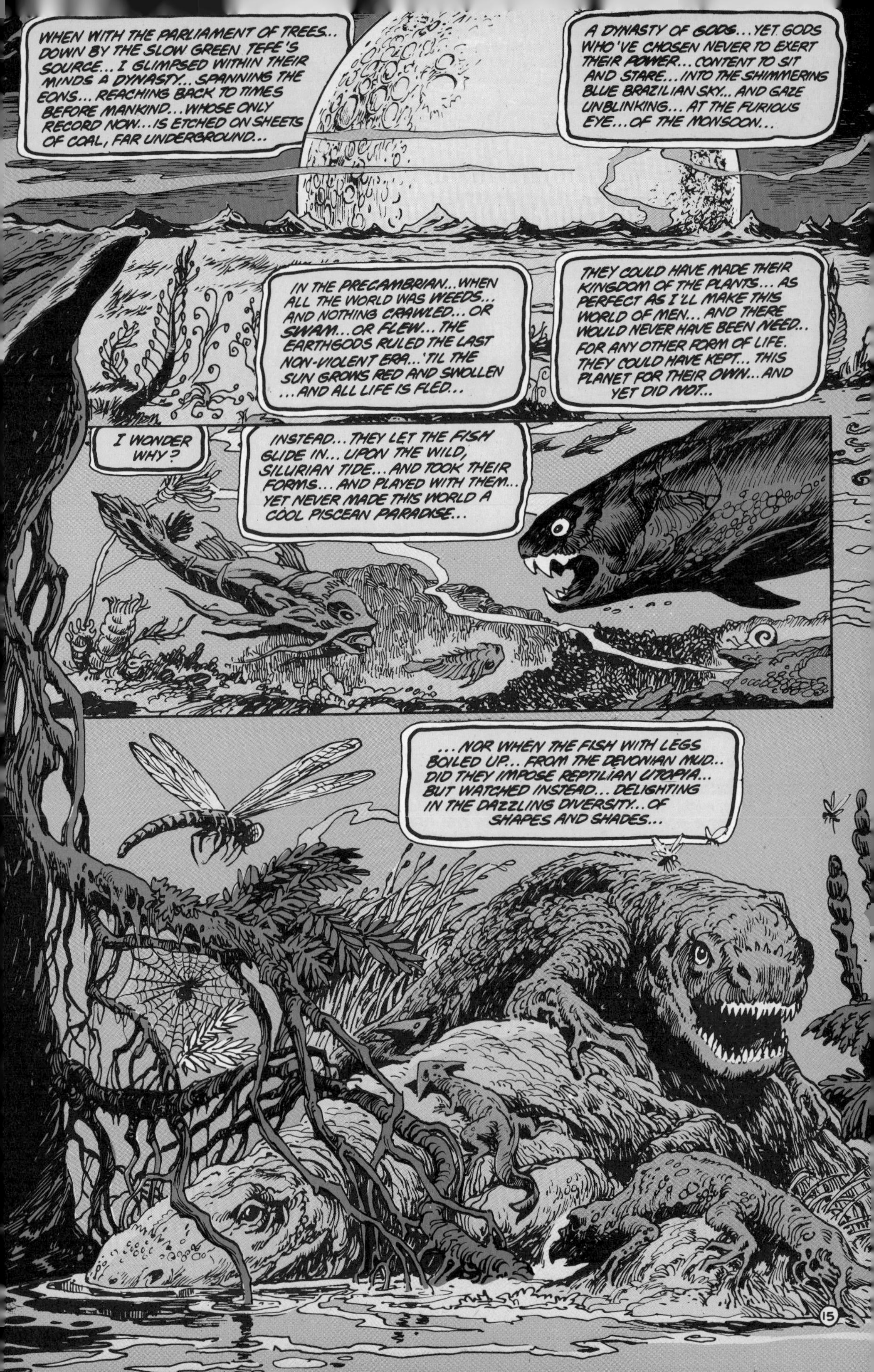
WHEN WITH THE PARLIAMENT OF TREES... DOWN BY THE SLOW GREEN TEFÉ'S SOURCE... I GLIMPSED WITHIN THEIR MINDS A DYNASTY... SPANNING THE EONS... REACHING BACK TO TIMES BEFORE MANKIND... WHOSE ONLY RECORD NOW... IS ETCHED ON SHEETS OF COAL, FAR UNDERGROUND...
A DYNASTY OF GODS... YET GODS WHO'VE CHOSEN NEVER TO EXERT THEIR POWER... CONTENT TO SIT AND STARE... INTO THE SHIMMERING BLUE BRAZILIAN SKY... AND GAZE UNBLINKING... AT THE FURIOUS EYE... OF THE MONSOON...
IN THE PRECAMBRIAN... WHEN ALL THE WORLD WAS WEEDS... AND NOTHING CRAWLED... OR SWAM... OR FLEW... THE EARTHGODS RULED THE LAST NON-VIOLENT ERA... 'TIL THE SUN GROWS RED AND SWOLLEN ...AND ALL LIFE IS FLED...
THEY COULD HAVE MADE THEIR KINGDOM OF THE PLANTS... AS PERFECT AS I'LL MAKE THIS WORLD OF MEN... AND THERE WOULD NEVER HAVE BEEN NEED... FOR ANY OTHER FORM OF LIFE. THEY COULD HAVE KEPT... THIS PLANET FOR THEIR OWN... AND YET DID NOT...
I WONDER WHY?
INSTEAD... THEY LET THE FISH GLIDE IN... UPON THE WILD, SILURIAN TIDE... AND TOOK THEIR FORMS... AND PLAYED WITH THEM... YET NEVER MADE THIS WORLD A COOL PISCEAN PARADISE...
...NOR WHEN THE FISH WITH LEGS BOILED UP... FROM THE DEVONIAN MUD... DID THEY IMPOSE REPTILIAN UTOPIA... BUT WATCHED INSTEAD... DELIGHTING IN THE DAZZLING DIVERSITY... OF SHAPES AND SHADES...

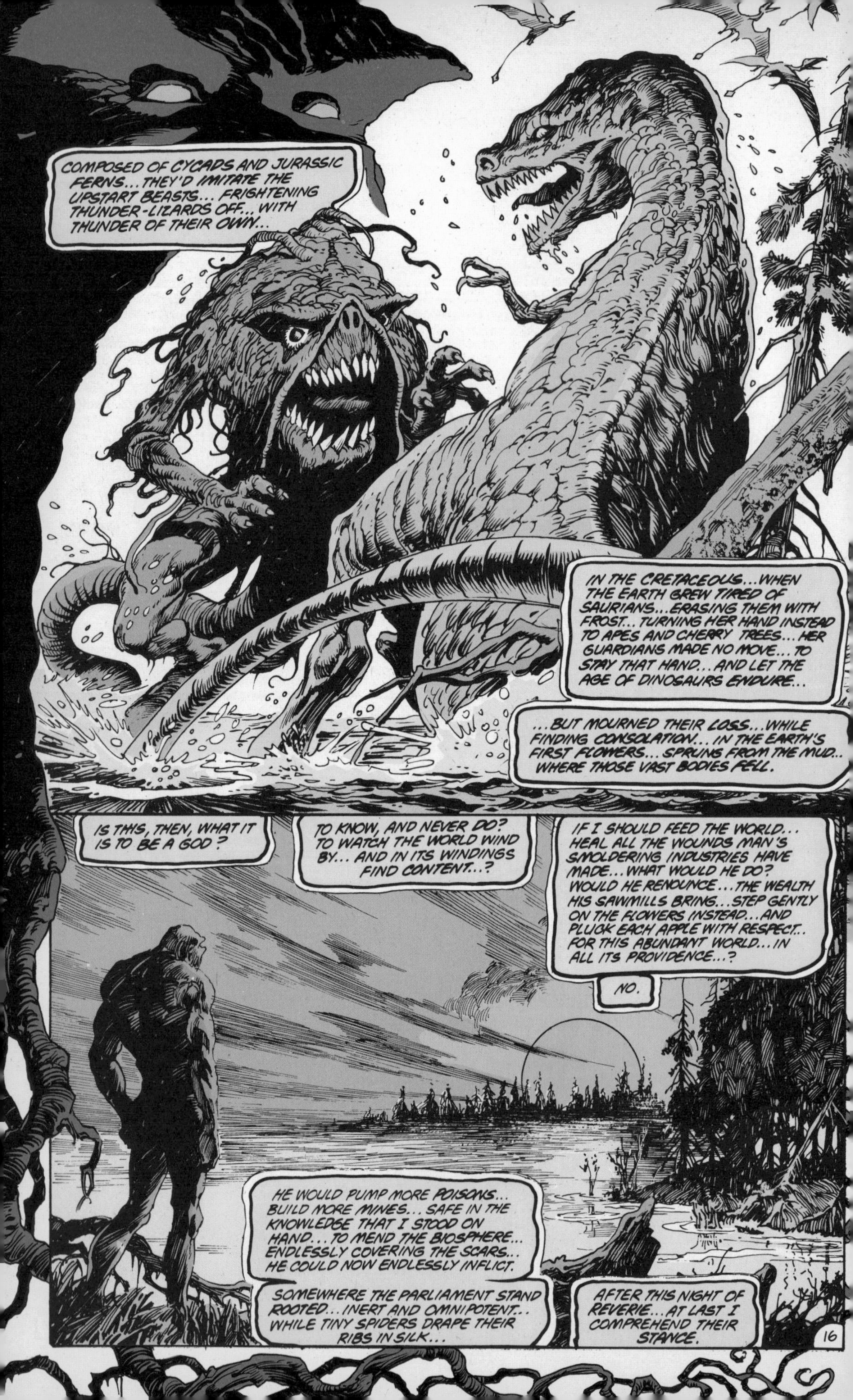
COMPOSED OF CYCADS AND JURASSIC FERNS... THEY'D IMITATE THE UPSTART BEASTS... FRIGHTENING THUNDER-LIZARDS OFF... WITH THUNDER OF THEIR OWN...
IN THE CRETACEOUS... WHEN THE EARTH GREW TIRED OF SAURIANS... ERASING THEM WITH FROST... TURNING HER HAND INSTEAD TO APES AND CHERRY TREES... HER GUARDIANS MADE NO MOVE... TO STAY THAT HAND... AND LET THE AGE OF DINOSAURS ENDURE...
...BUT MOURNED THEIR LOSS... WHILE FINDING CONSOLATION... IN THE EARTH'S FIRST FLOWERS... SPRUNG FROM THE MUD... WHERE THOSE VAST BODIES FELL.
IS THIS, THEN, WHAT IT IS TO BE A GOD?
TO KNOW, AND NEVER DO? TO WATCH THE WORLD WIND BY... AND IN ITS WINDINGS FIND CONTENT...?
IF I SHOULD FEED THE WORLD... HEAL ALL THE WOUNDS MAN'S SMOLDERING INDUSTRIES HAVE MADE... WHAT WOULD HE DO? WOULD HE RENOUNCE... THE WEALTH HIS SAWMILLS BRING... STEP GENTLY ON THE FLOWERS INSTEAD... AND PLUCK EACH APPLE WITH RESPECT... FOR THIS ABUNDANT WORLD... IN ALL ITS PROVIDENCE...?
NO.
HE WOULD PUMP MORE POISONS... BUILD MORE MINES... SAFE IN THE KNOWLEDGE THAT I STOOD ON HAND... TO MEND THE BIOSPHERE... ENDLESSLY COVERING THE SCARS... HE COULD NOW ENDLESSLY INFLICT.
SOMEWHERE THE PARLIAMENT STAND ROOTED... INERT AND OMNIPOTENT... WHILE TINY SPIDERS DRAPE THEIR RIBS IN SILK...
AFTER THIS NIGHT OF REVERIE... AT LAST I COMPREHEND THEIR STANCE.
16

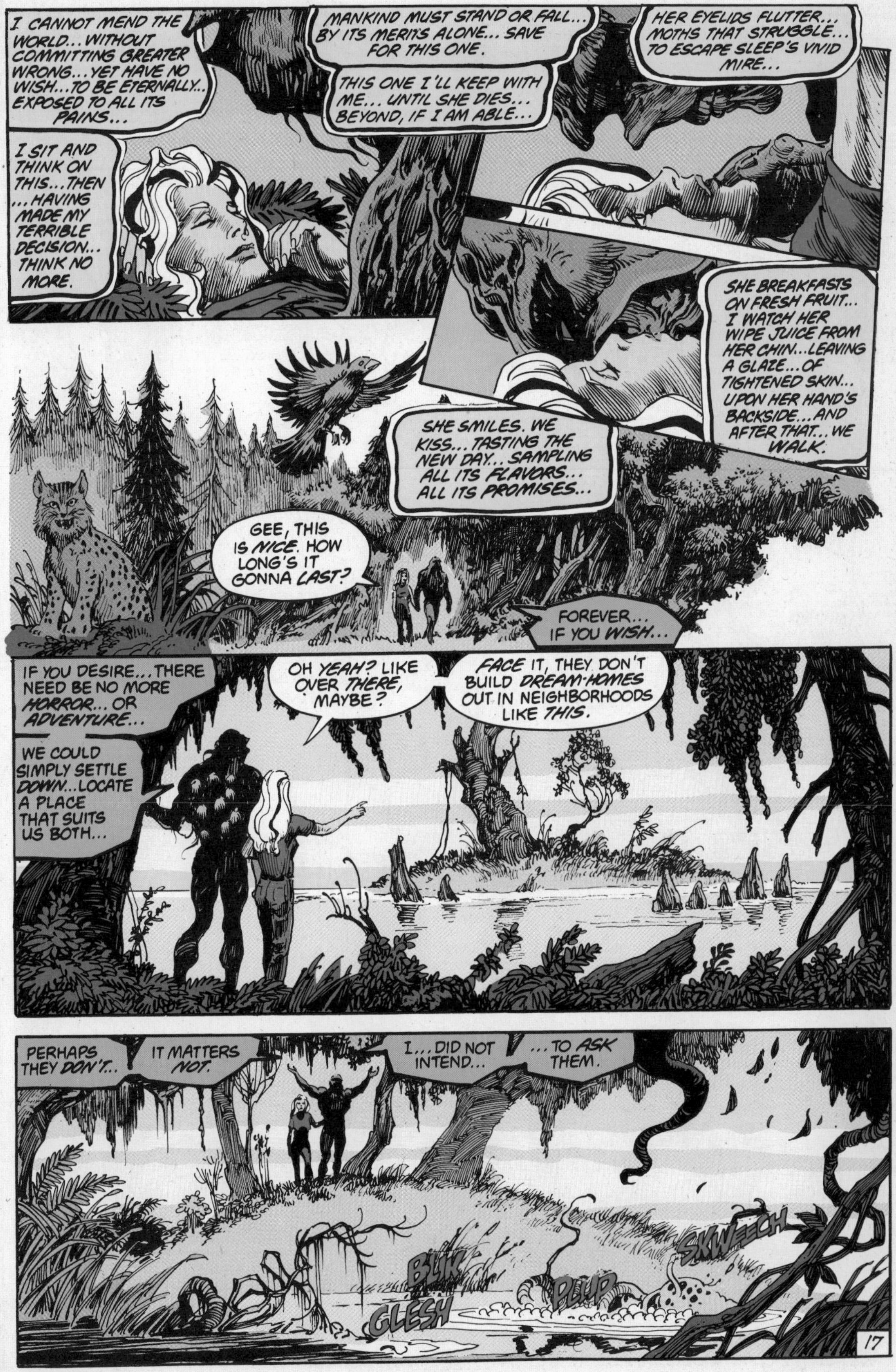
I CANNOT MEND THE WORLD... WITHOUT COMMITTING GREATER WRONG... YET HAVE NO WISH... TO BE ETERNALLY... EXPOSED TO ALL ITS PAINS...
I SIT AND THINK ON THIS... THEN ...HAVING MADE MY TERRIBLE DECISION... THINK NO MORE.
MANKIND MUST STAND OR FALL... BY ITS MERITS ALONE... SAVE FOR THIS ONE.
THIS ONE I'LL KEEP WITH ME... UNTIL SHE DIES... BEYOND, IF I AM ABLE...
HER EYELIDS FLUTTER... MOTHS THAT STRUGGLE... TO ESCAPE SLEEP'S VIVID MIRE...
SHE BREAKFASTS ON FRESH FRUIT... I WATCH HER WIPE JUICE FROM HER CHIN... LEAVING A GLAZE... OF TIGHTENED SKIN... UPON HER HAND'S BACKSIDE... AND AFTER THAT... WE WALK.
SHE SMILES. WE KISS... TASTING THE NEW DAY... SAMPLING ALL ITS FLAVORS... ALL ITS PROMISES...
GEE, THIS IS NICE. HOW LONG'S IT GONNA LAST?
FOREVER... IF YOU WISH...
IF YOU DESIRE... THERE NEED BE NO MORE HORROR... OR ADVENTURE...
WE COULD SIMPLY SETTLE DOWN... LOCATE A PLACE THAT SUITS US BOTH...
OH YEAH? LIKE OVER THERE, MAYBE?
FACE IT, THEY DON'T BUILD DREAM-HOMES OUT IN NEIGHBORHOODS LIKE THIS.
PERHAPS THEY DON'T...
IT MATTERS NOT.
I... DID NOT INTEND...
...TO ASK THEM.
BLIK
GLESH
PLUP
SKWEECH
17

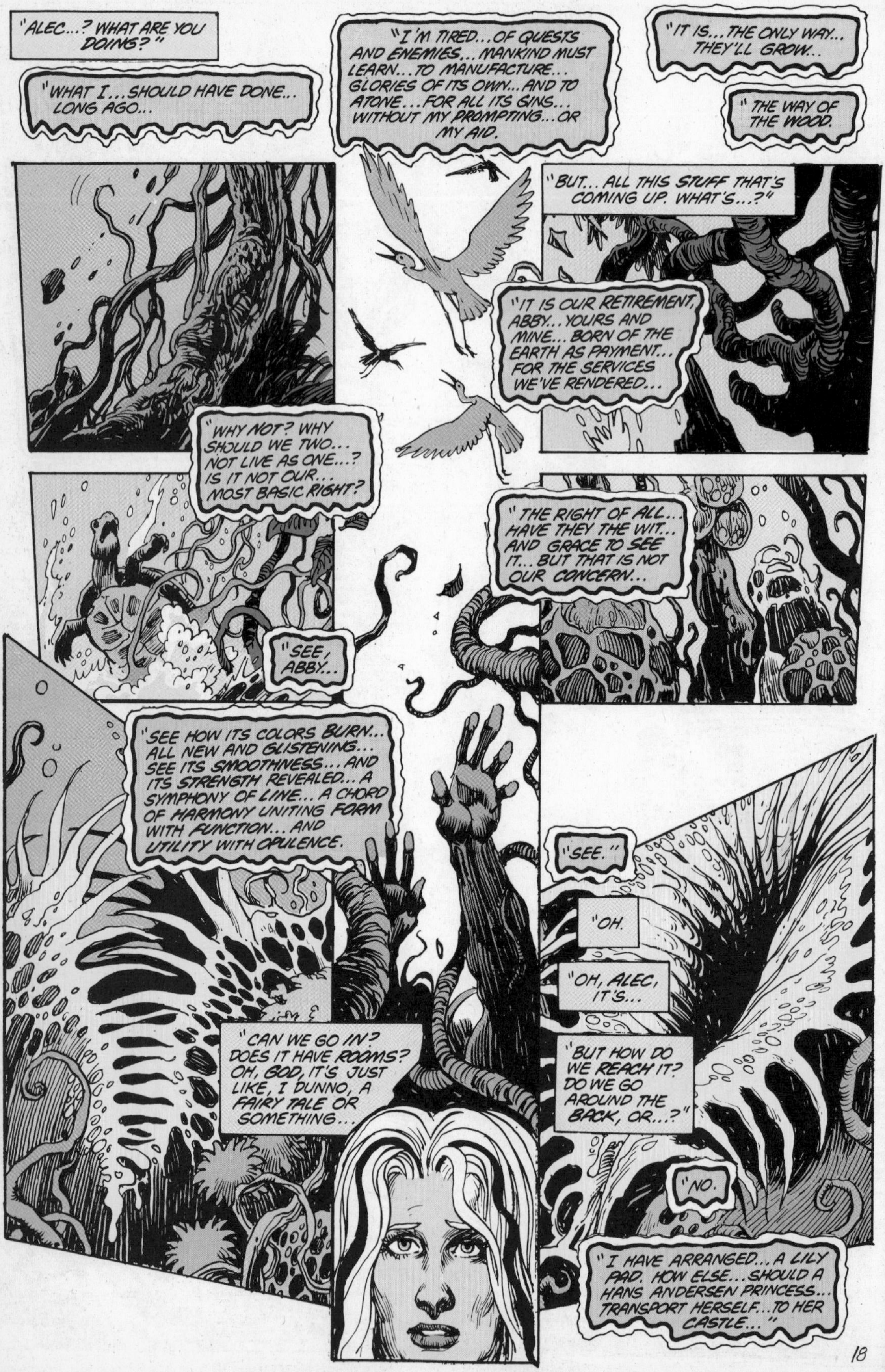
"ALEC...? WHAT ARE YOU DOING?"
"WHAT I...SHOULD HAVE DONE... LONG AGO...
"I'M TIRED...OF QUESTS AND ENEMIES...MANKIND MUST LEARN...TO MANUFACTURE... GLORIES OF ITS OWN...AND TO ATONE...FOR ALL ITS SINS... WITHOUT MY PROMPTING...OR MY AID.
"IT IS...THE ONLY WAY... THEY'LL GROW...
"THE WAY OF THE WOOD.
"BUT... ALL THIS STUFF THAT'S COMING UP. WHAT'S...?"
"IT IS OUR RETIREMENT, ABBY...YOURS AND MINE...BORN OF THE EARTH AS PAYMENT... FOR THE SERVICES WE'VE RENDERED...
"WHY NOT? WHY SHOULD WE TWO... NOT LIVE AS ONE...? IS IT NOT OUR... MOST BASIC RIGHT?
"THE RIGHT OF ALL... HAVE THEY THE WIT... AND GRACE TO SEE IT...BUT THAT IS NOT OUR CONCERN...
"SEE, ABBY...
"SEE HOW ITS COLORS BURN... ALL NEW AND GLISTENING... SEE ITS SMOOTHNESS...AND ITS STRENGTH REVEALED...A SYMPHONY OF LINE...A CHORD OF HARMONY UNITING FORM WITH FUNCTION...AND UTILITY WITH OPULENCE.
"SEE."
"OH.
"OH, ALEC, IT'S...
"CAN WE GO IN? DOES IT HAVE ROOMS? OH, GOD, IT'S JUST LIKE, I DUNNO, A FAIRY TALE OR SOMETHING...
"BUT HOW DO WE REACH IT? DO WE GO AROUND THE BACK, OR...?"
"NO.
"I HAVE ARRANGED...A LILY PAD. HOW ELSE...SHOULD A HANS ANDERSEN PRINCESS... TRANSPORT HERSELF...TO HER CASTLE..."
18

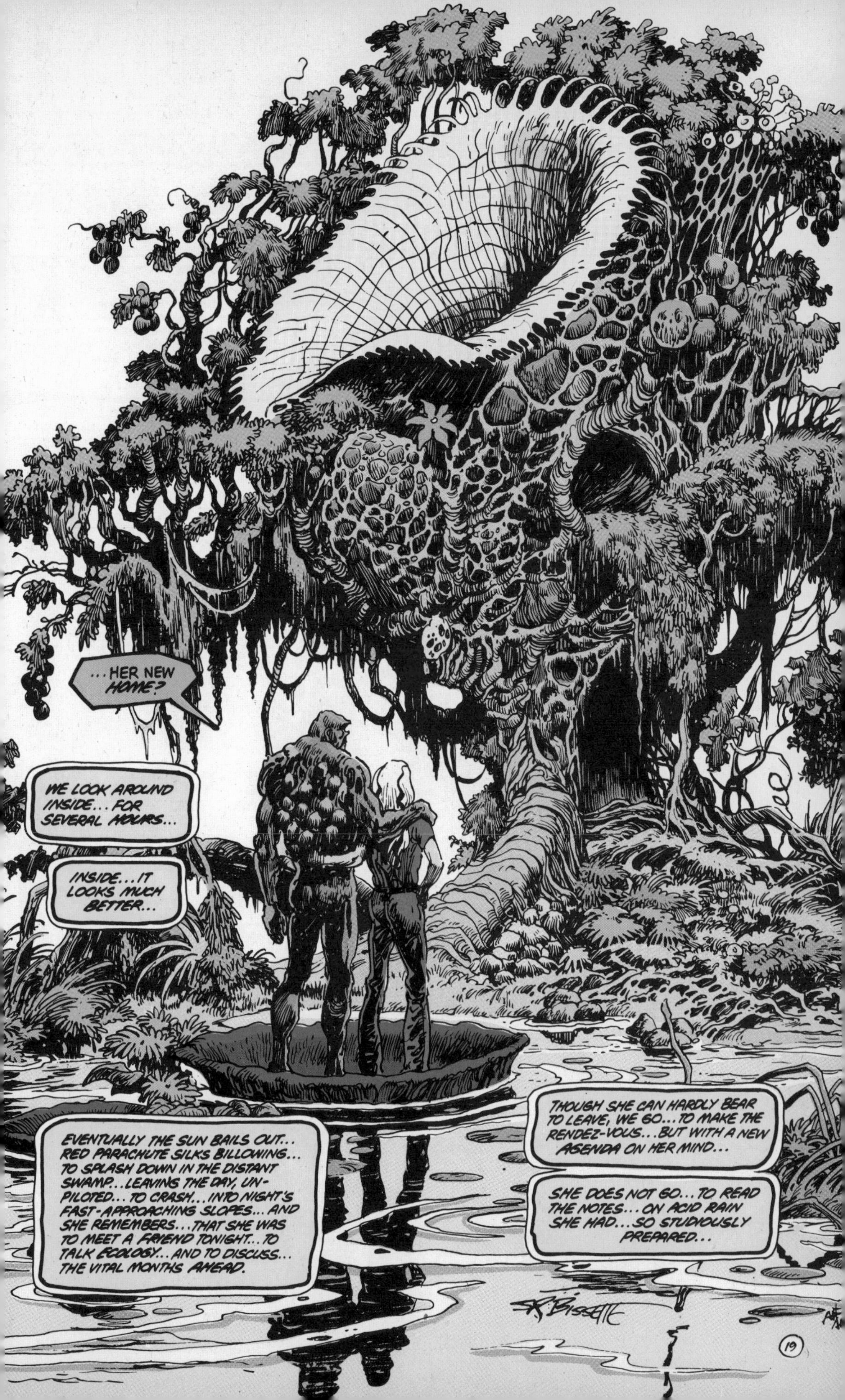

...HER NEW HOME?
WE LOOK AROUND INSIDE... FOR SEVERAL HOURS...
INSIDE... IT LOOKS MUCH BETTER...
EVENTUALLY THE SUN BAILS OUT... RED PARACHUTE SILKS BILLOWING... TO SPLASH DOWN IN THE DISTANT SWAMP... LEAVING THE DAY, UN-PILOTED... TO CRASH... INTO NIGHT'S FAST-APPROACHING SLOPES... AND SHE REMEMBERS... THAT SHE WAS TO MEET A FRIEND TONIGHT... TO TALK ECOLOGY... AND TO DISCUSS... THE VITAL MONTHS AHEAD.
THOUGH SHE CAN HARDLY BEAR TO LEAVE, WE GO... TO MAKE THE RENDEZ-VOUS... BUT WITH A NEW AGENDA ON HER MIND...
SHE DOES NOT GO... TO READ THE NOTES... ON ACID RAIN SHE HAD... SO STUDIOUSLY PREPARED...
S.R. BISSETTE

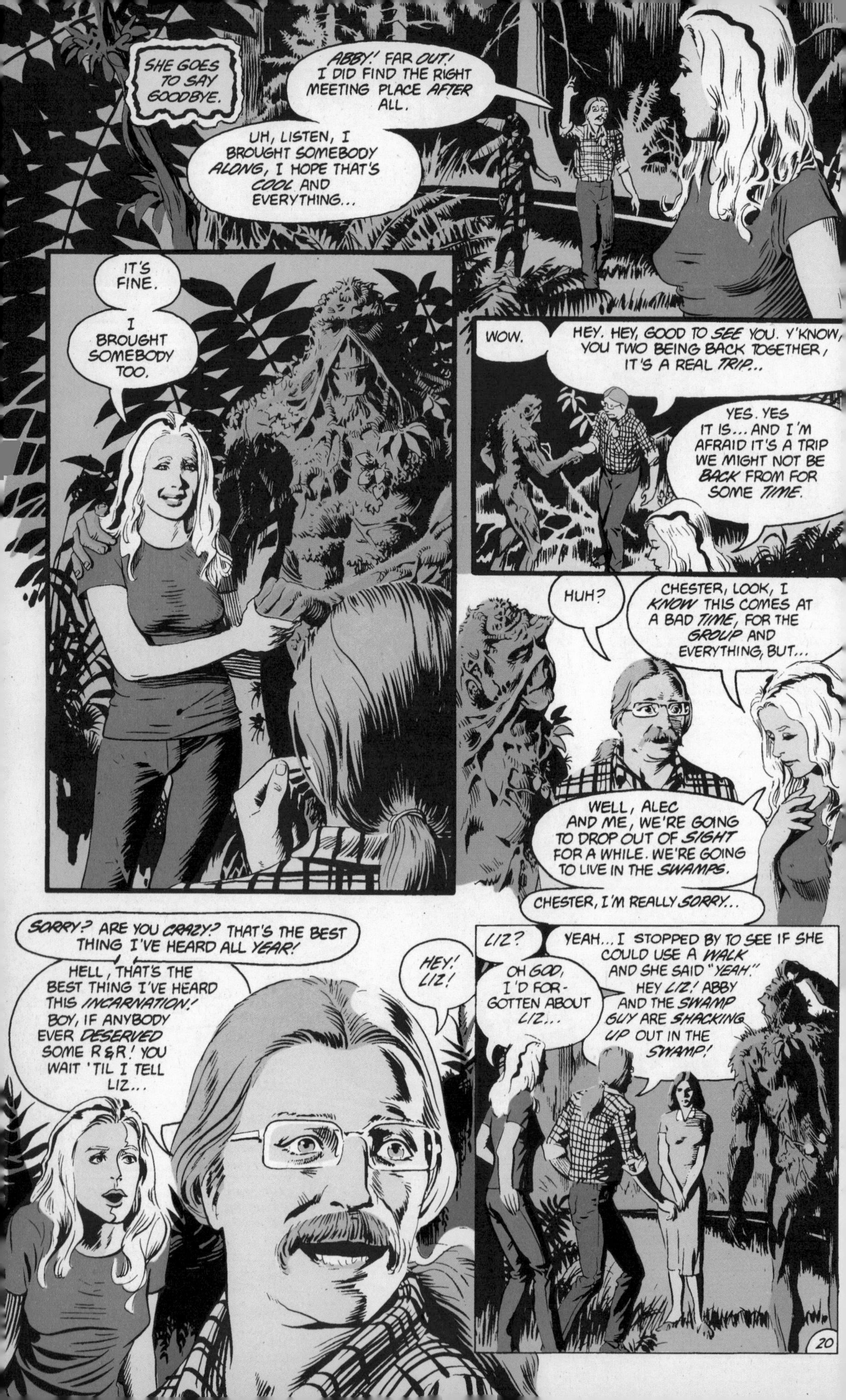

SHE GOES TO SAY GOODBYE.
ABBY! FAR OUT! I DID FIND THE RIGHT MEETING PLACE AFTER ALL.
UH, LISTEN, I BROUGHT SOMEBODY ALONG, I HOPE THAT'S COOL AND EVERYTHING...
IT'S FINE.
I BROUGHT SOMEBODY TOO.
WOW.
HEY. HEY, GOOD TO SEE YOU. Y'KNOW, YOU TWO BEING BACK TOGETHER, IT'S A REAL TRIP...
YES. YES IT IS... AND I'M AFRAID IT'S A TRIP WE MIGHT NOT BE BACK FROM FOR SOME TIME.
HUH?
CHESTER, LOOK, I KNOW THIS COMES AT A BAD TIME, FOR THE GROUP AND EVERYTHING, BUT...
WELL, ALEC AND ME, WE'RE GOING TO DROP OUT OF SIGHT FOR A WHILE. WE'RE GOING TO LIVE IN THE SWAMPS.
CHESTER, I'M REALLY SORRY...
SORRY? ARE YOU CRAZY? THAT'S THE BEST THING I'VE HEARD ALL YEAR!
HELL, THAT'S THE BEST THING I'VE HEARD THIS INCARNATION! BOY, IF ANYBODY EVER DESERVED SOME R&R! YOU WAIT 'TIL I TELL LIZ...
HEY! LIZ!
LIZ?
OH GOD, I'D FOR-GOTTEN ABOUT LIZ...
YEAH... I STOPPED BY TO SEE IF SHE COULD USE A WALK AND SHE SAID "YEAH." HEY LIZ! ABBY AND THE SWAMP GUY ARE SHACKING UP OUT IN THE SWAMP!

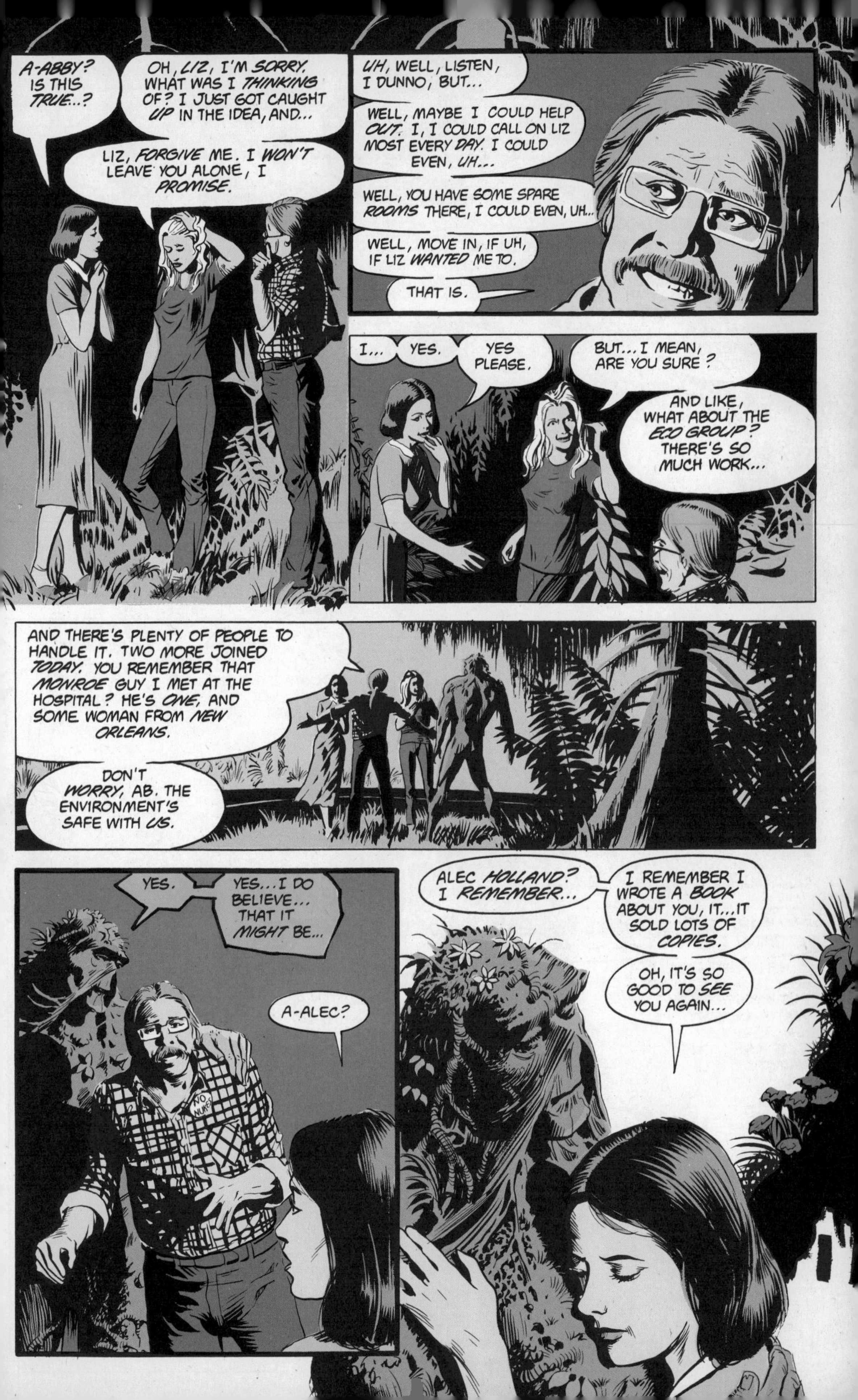
A-ABBY? IS THIS TRUE...?
OH, LIZ, I'M SORRY. WHAT WAS I THINKING OF? I JUST GOT CAUGHT UP IN THE IDEA, AND...
LIZ, FORGIVE ME. I WON'T LEAVE YOU ALONE, I PROMISE.
UH, WELL, LISTEN, I DUNNO, BUT...
WELL, MAYBE I COULD HELP OUT. I, I COULD CALL ON LIZ MOST EVERY DAY. I COULD EVEN, UH...
WELL, YOU HAVE SOME SPARE ROOMS THERE, I COULD EVEN, UH...
WELL, MOVE IN, IF UH, IF LIZ WANTED ME TO.
THAT IS.
I...
YES.
YES PLEASE.
BUT... I MEAN, ARE YOU SURE?
AND LIKE, WHAT ABOUT THE ECO GROUP? THERE'S SO MUCH WORK...
AND THERE'S PLENTY OF PEOPLE TO HANDLE IT. TWO MORE JOINED TODAY. YOU REMEMBER THAT MONROE GUY I MET AT THE HOSPITAL? HE'S ONE, AND SOME WOMAN FROM NEW ORLEANS.
DON'T WORRY, AB. THE ENVIRONMENT'S SAFE WITH US.
YES.
YES... I DO BELIEVE... THAT IT MIGHT BE...
A-ALEC?
NO NUKES
ALEC HOLLAND? I REMEMBER...
I REMEMBER I WROTE A BOOK ABOUT YOU, IT... IT SOLD LOTS OF COPIES.
OH, IT'S SO GOOD TO SEE YOU AGAIN...

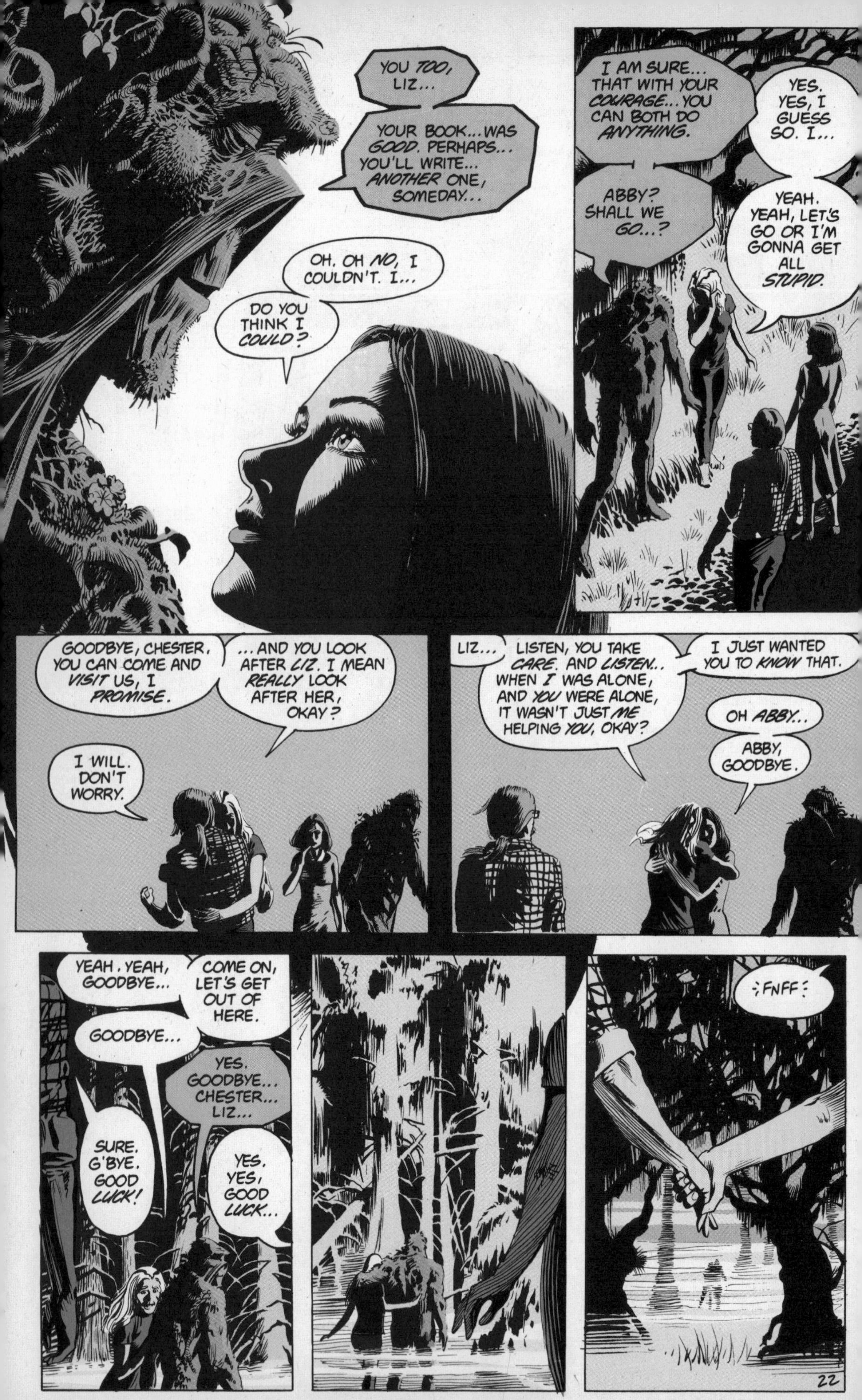
YOU TOO, LIZ...
YOUR BOOK...WAS GOOD. PERHAPS... YOU'LL WRITE... ANOTHER ONE, SOMEDAY...
OH. OH NO, I COULDN'T. I...
DO YOU THINK I COULD?
I AM SURE... THAT WITH YOUR COURAGE...YOU CAN BOTH DO ANYTHING.
ABBY? SHALL WE GO...?
YES. YES, I GUESS SO. I...
YEAH. YEAH, LET'S GO OR I'M GONNA GET ALL STUPID.
GOODBYE, CHESTER. YOU CAN COME AND VISIT US, I PROMISE.
...AND YOU LOOK AFTER LIZ. I MEAN REALLY LOOK AFTER HER, OKAY?
I WILL. DON'T WORRY.
LIZ...
LISTEN, YOU TAKE CARE. AND LISTEN... WHEN I WAS ALONE, AND YOU WERE ALONE, IT WASN'T JUST ME HELPING YOU, OKAY?
I JUST WANTED YOU TO KNOW THAT.
OH ABBY...
ABBY, GOODBYE.
YEAH. YEAH, GOODBYE...
COME ON, LET'S GET OUT OF HERE.
GOODBYE...
YES. GOODBYE... CHESTER... LIZ...
SURE. G'BYE. GOOD LUCK!
YES. YES, GOOD LUCK...
FNFF

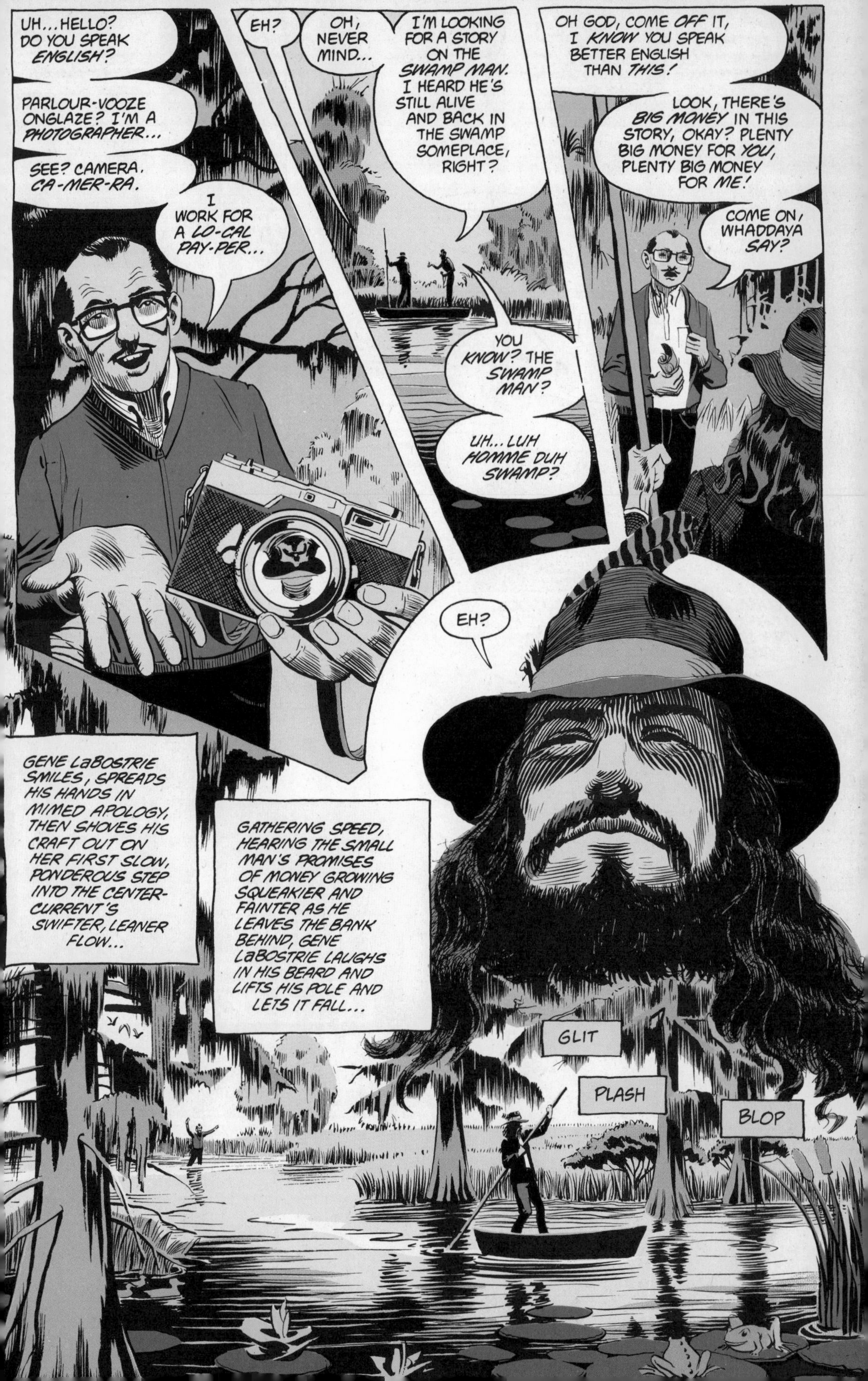
UH...HELLO? DO YOU SPEAK ENGLISH?
PARLOUR-VOOZE ONGLAZE? I'M A PHOTOGRAPHER...
SEE? CAMERA. CA-MER-RA.
I WORK FOR A LO-CAL PAY-PER...
EH?
OH, NEVER MIND...
I'M LOOKING FOR A STORY ON THE SWAMP MAN. I HEARD HE'S STILL ALIVE AND BACK IN THE SWAMP SOMEPLACE, RIGHT?
YOU KNOW? THE SWAMP MAN?
UH...LUH HOMME DUH SWAMP?
OH GOD, COME OFF IT, I KNOW YOU SPEAK BETTER ENGLISH THAN THIS!
LOOK, THERE'S BIG MONEY IN THIS STORY, OKAY? PLENTY BIG MONEY FOR YOU, PLENTY BIG MONEY FOR ME!
COME ON, WHADDAYA SAY?
EH?
GENE LaBOSTRIE SMILES, SPREADS HIS HANDS IN MIMED APOLOGY, THEN SHOVES HIS CRAFT OUT ON HER FIRST SLOW, PONDEROUS STEP INTO THE CENTER-CURRENT'S SWIFTER, LEANER FLOW...
GATHERING SPEED, HEARING THE SMALL MAN'S PROMISES OF MONEY GROWING SQUEAKIER AND FAINTER AS HE LEAVES THE BANK BEHIND, GENE LaBOSTRIE LAUGHS IN HIS BEARD AND LIFTS HIS POLE AND LETS IT FALL...
GLIT
PLASH
BLOP

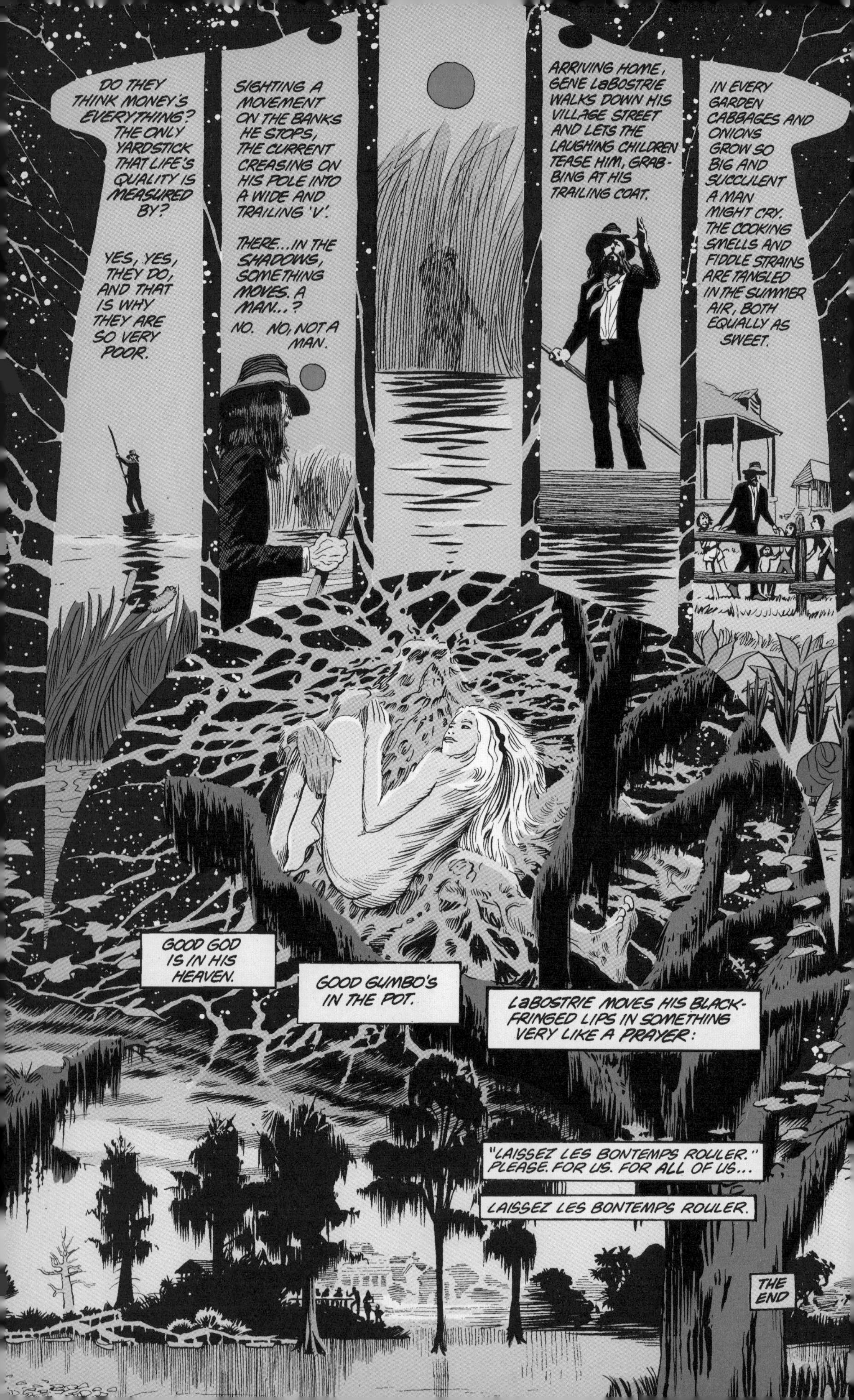

DO THEY THINK MONEY'S EVERYTHING? THE ONLY YARDSTICK THAT LIFE'S QUALITY IS MEASURED BY?
YES, YES, THEY DO, AND THAT IS WHY THEY ARE SO VERY POOR.
SIGHTING A MOVEMENT ON THE BANKS HE STOPS, THE CURRENT CREASING ON HIS POLE INTO A WIDE AND TRAILING 'V'.
THERE...IN THE SHADOWS, SOMETHING MOVES. A MAN...?
NO. NO, NOT A MAN.
ARRIVING HOME, GENE LaBOSTRIE WALKS DOWN HIS VILLAGE STREET AND LETS THE LAUGHING CHILDREN TEASE HIM, GRAB-BING AT HIS TRAILING COAT.
IN EVERY GARDEN CABBAGES AND ONIONS GROW SO BIG AND SUCCULENT A MAN MIGHT CRY. THE COOKING SMELLS AND FIDDLE STRAINS ARE TANGLED IN THE SUMMER AIR, BOTH EQUALLY AS SWEET.
GOOD GOD IS IN HIS HEAVEN.
GOOD GUMBO'S IN THE POT.
LaBOSTRIE MOVES HIS BLACK-FRINGED LIPS IN SOMETHING VERY LIKE A PRAYER:
"LAISSEZ LES BONTEMPS ROULER." PLEASE. FOR US. FOR ALL OF US...
LAISSEZ LES BONTEMPS ROULER.
THE END

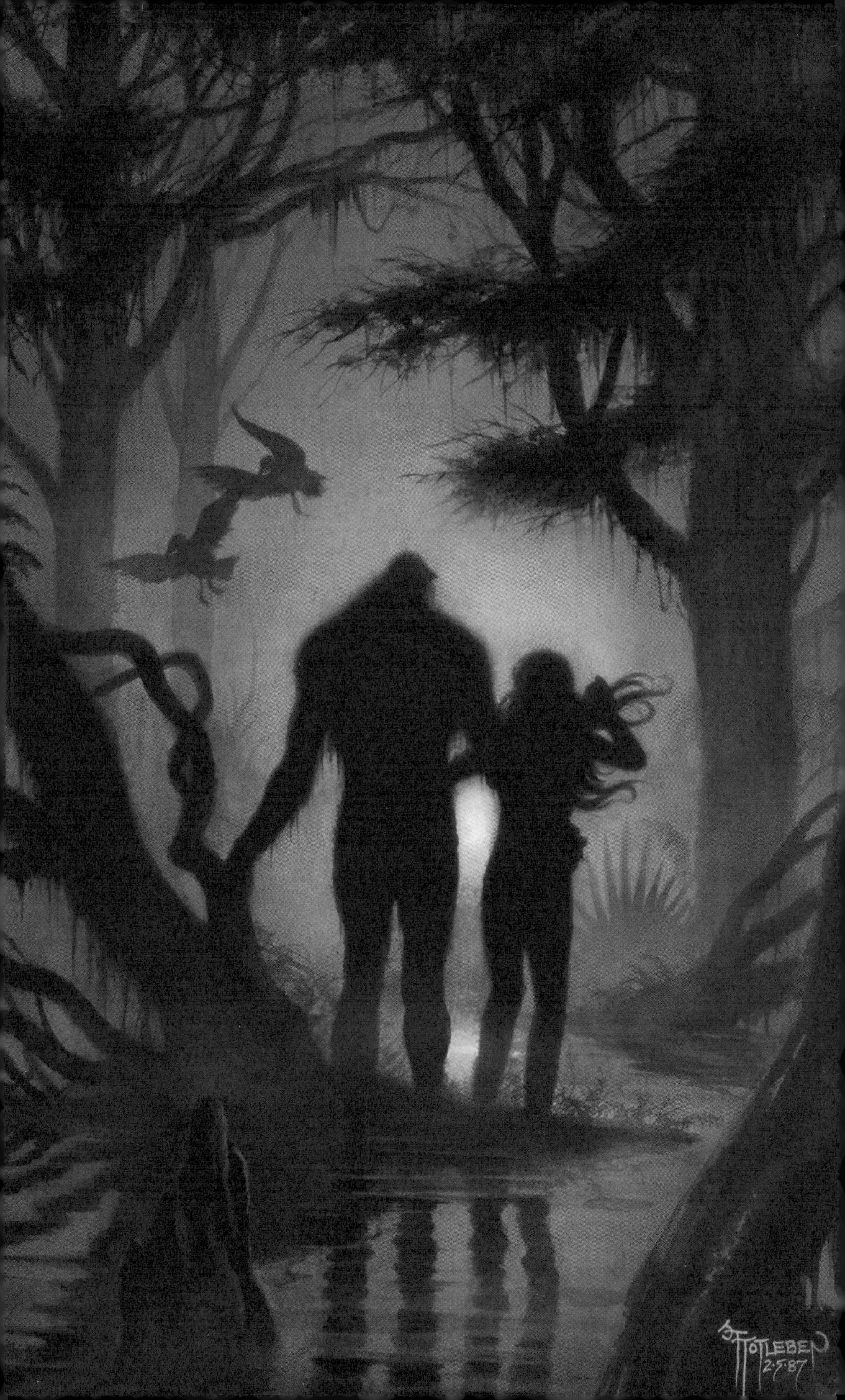
TOTLEBEN
2.5.87

ALAN MOORE is perhaps the most acclaimed writer in the graphic story medium, having garnered countless awards for works such as *Watchmen, V For Vendetta, From Hell, Miracleman* and *Swamp Thing*. He is also the mastermind behind the America's Best Comics line, through which he has created (along with many talented illustrators) *The League of Extraordinary Gentlemen, Promethea, Tom Strong, Tomorrow Stories* and *Top 10*. As one of the medium's most important innovators since the early 1980s, Moore has influenced an entire genera-tion of comics creators, and his work continues to inspire an ever-growing audience. He resides in central England.

RICK VEITCH worked in the underground comics scene before attending the Joe Kubert School of Cartoon and Graphic Art. After graduating, he worked with Stephen Bissette on *Bizarre Adventures* before creating and illustrating *The One*, the innova-tive Epic Comics miniseries. In addition to writing and drawing an acclaimed run on *Swamp Thing*, he is the creator/cartoonist of *Brat Pack, Maximortal* and the dream-based *Rare Bit Fiends*, and a contributing artist on *1963*. He is also the writer and artist of the miniseries *Greyshirt: Indigo Sunset* from America's Best Comics, and the creator of the critically acclaimed graphic novel *Can't Get No* and the spectacularly satirical series *Army@Love* from Vertigo.

After a childhood in Erie, Pennsylvania spent consuming a steady diet of comics, monster magazines and monster movies, **JOHN TOTLEBEN** went to the Joe Kubert School of Cartoon and Graphic Art where he met Stephen Bissette. Together they worked on *Bizarre Adventures* followed by *Swamp Thing*, which they drew for almost three years. Totleben is best known for his illustrative work on Alan Moore's *Miracleman*. His other credits include *1963, Vermillion* and *The Dreaming*.

ALFREDO ALCALA's graceful, moody inks helped maintain the style on *Swamp Thing* through many penciller changes. DC first employed Alcala's talents in its horror and war comics such as *Ghosts, Unexpected*, and *Weird War Tales*. Later he moved on to titles including *All-Star Squadron, Savage Sword of Conan, Batman, Swamp Thing* and countless others for both DC and Marvel. After a long battle with cancer, Alcala passed away in April, 2000.

STEPHEN R. BISSETTE has won many industry awards as cartoonist, writer, editor and publisher. A pioneer graduate of the Joe Kubert School of Cartoon and Graphic Art, he has been teaching at the Center for Cartoon Studies since 2005 and is renowned for his work on *Swamp Thing*, *Taboo* (in which Alan Moore's *From Hell* and *Lost Girls* first appeared), *1963* and *S.R. Bissette's Tyrant*. He illustrates books (including *The Vermont Monster Guide*) and writes fiction (including the Bram Stoker Award-winning novella *Aliens: Tribes*) and non-fiction (including co-authoring *Prince of Stories: The Many Worlds of Neil Gaiman*, *Comic Book Rebels*, and *The Monster Book: Buffy the Vampire Slayer*). His latest book is *Teen Angels & New Mutants: Rick Veitch's Brat Pack and the Art, Karma, and Commerce of Killing Sidekicks*, and his short story "Copper" appeared in the 2010 zombie anthology *The New Dead*. His papers reside in HUIE Library's Special Collections at Henderson State University in Arkadelphia, Arkansas.

TOM YEATES was one of the first graduates of the Joe Kubert School of Cartoon and Graphic Art (along with classmates Rick Veitch, Stephen Bissette, and John Totleben). Influenced primarily by classic adventure illustrators like Alex Raymond and Hal Foster, Yeates has contributed artwork to a host of titles and publishers, and has served as an editor for Eclipse Comics as well as illustrating a newspaper strip revival of *Zorro* from 1999 to 2000.

BILL SIENKIEWICZ has had a major impact on the comic book field with his innovative use of multimedia, collage, illustration techniques and storytelling. He has won nearly every major comics award in the U.S. and abroad, and has exhibited his art worldwide. Among his best-known works are the series *Elektra: Assassin*, for which he received the prestigious Yellow Kid Award, and the critically acclaimed *Stray Toasters*, which he both wrote and illustrated. He was nominated for two Emmy awards for his work on the animated series *Where in the World Is Carmen Sandiego?*, and he also worked on the Academy Award-winning film *Unforgiven* as well as contributing cover and interior illustrations for the DVD and Blu-ray releases of *The Venture Bros.* seasons one and three. He is currently doing covers for the special five-volume limited edition of *The Collected Stories of Philip K. Dick* and working on the trans-media project *Electro*Love*, which he co-created with musician and producer Dave Stewart.

TATJANA WOOD switched careers from dressmaking to comics coloring in the late 1960s and quickly established herself as one of the top colorists in the field, winning two Shazam awards in the early 1970s.

Over his long and prolific career, **JOHN COSTANZA** has lettered a huge number of comics and has won numerous awards along the way. A cartoonist in his own right, Costanza has also contributed stories and art to a variety of titles, beginning in the late 1960s and continuing right through to the new millennium.